CONSTITUTING CULTURAL DIFFERENCE THROUGH DISCOURSE

INTERNATIONAL AND INTERCULTURAL COMMUNICATION ANNUAL

Volume XXIII   **2000**

Editor

Mary Jane Collier
University of Denver

Editorial Assistants

Jennifer Thompson
Nichole Luciani
University of Denver

Consulting Editors for Volume XXIII

Dolores Tanno   Alberto González
University of Nevada, Las Vegas   *Bowling Green State University*

INTERNATIONAL AND INTERCULTURAL COMMUNICATION ANNUAL
VOLUME XXIII   2000

CONSTITUTING CULTURAL DIFFERENCE THROUGH DISCOURSE

editor
Mary Jane COLLIER

Published in cooperation with
National Communication Association
International and Intercultural Division

SAGE Publications
International Educational and Professional Publisher
Thousand Oaks London New Delhi

For information:

Sage Publications, Inc.
2455 Teller Road
Thousand Oaks, California 91320
E-mail: order@sagepub.com

Sage Publications Ltd.
6 Bonhill Street
London EC2A 4PU
United Kingdom

Sage Publications India Pvt. Ltd.
M-32 Market
Greater Kailash I
New Delhi 110 048 India

Printed in the United States of America

Library of Congress Cataloging-in-Publication Data

Main entry under title:

Constituting cultural difference through discourse / edited by Mary Jane Collier.
    p. cm.
Includes bibliographical references and index.
  ISBN 0-7619-2229-6 (cloth: alk. paper)
  ISBN 0-7619-2230-X (pbk.: alk. paper)
1. Intercultural communication. I. Collier, Mary Jane.
  HM1211.C66 2000
  303.48'2—dc21   00-009516

01 02 03 04 05 10 9 8 7 6 5 4 3 2 1

Acquiring Editor:	Margaret H. Seawell
Editorial Assistant:	Sandra Krumholz
Production Editor:	Diana E. Axelsen
Editorial Assistant:	Victoria Cheng
Typesetter/Designer:	Janelle LeMaster
Indexer:	Jeanne Busemeyer

Contents

Acknowledgments

I first want to thank my two editorial assistants, Jennifer Thompson, doctoral candidate in Human Communication Studies, and Nichole Luciani, master's candidate in International and Intercultural Communication, at the University of Denver. Both invested long hours in carefully reading manuscripts and attempting to overcome technological crises. I wish to add my thanks to the University of Denver's Dean of Arts, Humanities, and Social Sciences and the Provost for providing me with funding for the graduate student editorial assistants. Margaret Seawell, acquisitions editor at Sage, encouraged my vision and themes for Volumes XXIII through XXX and also advocated for the continued presence of the annual as a site of outstanding scholarship in international and intercultural communication.

The reviewers for this volume ensured that each essay submitted received thorough and supportive commentary. My sincere appreciation to Brenda Allen, Ben Broome, Donal Carbaugh, Victoria Chen, Robin Crabtree, Stan Deetz, Fernando Delgado, Natalie Dollar, Kristine Fitch, Lisa Flores, Brad Hall, Kathleen Haspel, Radha Hegde, Ronald Jackson, Lenore Langsdorf, Wen Shu Lee, Casey Lum, Judith Martin, Mark McPhail, Dreama Moon, Richard Morris, Tom Nakayama, Kent Ono, Diana Rios, and Bill Starosta. Finally I wish to thank the scholars who submitted their work to a volume that I think will make a noteworthy contribution to international and intercultural programs of research; stimulate dialogue among scholars, students, and practitioners; and inspire diverse discourses about informed social change.

1

Constituting Cultural Difference Through Discourse

Current Research Themes of Politics, Perspectives, and Problematics

MARY JANE COLLIER • *University of Denver*

INTRODUCTION AND OBJECTIVES

As we begin the year 2000, it is noteworthy that culture is a primary and recurring theme in the discourse of governmental spokespersons, politicians, heads of transnational corporations, officials from regional organizations, and community opinion leaders, as well as in everyday conversations among members of the public. Although globalization, transnational economic expansion, and technological access have provided increased information and contact between members of different cultural groups, the contact also includes exposure to and often conflict over ideologies, political policies, institutional practices, resources, and the forms of contact. Contemporary discourses produce and are the products of multiple cultural group identities, iluding those based on nation-state, ethnicity, race, sex, religion, and political standpoint. Such discourses take multiple forms, including speeches by political spokespersons, media images, and the conversations and narrations through which members of cultural groups make sense of their lives and changing social and contextual milieus.

The academic approaches brought to the study of how culture and discourse are related are as diverse as the social problematics and challenges facing different group members across the globe. One of the objectives of Volume XXIII of the annual, therefore, is to present timely and relevant research from a variety of perspectives on cultural difference as a contemporary social problematic.

A second objective of this volume is to respond to what has been called the "linguistic/communicative turn" in many disciplines (Anderson,

1

1996) and the emergence of social constructionism. Social constructionists, although very diverse in issues selected for inquiry and methods employed, are described by Burr (1995) as generally holding common assumptions. She describes social constructionists as scholars who
predominantly hold anti-essentialist and antirealist views, endorse the
historical and cultural specificity of knowledge, see language as a pre-
condition for thought and as a form of social action, and focus on interaction and social practices and processes. The theme of this volume, therefore, builds on the recognition of communication as a constitutive
practice outlined by Berger and Luckmann (1966), Gergen (1985), and
Shotter (1993), among others, and described by Giddens (1984) in his
call for scholars to engage in practical science about discursive systems.

In addition to presenting relevant research that focuses on relevant social problematics through discursive (and nondiscursive) texts, a third
goal of this volume is to incorporate research that reflects the increasing
prominence of critical de/reconstructionist approaches among those
who study culture in an increasingly complex and transnational world.
Postcolonial and critical scholars call for academics to broaden the character the voices speaking in scholarship on culture. Consequently, the
authors who are included in this volume and the respondents they involve in their research are from a variety of cultural groups, including
those from previously silenced or marginalized groups.

This volume also contains many different perspectives to discourse
analysis, ranging from localized, situated interpretations of group members' in-group dialogues to interpretations from informed critics of public
images and texts. Interpretations and conclusions reported reflect contradictions and multivocal contestations, patterns in avowal and ascription and divergent voices, individual respondents' descriptions of their
experiences, and mediated or public texts reflecting political ideologies
and broader social hierarchies, to name a few. Epistemological orientations that sometimes include combinations of media studies, cultural
studies, feminism, ethnography of communication, social interaction,
performance studies, poststructuralism, and postcolonialism are also included.

Many scholars in this volume are responding to the call for critical reflection that has emerged in the discipline. Several authors explicitly interrogate taken-for-granted assumptions; question the relevance of previous academic inquiry on particular topics; recognize that truths are
constructed; and, in an era of postmodern skepticism, pose alternative

readings of mediated and political public texts, as well as of everyday conversation.

Yet another goal is to showcase scholarly work on cultural difference in which authors recognize that the boundaries and distinctions between cultural groups, as well as the "territories" and academic camps within the communication discipline, are increasingly murky and overlapping (and perhaps better incorporated into research of intersections, hybridity, and fluctuating processes within broader institutional and structural constraints). Several chapters in this volume show the value of intertextual dialogue and dialogue across theoretical perspectives, in that some chapters are written by teams of scholars with different cultural voices and orientations to the discourse and contain themes addressing issues from more than one theoretical perspective.

CONCEPTUAL AND THEORETICAL ISSUES

Discourse and Texts

In this volume, the analysis of discourse focuses on the systems of texts and talk that range from public to private and from naturally occurring to mediated forms. Van Dijk (1997) describes 12 principles that are shared to some degree by the loose confederation of scholars committed to making sense of how discourse relates to identities, group membership, relationships among group members, structures, and contexts. These principles are shared by several of the scholars analyzing discourse in Volume XXIII. The interrelated principles are

1. The study of naturally occurring text and talk
2. The study of discourse as a constitutive part of local, global, social, and cultural contexts
3. Increasing variety of texts
4. An approach to discourse as social practice of group members
5. Attention to group members' categories of interpretation (as well as social and institutional practice)
6. Attention to sequentiality and analysis of functionality in sequences
7. Constructivity in hierarchical structures of forms as well as meanings
8. A focus on analytical levels, dimensions, and layers and the relationships between them
9. Attention to meanings as well as functions

10. Descriptions of how rules are violated, ignored, or changed and the consequences of such moves
11. Identification of interactional strategies
12. Incorporation of the role of social cognition (van Dijk, 1997)

Whereas the chapters in this volume by Yumiko Yokochi and Bradford 'J' Hall, by Yael-Janette Zupnik, and by Rivka Ribak exemplify the kind of discourse analysis described above, other researchers choose alternative types of texts. For example, in their chapters, Lisa A. Flores and Marouf Hasian Jr. apply a rhetorical and postcolonial lens to the discourse of a television show in the United States and to the speech of an African American leader, respectively. Raka Shome brings a postcolonial and feminist perspective to a television program in Great Britain, and her analysis includes discursive as well as nondiscursive imagery and nonverbal cues as text.

Intellectual Ferment and Changing Perspectives

Postmodernism is the backdrop and the character of the intellectual reexamination that informs scholarly issues and debates about culture in a variety of disciplines today. The authors in this volume recognize that their research occurs within a broader social and intellectual context, one characterized by increasing contradictions and questions about epistemological foundations. Although many orientations to postmodernism exist, broadly speaking, postmodernism has been described as a rejection of reason, rationality, and the search for Truth that arose during the Enlightenment. Burr (1995) notes that postmodernism rejects "both the idea that there can be an ultimate truth, and . . . structuralism, the idea that the world as we see it is the result of hidden structures . . . grand theories or metanarratives" (p. 13). Further, Prus (1996) characterizes the postmodern voice as "extreme skepticism in the viability of all forms of knowing (and presumably all interpretation as well)" (p. 217).

Because postmodern voices speak alongside modern voices, scholars in communication come from and orient their studies of culture and discourse from a plurality of perspectives and choose to study a variety of social problematics. The chapters in this volume are no exception and include those from critics, interpretivists, and ethnographers.

Language and Meaning:
Representation and Social Construction

Some scholars in this volume approach language and specific discourse as representative (Stewart, 1995), in that discourse texts are approached as apparently authentic representations of psychological states. In other words, scholars work toward coming to understand patterns of messages and signs because they represent cognitive orientations and affective states that respondents hold with regard to their own groups or toward others as members of cultural groups. For instance, several authors in this volume of the annual want to discover if, how, or to what degree previously identified cultural patterns emerge in particular situated discourse. Researchers from this tradition generally assume that such patterns of messages and their interpretations are learned through socialization as a member of a particular cultural group and are "brought to" interactions as well as, to some degree, negotiated in local situations.

Yokochi and Hall provide a rationale for their cross-cultural comparison of U.S. and Japanese cultural patterns that emerge in intercultural group discourse by outlining the literature describing general differences in cultural patterns of the two national groups. One goal of their study is to uncover any of those or additional patterns that emerge in intercultural group discourse. Their approach to language evidences an assumption that respondents bring knowledge of what their language code is and of how to use the code in order to be an accepted member of the group. They also assume that interpretations emerge in situated contexts and may change, to some degree, over time. They define culture accordingly as a sense-making system with reflexive force used to produce and interpret action. One conclusion they reach is that culture constitutes communication; they also conclude that communication and the emergent patterns of negotiated norms and values constitute culture.

Trudy Milburn describes the use of time by Puerto Ricans in the United States in her ethnographic study. Two assumptions seem to be implicit: first, that the respondents bring to interactions an a priori sense of appropriate use of time based on being socialized as Puerto Ricans, and second, that the patterns and interpretations of the use of time emerge in the communal enactment of the norms about time at the Cultural Center.

The chapters by Milburn and by Yokochi and Hall reflect an implicit assumption that patterns in the discourse will covary with cultural group affiliation. Other authors who address cultural group distinctions and respondent discourse make the additional assumption that it is appropriate for researchers to ask insider members of groups to reflect on and describe their interpretations of discourse and experiences as group members; for example, Mark P. Orbe, Kiesha T. Warren, and Nancy C. Cornwell ask African American males to talk about their everyday experiences and treatment by outsiders, and Jolanta A. Drzewiecka invites Polish immigrants to describe conduct that indicates being Polish.

A "crisis of representation" has emerged among anthropologists and ethnographers that includes concerns relevant to intercultural communication researchers. Ethnographers and interpretivists have been criticized on several grounds. For instance, they are often criticized for creating a form of cultural domination, incorrectly assuming that all people are equally able to inform researchers about their lived experiences and failing to realize that there are problems with ethnographic accounts caused by their imposed form and structure (summarized in Prus, 1996). More generally, the "crises of representation" (Clifford & Marcus, 1986; Marcus & Fischer, 1986) have to do with questioning assumptions researchers make about symbolic activity; "representing" psychological orientations or behavioral intentions; and making assumptions about who can speak "for" or "as" a member of a cultural group and about what our scholarly identities and reports "represent" in terms of unspoken biases, privileged standpoints, and taken-for-granted structures. Authors in this volume address some of these issues through their acknowledgment of the limitations of their interpretivist-critic role, their increased reflexivity, and their use of numerous examples from the voices of respondents. Such moves improve the representative validity of their research studies.

Several authors in this volume also approach language as the site/process in which meanings are socially constructed. Social constructionists who study culture and cultural difference, for example, focus on interactions that occur between people and the communication process as the social problematic. Such an orientation contrasts with psychological explanations of conduct, which are based on cognitive variables, and with sociological explanations of conduct, which are based on social institutions and structures.

In her chapter, Ribak addresses how Israeli Jews and Arabs construct their respective histories, the political event of the *intifada,* and their own group identities through their social contact. She places emphasis upon interpretive repertoires, which are not always consistent with national, generational, or political identity. In addition, her chapter highlights the fact that differences in discursive practice are not necessarily predictable by social group membership; rather, they may covary with local practices and purposes underlying the discourse. Yoko Nadamitsu, Ling Chen, and Gustav Friedrich also employ a social-constructionist perspective in their orientation to the processes through which long-term Chinese sojourners and residents construct Japanese cultural identity in their discourse about the Japanese.

Interpretivist Perspectives

One of the major orientations to discourse and culture reflected in the scholarship of Volume XXIII is the broad category of interpretive approaches. The interpretive studies in this volume are consistent with what Anderson (1996) describes as a recognition of the linguistic/communication turn in academic scholarship. Within this perspective, language is viewed as articulate contact (Stewart, 1995), and the authors seek to build knowledge about the ways in which humans use language to construct their "realities" and identities with one another (Shotter, 1993).

A major thrust of this body of scholarship is the study of discourse in which members of groups negotiate and enact their cultural identities in interaction with members of other groups. The range of interpretive perspectives adopted in this volume of the annual includes those concentrating on the social construction of cultural group membership and on communication processes that produce/reproduce/affect meanings and structures and patterned social practices.

Ethnography of communication approaches fall under the general rubric of interpretivism in that the goal of ethnographers, generally, is to answer questions related to how participants in communities achieve "membering" (Philipsen, 1989) and to the communication means and meanings that are associated with communal life (Carbaugh, 1990). Assumptions brought to inquiry by ethnographers include the ideas that communication is contexted, locally designed, situationally managed, and individually applied (Carbaugh, 1990).

Milburn's chapter on enacting "Puerto Rican Time" in this volume is written within an ethnographic framework, and several other scholars in this volume seek to build understanding of the coherence, codes, and meanings in use by group members through broader interpretive approaches. Examples of such approaches in this volume include chapters by Zupnik on Israeli-Palestinian "dialogue" events, by Ribak on Israeli Jews and Arabs constructing *intifadas* and selves, and by Yokochi and Hall on Japanese and U.S. intercultural group discourse. Other examples include studies of discourse in which group members describe outsiders (as in the chapter by Nadamitsu, Chen, and Friedrich, in which Chinese respondents describe their experiences with and ascriptions of the Japanese, as well as their own avowed Chinese group identity); discourse in which in-group members negotiate and contest their positions and distinctions (as in the chapter by Drzewiecka on ethnic immigrants); and finally, discourse in which insider-outsider boundaries are challenged and questioned by individuals (as in the chapter about interclass travel, adaptation, and "passing" among white women in the United States by Dreama Moon).

Critical/Deconstructionism

In addition to recognizing the role of language in constituting group identities, multiple truths, claims to resources, and the nature of our relationships with one another, it is becoming more common to hear critical scholars speak to the need for deconstruction of our taken-for-granted assumptions about "objectivity, neutrality, discovery," and prediction/ explanation. Characteristic of critical scholars is skepticism about overriding metanarratives (Lyotard, 1984), questions about knowledge and power (Foucault, 1980), and skepticism regarding the role of the researcher. Scholars who articulate assumptions consistent with what has been labeled critical/deconstructionism by Mumby (1997) are primarily concerned with issues of exploitation, power, and empowerment; with the development of rhetorical tools to deconstruct and critique linguistically constructed and textually mediated social realities; and with providing alternatives to universalist interpretations of texts. Hegde (1998) describes a more specific critical stance, that of postcolonialism, as "a global discourse that emphasizes interdependencies and dialectical interconnections . . . offering ways . . . of situating and historicizing difference . . . dismantling binaries of 'West-Rest' and colonizer-colonized . . . and problematizing culture as impure and heterogeneous" (p. 283).

Several of the chapters in Volume XXIII reflect such a critical perspective. In her chapter on challenging the myth of assimilation, Flores contributes an oppositional reading of a popular television text and invites a Chicana feminist literary critic into the dialogue. In this way, insider feminist voices critique the master narrative of assimilation being reified in the discourse of the television program. Shome uncovers the colonialist, nationalist, and sexist cultural narratives in a popular television program, *The Jewel in the Crown,* which was aired in the 1980s in Great Britain. Shome situates her chapter as a postcolonialist endeavor in her focus on the critical examination of imperialism and the imperialist subject in the media text, and she provides an alternative reading of the text through the additional lens of feminist critic. Hasian provides an alternative, subaltern reading of the Million Man March speech by Louis Farrakhan. In addition, through attention to the texts of the responses of political commentators after the speech, Hasian demonstrates how readings in the public sphere are constructed to prevent and silence those who might offer alternative readings.

The Absence of Positivism

In intercultural communication research, positivist approaches have a strong legacy, and what Martin and Nakayama (1999) describe as functionalist approaches to intercultural communication have been a dominant paradigm. Anderson (1996) notes the increasing questions that are emerging with regard to objectivist theories and their foundational principles of empiricism, materialism, determinism, and objectivity. Previously unexamined assumptions now require interrogation. The scholars in this volume choose other approaches to guide their respective endeavors, and it is noteworthy that none of these authors oriented his or her study of discourse based on discovery or predictions and explanations of causal relationships.

Appropriateness of Combining Perspectives

Perspectives are developed because of some degree of internal coherence and consistency in assumptions guiding inquiry about particular types of questions (Deetz, 1994; Martin & Nakayama, 1999). It is becoming more common to see scholars express appreciation for identifying assumptions explicitly and translating them across perspectives. Rawlins (1998) notes that juxtaposing his interpretive research program on friendship with descriptions of traditional social scientific studies strengthened his research; although his preference for interpretivism remains the dominant voice in his work, he views the intertextual dialogue among scholars and among theoretical perspectives as informative and worthwhile.

Intertextuality (Bakhtin, 1984) may also be applied in order to strengthen traditional or dominant perspectives that are based on assumptions that may or may not be appropriate to all research endeavors, moments in time, and geopolitical and social spaces. For example, the canons of Western philosophy and rhetoric that guide many of the models of public speaking reflected in textbooks today arose in a socio/cultural/political moment of history that was decidedly male and controlled by an elite group with power and privilege (Foss & Foss, 1994; Powell & Collier, 1990). Notably, the chapters of Hasian and of Flores illustrate the value of combining rhetorical and critical approaches. Such integrated approaches illustrate that translation between approaches is not only possible, but useful, and that modification of more traditional rhetorical assumptions about purpose, roles of participants, social and institutional contexts and constraints, and the extent of agency and power can be beneficial in increasing the relevance of such models to the study of diverse voices in public discourse today.

Dialogue across perspectives and critique based upon familiarity with multiple epistemological perspectives is not the same as a call for methodological "triangulation," which is only appropriate when scholars clearly articulate their ontological and epistemological assumptions and persuasively demonstrate that the use of multiple methods is justified and consistent. Nor is this call for examination of multiple epistemological perspectives an oversimplified "pluralistic" position that "all perspectives are equal," or what Hegde (1998) calls a "relativistic accommodation . . . I'm OK, You're OK" viewpoint. This kind of translation and dialogue is also different from the "interparadigmatic borrowing" that Martin and Nakayama (1999) describe, because new perspectives are constructed rather than constructs being imported or "borrowed" and integrated into existing perspectives and paradigms.

Drzewiecka's perspective on building knowledge about Polish immigrant identities is consistent with Hegde's (1998) view of communication from "elsewhere" and is an exemplar of theoretical development based on intertextuality that appropriately incorporates assumptions from postcolonial critique and intercultural-transnational communication. Shome's chapter is an intertextual analysis that adds feminism to postcolonial critique and intercultural-transnational communication. In both of these studies, we see not simply an integration of multiple perspectives, but an explicit outline of assumptions and a justification of how such assumptions have an internal coherence (Anderson, 1996; Deetz, 1994) and breadth of correspondence.

The quality of our scholarly work about discourse is strengthened when readers see multiple perspectives appropriately applied to a research problematic and are able to evaluate the consistency of philosophical assumptions, recognize and translate across the language games in use, and situate the critique within a context and set of goals. Whether seeking emancipation within a critical feminist viewpoint or substantiation of conditional, contextual accounts about women's abilities to "pass," researchers' efforts can be strengthened from this kind of dialogue. Finally, if the overall goal of scholarship is knowledge production and praxis to deal with social problematics in some form (Deetz, 1994), then dialogue across perspectives may help to decrease the reproduction of racism, sexism, and myths of homogeneity and equal agency in our scholarly discourse.

Questions related to the issue of when to translate across perspectives include the extent to which researchers should be expected to undertake structural analysis in the form of attention to ideological/institutional-level histories and forces and the extent to which they should be expected to analyze microlevel social practices and discourse. Van Dijk (1987, 1993) established a research program examining the social, political, and cultural reproduction of racism by giving attention to the intersections of microlevel interactions and the social macrostructures, that is, socially shared strategies and representations of power, dominance, and access evident in everyday conversations and interview discourse.

Ribak and Zupnik incorporate macrostructural features of political history and religion into their analyses of discourse and microlevel interactions among groups in the Middle East. Orbe, Warren, and Cornwell conduct two separate analyses by first critically addressing the mediated text and structural processes, such as racism and the promotion of negative stereotypes of African American males, in a public text, the television program *The Real World*. They then supplement that analysis by adding respondents' descriptions and interpretations of their everyday experiences as African American men in the United States.

Reflexivity and Acknowledging Researcher Positionality

The current volume incorporates research about issues that feature overlapping and intersecting contexts and varied orientations to the analysis of discourse; in addition, many of the authors explicitly discuss or imply that they have interrogated previously taken-for-granted assumptions about what should be studied, the role of multiple cultural group and scholarly identities in the research process, and the need to examine their relationships with respondents, as well as the benefits from increasing the relevance of research to wider numbers of cultural groups. The scholars in this volume demonstrate that, as researchers, our positionality and the spaces from which we speak as scholars are important, as are the assumptions we make about the people we speak to, with, and about in our research.

Delgado (1994) describes the need for scholars of culture to be open for others to critique their work and question implicit assumptions. According to Delgado, openness to criticism is "a positive step, representing both interest and reflective inquiry that potentially can lead to more and better scholarship" (p. 77). Conquergood (1992) also maintains that scholarly discourses can benefit from reflexivity, criticism, and recognition of the rhetorical strategies involved in creating a voice of authority.

Postcolonial scholars in general, and in this volume, raise important issues about positionality, including the need to expand the cultural identities of the scholarly voices most often speaking and most often the objects of study, and about the implications of the prominence of particular elite voices. Also, they acknowledge the notion that disciplinary training and what Anderson (1996) calls "indoctrination" create epistemological and ontological orientations. Such orientations can become genealogies of power and regimes of truth by reifying particular norms and ways of languaging (Foucault, 1980), silencing marginalized voices, and discouraging nontraditional ways of knowing.

A need for reflexivity is underscored in several of the studies in this volume. Each researcher interested in culture holds two sets of ontological claims: a set of claims about how humans produce, constitute, negotiate, contest, and make sense of their cultural group memberships, as well as a set of claims about his or her own identity construction within the academic, historical, socioeconomic, and disciplinary milieu.

National, religious, and political identities may easily influence labels, terminology for themes, and interpretations of discourse in ways that may not be immediately clear to authors without an outsider to question them. Therefore, authors comment explicitly on the rationales guiding their choices of labels for groups and on those that affect conclusions drawn from the analysis. For example, Ribak, Zupnik, and Flores, among others, present their rationale for using particular group labels such as Palestinian, Arab Israeli, Latina, and Chicana. In addition, Milburn explains her use of the word "American" (including the use of quotation marks) as the label in use by respondents and as consistent with the use of "popular American" in other ethnographies of communication in the United States. In this way, she acknowledges that some readers may be offended by the ethnocentric use of "America," a label denoting a continent, as if it signifies the country of the United States. She also demonstrates that ethnographers in particular, as well as interpretivists in general, need to take care in the labels chosen to stand for groups and to reflexively examine assumptions being made by both respondents and scholars about those labels.

Scholars in this volume are a diverse group of academics who have a range of group identities, histories, ideologies, political views, and orientations to scholarship. Many choose to recognize their intimate engagement with the research process and to speak from a first-person rather than a third-person voice. Speaking from a space of intimately engaged participant-researcher recognizes that scholarly inquiry emerges from a political and personal history (Collier, 1998). The chapter by Orbe, Warren, and Cornwell includes an explicit description not only of the authors' cultural backgrounds in terms of race and sex, but also of their experiences and relationships with insiders and the media featuring African Americans.

Ontological and epistemological assumptions that researchers bring to inquiry are interrelated and are developed in institutions and through academic structures that reflect histories, traditions, and political constraints, as well as personal preferences (Collier, 1998). As researchers and practitioners who have lives and identities inside and outside of the academy, we are immersed in doing and living what we are attempting to study. Several of these scholars study groups whose voices are underrepresented in the literature and describe the role of unearned privilege in the creation of elite group readings of public texts as well as more situated conversational discourses. For example, both Flores and Drzewiecka, as members of marginalized groups, point to the ideas that identities are multiple, dynamic, and politicized and that U.S. American scholars learn ethnocentrism—whites learn racism, males learn sexism, and women of color learn what it feels like to be marginalized. Such ontologies frame and shape epistemic assumptions and methodological moves. The researchers in this volume are examples of how we are all beginning to wrestle with the need to interrogate and make our assumptions consistent about who we are and how we practice scholarship and build knowledge about our own and other groups.

Researcher Point of View

When studying discourse, scholars face an epistemological issue regarding the consistency of assumptions being made about what constitutes knowledge and about how knowledge is acquired within the context of the particular goals and questions driving the scholarly effort. Scholars working with discourse and texts must select a researcher point of view in order to make sense of the communicative text and point of view that is driven by theoretical perspective and overall goals.

Many scholars speaking from a critical or cultural studies standpoint conduct their analyses on public or mediated texts from an individual researcher's point of view (Anderson, 1996); in this volume, the chapters of Shome and Hasian can be broadly categorized as reflecting this overall perspective. Zupnik and Ribak approach their analyses through a broad critical discourse analysis orientation (van Dijk, 1997). Thus, they choose to act as individual interpretivists. They also use analytical frames that incorporate macrostructural factors, such as political and religious ideologies, and apply them to micropractices that emerge in intercultural and cultural group discourse.

Orbe, Warren, and Cornwell first adopt a critical view to the portrayal of African American men in a media text. The three researchers collaborate in an overall critique. The researchers also analyze the additional text of responses from African American men describing their everyday experiences as African American men. Their chapter illustrates the value of having multiple researcher and respondent viewpoints. Drzewiecka and Flores choose to bring their own subjective, personal experience into their interpretations in order to lend a different kind of first-hand credibility to their analyses.

The chapters in this volume exemplify the fact that strong, theoretically grounded research on the discourse of cultural difference can be approached from a variety of theoretical orientations and researcher points of view. All of the authors allow the voices in the communicative texts to "speak" and provide examples for the reader to "hear." This is essential for readers to judge the appropriateness of interpretive and critical claims.

Borders and Contexts as Contested Spaces

As we begin the 21st century, the borders and boundaries between the traditional context areas of the communication discipline are beginning to intersect, overlap, and become more permeable. Culture, whether approached as a social-psychological set of dimensions, as a socially constructed identity, or as a site of institutional power, transcends and incorporates multiple contexts in any traditional sense. As the chapters in this volume demonstrate, many intercultural communication questions being investigated today require examination of intersections of what have been known for several decades as interpersonal, group, rhetorical, mediated, and organizational contexts.

The areas of the discipline of international and intercultural communication have also undergone change. The traditional distinction between international communication—that which crosses national borders through mediated or policy/product-oriented means—and intercultural communication—interpersonal or intergroup communication between people from different places or backgrounds—is no longer useful. For instance, contemporary international and intercultural communication scholars study diverse issues and problematics, including those who critique globalism as an economically normative agenda and critique development efforts as creating dependence, those who have transformed their approaches to culture by making it an independent rather than a dependent variable, and those who focus on rhetoric and the processes though which we constitute knowledge (Keith, 1997). International and transnational/global communication has become conceptualized as communicative contacts taking various forms in which national, ethnic, economic, local, and global identities are constituted and contested, power and influence are evident in ongoing struggles, and a myriad of people negotiate the contradictions and tensions in their relationships and "borders" (Friedman, 1994).

The work of Drzewiecka, Shome, Ribak, and Zupnik, among others, are exemplars of how national, ethnic, and immigrant identities and relationships intersect and exist within broader historical and structural constraining forces. The chapters in this volume reflect current sociopolitical complexities, contradictions, and changes. Borders between countries and claims to territories can change rapidly and are regularly negotiated through violence as well as diplomacy. Israelis and Palestinians claim the same piece of land in which settlements and refugee camps are located side by side. The geographic borders between countries as well as the racial and ethnic boundaries between groups are sometimes muddy and "bleed" into one another (Conquergood, 1991).

The chapters in this volume include attention to current social problematics and emerging trends for intercultural scholars to study the ways in which a wider cross-section of peoples across the globe wrestle with multiple group identities, competing social hierarchies, differences in ideologies, and practices of justice and morality. The authors acknowledge that although technological advances and political exigency, in addition to higher socioeconomic standards for some, help provide increased opportunities for intergroup contact, at the same time, dominant group histories, institutions, and ideologies continue to constrain intergroup social practices. Consequently, contradictions and paradoxes characterize group and intergroup contact.

More specifically, some of the authors see that paths in and out of occupied territories are sometimes hidden and sometimes marked with checkpoints and military police. Whereas Moon shows the reader how individuals engage in passing as members of a particular social class, Orbe, Warren, and Cornwell; Hasian; and Shome reinforce the conclusions that physical appearance is often an indisputable racial marker and that mediated, public, and conversational practices are a means through which identities are negatively constituted and constrained. Conversational markers may feature distinctions that showcase sociopolitical identity distinctiveness from or similarity to Others, as Zupnik describes in her chapter about Israeli-Palestinian dialogues. Mediated portrayals of cultural groups, such as those found in *The Jewel in the Crown* or *The Real World,* reify negative generalized images of the Other when they focus on "colored . . . immigrants" defiling the national, colonial body of England, as Shome points out, or when they show African American males as angry, violent, and sexually aggressive in *The Real World,* as Orbe et al. argue.

The nature of the social problems being addressed by authors in this volume demonstrates the increasing trend toward an expanded and revisioned disciplinary orientation in communication in which scholars focus on anomalous problematics that cannot be explained by other disciplinary orientations and focus on processes of communication rather than information (Deetz, 1994). Furthermore, these authors embrace the communicative turn from philosophy, challenge the unitary social order, critique hierarchical social processes, and produce work that demonstrates the value of approaching culture as a constitutive process. Therefore, the themes addressed in these chapters challenge intercultural scholars to de/reconstruct traditional views of what were defined previously as the parameters and boundaries of the discipline.

Issues of the Centrality of Culture

Debate regarding the centrality of culture and the appropriateness and scope of cultural "versus" intercultural communication approaches has reemerged during the past few years. A decade ago, Gudykunst (1988) persuasively pointed out the merits of developing intercultural communication theory and the need for culture-general and context-general analytical frameworks. He called for scholars to develop an additional theoretical trajectory, that of intercultural axiomatic theory based on explanatory and generalizable variables. Shuter (1990, 1998) has argued for scholars to return to what he calls the "centrality of culture," to inquiry focused on intracultural communication and emic frameworks within a country, society, or world region. Chapters in this volume reflect a variety of approaches, including those concentrating on the discourse of a single cultural group of Puerto Ricans in the United States, intergroup conversations between Palestinians and Israelis and between Japanese and U.S. students, views of Chinese long-term "visitors" toward their Japanese "hosts," and accounts of how Polish ethnic immigrants and white women constitute their cultural identities in contexts with Others.

Shuter's call for a focus on "nation" or residents in a particular geopolitical space is based on a definition of culture as "common unstated experiences which members of a given culture share, communicate without knowing, and which form the backdrop against which all other events are judged" (Hall, 1966, quoted in Shuter, 1998, p. 42). Nadamitsu, Chen, and Friedrich, as well as Yokochi and Hall, show that national identity is marked, distinct, and salient within the discourse of some groups. However, the postcolonial critique of the nation-state that brings attention to the problematic nature of such concepts as nation, colony, community, and national tradition as cultural boundaries (Ono, 1998) is echoed by Hasian, Shome, and Drzewiecka, among others. Hegde (1998) also points out that during globalization, communities "reterritorialize"; furthermore, privileging the cultural as based on geopolitical spaces may result in overlooking the experiences from those "moving in" and "moving out," as well as the voices of the "marginalized" (Parry, 1995).

When the focus is placed on discourse, as it is in this volume, whether from social-constructionist/interpretive perspectives or from critical perspectives, cultural similarities and differences are constituted and take form and shape throughout the contexts. Contested identities (including national, racial, ethnic, gender, and social class) emerge and are negotiated; enactments of power and dialogic relationship are constructed among insider group members and between insiders and outsiders. All of the contested and overlapping ways in which respondents define themselves are also defined by institutions, ideologies, and social structures. More often than not, the authors point their epistemological lenses toward the intersections, the spaces "between," that are the sites of the communicative process, rather than toward the psychological frame that individuals supposedly share when they live in or come from the same geopolitical space. To argue that this contact should not be studied, or that intracultural communication should be studied prior to studying intercultural contact, is not ontologically consistent with the assumptions being made by researchers who are interested in intergroup histories and processes, such as conflict management or problem solving, nor is it epistemologically consistent with a goal of building understanding about how identities are coconstructed.

Multivocality and Interpellated Cultural Identities

The scholars of cultural and intercultural discourse in this volume have made informed choices about when to focus on one group identity, such as nationality or sex, and when to recognize that cultural group identities are social constructions that are multiple, overlapping, intersecting, and continually contested. The challenge for researchers is to ascertain ways to avoid essentializing members of national, ethnic, gender, or corporate cultures; to recognize multivocality and within-group diversity; and to appropriately describe group trends. For instance, Drzewiecka's description of ethnic immigrant identities among Polish in the United States, as well as the challenge of U.S. assimilation myths discussed by Flores, are consistent with claims by Halualani (1998) that intercultural scholars are able to benefit from deconstructing homogenized, generalized versions of "America," as well as from accounts of individuals about their overlapping cultural identities and experiences, thus bringing to light multiple and contested "Americas" and truths.

McClintock (1995) points to the feminist critique of the social sciences and humanities to stress that researchers should recognize the interrelationships among gender, race, and class. She describes women of color who challenge Eurocentric feminists who claim "to give voice to

an essential womanhood (in universal conflict with an essential masculinity) and who privilege gender over all other conflicts" (p. 7). She explains that the categories of race, ethnicity, and class are fundamental
constructions that emerged during Western, industrial modernity and
that still benefit the middle and upper classes. Consistent with such arguments, Flores, Drzewiecka, Moon, and Shome point the reader to focus
on issues of hybridity and the study of multiple cultural identities
through attention to intersections of race, sex, and class.

Both hooks (1989) and McGoldrick (1994) acknowledge that sex,
race, and class are interpellated, most often defined from a white point of
view. They argue that scholars need to begin a discourse on race that in-
terrogates what has been the central or implicit standard in the past.
Moon's discussion of whiteness and social class is an example. Hall
(1995) adds the need to situate such conceptualizations of group identities within the broader social and historical context. He points out that
when studying cultural affiliation or a designation like ethnicity, scholars should recognize "the place of history, language and culture in the
construction of subjectivity and identity, as well as the fact that all discourse is placed, positioned, situated, and all knowledge is contextual"
(p. 226). Drzewiecka's analysis of ethnic immigrant identities as heterogeneous and contested and as "symbolic capital . . . not what people have
or to which they belong," but a set of fragmented social positions, symbolic values, and dynamic habitus, meets these criteria.

Although Nadamitsu, Chen, and Friedrich, as well as Yokochi and
Hall, study the discourse used by individuals who affiliate with particular national groups, they also provide examples in their analyses of divergent voices within the groups. Thus, the authors do not presume a generalized "consensus" among all those sharing a national affiliation (Fiske,
1991). In addition, the authors discuss similarities between the national
groups as well as differences between groups.

Issues of Power, Privilege, and Agency

Critical scholars from many areas of the discipline recommend that in
order to study culture in ways that are more relevant to the experiences of
respondents, researchers should recognize and engage intersubjective
and collective interpretations of power and resistance and should endeavor to study "a more diverse politics of agency, involving the dense
web of relations between coercion, negotiation, complicity, refusal, dis-
sembling, mimicry, compromise, affiliation, and revolt" (McClintock,

1995, p. 15). Such a dialogue incorporates the ontological and epistemological recognition that we need to conduct inquiry about power and agency as part of the doing-being (Sacks, 1984) and becoming (Baxter & Montgomery, 1996) of culture and cultural identities.

In addition to interrogating the ways in which scholars create and reify what is considered to be "Truth/truth/truths," as well as what constructs such as race, ethnicity, and sex mean, postcolonial scholars argue that categorizing groups into dualistic extremes of the "powerful imperialist" versus the "powerless colonized" is an unacceptable oversimplification and that there is no center or "standard" to which "outsiders" or the "marginalized" should be held (Bhabha, 1995). For example, Ashcroft, Griffiths, and Tiffin (1995) describe the binarism of settler/colonized or center/margin as a fallacy, because all cultures change, adapt, affect, and are affected by one another. Parry (1995) adds to this issue by stating that counterhegemony is inseparable from hegemony. She illustrates her argument by giving examples both of hybridity, in which groups challenge colonial authority by continual and mutual development of independent cultural traditions, and of adaptation to new cultural forms and practices with the maintenance of established cultural forms. The chapters of Flores and of Moon are consistent with a call for more complex views of hierarchy, assimilation, and adaptation.

McPhail (1997) and Dace and McPhail (1998) point out the danger of complicity that occurs among scholars when group members become essentialized or when theoretically suspect binary descriptions are used to refer to group members in either-or fashion without acknowledging "the fluid character of personal and social identity or the extent to which they are implicated in each other" (McPhail, 1997, p. 163). The suggestion offered is a move toward implicature, embracing multivocality and the intersections between the social and personal and moving into emancipatory and reconstructive political practice.

Assumptions about such issues as agency and the freedom of group members to choose modes of conduct and interpretation are as varied as the questions being addressed by the authors in this volume. For example, Shome, Hasian, and Flores conduct postcolonial-oriented inquiries into the constitution of culture in public media and political speech texts. Their perspective requires that they acknowledge the ways in which the individual agency of group members defined as immigrant or Other is constrained because of elite group ideologies that are produced, consumed, and reinforced across multiple institutions and regulated social practices. On the other hand, Yokochi and Hall, as well as Milburn, implicitly emphasize individual and intersubjectively negotiated and contextualized agency that is grounded in an interpretive perspective. Their goal is coming to understand how Japanese and U.S. American students and Puerto Ricans in the United States, respectively, conduct themselves as members of national groups in situated and local interaction. The extent to which scholars who seek to uncover privilege and emancipate members of oppressed groups seem to downplay the role of individual agency in emancipatory action, and, alternatively, the extent to which scholars who seem to privilege individual agency at the expense of acknowledging structural constraints may benefit from interperspective dialogue about individual agency and structural hegemony are issues for future research and deliberation.

Dialectical Tensions and Contradictions

Several authors in this volume critique and transform the tendency to dichotomize approaches, constructs, and processes that were presented as polar opposites and dualistic extremes in past research. Binary categorizations such as masculine/feminine and high/low power distance were common in analytical frames and dimensions that had been imported and adapted from social psychology (Hofstede, 1980). Such dichotomies appeared in a good part of our cross-cultural research in the past (Martin, Nakayama, & Flores, 1998) in the form of East-versus-West comparisons, in epistemological orientations as subjective/objective, and in views of researcher/respondent as corresponding to object/subject. Although the dualistic orientations to knowledge building in intercultural communication have a strong legacy in Western philosophy, Bernstein (1983) describes the dangers of the "Either/Or" and argues that "we need to *exorcize* the Cartesian Anxiety and liberate ourselves from its seductive appeal" (p. 19). Martin and Nakayama (1999) also argue that a dialectical perspective stresses the "relational, processual and contradictory nature of knowledge production" (p. 13), and they describe the merits of an epistemological frame that embraces multiple but distinct research paradigms.

Scholars in this volume who call for transforming the binary categorizations into more complex, if not dialectical, approaches in contemporary intercultural communication include Moon, in her discussion of passing as inter/cultural practice. In addition, Nadamitsu, Chen, and Friedrich describe Chinese experiences of Japanese culture in ways that call into question many of the existing descriptions of the Japanese and

Chinese as similar to one another and as typical of "Eastern" cultures. Drzewiecka also describes the challenges as well as the benefits that accrue when researchers must be simultaneously "inside" and "outside," when they must understand the experiences of "insiders" while remaining "outside" enough to theorize and draw conclusions relative to other phenomena (McPhail, 1997).

Overall, if the voices of the authors in this volume are to be acknowledged, the either-or dualisms and distinctions between groups and categories sometimes can be useful because they emerge in the discourse describing differences between Chinese and Japanese, for example. At other times, such identifications are based on contradictory tensions, such as habitus as a dynamic structure for Polish immigrants in the United States, and what Drzewiecka describes as a key to economic success as well as maintenance of traditions and history, a transformed "both-and option," a "borderland" (Anzaldúa, 1987), and an "elsewhere" (Hegde, 1998). Moon describes another borderland constructed by white women in the United States when they use passing as a strategy of both resistance and acquiescence within the context of class-based ideologies and structural constraints.

CONCLUSION

Three major themes characterize the scholarship in this volume on the relationships among culture and discourse. First, many of the researchers make politics an object of study or critique. The researchers in this volume speak from varied political points of view and have different orientations toward analysis of political standpoints articulated and taken for granted in the discourse texts and previous programs of research on culture. Although most acknowledge their own politics and positions, they also differ in the extent to which they wish to emancipate others. A second theme demonstrated here is that not only are multiple perspectives to knowledge building appropriate within programs of research, but also careful translation across perspectives and interperspective dialogue may strengthen theoretical scope and disciplinary value. Furthermore, the role of the communication turn and orientation toward culture as a socially constructed process is a foundational development and an increasingly common perspective. A third theme is that scholars examining culture today are addressing a variety of relevant social problematics reflected in diverse discourses. The scholarly work in this volume demonstrates that research on discourse and culture is relevant to the dynamic global and local sociocultural milieu, as well as to researchers and students in a variety of fields. In addition, the problematics approached by these researchers are evidence of the need for a communication disciplinary lens and of the value in incorporating diverse voices and a diversity of discourses about culture.

REFERENCES

Anderson, J. A. (1996). *Communication theory: Epistemological foundations.* New York: Guilford.

Anzaldúa, G. (1987). *Borderlands/la frontera: The new mestiza.* San Francisco: Spinsters/ Aunt Lute.

Ashcroft, B., Griffiths, G., & Tiffin, H. (1995). Ethnicity and indigeneity: Introduction. In B. Ashcroft, G. Griffiths, & H. Tiffin (Eds.), *The post-colonial studies reader* (pp. 213-214). New York: Routledge.

Bakhtin, M. M. (1984). *Problems of Dostoevsky's poetics* (C. Emerson, Ed., Trans.) Minneapolis: University of Minnesota Press. (Original work published 1929)

Baxter, L., & Montgomery, B. (1996). *Relating: Dialogues and dialectics.* New York: Guilford.

Berger, P., & Luckmann, T. (1966). *The social construction of reality: A treatise in the sociology of knowledge.* New York: Doubleday.

Bernstein, R. J. (1983). *Beyond objectivism and relativism: Science, hermeneutics, and praxis.* Philadelphia: University of Pennsylvania Press.

Bhabha, H. (1995). Signs taken for wonders. In B. Ashcroft, G. Griffiths, & H. Tiffin (Eds.), *The post-colonial studies reader* (pp. 29-35). New York: Routledge.

Burr, V. (1995). *An introduction to social constructionism.* London: Routledge.

Carbaugh, D. (1990). Intercultural communication. In D. Carbaugh (Ed.), *Cultural communication and intercultural contact* (pp. 151-176). Hillsdale, NJ: Lawrence Erlbaum.

Clifford, J., & Marcus, G. E. (Eds.). (1986). *Writing culture: The poetics and politics of ethnography.* Berkeley: University of California Press.

Collier, M. J. (1998). Researching cultural identity: Reconciling interpretive and postcolonial perspectives. In D. V. Tanno & A. González (Eds.), *Communication and identity across cultures* (International and Intercultural Communication Annual, Vol. 21, pp. 122-147). Thousand Oaks, CA: Sage.

Conquergood, D. (1991). Rethinking ethnography: Towards a critical cultural politics. *Communication Monographs, 58,* 179-194.

Conquergood, D. (1992). Ethnography, rhetoric and performance. *Quarterly Journal of Speech, 78,* 80-123.

Dace, K., & McPhail, M. (1998). Crossing the color line: From empathy to implicature in intercultural communication. In J. Martin, T. Nakayama, & L. Flores (Eds.), *Readings in cultural contexts* (pp. 434-441). Mountain View, CA: Mayfield.

Deetz, S. (1994). The future of the discipline: The challenges, the research and the social contribution. In S. Deetz (Ed.), *Communication yearbook: Vol. 17* (pp. 115-147). Thousand Oaks, CA: Sage.

Delgado, F. P. (1994). The complexity of Mexican American identity: A reply to Hecht, Sedano and Ribeau and Mirande and Tanno. *International Journal of Intercultural Relations, 18,* 77-84.

Fiske, J. (1991). Writing ethnographies: Contribution to a dialogue. *Quarterly Journal of Speech, 77,* 330-335.

Foss, S. K., & Foss, K. A. (1994). Inviting transformation: Presentational speaking for a changing world. Prospect Heights, IL: Waveland.

Foucault, M. (1980). *Power/knowledge: Selected interviews and other writings, 1972-1977* (C. Gordon, L. Marshall, J. Mepham, & K. Soper, Trans.). New York: Pantheon.

Friedman, J. (1994). *Cultural identity and global process.* Thousand Oaks, CA: Sage.

Gergen, K. J. (1985). The social constructionist movement in modern psychology. *American Psychologist, 40,* 255-275.

Giddens, A. (1984). *The constitution of society: An outline of the theory of structuralism.* Cambridge, MA: Polity.

Gudykunst, W. B. (1988). Theorizing in intercultural communication: An introduction. In W. Gudykunst (Ed.), *Intercultural communication theory* (International and Intercultural Communication Annual, Vol. 7, pp. 13-20). Thousand Oaks, CA: Sage.

Hall, S. (1995). New ethnicities: The myth of authenticity. In B. Ashcroft, G. Griffiths, & H. Tiffin (Eds.), *The post-colonial studies reader* (pp. 223-227). New York: Routledge.

Halualani, R. T. (1998). Seeing through the screen: A struggle of "culture." In J. Martin, T. Nakayama, & L. Flores (Eds.), *Readings in cultural contexts* (pp. 264-274). Mountain View, CA: Mayfield.

Hegde, R. (1998). A view from elsewhere: Locating difference and the politics of representation from a transnational feminist perspective. *Communication Theory, 8,* 271-297.

Hofstede, G. (1980). *Culture's consequences.* Beverly Hills, CA: Sage.

hooks, b. (1989). *Talking back: Thinking feminist, thinking Black.* Boston: South End.

Keith, N. W. (1997). *Reframing international development.* Thousand Oaks, CA: Sage.

Lyotard, J. (1984). *The postmodern condition* (G. Gennington & B. Massumi, Trans.). Minneapolis: University of Minnesota Press.

Marcus, G. E., & Fischer, M. (1986). *Anthropology as cultural critique.* Chicago: University of Chicago Press.

Martin, J. N., & Nakayama, T. K. (1999). Thinking dialectically about culture and communication. *Communication Theory, 9,* 1-25.

Martin, J. N., Nakayama, T. K., & Flores, L. A. (1998). A dialectical approach to intercultural communication. In J. Martin, T. Nakayama, & L. Flores (Eds.), *Readings in cultural contexts* (pp. 5-14). Mountain View, CA: Mayfield.

McClintock, A. (1995). *Imperial leather.* New York: Routledge.

McGoldrick, M. (1994). Culture, class, race, and gender. *Human Systems: The Journal of Systemic Consultation and Management, 5,* 131-153.

McPhail, M. (1997). (Re)constructing the color line: Complicity and black conservatism. *Communication Theory, 7,* 162-177.

Mumby, D. (1997). Modernism, postmodernism, and communication studies: A rereading of an ongoing debate. *Communication Theory, 7,* 1-28.

Ono, K. (1998). Problematizing "nation" in intercultural communication research. In D. V. Tanno & A. González (Eds.), *Communication and identity across cultures* (International and Intercultural Communication Annual, Vol. 21, pp. 193-202). Thousand Oaks, CA: Sage.

Parry, B. (1995). Problems in current theories of colonial discourse. In B. Ashcroft, G. Griffiths, & H. Tiffin (Eds.), *The post-colonial studies reader* (pp. 36-44). New York: Routledge.

Philipsen, G. (1989). Speech and the communal function in four cultures. In S. Ting-Toomey & F. Korzenny (Eds.), *Language, communication, and culture: Current directions* (International and Intercultural Communication Annual, Vol. 12, pp. 79-92). Newbury Park, CA: Sage.

Powell, R., & Collier, M. J. (1990). Public speaking and cultural bias. *American Behavioral Scientist, 34,* 240-250.

Prus, R. (1996). *Symbolic interaction and ethnographic research.* Albany: State University of New York Press.

Rawlins, W. (1998). Writing about *Friendship Matters:* A case study in dialectical and dialogical inquiry. In B. Montgomery & L. Baxter (Eds.), *Dialectical approaches to studying personal relationships* (pp. 63-82). Mahwah, NJ: Lawrence Erlbaum.

Sacks, H. (1984). On doing "being ordinary." In J. M. Atkinson & J. Heritage (Eds.), *Structures of social action: Studies in conversation analysis* (pp. 413-429). Cambridge, UK: Cambridge University Press.

Shotter, J. (1993). *Conversational realities: Constructing life through language.* London: Sage.

Shuter, R. M. (1990). The centrality of culture. *Southern Communication Journal, 55,* 237-249.

Shuter, R. M. (1998). Revisiting the centrality of culture. In J. Martin, T. Nakayama, & L. Flores (Eds.), *Readings in cultural contexts* (pp. 38-48). Mountain View, CA: Mayfield.

Stewart, J. (1995). *Language as articulate contact.* Albany: State University of New York Press.

van Dijk, T. (1987). *Communicating racism: Ethnic prejudice in thought and talk.* Newbury Park, CA: Sage.

van Dijk, T. (1993). *Discourse and elite racism.* London: Routledge.

van Dijk, T. (1997). The study of discourse. In T. van Dijk (Ed.), *Discourse as structure and process* (pp. 1-34). Thousand Oaks, CA: Sage.

2

Challenging the Myth of Assimilation

A Chicana Feminist Response

LISA A. FLORES • *University of Utah*

> Oppressed people resist by identifying themselves as subjects, by defining
> their reality, shaping their new identity, naming their history, telling their
> story.
>
> —hooks, 1989, p. 43

In *The Last Generation,* Cherríe Moraga (1993) argues that the Chicana/o culture, after more than a century of attack, is dying.[1] Cultural genocide, resulting from politics of assimilation, silence, and oppression, is inevitable. Her response, her resistance, comes in the form of writing, for it is in writing and thus telling the history of Chicanas/os that Moraga hopes to extend the life of the culture. Envisioning in her words and the words of other Chicanas/os the creation of a Chicana/o history, Moraga (1993) writes,

> Our codices—dead leaves unwritten—lie smoldering in the ashes of disre-
> gard, censure, and erasure. . . . I write [*The Last Generation*] against time, out
> of a sense of urgency that Chicanos are a disappearing tribe.
>   My tíos' children have not taught their own children to be Mexicans. They
> have become "Americans." And we're all supposed to quietly accept this
> passing, this slow and painless death of a cultura, this invisible disappearance
> of a people. But I do not accept it. I write. (p. 2)

Moraga's desire to maintain a dying culture by relating a counternarrative contesting assimilation is shared by other Chicanas/os who offer
their words as a means of rejecting dominant discourses (Anzaldúa,
1987; Gutiérrez-Jones, 1995; Rebolledo, 1995). Her position is also em-
braced by hooks (1989), who argues that the dominant authoritative his-

tories of marginalized communities need to be contested and critiqued through the inclusion of histories that come from the members of those marginalized communities.[2] As Moraga (1993) and hooks (1989) both explain, rewriting history from the perspectives of the traditionally disenfranchised positions those who have been objects as subjects. In this chapter, I argue that when members of marginalized communities, including those of us in academia, produce oppositional readings of popular texts, we participate in the critique of master narratives and in so doing contribute to the recording and voicing of the histories of marginalized groups.

Oppositional readings of dominant or mainstream texts have long been recognized as a strategy of resistance. Illustrating how communities that see themselves as outside of the acceptable norms established in popular culture respond to such texts, media critics have argued that audiences claim texts as their own by revising, revisiting, and rejecting texts that they find problematic.[3] Differences in gender, class, and politics affect readings of mass-mediated texts (Bobo, 1995; Condit, 1989; Press, 1991). Although some recognize these oppositional readings as strategies of resistance, others question the supposed critical consciousness of resistive readings that do not alter the existing power structures (Cloud, 1994).[4]

This chapter draws on theories of oppositional readings and argues for an understanding of material change and liberatory power within the act of reading cultural discourses from oppositional positions. I argue both that we can use cultural narratives as frames for oppositional discourses and that such oppositional stories enact and record the cultural history of marginalized peoples. In particular, I offer an oppositional critique of assimilation and draw on Chicana feminist writings, which by their very definition are anti-assimilation, to ground this critique.

I begin by reviewing discussions of oppositional readings of mass media, noting their prevalence among groups whose stories are less likely to be heard in mass-mediated texts. I then argue that we can extend our understanding of oppositional readings by locating this discussion within a specific cultural context. Here, I maintain that there is a growing need to create theories that are culturally positioned. Using the idea of "theory in the flesh" (Moraga & Anzaldúa, 1983, p. 23), I contend that feminists of color revise theory by beginning with the personal and that such theories are essential to feminist scholarship. From this section I move to a case study in which I use Chicana feminist discourse to frame a possible oppositional reading of an assimilation narrative in mass media. Finally, in the conclusion, I argue that when critics reread dominant narratives through marginalized perspectives, we gain broader understandings of resistance.

THEORIZING OPPOSITIONAL READINGS

Arguments over the multiplicity of meanings within particular texts emerged within the debate over approaches to mass media and the move to recognize the role of the audience in the interpretation of texts (Condit, 1989; Fiske, 1986; Hall, 1980). Hall (1980) convincingly argued that audience responses to a text range from "preferred" readings, which cohere with "intended" meanings, to "oppositional" readings, which negate intended meanings. Fiske (1986) contributed to this dialogue on text, audience, and meaning, noting that the combination of the diversity of cultures and societies along with inevitable inequity in power and thus in representation results in "divergent and resistant subcultures . . . alive, well and kicking and exerting various forms of pressure and criticism upon the dominant ideology of Western capitalist societies" (p. 392). Coalescing around the idea of polysemy, media and rhetorical critics offered varying illustrations on the making of meanings (Ceccarelli, 1998; Cloud, 1992; Condit, 1989; Fiske, 1986). This turn to the audience necessitates a rethinking of our understandings of text, context, and meaning.

As critics, when we begin with audience interpretations and understandings of texts, we must recognize the collapse of text into context (McGee, 1990). Audiences approach texts from specific historical and cultural locations, bringing with them experiences that may or may not be widely shared. The positionality of audiences informs and frames the construction of meaning. As text and context begin to merge, the politics of position surface as key in resistance to mass-mediated texts. Individuals and groups who recognize themselves as outside of mainstream culture and as having a history of oppression by mainstream culture develop decoding skills that facilitate oppositional readings.[5]

In the United States, individuals and groups who are outside the mainstream are often able to see through texts and find the "ideological seams" (Radway, 1986).[6] Bobo (1995) offers powerful examples depicting Black women's responses to African Americans in mass media, noting in her study that African American women are quite skilled at resisting images of themselves imposed by mainstream culture. Brown (1994) and Radway (1984/1991) uncover part of the appeal of "women's" texts (i.e., soap operas and romance novels) and reveal how women have used such texts to develop oral networks, to gain historical knowledge, and to build spaces for themselves that cannot be invaded by demands from families. And Fiske (1991) illustrates how men in a homeless shelter subvert traditional relations of hero and villain, cheering at media depictions of violence toward law officers. Surfacing in research on audiences and oppositional readings, then, is the link between audience and the potential for oppositional readings. As people of color have argued for years, living within structures of power and oppression teaches strategies of resistance, and oppositional readings are one such strategy.[7]

Contained within oppositional readings, and contributing to their emancipatory potential, is the speaking of the unspeakable and ignored. The practice of close textual reading, which often privileges authorial intent, has the potential to highlight a rhetor's vision of the world and to elucidate the aesthetics of discourse.[8] Simultaneously, however, such an approach can perpetuate the silencing of alternative views. Still today, the voices we are most likely to hear in public discourse are not the voices of the marginalized and disenfranchised. Their visions are not likely to be contained in those who have the power and resources to speak (Condit, 1990).[9] McGee (1990) notes that in our current postmodern, and I would add, postcolonial society, we cannot afford to assume that audiences interpret texts as they are supposed to. For many audiences, texts become meaningful through what is not said as much as through what is said (McGee, 1990; Wander, 1984).

Where then, is the liberatory potential? Said (1994) argues that "each cultural work is a vision of a moment, and we must juxtapose that vision with the various visions it later provoked" (p. 67). Although many texts are produced with specific audiences in mind and with no real recognition of the complexities of the audiences that are not addressed directly, as critics in a postcolonial world, we do not have to continue to reproduce this politics of silence. By interrogating the texts and uncovering dimensions that might resonate with audiences that are not addressed, we understand processes of colonialism and cultural imperialism (Said, 1994, pp. 66-67). In recognizing both the role of discourse in the perpetuation of power and oppression and the role of the ability of disenfranchised groups to develop strategies of resistance, we begin to see how marginalized groups build cultural discourses that can contest oppressive ones.[10] Moreover, with an emphasis on the multiplicity of audiences, we move away from a speaking-for and toward a speaking-to (Alcoff, 1991).

Although much of the work on oppositional readings is done through media reception studies, rhetorical analyses can also forward counternarratives. Rhetorical critics can participate in the debate over polysemy and oppositionality by uncovering the symbolic workings within a text and between text and audience. As Campbell (1989) states, "Rhetorical critics attempt to function as surrogates for audiences. . . . Based on their general knowledge of rhetorical literature and criticism . . . critics attempt to show how a rhetorical act has the potential to teach, to delight, to move, to flatter, to alienate, or to hearten" (p. 2). Solomon (1988) concurs and argues that rhetorical critics would do well to follow the insights of deconstruction theory and use their critical skills along with "'fresh' eyes" to uncover possible meanings that might emerge between audiences and texts (p. 32).[11] She argues that, ultimately, the critic alone can use her critical skills to offer an informed reading of a text (Solomon, 1988). Indeed, armed with the tools of rhetorical criticism and critical theory, we can investigate the role of discourse and the management of meanings (Brummett, 1991, p. 28). Part of the obligation of the critic as surrogate is to bring to light the symbolic patterns of the projected audience. Here we can turn to McGee (1990), who argues that different communities within a large society, such as the United States, are likely to bring different symbolic meanings to a reading.

This perspective on the role of the rhetorical critic opens the door for rhetorical critics to construct possible oppositional readings. Informed by cultural communities, we can act as surrogates and uncover symbolic patterns. One such cultural community is Chicana feminists. The Chicana feminist community, although unarguably a diverse group, does share some symbolic knowledge that allows for a common bond among Chicana feminists. As a Chicana feminist rhetorical critic, my position as a critic is informed by Chicana history and culture. As a Chicana, my lived experiences are of Chicana history and culture and of Mexican American history and culture. My voice, echoed by the voices of those Chicana feminists I bring to my analysis, allows me to stand as a surrogate for a Chicana feminist audience, and to bring forward this shared symbolic knowledge. Brummett (1991) argues that the critic, informed by the cultural knowledge of the audience she hopes to represent, uncovers possible readings. He states,

> The critic's business is to show how *patterns* available in a cultural repertoire could have been used to order the symbolic environment within a rhetorical transaction. What the critic should discover is how the environment of bits available during a transaction might be ordered to create a mosaic of text, context, and subjects for text and context. (Brummett, 1991, p. 95)

As a Chicana feminist rhetorical critic, then, I have at my disposal the critical and analytical tools that enable me to uncover the "patterns" and the "cultural repertoire" as a Chicana feminist critic and as a rhetorician.[12] The Chicana feminist oppositional reading I offer here, although presented as possible orderings rather than as an absolute interpretation, reflects my critical position as a rhetorician and as a Chicana feminist.

Although communication and media scholars explore the oppositional readings of marginalized groups from both rhetorical and audience reception perspectives, the theory and criticism remain largely within a dominant paradigm. Scholars have begun to consider how theory developed within marginalized communities might extend our understanding of oppositional readings, but more exploration remains to be done. Thus, I turn now to a discussion of the need to develop culturally specific theories.

MOVING TOWARD CULTURALLY LOCATED THEORIES

Feminist scholarship can generally be classified as scholarship that is suspicious of or cautious toward the desire for universal theory. The need to recognize differences and the need to avoid essentialism are by now commonly accepted (e.g., Butler, 1990; Fuss, 1989; Trinh, 1989). Beyond the call to recognize differences among women, however, is the need to address other differences, such as those of race, class, and sexuality (Valdivia, 1995). Feminists of color and lesbian feminists have heralded the cry for theory and criticism that begin within culturally specific contexts and that bring critical attention to the differences that separate women.[13] Among Chicana feminists, such demands for theories from within cultures are often predicated upon a distrust of theories generated by whites (Chabram, 1994; Pérez, 1993; Saldívar-Hull, 1991).

Feminist theory that begins within a cultural context creates spaces for women of color to explore the ways in which the material realities of our lives structure our identities, relationships, and understandings of our worlds. These realities are not adequately represented by essentialist feminist positions that homogenize and create monolithic feminisms. Such culturally specific theories also have the potential to become barriers between those women of color who have the material luxuries that allow them to theorize and those who do not have such time. Women of color within the academy can use theory to bring to women in the community an understanding of different ways of knowing, power structures, and histories of resistance that affect our lives. Such theory, written accessibly, becomes a means of uniting women of color and theory so that women of color have forums for expressing our ideas (Collins, 1988, p. 302; Madison, 1993, p. 214). Experiences of oppression teach women of color to create our own spaces wherein we build and maintain our communities. These spaces and communities enable cultural survival, for it is in these spaces that women of color share our knowledge, strategies of resistance, and means of cultural survival (Collins, 1988; Madison, 1993).

Reflecting on the need to begin with the histories and experiences of a people, Moraga and Anzaldúa (1983) call for "theory in the flesh" (p. 23). Theory in the flesh is that which begins with stories of oppression, resistance, identity, and power told "in our own words" (Moraga & Anzaldúa, 1983, p. 23). Theories in the flesh privilege the situatedness of knowledge within cultural structures and institutions. They help explain differences in experiences, such as understanding home as a "safe" space, where strategies of resistance can be enacted outside of the eyes of the mainstream (Madison, 1993, p. 214). In addition, theories in the flesh "privilege agency and interrogate notions of the . . . 'voiceless victims'" (Madison, 1993, p. 214). Beginning with cultural experiences brings a greater understanding of means of coping with and resisting oppression. Illustrating such theory, Pérez (1993) explains that as a young child she felt alienated and ridiculed in the largely white school she attended and that coming home to her mother after school restored a sense of calmness and tranquility. Talking with her mother in Spanish and singing songs with her mother in Spanish reconstructed cultural pride and location (Pérez, 1993). As Rebolledo (1995) explains, theoretical knowledge about Chicanas should come from those who know Chicana customs. These culturally located stories or theories chronicle the resistance of a people.

By turning to the writings of particular cultural groups and using this discourse to inform our analyses, scholars can begin to meet the need for culturally specific theories. To illustrate, I turn to a particular mainstream narrative of assimilation and reread that narrative from a Chicana feminist perspective.

ASSIMILATION POLITICS AND CULTURAL SURVIVAL: A CHICANA FEMINIST PERSPECTIVE

Chicana feminism as a political identity provides a lens or framework through which oppositional discourses can be created. In this section, I build on theory about oppositional readings by introducing Chicana feminism. Drawing on ideas and arguments from Chicana feminists, I provide two perspectives on assimilation. The first uses a recent mainstream text, the television program *Matt Waters,* as an instance of a contemporary mainstream narrative of assimilation. I then counter that story with a Chicana feminist reading that illustrates how the anti-assimilation position of Chicana feminists enables the rupturing of the dominant assimilation story as manifested in *Matt Waters.*

The program *Matt Waters* is a drama set in an ethnically mixed high school in a large city. Starring Montel Williams as Matt Waters, a high school teacher, the program offers a view of an integrated and well-adjusted society. Watching the program *Matt Waters,* although it was a short-lived series, gives viewers an enticing vision of the new world.[14] In the midst of an inner city, which today has become synonymous with gangs, drugs, and crime, there is hope. In *Matt Waters* we find the multicultural ideal, an ethnically diverse school where teachers and students learn about similarities and differences and choose to join together as members of the human race. Reviewers consistently compared the program to earlier programs, such as *Room 222* and *The White Shadow,* in which caring teachers help troubled students (O'Connor, 1996; Schleier, 1996; Zurawik, 1996). Williams seems to agree with the analogy and adds that the title character is based on his own life and his desire to give back to the community (Kelleher, 1995; "Montel Williams' new series," 1996).

In the two episodes under analysis here, Angela, a Puerto Rican high school student, questions identity and her position in the world. In each of the story lines that features Angela, she struggles with her place and her future.[15] From a "preferred" perspective, we can view Angela's struggles with her view of herself and her place in the world as her movement toward assimilation. This choice seems reasonable given the environment in which she lives. Her classmates are Latina/o, African American, Asian American, and white. They are gay and straight. Her teachers are African American and white.[16] Problems in school, whether in class assignments or interpersonal relations, do not center on racial or sexual politics. Instead, they are the "normal" high school problems of dating and doing well in school.[17]

The discourse surrounding Angela begins in science class, where Waters talks to the diverse class about genetics, evolution, and adaptation. One class discussion revolves around genetics and the many links that unite all humans. Waters divides the class into two groups, those who can curl their tongues and those who cannot. Speaking to those who can curl their tongues, Waters tells the class to greet their long-lost relatives. One African American student responds that they are not related because they are all of different races. Waters replies: "Yes, you may be different races, but those people who can curl their tongues, all share a common gene. As a matter of fact, 99.99% of our genes are all actually identical. There's no difference between Tyler, Don, Chloe . . . none whatsoever." Waters's lecture promotes a joining in similarities over differences, and viewers who are uneasy about what they see as growing cultural separatism in the United States can take comfort in this call for membership in the human race. In this celebration of a pluralism that is united in harmony and similarity, dominant social relations go unquestioned, and a society confronted with difference and fragmentation can be reassured by this liberal universalist message, which ultimately contributes to the maintenance of the hegemonic order (Gray, 1995).

The discourse of assimilation continues in *Matt Waters* as Waters and his science class proceed in their exploration of evolution. Teaching students that it is through adaptation and the development of favorable traits that species survive, Waters argues that without adaptation, species die out.

> Waters: Now look, 99% of the life forms that have ever existed are dead and gone, why?
>
> Angela: Because they couldn't adapt to change.
>
> Waters: It is a brutal world out there. If you don't change and adapt, let's say physically or biologically, the natural selection process is going to weed you out. . . . Adaptation to environment. The willingness to face change.

In this discussion of adaptation, the underlying message is assimilation. The happy world in *Matt Waters,* where differences blend into community, works because the postcolonial "Other" sheds those differences that impede community, choosing to adapt to the multicultural U.S. America. Angela's response to Waters signifies her recognition of the need for adaptation and thus her commitment to assimilation.

Angela's decision to adapt becomes clear in her interactions with her friends. In particular, in conversations with her friend Russ Ochoa and with her romantic interest "T" Rodriguez, Angela chooses assimilation over cultural maintenance. Following science class, Angela and her friend Russ head outdoors to eat lunch from a freestanding lunch cart, run by T Rodriguez. While they are walking, Angela and Russ discuss their science class and the assignment to write a paper about an inherited trait. Angela remarks, "I don't know, sometimes I come home and I look at my family, and I feel like we're from different countries, like we're not even related." In this statement, Angela distances herself from her "ethnic" heritage and marks her chosen position within a unified, and thus, mainly white culture.

Angela continues this separation from her ethnicity in her choice of lunch. T, flirting with Angela, says, "I've got a special on black beans to-day," to which Angela replies, "You know I don't like those, why don't you just give me a hamburger." In this juxtaposition of two quintessential ethnic markers, black beans and hamburgers, Angela moves away from one of the few acceptable signs of difference, ethnic food, and establishes herself as American in her consumption of the paradigmatic emblem of American culture, the hamburger. In a later scene, again with Russ, Angela's struggle with her identity continues to go in favor of an American ideal and away from an ethnic heritage. Angela debates whether to date T:

Angela: He's not my type, he's too . . .

Russ: Puerto Rican.

Angela: Exactly.

Russ: You better check your genes girl because aren't you?

As *Matt Waters* progresses, Angela moves away from her ethnic heritage and toward adaptation and assimilation into a generic (read white) American culture.

The discourse that connects assimilation with success is supported throughout the show in the character of Matt Waters, who becomes a sign for success in spite of obstacles. Viewers learn in the show that Waters faced discrimination as a student from a teacher who failed him largely because he is Black. Williams supports this reading in his discussion of the deliberate connections between his life and the character's life. Whereas Waters comes to teaching after retiring from a 20-year career as a Navy SEAL, Williams's military career included enlisting in the Marines and then graduating from the Naval Academy (McCabe, 1995). Other connections between the character and the actor include a determination to overcome social obstacles, a commitment to education, and a commitment to making a difference (Dorsey, 1996; Pennington, 1996; Schleier, 1996). Williams comments on the need to face adversity in his references to the work ethic of his father, who held multiple jobs to compensate for the low wages paid to Blacks (Schleier, 1996). Schleier (1996) describes Williams's ability to succeed in spite of racism: "Fortunately, he [Williams] comes from a family that does not allow racism to stand in its way. His dad is currently chief of the Baltimore Fire Department. And when the family moved to a suburb where Montel was bused to primarily white schools, he essentially took over, serving as president of his high school junior and senior classes, student representative to the board of education and in other local and regional posts" (p. 2). This discussion of Williams and his family, which appears in multiple articles about the show, supports the argument that when social minorities work hard and refuse to be "victims," they can find success.[18] Thus, both Angela and Williams/Waters are examples of a system that works.

In contrast to Angela, who becomes a sign of success through assimilation (she appears to do well in school, and we learn that she maintains a part-time job while going to school), is T, who acts as a reminder of the dangers of cultural maintenance. In his language and his manner, T signifies Latina/o culture. Unlike Angela, T is comfortable code switching. He proposes to Angela that they go dancing to "Latin" music, and he exhibits the assertive street flirting commonly attributed to Latinos (Lozano, 1994). At the same time that T comes to represent ethnicity, that ethnicity is equated with difference and then with problems, illustrating the common mass-mediated response to difference (Cuklanz, 1995).

The conflation of ethnicity with difference and problem in T is manifested in T's struggle to maintain his job. As Angela, Russ, and their multicultural classmates are learning the lessons of assimilation, T is facing impending unemployment. After another science lecture on adaptation and cultural survival, Angela ventures outdoors to visit T, who is alone in the rain trying to fix a problem with his lunch cart. Angela, having internalized the class lecture, encourages him to "adapt," to go back to school and graduate, arguing that his job is menial and that if he tried he could do better. T explosively refuses to consider going back to school, and viewers begin to see T setting himself up for unemployment. In his refusal to adapt, T becomes an example of death from failure to assimilate.

In the next scene between Angela and T, T stands outside his desolate lunch wagon, looking out over the water. Angela approaches but stops short, watching him. She stands on one side of a chain-link fence, with the school behind her; on the other side is T—cold, wet, and alone. Angela goes to T, and he explains that when he and his friends dropped out of school, they swore they would never go back. She asks what his life will be like in 20 years and then says, "I'm going inside, it's starting to rain harder." This scene serves to emphasize to viewers that assimilation, and particularly formal education, is the route to survival and success. Angela's verbal messages combine with nonverbal ones to create a visual argument for assimilation. T, with his mobile lunch cart, now empty of customers, represents isolation. The strategic placing of Angela and T on opposite sides of a chain-link fence reminds viewers of boundaries that can separate cultures and countries. Angela's position on the "inside" of the fence is further evidence of her alignment with dominant culture, whereas T, on the outside and in symbolic danger of drowning, must make a choice between assimilation and survival or separation and death. Angela's final comment to T, "I'm going inside, it's starting to rain harder," seals the assimilation discourse. Inside is the safe haven of the ideal pluralistic world, of which Angela is now a member. T, alone in the rain, can choose to engage in a futile battle against forces of nature. Should he opt for difference, he will likely fail. There is little room in either character, Angela or T, for a position in between assimilation and separation. Each character is positioned as a commitment to only a select group of cultural markers, including food, music, and language. The power of particular choices, most specifically the food and the music, comes from the general social acceptance of ethnic food and music, for if Angela must reject even food and music, what room is left for her to maneuver in between assimilation and cultural maintenance? The choices here seem limited.

The markers for finding a discourse on assimilation in *Matt Waters* abound. However, to follow the seeming logic of this assimilationist politics requires an initial belief in the goal of a single, unified American culture expressed in a harmonious community such as that found within the *Matt Waters* community. The assimilationist perspective also mandates an assumption that ethnic minorities cannot maintain cultural difference except in rejection of all of dominant or mainstream society, as is evidenced by T.

If, however, audience members are initially suspicious of assimilation, they might read through and consciously reject this argument, finding instead a counterdiscourse that equates assimilation with cultural death. One such group of audience members might include Chicana feminists, because the narratives and writings of Chicana feminists are grounded in a rejection of assimilation. Many Chicana feminists find that their life stories and experiences shape their perspective on assimilation, illustrating the call by Moraga and Anzaldúa (1983) for "theory in the flesh." For instance, Moraga writes of how her success in school and her fluency in English offered her the opportunity to interact in an Anglo world but also alienated and distanced her from Chicana/o communities. In hindsight, she notes that assimilation comes at a price that is too high to pay, and thus she rejects assimilation: "To be a Chicana is not merely to name one's racial/cultural identity, but also to name a politic, a politic that refuses assimilation into the U.S. mainstream" (Moraga, 1983, p. 56). Similarly, Fregoso and Chabram (1990) argue that the very term *Chicana/o* entails "the rejection of assimilation, acculturation, and the myth of the American melting pot" (p. 205). Thus, the writings of Chicana feminists offer possible insight into what counternarratives to assimilation might look like.

Although the argument for assimilation in *Matt Waters* includes everyone but T, much of the story is played out through the character Angela. A clear tension in Angela's life is her ethnic identity. Whether it is in her caution about dating a young man because he is "too Puerto Rican," her rejection of black beans for lunch, or her sense that her family is of a "different race," her distancing of herself from her Puerto Rican identity is clear. And yet, her choice to blend is not surprising. The environment in which she lives privileges assimilation as the key to survival. This survival, consistent with U.S. American ideology, is an individual one. Angela can make personal choices—in her food, her relationship partners, and her education—that will increase her chances of making it.

However, for many Chicana feminists, individual success attained through assimilation is akin to cultural death. The voices of Chicana feminists might tell a different story than the one Angela and her classmates hear in science class. I draw on these voices, read through my own, to illustrate another narrative, which questions the call for assimilation.

Angela's quest for identity in *Matt Waters* positions assimilation as the key that allows entry into the public sphere. Unlike T, who stands outside in the rain, Angela chooses to go inside into a seemingly more hospitable climate. And yet, many Chicanas might question the alleged opportunities indoors. Lamenting her inability to speak Spanish and linking this absence to a racist and colonial practice that punished her father for speaking Spanish, Martinez (1999) might point to the ability of both T and Russ to code-switch and the seemingly greater comfort both exhibit with their ethnic identity. In talking with Angela about her reluctance to research her cultural and familial history, Martinez might well say, "I am reminded of the profound silences that capture our histories and keep them bound to the Anglo-racist accounts" (p. 77). For Moraga, the type of choices Angela makes are some of the very choices that lead to cultural e/race/sure. Often able to "pass" because of her Anglo surname and her access to the tools of the English language and of education, Moraga found that it was only in turning back to her culture and history that she began to regain her voice and her self. Cautioning that in assimilation comes silence, Moraga might say to Angela, "In returning to the love of my race, I must return to the fact that not only has the mother been taken from me, but her tongue, her mothertongue. I want the language, feel my tongue rise to the occasion of feeling at home, in common. I know this language in my bones ... and then it escapes me" (Moraga, 1983, p. 141).

Rather than joining in the "human race" and so turning away from history and culture, Chicana feminists advocate a movement toward Chicana feminism. In Chicana feminism, remembering the past is not about cultural separatism but about reenvisioning the future through the past so as to assure survival. This retention of culture includes a recognition of multiple forms of knowledge, which extend beyond what is learned in formal institutions. Chicana feminists call for a "corrective history" (Gutiérrez-Jones, 1995) that necessitates culturally located history. A part of this corrective history is remembering the "once-freedom" days before the 1848 war that resulted in a border separating Mexicanas/os from other Mexicanas/os and remembering the glory days of the Aztecs before Spanish colonization of Mexico (Moraga, 1993, p. 60). Moraga argues that it is only in the turn backward to the knowledge of the past that we can imagine, and so create, a future in which we still exist (1993, p. 60). Castillo (1995) echoes this sentiment and demands that we "be archaeologists and visionaries of our culture" (p. 220). This education in cultural history stands in contrast with Waters's grounding in science, for adaptation to change à la *Matt Waters* and evolutionary theory promises cultural genocide if this adaptation involves forgetting and moving away from obstacles and difficulties. Where Waters envisions a new species, a "human race," Moraga (1993) and Castillo (1995) both ground identity in the history and the lived experiences of a people.

And yet, a re/turn to history does not require one to reject formal education. Instead, it can be a questioning of the false dichotomy of the mainstream assimilation narrative, in which the only two options are assimilation and separatism. For instance, Chicana feminist Orozco (1999) emphasizes *ganas* or desire. The daughter of poor Mexican immigrants and the mother of college-educated professionals, Orozco might be able to offer a different perspective on the choices Angela and T face regarding education and work. For Orozco, the binary choice presented in *Matt Waters* is a fiction that can endanger those who buy into it. Rather than choosing between cultural maintenance and its attendant failure, as signified by T, and assimilation and success, as encoded onto Angela, Orozco (1999) might simply reject this narrative and say instead, "Teach [our . . . future generations] the importance of education. While they are at home, read to them in English *and* in Spanish. Teach them to be proud of their heritage, and tell them that going to school gives them the opportunity to be anything they want" (pp. 119-120).

For many Chicanas, the individualism at the core of assimilation politics ignores and threatens marginalized communities (Rebolledo, 1995; Yarbro-Bejarano, 1988). This individualism signifies the cultural isolation that many Chicanas/os and Latinas/os struggle against, and it precludes the re/turning to community. In addition, individualism allows for a social lack of recognition of oppression and discrimination (Gutiérrez-Jones, 1995). When we highlight what one person has accomplished, we also ignore systematic and institutional discrimination, because we turn our attention to the examples that seem to illustrate equality. Returning to Angela in *Matt Waters,* when Angela espouses to T achievement in school as the key to a better life, the show is then able to locate responsibility for "failure" on T. Such a discourse is dangerous, for the successes of the one eclipse the continuing struggles of the many. Moraga recalls the battles her Chicana/o students face: "Even if *they* got to UC Berkeley, their brother is still on crack in Boyle Heights, their sister had three kids before she's twenty, and *sorry but they can't finish the last week of the semester cuz Tío Ignacio just got shot in front of a liquor store*" (emphasis in original; Moraga, 1993, p. 155). The assimilationist discourse in *Matt Waters* requires a choice between self and family, between self and community, which is seen in Angela's distancing of herself from those who are "too Puerto Rican." For Chicana feminists, this option is short-sighted and flawed. Ultimately, Chicana feminists deconstruct the myth of assimilation. Denouncing its dangers and uncovering its fallacies, Chicana feminists offer another option, in which identities are complex and culturally specific. Indeed, for many Chicana feminists, it is the empty promise of assimilation that must be made visible. Castillo (1995) argues that the melting pot myth does not work, in large part because people of color in the United States are denied the option of claiming an "American" identity. The life experiences of Chicana feminists as well as those of many people of color form the theoretical foundations through which counternarratives to assimilation are formed.

CONCLUSION

For cultural and intercultural scholars, the theory and practice of reading against the grain, as developed by media and rhetorical scholars, has much to offer. As scholars interested in cultural relations and the role of power in those relations, the analysis of dominant or master narratives from marginalized perspectives offers a means of uncovering the implicit messages that help to maintain the status quo. By charting oppositional readings through both audience reception studies and rhetorical analyses, scholars can bring forward the multiple histories and counternarratives that both supplement and contest existing ones. Such a process is an important part of the recording of multiple voices.

Chicana feminism offers a particular instance of opposition through the challenging of the mainstream assimilation narrative. Identifying and articulating this counternarrative breaks the silence that comes within the myth of the happy multicultural community. This counternarrative emerges in the writings of Chicana feminists, and it becomes a resource, a strategy of resistance, and a lens through which we can uncover the symbolic patterns of a particular marginalized group. Although this counternarrative might not replace others in circulation, it can be shared among generations so that children and grandchildren gain insight into the collective memory and future visions of a people. In growing assimilation, when second-generation immigrants are more likely to lose their "native" tongue than to retain it and when history books continue to perpetuate one-sided versions of the past, the histories of marginalized groups are in danger. Arguments such as those that deny the Holocaust magnify the need for culturally specific histories, and in the sharing of oppositional perspectives, individuals and communities within and without the academy can engage in historical correction.

NOTES

1. Following current practice among Chicana/o critical scholars and feminists of color, I use the term *Chicana/o* as a gender-inclusive term. When I use "Chicano," I refer to men or male perspectives, whereas when I use "Chicana," I refer to women or female perspectives. The terms *Chicano, Chicana, Chicana/o,* and *Chicano/a* also refer in this chapter to a self-claimed ideological identity position. As Alarcón (1990) argues, "The name Chicana, is not a name that women (or men) are born to or with, as is often the case with 'Mexican,' but rather it is consciously and critically assumed and serves as point of redeparture for dismantling historical conjunctures of crisis, confusion, political and ideological conflict and contradictions" (p. 250). The term *Mexican American* denotes descent and U.S. citizenship, and *Mexicana/o, Mexicano/a,* and *Mexican* also indicate descent and Mexican citizenship.

2. See also Madison (1993) and Trinh (1989) for further support for the importance of telling one's story.

3. See, for example, Bobo, 1995; Brown, 1994; Condit, 1989; Fiske, 1986; Hall, 1980; Press, 1991; and Steiner, 1988.

4. Cloud (1994) argues that theories of materialism in discourse overstate claims to resistance and change. Her position is that although audiences may respond in critical and questioning ways to mass media and popular culture, such response does not alter the living conditions of the people. She argues further that critics who claim to be materialists should look to such things as strikes or political battles if they wish for material change.

5. Condit (1989) argues that it is considerably more difficult to decode mass-mediated texts in oppositional ways than in preferred ways.

6. For some examples of audience studies that illustrate oppositional decoding, see Bobo, 1995; Brown, 1994; Dow, 1992; Liebes, 1990; Press, 1991; and Radway, 1984/1991.

7. For many marginalized groups, one strategy of resistance has been the development of what Black feminist Patricia Hill Collins (1990) calls "dual consciousness." She argues that Black women learn to see through the "lens of the oppressor" and to hide themselves from the dominant gaze.

8. See, for example, the collection of essays in Leff and Kauffeld (1989), which provides insight into the complexities of public texts.

9. Here, I am using the word *speak* broadly to encompass public discourse, which includes, of course, the mass media. Although I recognize that more people of color are gaining access to the production of public texts, I maintain that the overwhelming majority of "public" discourse still comes from a predominantly white male center.

10. Bobo (1995) clarifies that to argue that marginalized and disenfranchised communities appropriate mass-mediated texts, finding in those texts image resources that can be reconstructed in culturally affirming ways, does not mitigate against the potential power of such texts to perpetuate restrictive and stereotypical images.

11. See also Rosenfield (1990), who proposes the critic as surrogate as one of the available positions from which to do rhetorical criticism.

12. Clearly, I cannot extrapolate from my critical analysis to a definitive Chicana feminist reading. To do so would be to fall into an essentializing trap and to position my voice as the voice of Chicana feminists. This type of argument requires a belief in an authentic Chicana voice. I have no wish to attempt to speak for all Chicana feminists or to try to locate authenticity; it does not exist. However, what I, as a rhetorical critic and a Chicana feminist, can do is speak as one member of the Chicana feminist community.

13. Some scholars of color who support the development of culturally specific theories include Anzaldúa, 1987; Castillo, 1995; Collins, 1990; Moraga, 1993; Radford-Hill, 1986; Smith, 1985; and Wong, 1991.

14. The program ran on CBS during the spring of 1996. It was produced by Christmas Tree Entertainment and James D. Parriott Productions. Williams began working on the show in August 1991 ("Montel Williams' new series," 1996; O'Connor, 1996).

15. For the purposes of this analysis, it is coincidental that the central character in this assimilation discourse is Puerto Rican. Because the intent of this chapter is to offer a Chicana feminist analysis of a mainstream assimilation discourse, the cultural, historical, political, and social specificities that certainly influence experienced choices regarding modes of adaptation are less relevant than the larger discourse of assimilation and survival. Indeed, what is most compelling about this particular instance of a mainstream discourse on assimilation is the explicit attempt to address a diverse audience and to tackle difficult questions. I do not mean to suggest in my analysis that the differences between Puerto Ricans, Mexican Americans, Chicanas/os, other Latinas/os, and other people of color are irrelevant. Rather, I draw attention to the overarching theme of assimilation that has resonance to a Chicana feminist community, because central to one's decision to self-label as "Chicana" is one's opposition to assimilation. Although this particular instance of the mainstream melting pot myth centers on a Puerto Rican woman, I maintain that the narrative would still have resonance for Chicanas who would be likely to critique it.

16. In one interview, Williams describes the case as "almost a U.N. cast" (Solomon, 1996), and a reviewer describes the students as an "appealing, rainbow-coalition core group of teenagers" (Johnson, 1996).

17. Other episodes feature problems associated with "urban" schools, including gangs and drugs.

18. Articles that discuss Williams's achievements include Dorsey, 1996; Johnson, 1996; Jones, 1996; Kelleher, 1995; McCabe, 1995; Pennington, 1996; Schleier, 1996; Solomon, 1996; and Zurawik, 1996.

REFERENCES

Alarcón, N. (1990). Chicana feminism: In the tracks of "The" native woman. *Cultural Studies, 4,* 248-255.

Alcoff, L. (1991). The problem of speaking for others. *Cultural Critique, 10,* 5-32.

Anzaldúa, G. (1987). *Borderlands/la frontera: The new mestiza.* San Francisco: Aunt Lute.

Bobo, J. (1995). *Black women as cultural readers.* New York: Columbia University Press.

Brown, M. E. (1994). *Soap opera and women's talk: The pleasure of resistance.* Thousand Oaks, CA: Sage.

Brummett, B. (1991). *Rhetorical dimensions of popular culture.* Tuscaloosa: University of Alabama Press.

Butler, J. (1990). *Gender trouble: Feminism and the subversion of identity.* New York: Routledge.

Campbell, K. K. (1989). *Man cannot speak for her: A critical study of early feminist rhetoric: Vol. 1.* New York: Praeger.

Castillo, A. (1995). *Massacre of the dreamers: Essays on Xicanisma.* New York: Plume.

Ceccarelli, L. (1998). Polysemy: Multiple meanings in rhetorical criticism. *Quarterly Journal of Speech, 84,* 395-415.

Chabram, A. (1994). Conceptualizing Chicano critical discourse. In H. Calderón & J. D. Saldívar (Eds.), *Criticism in the borderlands: Studies in Chicano literature, culture, and ideology* (pp. 127-148). Durham, NC: Duke University Press.

Cloud, D. L. (1992). The limits of interpretation: Ambivalence and the stereotype in Spenser: For Hire. *Critical Studies in Mass Communication, 9,* 311-324.

Cloud, D. L. (1994). The materiality of discourse as oxymoron: A challenge to critical rhetoric. *Western Journal of Communication, 58,* 141-163.

Collins, P. H. (1988). The social construction of Black feminist thought. In M. R. Malson, E. Mudimbe-Boyi, J. F. O'Barr, & M. Wyer (Eds.), *Black women in America* (pp. 297-325). Chicago: University of Chicago Press.

Collins, P. H. (1990). *Black feminist thought: Knowledge, consciousness, and the politics of empowerment.* New York: Routledge.

Condit, C. M. (1989). The rhetorical limits of polysemy. *Critical Studies in Mass Communication, 6,* 103-122.

Condit, C. M. (1990). Rhetorical criticism and audiences: The extremes of McGee and Leff. *Western Journal of Speech Communication, 54,* 330-345.

Cuklanz, L. M. (1995). News coverage of ethnic and gender issues in the Big Dan's rape case. In A. N. Valdivia (Ed.), *Feminism, multiculturalism, and the media: Global diversities* (pp. 145-162). Thousand Oaks, CA: Sage.

Dorsey, T. (1996, January 3). CBS' *Matt Waters* looks as if it will sink. *Courier-Journal* (Louisville, KY) [On-line], pp. 1-3. Available: http://proquest/umi.com/pqdweb

Dow, B. J. (1992). Femininity and feminism in *Murphy Brown. Southern Communication Journal, 57,* 143-155.

Fiske, J. (1986). Television: Polysemy and popularity. *Critical Studies in Mass Communication, 3,* 391-408.

Fiske, J. (1991). For cultural interpretation: A study of the culture of homelessness. *Critical Studies in Mass Communication, 8,* 455-474.

Fregoso, R. L., & Chabram, A. (1990). Chicana/o cultural representations: Reframing alternative critical discourses. *Cultural Studies, 4,* 203-212.

Fuss, D. (1989). *Essentially speaking: Feminism, nature & difference.* New York: Routledge.

Gray, H. (1995). *Watching race: Television and the struggle for "Blackness."* Minneapolis: University of Minnesota Press.

Gutiérrez-Jones, C. (1995). *Rethinking the borderlands: Between Chicano culture and legal discourse.* Berkeley: University of California Press.

Hall, S. (1980). Encoding/decoding. In S. Hall, D. Hobson, A. Lowe, & P. Willis (Eds.), *Culture, media, language* (pp. 128-138). London: Hutchinson.

hooks, b. (1989). *Talking back: Thinking feminist, thinking Black.* Boston: South End.

Johnson, S. (1996, January 10). Murky *Waters*: Montel Williams' new series gets stranded on the shoals of familiar situations. *Chicago Tribune,* Tempo, p. 3.

Jones, B. (1996, January 3). "Welcome back, Montel"? School drama stars talk jock. *The Arizona Republic,* p. C6.

Kelleher, T. (1995, December 31). Teaching in the school of hard knocks. *Newsday,* TV-Plus, p. 3.

Leff, M. C., & Kauffeld, F. J. (Eds.). (1989). *Texts in context: Critical dialogues on significant episodes in American political rhetoric.* Davis, CA: Hermagoras Press.

Liebes, T. (1990). Cultural differences in the retelling of television fiction. In B. L. Brock, R. L. Scott, & J. W. Chesebro (Eds.), *Methods of rhetorical criticism: A twentieth-century perspective* (3rd ed., pp. 461-476). Detroit, MI: Wayne State University Press.

Lozano, E. (1994). The cultural experience of space and body: A reading of Latin American and Anglo American comportment in public. In A. González, M. Houston, & V. Chen (Eds.), *Our voices: Essays in culture, ethnicity, and communication* (pp. 140-145). Los Angeles: Roxbury Press.

Madison, D. S. (1993). "That was my occupation": Oral narrative, performance, and Black feminist thought. *Text and Performance Quarterly, 13,* 213-232.

Martinez, J. M. (1999). Speaking as a Chicana: Tracing cultural heritage through silence and betrayal. In D. L. Gallindo & M. D. Gonzales (Eds.), *Speaking Chicana: Voice, power, and identity* (pp. 59-84). Tucson: University of Arizona Press.

McCabe, B. (1995, December 31). From talk-show host to teacher. *The Boston Globe,* TV Week, p. 4.

McGee, M. C. (1990). Text, context, and the fragmentation of contemporary culture. *Western Journal of Speech Communication, 54,* 274-289.

Montel Williams' new series gets the message across. (1996, January 3). *Chicago Tribune,* Tempo, p. 7.

Moraga, C. (1983). *Loving in the war years: lo que nunca pasó por sus labios.* Boston: South End.

Moraga, C. (1993). *The last generation.* Boston: South End.

Moraga, C., & Anzaldúa, G. (Eds.). (1983). *This bridge called my back: Writings by radical women of color.* New York: Kitchen Table.

O'Connor, J. J. (1996, January 3). Tough-guy teacher with cash to spare. *The New York Times,* p. C16.

Orozco, A. E. (1999). Mexican blood runs through my veins. In D. L. Gallindo & M. D. Gonzales (Eds.), *Speaking Chicana: Voice, power, and identity* (pp. 106-120). Tucson: University of Arizona Press.

Pennington, G. (1996, January 10). Overlooking preachiness of TV's new *Matt Waters. St. Louis Post-Dispatch* [On-line], pp. 1-3. Available: http://web.lexis-nexis.com/universe

Pérez, E. (1993). Sexuality and discourse: Notes from a Chicana survivor. In N. Alarcón, R. Castro, E. Pérez, B. Pesquera, A. S. Riddell, & P. Zavella (Eds.), *Chicana critical issues* (pp. 45-69). Berkeley: Third Woman Press.

Press, A. L. (1991). *Women watching television: Gender, class, and generation in the American television experience.* Philadelphia: University of Pennsylvania Press.

Radford-Hill, S. (1986). Considering feminism as a model for social change. In T. de Lauretis (Ed.), *Feminist studies/Critical studies* (pp. 157-172). Bloomington: Indiana University Press.

Radway, J. A. (1986). Identifying ideological seams: Mass culture, analytical method, and political practice. *Communication, 9,* 93-123.

Radway, J. A. (1991). *Reading the romance: Women, patriarchy, and popular literature.* Chapel Hill: University of North Carolina Press. (Original work published 1984)

Rebolledo, T. D. (1995). *Women singing in the snow: A cultural analysis of Chicana literature.* Tucson: University of Arizona Press.

Rosenfield, L. W. (1990). The anatomy of critical discourse. In B. L. Brock, R. L. Scott, & J. W. Chesebro (Eds.), *Methods of rhetorical criticism* (3rd ed., pp. 96-116). Detroit, MI: Wayne State University Press.

Said, E. W. (1994). *Culture and imperialism.* New York: Vintage Books.

Saldívar-Hull, S. (1991). Feminism on the border: From gender politics to geopolitics. In R. Trujillo, J. D. Saldívar, & H. Calderón (Eds.), *Criticism on the borderlands: Studies in Chicano literature, culture, and ideology* (pp. 203-220). Durham, NC: Duke University Press.

Schleier, C. (1996, January 3). Next on Montel . . . Talk show hosts who become prime-time actors. *The Detroit News* [On-line], pp. 1-3. Available: web.lexis-nexis.com

Smith, B. (1985). Toward a Black feminist criticism. In E. Showalter (Ed.), *Feminist criticism: Essays on women, literature, & theory* (pp. 168-185). New York: Pantheon.

Solomon, H. (1996, January 3). Montel Williams rescues tough classroom drama after it was adrift in . . . rough "Waters." *The Boston Herald,* [On-line], p. TV. Available: http://web.lexis-nexis.com/universe

Solomon, M. (1988). "With firmness in the right": The creation of moral hegemony in Lincoln's second inaugural. *Communication Reports, 1,* 32-37.

Steiner, L. (1988). Oppositional decoding as an act of resistance. *Critical Studies in Mass Communication, 5,* 1-15.

Trinh, T. M. (1989). *Woman native other.* Bloomington: Indiana University Press.

Valdivia, A. N. (Ed.). (1995). *Feminism, multiculturalism, and the media: Global diversities.* Thousand Oaks, CA: Sage.

Wander, P. (1984). The third persona: An ideological turn in rhetorical theory. *Central States Speech Journal, 35,* 197-216.

Wong, N. (1991). Socialist feminism: Our bridge to freedom. In C. T. Mohanty, A. Russo, & L. Torres (Eds.), *Third world women and the politics of feminism* (pp. 288-296). Bloomington: Indiana University Press.

Yarbro-Bejarano, Y. (1988). Chicana literature from a Chicana feminist perspective. In M. Herrera-Sobek & H. M. Viramontes (Eds.), *Chicana creativity and criticism: Charting new frontiers in American literature* (pp. 139-146). Houston, TX: Arte Publico Press.

Zurawik, D. (1996, January 3). Give *Matt Waters* an F: New classroom drama plays more like a TV talk show with characters behaving like dysfunctional guests. *The Baltimore Sun,* p. E1.

3

Enacting "Puerto Rican Time" in the United States

TRUDY MILBURN • *Baruch College*

Through communication people constitute communities. Carbaugh (1994) describes this as the process of "linking individuals into communities of shared identity" (p. 24).[1] Various communicative forms are used to enact and enable the creation of communities and shared identities. Within communities, however, there is often competing cultural knowledge or symbols upon which participants draw to structure their activities. I will describe one such symbol, which can be said to have had competing, or at least disparate, cultural value as it occurred within two events at a Puerto Rican cultural center (PRCC). The symbol of communication described here is the use of "time."

I take as my base a perspective that stems from ethnography of communication literature: namely, that communication is primary, that communicative practices have cultural components, and that through communication a sense of what it means to be a "Puerto Rican" or any other type of person or group member is constructed. I used the following literature to form a conceptual framework through which to distinguish and explicate the particular components addressed in this study.

COMMUNICATION

Sapir (1931) describes communication as something that occurs day to day among individuals. Although it is a mundane process, Sapir tells us that "language is the communicative process par excellence in every known society" (p. 105). Through language, communication reaffirms society. Communication also varies in form and meaning depending on particular personal relationships.

Not only is communication an everyday process, it also symbolically produces, maintains, repairs, and transforms reality (Carey, 1975, p. 10). Based on the assertion that communication creates reality, communication researchers should ask questions such as how do we create, express, and convey our knowledge of and attitudes toward reality (Carey, 1975, p. 17). Expressed in another way, Carbaugh (1989) defines *communication* as "a spoken system of symbols, symbolic forms, and meanings" (p. 14). Carbaugh builds on the foundation established by Hymes (1972, 1974) and posits four components of communication, all of which are relevant to discourse at a PRCC: it is socially negotiated, individually applied, culturally distinct, and historically grounded. Many authors have defined and relied on symbols as a way to examine the communicative practices of a culture. For Geertz (1973), *symbols* are broad categories to describe social organization (p. 17). Schneider (1976) approaches culture as a large symbolic system. Given the importance of symbols, symbolic actions, and their meanings, one can attend to the significant symbols through and with which participants in a given speech community make meaning. These symbols can partially constitute membership[2] and can function to organize actions. In summary, the fundamental question in my ethnography of communication study is, what forms and meanings of communication related to time are used by Puerto Ricans in a particular site?

COMMUNICATION AND CULTURE

Given the constitutive nature of communication, we can speak of communication as creating culture. Carey (1975) defines communication as the "construction and maintenance of an ordered, meaningful cultural world" (p. 6). While creating culture, communicative practices can also be described as cultural. Carbaugh (1994) refers to Philipsen (1992) when he states, "to speak is, fundamentally, to speak culturally" (p. 8). Therefore, communication in part constitutes culture and can be heard as a cultural phenomenon.

Culture in the United States has become a particularly salient area of investigation given current social attention to "multiculturalism" (Hilgers, Wunsch, & Chattergy, 1992; Lynch, 1989; Phelan & Davidson, 1993; Thompson & Tyagi, 1993). However, much writing about multiculturalism is "narrow and ethnocentric" (Lynch, 1989) and does not focus on the communicative construction of culture. Therefore, an examination of particular communicative constructions of culture adds to our knowledge of multiculturalism and diversity.

Understanding "native" (Geertz, 1973, p. 15) meanings, or those meanings particular to a specific group at a specific time and place, is an important starting point for developing intercultural or cross-cultural communication theories. Geertz (1973) defines *culture* as

> an historically transmitted pattern of meanings embodied in symbols, a system of inherited conceptions expressed in symbolic forms by means of which [people] communicate, perpetuate, and develop their knowledge about and attitudes toward life. (p. 89)

This interpretation highlights the communicative creation of culture. As a communicative accomplishment, culture can be studied as "contested, temporal, and emergent" (Clifford & Marcus, 1986, p. 19). Juan Flores (1993) echoes this sentiment in his description of Puerto Rican culture. He describes culture as "the vibrant, living expression of the 'soul' of a people or an epoch" (p. 47). To research cultural communication conceived of in this way, one can examine the components of culture described by Philipsen (1987): code, conversation, and community (p. 249). These elements refer to the deeply held beliefs (code) that tie a culture together through various communicative acts (conversation) that compose a community. The description of cultural communication used in this study is also consistent with that of Carbaugh (1990), who proposed the usefulness of focusing on three important issues: "shared identity," "common meaning" (p. 5), and the role communication plays in the development of each.

A CALL TO STUDY PUERTO RICAN COMMUNICATION PRACTICES

Flores (1993) calls for ethnographic research about Puerto Ricans when he describes current research as "missing . . . any resonance of the community's own language practice" (pp. 148-149). He describes Puerto Rican speech in the United States as an "intricate mixing and code switching" (pp. 148-149). Because the communicative practices are so richly complex, Flores (1993) advocates for the use of an "obvious source of evidence: the firsthand cultural production of Puerto Ricans in the United States and their linguistic practices" (p. 159).

Although this type of research is called for, Flores (1993) also warns us about trying to find the essence of Puerto Ricans. He believes that Puerto Rican identity is constructed through a dynamic process rather than through a researcher's or individual's quest for a "primordial *que somos?*" (who are we?). Flores (1993) indicates that the question of who we are and how we are is defined through a "relational, non-essentialist approach" that accounts for "diversity and complexity" (p. 100).

Morris's (1981) research points to the complexity of Puerto Rican identity, as his research methods have been an attempt to observe and understand the "sayings and meanings" of Puerto Ricans in Puerto Rico. According to his conclusions, the words Puerto Ricans use do not make clear and direct reference to places and things. Morris criticizes Puerto Rican language imprecision, and thus Puerto Ricans themselves, from an ethnocentric "ethnographic" study of discourse. Thus, he fails to attend to the significance of the usage for the people using the language (and how they would define themselves). His work, though perhaps missing the mark about cultural interpretations and understandings, does provide a useful background and analysis of certain cultural forms. For example, Morris (1981) concludes,

> In Puerto Rican society, one's place and one's sense of oneself depend on an even, disciplined and unthreatening style of behavior. Aggressiveness, open conflict, contradiction, or confrontation, or the appearance of any of these, breaks the tacit agreement of respect. Puerto Ricans must not appear to separate themselves from others, thrust themselves forward, or directly push others down. (p. 135)

This passage refers to the social norm of "respect" in the communal sense ("not . . . separate themselves from others"), which is quite significant to Puerto Ricans. However, this passage also illustrates Morris's emphasis on how Puerto Rican behavior is interpreted by others (what the behavior "appears" to be), rather than how behavior is given meaning by the participants themselves. Yet, despite its limitations, Morris's (1981) work does provide useful background information about some cultural beliefs that can be significant when interpreting the norms of time practices.

Although Puerto Rican identity can certainly be further examined on the island itself, Puerto Ricans occupy a particularly unique position within the United States. As Flores (1993) describes, the "uneven clash of cultures can only be understood in its full magnitude when account is taken of the political and cultural life of Puerto Ricans in the metropolitan United States" (p. 55). Because Puerto Rico is a U.S. commonwealth, Puerto Rican national identity includes the experience of mobility from the island to the states and back again. Consequently, Puerto Ricans identify with (and are constructed from) this blending of different experiences and contacts in both places (Flores, 1993, p. 98).

CROSS-CULTURAL COMPARISONS

In order to demonstrate what is unique about the cultural symbols and meanings of one particular cultural group, it is often useful to make reference to the ways that other cultures communicate, enact roles, and attribute meaning to similar actions or ways of speaking. For example, Carbaugh (1989) describes "popular American"[3] talk as using key symbols such as *selves* and *individuals.* Persons in this culture vacillate between difference and commonality. He posits that when speaking this way, "Americans" act based on a code of dignity (respect for individual rights, autonomy, freedom, equality). The cultural premises include: (a) one is an individual, (b) everyone should be unique, and (c) cultural commonalities should be dispelled. If it is a group norm to be unique and yet one is supposed to give recognition not to group values but to individual ones, then the three premises seem contradictory. Yet they form the complex web of communication rules that persons follow nonetheless (Carbaugh, 1990, pp. 123-132). By examining personhood in this way, we learn not only that there are specific terms that "Americans" use to refer to persons, but also that these terms signify the roles and positions that these persons have (and can have) toward themselves and one another.

Another example is given by Weider and Pratt (1990), who explain personhood by the actions in which one engages. Weider and Pratt describe the problem of "recognition and being recognized" as a "real Indian" in the United States. The "real" Indian will know when and how to play the proper roles (p. 60). Knowledge and respect as a "real" Indian become evident in several courses of action, such as approaching strangers, razzing, face-to-face encounters, displaying modesty, recognizing quasi-kinship relationships, and public speaking. By recognizing these actions as culturally distinct and significant, one is better able to understand Indian "personhood." Weider and Pratt (1990) explain that "being a real Indian is not something one can simply be, but is something that one becomes and/or is, in and as 'the doing' of being and becoming a real Indian" (pp. 49-50).

Carbaugh (1989) and Weider and Pratt (1990) have fruitfully explored different speech patterns to better understand "insider" meanings within "American" and American Indian groups in the United States. When communication occurs, it explicates and constitutes cultural order, social organization, and cultural meanings in the occasion (Carbaugh, 1990). It is particular with regard to persons, places, nature, function, and structure. The nature of the cultural communication practices helps to constitute a sense of what it means to be a person in that particular context within that particular speech community.

This study was undertaken to add to the literature about how members of a speech community enact practices that comment on and construct their sense of identity and membership through closely examining references to and uses of the concept of *time*. My analysis examines two speech events and the symbols and norms that help to form a way of speaking.

The general research questions guiding this analysis were as follows: How do the use and practices of communicative acts, related to time, help to shape what it means to be a member of this group? How do the members understand the practices that have intercultural implications (and differing meanings) that need to be negotiated among members in this group, a Puerto Rican organization within the United States, in ways that differentiate "members" from nonmembers.

SOCIAL-ENVIRONMENTAL CONTEXT

I began as a volunteer at a PRCC in August 1994. The center is located in the northeast United States in a city that hosts the fourth-largest population of Puerto Ricans in the United States (Rivera-Batiz & Santiago, 1994, p. 20). The cultural center is located in the north end of the city, a section that is demographically predominantly Puerto Rican. The cultural center was founded in 1976 to: (a) conduct educational and cultural activities, (b) facilitate the adjustment of Hispanic people into the mainstream of American society without sacrificing their cultural values, (c) promote and preserve the Puerto Ricans' cultural heritage, and (d) help develop a better understanding and improve the relationship between the Puerto Rican community and other ethnic groups in the city. The vision of the center is to enhance pride and self esteem within the Puerto Rican and other Spanish speaking communities by promoting, maintaining, and sharing our rich cultural heritage, to promote community involvement and foster leadership development, to meet the diverse social and economic needs of a growing community by providing comprehensive services and to act as an advocate in shaping and influencing the issues that affect our people. (PRCC Vision Statement)

A board of directors, consisting of 13 members, defines the direction, goals, and tone of the organization. The staff includes an executive director, who runs the daily operations of the center. The executive director has an assistant. Each component of the center has a coordinator: There is an education coordinator, a cultural activities coordinator, and a youth leadership development coordinator. The Education component employs an assistant education coordinator, two General Equivalency Diploma teachers, a case manager, three English as a second language teachers, an adult basic education teacher, and a childcare provider; the Education component currently holds courses for local adults at the Young Men's Christian Association. The Cultural component employs a staff that consists of a folklore dance instructor, a gym instructor, a bridge-building instructor, and a drumming instructor; the Cultural component holds afterschool programs for middle school children. The other staff member is the program development specialist, who researches and writes grants for the center. Three volunteers, myself included, assist with communications, computer programming, and organizing the festival.

METHODOLOGY

During my first encounter with the director and the cultural events coordinator, I advanced a proposal to volunteer at the center to conduct ethnographic investigation in interpersonal communication. I described my research interest as trying to determine how interaction creates identity. The director of the center told me that he was interested in my expertise in communication and asked me if I would be interested in helping to promote upcoming events, beginning with the Annual Dinner. In this capacity, I began my fieldwork.

My interactions at the center were conducted in English, which is the language most participants at the center used (either as a first or second language). I listened when Spanish was spoken by others and when I was addressed in Spanish, at which times I responded in English.[4]

After being in the field for two and a half months, I was elected to sit on the board of directors. This position gave me access to the monthly board meetings. I informed the other board members at our first gathering of my researcher position. Members of the board gave their permission for me to audiotape the board meetings.

DATA COLLECTION

In August 1994, my volunteer work took place during the morning on Tuesdays and Wednesdays. Between September and December, I volunteered Wednesday mornings. From January through May 1995, I attended monthly board meetings, special meetings, and retreats. I also spoke weekly with members of the staff by telephone. Initially, I worked closely with the cultural activities coordinator. Over time, I had the opportunity to have conversations with all those employed at the center. I took field notes throughout my 10 months at the center. I videotaped the Annual Dinner and audiotape-recorded the monthly board meetings (which occur on the third Thursday of every month).

I recorded observational data of my weekly interactions at the center with the staff through written field notes. These notes were written according to the method proposed by Schatzman and Strauss (1973). This system includes indicating and differentiating "Observation Notes," "Methodological Notes," and "Theoretical Notes" (p. 99). Segments of the audio- and video-recorded material have been transcribed using a version of the system proposed by Sacks, Schegloff and Jefferson (1974). I attended to the aspects of their coding system (as well as referencing Goodwin, 1990, p. 25) that were most relevant to my data and to the type of analysis I conducted. The amount of transcription detail used in each segment transcribed follows the analysis I make of each instance.

DATA ANALYSIS

The conceptual tools that I chose were derived from my theoretical attention to cultural communication. Following Hymes (1972), I attended to cultural scenes, communication activities, and norms. I based my analysis primarily on two scenes: an Annual Dinner Dance and monthly board meetings. First, I will describe the theoretical premises and assumptions upon which each methodological tool is based; next, I will describe the procedure that I employed in the following analysis.

My basic unit of analysis, within which I examined the symbols, norms, and ways of speaking, was what Hymes (1972) referred to as a "speech event." A speech event is bounded by a beginning and an end, and it refers to activities that are governed by rules or norms for speech (Hymes, 1974, p. 52). Communication events provide focal activities for discovering what is of significance for a particular speech community. Discovering the boundaries of communicative events is the basis for understanding how members of a particular speech community communicate.

Hymes's (1980) definition of speech community includes the means and meanings of various symbols. Therefore, I began my analysis by documenting instances of the symbol *time.* Because Hymes (1972) describes the speech community as people who share "rules for the conduct and interpretation of speech, and rules for the interpretation of at least one linguistic variety" (p. 54), I examined the rules and norms of time use. Finally, Hymes (1974) states that for one to be counted as a member of a speech community, one must share at least one "way of speaking" with others. To describe how concepts of *time* can be considered a "way of speaking," I will present a summary of cultural practices as evidence that these components are constitutive features of the community of participants from the PRCC.

I looked for key symbols in the talk produced by participants at the PRCC. I located these symbols through their prominence, repetition, and co-occurrence with like words. I tried to further substantiate each key symbol by locating a form of enactment that relied, at least in part, for its coherence upon that key symbol. *Symbol,* then, is taken to be a prominent and recurring term; symbols form clusters of co-occurrence around the prominent terms, creating a galaxy in Schneider's (1976) analytical scheme. In this analysis, my focus was on the key symbol of *time.*

Time was a key symbol through which conversations occurred. This key symbol has been the target of investigation by other researchers, and a body of literature can be called on to describe other ways of examining time and chronemics. After locating several instances of this symbol, I reviewed the relevant literature and began to discriminate the ways in which the symbol was used in the PRCC scenes and the ways in which the literature constructs each symbol.

NORMATIVE AND CODE RULES

To get at beliefs and standards for action, I followed Hymes's (1972) suggestion to search for norms or rules. Carbaugh (1990) has proposed a refined way of analyzing and articulating beliefs about action. He distinguishes between two types of rules: normative and code. "They are alike in that they both refer to socially patterned communicative action, capture some consensual imperative for interlocutors, and have practical force in identifiable contexts" (p. 139).

Normative rules refer to standards for action. They describe appropriate behavior and imply an evaluation of actions. They answer the question, "what behavioral acts are appropriate in this context? . . . Normative rules function to guide actions in social contexts" (Carbaugh, 1990, p. 141). When rules are violated, they may be explicitly stated. Normative rules follow the form: "in context C, if X, one should/not do Y" (Carbaugh, 1990, p. 142). It is important to note that "one cannot abstract normative rules . . . without also abstracting codes" (Carbaugh, 1990, p. 142).

Code rules refer more specifically to patterns of meaning constructed by symbols and symbolic forms. Code rules function "in conversation to frame actions, to define contexts, to construct a coherent sense" (Carbaugh, 1990, p. 139). They are components of a belief system and can be stated in the form, "in context C, the unit, X, counts as meaningful on another level as Y" (p. 140).

Carbaugh (1990) notes that the idea that children should address elders with respect is an example of a normative rule for conduct (who *should* address whom). In addition, the statement of the norm includes terms for which one can formulate code rules about who counts as an elder and a child (those who so address and those who are addressed as such). Many times, code rules are intertwined with normative rules. Both kinds of rules operate within a particular cultural context.

I began searching for normative rules that governed each event. Next, I searched for the ways in which rules (of either type) were explicitly articulated. Usually, norms can be located by the presence of a normative force (Carbaugh, 1990), such as the terms *should* or *ought*. Frequently the norms that were explicated were of the "normative rule" type. After examining these two types, I began to use the form proposed by Carbaugh (1990) to restate my findings into both normative and code rules. Finally, when many of the rules began to form a pattern, I was able to establish with more certainty the broader normative and code rules for each scene.

WAYS OF SPEAKING

In order to assess differences between speech communities, I relied on Hymes's (1972) broader category, "ways of speaking." Ways of speaking are distinct to particular speech communities and particular occasions (Hymes, 1972, p. 58). I identified PRCC ways of speaking by noting the way action was regulated and determined. Furthermore, I noted events in which particular ways were identified by participants. Throughout this study, I describe one prominent way of speaking, which uses and makes reference to the symbol *time*.

I relied upon Sacks's (1992) and Carbaugh's (1990) assumptions that sequences may be "doing something." In addition, I attended to the implications that when utterances were strung together, they formed some outcome. While keeping the question open as to what type of outcome certain conversational sequences might be leading toward, I carefully documented the ways in which participants strung together bits of utterances in conversations to form a kind of characteristic sequence. This type of documentation provides the details for enactments that may form a culturally based way of speaking, such as establishing quorum in a board meeting.

It was through this methodological procedure—an analysis of *time* as a key symbol, regulated by norms and rules, that characterizes a prominent way of speaking—that I began to unravel what it means to be a member of the community in the two primary scenes of the PRCC. The following description sets the scenes that were the basis of my analysis. I also explain the detailed analysis that I conducted based on these various methodological procedures.

TWO SYMBOL SYSTEMS: "PUERTO RICAN" AND "POPULAR AMERICAN" WAYS OF REFERRING TO AND USING TIME

The cultural symbol of time emerged as important in many speaking situations within the center, including two events, the Annual Dinner Dance and the monthly board meetings. A general Puerto Rican sense of time has been described as a fluid sense of time (Morris, 1981). Edward Hall (1976) described "American" time as "monochronic" (MC), "emphasiz[ing] schedules, segmentation and promptness" (p. 17). In contrast, he considers Latin America and the Middle East to operate on "polychronic time" (PC), which is "characterized by several things happening at once" (p. 17). Hall explains that when people operating with different time orientations come into contact, there can be confusion and misunderstandings. Hall's (1976) definitions of time (PC and MC) are described through personal examples. However, the present study seeks to capture more detailed and descriptive evidence of "time usage" through analyzing naturally occurring discourse conversations in situations. Whereas Hall suggests that appointments are flexible in cultures that operate on polychronic time, the goal of this study it to examine the texture of recounting detailed evidence of when, under which conditions, and for which participants this flexibility is meaningful. Hall (1976) described one specific scenario, in which he suggested to American foreign service officers who were assigned to Latin America that they "should be out *interacting* with the local people" instead of "being cut off from the people with whom they should be establishing ties" because of the strict time regulations binding them to an office (Hall, 1976, p. 19). Hall (1976) suggested that in these types of situations, the officers would not be able to be "*effective*"—an "American" monochronic norm—by complying with the "American" norm for time (p. 19). Evidence is needed about how one sense of time is meaningful to other groups of participants and about the normative implications of not abiding by one group's time rules in other situations and scenes. The "Puerto Rican" sense of time does not rely on fixed boundaries but rather has more flexible boundaries.

To overview, I found that the way time is described and enacted by Puerto Ricans at the PRCC is distinct. Across situations, participants orient to time differently, abiding by different norms and rules in different contexts and for different purposes. Second, time references and practice appear to be based on certain historic and cultural roots, which, when enacted, demonstrate that the participants base their actions on some shared cultural knowledge.

The two senses of time—Puerto Rican and "popular American"—will be described before looking at each event in particular. There are at least two meanings for the symbol *time* that is operative in each event.

During the Annual Dinner Dance,[5] the following statement was made:

1 JG: hopefully we won't be operating on Puerto Rican time this evening, so
we have more time to enjoy the social part of the program.

Puerto Rican time was also referred to directly during a board meeting.[6]
Consider the following example:

245 JG: The parade doesn't start until twelve o'clock.

246 It doesn't get going until twelve thirty, probably:: one o'clock,

247 which is always Puerto Rican time.

248 Uh, by the time it finishes up,

249 and everybody gets downtown

250 and everybody goes through the reviewing stand, do their thing

251 It's three o'clock

252 On any given day, it's three o'clock. (March board meeting)

In Lines 1 and 247, "Puerto Rican time" is labeled directly. PRCC participants talk about a fluid sense of time as "Puerto Rican." They refer to
this sense of time and define its recognizable characteristics. The
"clock" time "twelve thirty" becomes "one o'clock" (Line 246) to "three
o'clock" (Lines 251-252) in Puerto Rican time. Thus Puerto Rican time
seems to start and end later, taking more time (two hours in this example)
than what is indicated by a clock.

The reference to "any given day" (Line 252) indicates that this is a generalized sense of time that is not just specific to one occasion but to many,
including the festival[7] (to which Lines 245-252 refer).

This sense of time not only is referred to directly by name but also is
enacted. Further, this sense of time prominently factors into decision
making, because participants are aware that others in the community will
act with the cultural knowledge that Puerto Rican time is governing
events. For instance, Lines 247-250 suggest that Puerto Rican time can
be identified and that "everybody" will enact it by "doing their thing."

What distinguishes the references to time in these scenes from other
"popular American" scenes is the distinction between two different
kinds of time operating in these scenes. The first was referred to directly
as "Puerto Rican time" (Line 1). When he first took the microphone, the
master of ceremonies said that he did not want the dinner to be governed
by Puerto Rican time. Labeling time as "Puerto Rican" recognizes the
fact that it must stand in contrast to some other sort of time that is not

named. The second sense of time is referred to as "American time." It is my interpretation that when events are governed "by the clock," so to speak, Puerto Ricans refer to this as *"hora Americana."*[8]

The Puerto Rican time described here can be likened to a "relaxing the rules" of "American" time. "Relaxing the rules" is a phrase Lauria (1964) uses to describe the way *relajo* (joking) transforms *respeto* (respect), whereby jokes are made on the basis of relaxing the "respect" rules. In a similar way, the "American" time rules can be said to be relaxed when Puerto Rican time is operating. Both senses of time are ways of socially organizing actions in the scenes of the cultural center.[9]

Knowing that these two senses of time govern various events, the question becomes, what senses of *time* are invoked at PRCC events such as the Annual Dinner and the board meetings? If both senses of time are invoked during a single event, when is each sense invoked, and for whom is each sense of time most significant?

WHEN AND HOW PARTICIPANTS
ORIENT TO TIME

Several instances of time talk and enactment occurred during the two significant events of this study. First, I discuss those instances separately, as time references emerged in each event. Then I discuss the common features of the way time becomes meaningful across events.

Annual Dinner

Throughout the Annual Dinner Dance, time was used as an event regulator. For example, the executive director, who served as master of ceremonies, repeatedly referred to time as something that was in short supply. The continual focus on time ("for the sake of time," "at this time," "kept . . . to two minutes," "we're running behind time," and "there's plenty of time and there isn't") illustrates the organizing function and symbolic significance of time in this episode.

This particular use of time during the Annual Dinner Dance was illustrated by several instances. In fact, this type of talk occurred at the beginning of the dinner.

8 JG: But if we're going to keep this on time and we have quite a lengthy program, we need to start.

To repeat an earlier example,

> 1 JG: hopefully we won't be operating on Puerto Rican time this evening, so
> we have more time to enjoy the social part of the program.

For members, the social portion, centered around music and dancing, is the most significant part of the dinner. The spoken portion can be understood as something that needs to be hurried through to get to the enjoyable part—the social part. JG pointed to the significance of the "social portion" as opposed to the "speaking portion" in his introductory remarks:

> 22 We are asking that you stay,
> 23 not only for the spoken part of our program,
> 24 but also for the social event,
> 25 to get to know your neighbor next to you.

This passage suggests that those who normally stay for the social portion of the dinner are not the ones being addressed in this passage. Rather, they may be the "neighbors" referred to in Line 25. Because the Annual Dinner is an attempt to make bridges between two cultural groups, public figures and the Puerto Rican community, the passage above and the references to the "spoken portion" of the dinner address the public figure types, who are generally not members of the center and who would not ordinarily stay to socialize. When the master of ceremonies says "get to know your neighbor next to you," he is advocating that the nonmembers get to know the members, or those who would ordinarily stay to socialize. This statement points to the significance of the social portion for members and is one clear way of differentiating the two groups at the dinner, who usually orient to time differently. Because these differences are recognized, the way that time is being used must be stated and labeled in order that all participants can recognize how the activities of the event should unfold.

The first sense of time discussed during the dinner suggests an "American" time frame. References to *time* are used to segment activities into brief, "short" slots at the beginning, the "speaking portion," of the dinner. This was done in order to get to the "social portion" of the dinner, the more enjoyable and preferred part of the dinner for the members. The "second half" of the dinner was not bound by time slots, but rather by participants and their activities (dancing), which lasted into the evening.

Puerto Rican time was again shown in the fact that the end of the event was based on whenever participants chose to leave.

Other examples of time talk could be heard when the master of ceremonies introduced the speakers.

122 JG: I'd like at this time to present to you,

123 an individual who's really worked hard

124 to develop the hearts and minds of the young people . . .

125 we have to make it short and sweet and to the point, cause

126 otherwise I will not be responsible for the actions of the masses.

The segment (Lines 122-126) illustrates two instances of time talk operating at the dinner (both of which are based on "American" time). When, in Line 122, JG says, "at this time," he is talking about the way in which his words organize the "speaking portion" of the dinner. As the master of ceremonies, JG is able to designate which times will be allotted to which purposes. This instance also illustrates how time is used to frame the actions of participants in the dinner. Because of the limited amount of time, it must be tightly controlled, as shown in the instance above: "make it short and sweet" (Line 125).

Lines 122-126, in particular, illustrate the way that time is used to organize the dinner as an event as well as to organize the actions of participants. When JG introduced the dinner speakers, he not only commented upon the "work" they had done for the Center (Line 123), he also commented upon the "time" available for the speakers to address the audience (described as the "masses" in Line 126). JG's statement served as an overt reference to a dinner norm (keeping the speech short) with a particularly strong force as defined by its potential enforcement (which was left vague—we do not know what "actions" the "masses" would take in the case of a norm violation here). Consequently, it is the masses who are also appealed to when JG states the norm. It is for this reason that the masses are able to dictate and enforce the time norms as participant regulators, even though at the event level, an agenda (reflected in the dinner's program) has been prepared previously (by PRCC staff) and would presumably regulate the time of the event.

The tension between two types of time is operating here as illustrated by the two groups addressed: the speakers and "the masses." The dinner speakers, as public figures, are known for making extended speeches, which the masses do not prefer.

142 JG: I'm not going to hear the end of this,

143 this is the first time we've kept him under two minutes.

As illustrated in Line 143, the speaker has previously spoken at great length during past Annual Dinners. The reference to lengthy speeches refers to a "popular American" norm that public figures will address an audience for an extended period. The assumption is that this way of speaking may be common or expected at some "American" dinners. At the Annual Dinner, there may have been tension due to the mixed audience—part of which prefers the social portion (those operating on Puerto Rican time) and part of which is present "merely" for the spoken portion (invited guests and members of "the community" who are presumed to operate on "American" time). The dinner is held for both audiences and actually may privilege the "American" time norms for speaking because of the emphasis on showcasing the cultural center.

Board Meetings

A sense of "American" time was also used to regulate the board meetings. In these meetings, *time* was referred to and was considered in short supply, as it was during the dinner. I heard the following statements toward the end of several meetings:

404 HT: P, P

405 we don't have that much time. (January board meeting)

489 HT: o.k. we don't have much time left. (April board meeting)

627 HT: we are running short on time, there's a list, there should be a list in

628 everyone's folder in regards to committees, and I appreciate if the

629 committee chairs talk to their people. (April board meeting)

41 JG: and finally, the last piece [of business] that we're cause we're running

42 out of time. (May board meeting)

These instances all refer to the "time" "running out" (Lines 41-42) or being "short" (Line 627) or not having much time left (Line 489) at the end of meetings. Time is something that board members "don't have" (Line 405). It is interesting that the same attention to time is not strictly adhered to at the beginnings of meetings. *Time* is talked about at the beginning of meetings in regard to attaining a quorum. Because not all board members arrive "on time" (according to "American" time), then, all the business issues that need to be discussed are rushed through in order to end meetings on time.

There are several rules or norms participants followed:

1. An "American" time preference is advocated for what is considered business (both in the Annual Dinner and the board meetings).

2. When socializing is valued and is the goal of actions, Puerto Rican time is operative (such as in the social portion of the Annual Dinner).

3. In each event (board meetings and the Annual Dinner), there is a movement between an "American" conception and enactment of time and a Puerto Rican one.

4. In the movement from one sense of time to another (i.e., from the Puerto Rican time guiding socializing to the "American" time needed to regulate business), it becomes necessary to clearly label and make an assertion that Puerto Rican time (which is otherwise preferred and regulates action) will then become dispreferred and will no longer serve to regulate actions (on "American" time).

The boundaries of the speech event at monthly board meetings were regulated by a loose sense of time. The particular way that the symbol *time* functioned was through the device of reaching quorum. As I detailed previously, meetings do not begin on time unless quorum is reached. However, meetings end at the designated time, 9:15 a.m., regardless of when they begin.[10] For instance, near the end of a meeting, HT states, "o.k. we don't have much time left" (Line 489). The beginning and end of the meeting function conjointly, such that it is necessary for quorum to be accomplished for the meeting to proceed and for all the business to be accomplished by the fixed end of the meeting.

The norms that help regulate the boundaries of board meetings are as follows:

- An official board meeting occurs when quorum is reached. One half plus one of the board members should be present to make quorum.
- Meetings end on time.
- Some board members can (and do) leave early.

These normative rules guide the actions of board members. Because the described norms are based on a particular sense of time, they may also explain the ways that the symbol *time* is enacted during board meetings. It is interesting to note that, because time is constructed loosely, the boundary norms are also loosely held norms of preference. Violating the norms does not result in severe repercussions, because there is an understanding that the participants may have been operating on Puerto Rican time.

Using time as a scheduling mechanism also occurred in the following instance. When discussing plans to move to a new building, the center's director made the following request to board members:

675 JG: I'd like to set a time for you folks could go through it and it might be
676 something you might be interested in. (May meeting)

Although JG indicates that time can be something that is "set" (Line 675), the accomplishment of this goal was another matter. In my experience at the center, when meetings were set to view other buildings, they were changed frequently and often occurred at what seemed to be the 'spur of the moment' (from an "American" time perspective). I experienced this when I was called to see a building on the day of the viewing. When I happened to call the center on the day people were out seeing the building, I was told of a plan to visit a site that day. This lack of advance warning did not facilitate my being able to change my day's plans suddenly to accompany members (staff or board) on these visits. Whoever was available to make the trips did.

Another example related to scheduling time occurred during the January board meeting, as members tried to clarify the time at which a meeting would take place with United Way representatives.

221 PR: what time?
222 HT: at nine o'clock
263 HT: they're supposed to meet us there at nine
264 should we schedule it for a quarter of nine?
265 PR: we'll all be there by the time they make it there
266 PL: make it 8:30 and
267 we'll all be there on time
268 AB: the morning before
269 AB: it's about an hour right?
270 JG: yea, its a little longer than an hour

271 but those that can be there for an hour

272 or any part of the interview

273 would be great. (January board meeting)

This segment illustrates the way that time helps govern the behavior of board members. When one board member asks, "should we schedule it for a quarter of nine?" (Line 263), he is acting based on his cultural knowledge that the other board members may be operating on Puerto Rican time. His suggestion is based on the belief that if the board members are going to attend a meeting with others who operate on "popular American" time, then board members should be told to arrive at "8:30," in order to be there "on time" for the "American" schedule to be met. The phrase *on time* leads to the question, "whose time are we 'on?'" In this case, the time would refer to that of the people from the United Way. And, presumably, they would be operating on "American" time.

The next instance demonstrates the way that participants orient to the concept of *time* as it is used to regulate participants.

461 SH: maybe we need more time to think about it, after this discussion,

462 maybe he had not heard our concerns and maybe he may want to rethink about this decision. (April board meeting)

"Time" in this instance is something that is "needed" (Line 461). It has a more/less quality. It is something that "we" and "he" may need in order to think (or rethink) decisions. Decisions need time. Decisions that are based on a current "discussion" need "more time." Presumably, in that space of time, decisions may be changed. It is the participants in this instance, "we" and "he," who are regulated by a potentially expandable measure of time to "think about" "concerns" and possibly to change decisions.[11]

As a regulator of participants, time is something people "have" or do not have. It is something that people (in addition to events) are bound by. If they operate on Puerto Rican or American time they are regulated differently, and they may have different ends for their actions: to be social (Puerto Rican time) or to complete an action on time within a time frame ("American" time). As something that people have, time was also referred to as something that people could "commit" to (Line 227) or "contribute" in place of money[12] (see Line 12).

227 JG: because we need someone [i.e., a retreat facilitator] that's going to
commit their time. (December board meeting)
10 JG: but what is happening is that in lieu
11 of the fact that now that the monies are not being raised, we have to look
12 at cutting back some of those paid positions, so that what I have to
13 suggest is that some board members, or all board members will have to
14 contribute some time because otherwise, you know, we can't pay these
15 positions. (May board meeting)

Throughout the board meetings and the Annual Dinner, time was talked about as something that regulates participants or that can be used to regulate other participants' activities.

In addition to being a social quality, which regulates events and participants who act within those events, time is also used as a larger component of cultural history, the knowledge of which participants use to further guide actions and make decisions.

CULTURAL/HISTORICAL REFERENCES TO TIME

Another way that the concept of *time* operated for cultural center members was based on an understanding of cultural history. One particular time frame (or, perhaps more accurately from within a Puerto Rican time conception, a space of time) was described during the March board meeting as "*hora muerta.*"

413 SH: my point is that we were going on the assumption that
414 we were going on the assumption that usually from three to six,
415 *nuestra hora muerta,*
416 it's not going to be this year

What SH is referring to is the "dead hour" (Line 415 translation) more commonly known as downtime. Her use of Spanish here seems to indicate that this is a culturally identifiable understanding of time. Prior to this remark, this space of time was described by other board members as "slow":

323 JG: so, when we discussed from three to six,
324 that's a slow, that's a slow hour

358 RM: not only are they going to be benefiting us,
359 by bringing a lot of people at a time that is normally slow for the festival
360 but also in terms of [the cultural center] in terms of supporting the parade
361 and bringing it back to the North End

The time talk during this segment of the board meeting changed from "slow" to a "dead hour." This "hour" refers to three hours (by the clock). There are two cultural traditions one should bear in mind when trying to understand this sense of time.

"*Tiempo muerto*" (Line 415) translates to "dead time." In the recent past, the main industry in Puerto Rico was raising sugar cane. *Tiempo muerto* referred to the off season, when there was no work. During this time, when people were out of work, they needed to borrow money and credit (or tabs) in the stores to buy food. This arrangement kept them in a perpetual state of indebtedness and poverty. Therefore, when SH says "*hora muerta,*" with the indication that she refers to the time from 3 to 6 p.m., others may hear her alluding to a culturally known downtime. This "dead time" has negative connotations.

Another tradition or cultural event based on a similar use of time is *café a las tres,* a coffee break that begins in midafternoon at around 3 p.m. Based on my knowledge of Puerto Rican cultural history and customs, making reference to hours (or an "hour") from 3 to 6 p.m. would suggest a time of day when people sit down and drink coffee (as opposed to going to a festival). On a related note, *café a las tres* may occur during that particular "time slot," (to use an American idiom of time) from 3 to 6 p.m., because of the rise in temperature in the afternoon and the natural decline in physical energy that follows biological circadian rhythms. It would be similar to the way other cultures take an afternoon break (such as a Mexican *siesta*). However, in Puerto Rico, this reference to time is normally reserved for socializing with others while sitting on one's porch.

Therefore, when a Spanish phrase is introduced into a meeting that was otherwise conducted in English, the cultural/historic connotations become salient to the current event under discussion. The "dead hour," so to speak, was one significant instance of this type of time talk.

RELEVANCE AND MEANING OF TIME

In summary, there are two types of time around which activities are oriented, "American" time and Puerto Rican time. "American" time can be characterized as static and definitive; it signals prompt beginnings and endings where the activity within its schedule is of most importance. Puerto Rican time can be characterized as fluid and flexible. In Puerto Rican time, the relationships between participants take precedence over the scheduled activities.

Participants are aware of differences between Puerto Rican and "American" time and can move from one type of time to another (when instructed to or when the context calls for it). Business seems to follow "American" time, whereas socializing follows Puerto Rican time.[13]

In Table 3.1, the features of "American" time are distinguished from those of Puerto Rican time. First, the two senses of time have differing normative forces (i.e., different repercussions for not adhering to the norms). "American" time has a medium normative force, such as when participants recommend that others "should" be "on time." In contrast, Puerto Rican time has a relatively low normative force,[14] in that there are no repercussions for not being on time. The norm for participants acting within Puerto Rican time is to know when and under what circumstances to change to "American" time (or from one sense of time to the other).

Socializing is measured by the clock in "American" time and within Puerto Rican time. Socializing is not an activity that needs to be measured in the same way by the clock. Rather, it is an activity that is engaged in to be enjoyed (time is much less relevant). "American" time creates people (identities) that act in segmented slots. Each action is compartmentalized, as is seen in the examples "have a few minutes" to speak and "keep it short, sweet and to the point." Consequently, one speaks in time slots. Puerto Rican time is like a sea into and out of which people and actions flow. The mere happening of it is important. This sense of time creates people who value relationships irrespective of time constraints.

Puerto Rican time is neither an "amount" of time nor an "on-time" enactment, but a "quality" of time, where time is spent on the important aspects of life, such as socializing and building relationships. In this way, it has implications for being/doing membership in the Weider and Pratt (1990) sense of who counts as a "real" Puerto Rican. Therefore, conceptualizations of *time* can be said to be a significant component of membership in the PRCC. Persons orient to it and use it to structure their lives. Knowing how and when to use which type of time ("American" time or Puerto Rican time) becomes a differentiating factor in the quest to know who counts as a real Puerto Rican here.

TABLE 3.1 Characteristics of Two Symbols of Time: American Time and Puerto Rican Time

Characteristic	Hora Americana	Puerto Rican Time
Character	Static/definitive	Fluid/flexible
Features of events	Boundary marker that signifies beginnings and endings; events are "on time."	Socializing; "people time"; "social hour."
Rules/norms	Time markers regulate events; participants act with this awareness and schedule events to occur within specific time frames.	Both Puerto Rican and American time exist; participants are aware of the differences and (when instructed or when context calls for it—business on American time, socializing on Puerto Rican time) can move from one into the other.
Normative force	Medium normative force; can be broken; "should" be "on time."	Low normative force because the boundaries can never be broken—always in flux; people should know when to orient to each sense of time.
Goals	To ensures that activities do not fall outside their discrete boundaries so that other activities can take place.	To be with others.
Implications for identities	Creates people (identities) who act in segmented slots; each action is compartmentalized: "few minutes" to speak; "short, sweet and to the point."	Time is like a sea into and out of which people and actions flow; the mere happening of it is important; creates people who value relationships regardless of time constraints.
Socialization	Measured by a clock.	Not measured, just is.

TIME: CROSS-CULTURAL COMPARISON

Other authors have also examined different senses of time as they are used and understood in different cultures. Shotter (1993) describes Whorf's work with the Hopi Indians. The Hopi's sense of time structures their world and possible ways of acting and being. "Americans" might say that they did something in the "morning." Such a statement would refer to an action that occurred in the past. The sense of completion is connoted by the combination of the past tense of the verb with the word "morning" in the object position of the sentence. In contrast, Hopi would use time words as adverbs and would use a form that in English would be translated into "morning-ing." By using time words in an adverb form, "morning-ing" describes an activity that is in the process of occurring. This way of speaking does not "contain" time at all. There is no sense of fixed boundaries between, say, morning and afternoon, as the "popular American" form connotes. Hopi are not bound by "structured" time, because time is not described or talked about as a "thing" or object. This has very different implications for acting in the world.

Puerto Rican time can be compared to Hopi time in the use of the Spanish words *atardeciendo, anocheciendo,* and *amaneciendo,* which can be translated into "it is becoming afternoon," "it is becoming night," or "it is becoming morning," respectively. Similar to the Hopi, the Spanish words function as adverbs. Furthermore, one can say that it is "becoming morning"—or, as in the description of Hopi, "morning-ing," which means something close to "while morning-phase is occurring" (Shotter, 1993, p. 143). By using the term *amaneció,* one conveys the past sense of it being morning, or "it morninged." For the Hopi, "nothing is suggested about time except the perpetual 'getting later' of it" (Shotter, 1993, p. 143). This is similar to the Spanish words such as *amaneciendo,* meaning, "it's getting morning."

CONTRIBUTION TO THE FIELD

Other research into Puerto Rican speech (Morris, 1981) has been performed through or from a "popular American" frame of reference, which led the researcher to make interpretations about the meaning of the talk heard as not adhering to "popular American" speaking norms. For example, when describing Puerto Rican speech practices, Morris (1981) speaks repeatedly about a "diffuseness" and "fluidness" (p. 62). He attributes this to a lack of meaning, rather than attending to which communication practices were diffuse and fluid (such as references to time) and what it meant to communicate in that way. Although Morris's interpretations did not match what the participants in the conversations thought they were doing, through his research he was able to identify prominent values associated with talk in Puerto Rico. For example, talk is a key to membership (Morris, 1981, p. 15), in that "shared experience" is the "basis for understanding" (p. 112).

The findings presented in this report can be supported by some features of Morris's (1981) reports of some Puerto Rican ways of speaking, especially because his findings were based on conversations conducted in Spanish, whereas my research was based on conversations conducted in English. Therefore, this study, while specifically attending to the communicative practices of a specific PRCC, does suggest that cultural communication practices transcend some scenes and are differently enacted in others. According to *Puerto Ricans in the United States: A Changing Reality,*[15] the number of Puerto Ricans living in the United States is increasing,

> from close to 2 million in 1980 to over 2.7 million in 1990. This growth, which led to a population 35 percent larger in 1990 than in 1980, was more than three times the rate of growth of the overall American population during the decade. (Rivera-Batiz & Santiago, 1994, p. v)

Therefore, those trying to understand communication within the United States would do well to attend to the communication practices of Puerto Ricans.

CONCLUSIONS

This research is based on broader assumptions about language, speech, and communication. More specifically, cultural communication becomes apparent when one begins to recognize the meanings that are attached to actions.

Two cultures and symbol systems are intertwined in the scenes presented. Participants display cultural competence on these occasions in different, culturally strategic ways by responding to each cultural norm as it becomes relevant to do so. Any one person or social scene may be organized through different cultural symbols. Through a detailed and systematic methodology (based on Hymes and Carbaugh), strong intercultural characteristics and the seemingly polemical tensions between the different cultural norms for interacting were explored.

This study contributes to a growing number of research projects that feature situated communication practices. The data generated in this study illustrate how cultural communication shapes a sense of communal membership at this PRCC.

NOTES

1. The sense of community enacted within the Puerto Rican Cultural Center is very similar to the definition given by Bellah, Madsen, Sullivan, Swidler, and Tipton (1985): "Community is a term used very loosely by Americans today. We use it in a strong sense: a community is a group of people who are socially interdependent, who participate together in discussion and decision making, and who share certain practices that both define the community and are nurtured by it. Such a community is not quickly formed. It almost always has a history and so is also a community of memory, defined in part by its past and its memory of its past" (p. 333).

2. Mead (1934) describes the way that significant symbols help to constitute the "self" (pp. 138-139).

3. The use of the term *"American"* henceforth refers to what Carbaugh has called a "popular American" way of speaking. Since not everyone who considers him or herself American speaks the same way, I will continue to use the term *"American"* with quotation marks around it to refer to the particular sense of *American* as described by Carbaugh and others.

4. Although I am not fluent in Spanish, I have listened to the language spoken by my relatives and others since I was a child. I reached the second-year level of Spanish language proficiency in courses as an undergraduate.

5. The Annual Dinner Dance is an event that occurs as a single-evening occasion; it is bounded by a beginning and an end and is summarized by the program handed out to each person who attends the dinner. By exploring patterns of communication that occurred within this speech event, I found repeated references to time.

This event takes place at different locations each year. The setting for the 1994 dinner was at Chez Joseph. Various persons involved with the center are invited, as are those who should be made aware of the center's activities who provide much service to the city, namely, prominent government officials and businesspersons. This event is held each year to review the past year's accomplishments and to elicit the continuing support of the community in the center's activities.

6. The monthly board meetings took place in an old Victorian-style building. This building housed the center's offices on the second and third floors and a loan-type business on the first floor. The board meetings took place in the executive director's office on the third floor. During the board meetings, board members sat around a rectangular metal table, which was located just inside the door. Folding chairs were set up around the table, which took up most of the space in the room. The seating arrangement of board members varied for each meeting and depended on the time that each member arrived. The director's

desk is further into the room, directly in front of the windows. Award plaques and pictures of Puerto Rico cover the walls. In addition, a clock is located on the wall above the table where the participants sit.

The participants at board meetings, referred to as "board members" and "staff persons," dress in formal business attire. The attire indicates a "formal" social setting, which invokes positional identities based on code structuring (Irvine, 1979). Many men wear suits and more formal shirts and ties. Women dress professionally in pant or skirt outfits or dresses. Attire seems to be regulated by the work that participants conduct after the morning board meeting.

The board meetings were bounded speech events, including norms, goals, and speech acts.

7. The "festival" was an annual event, held each summer. Much of the content of board meeting conversations centered around the tasks to be completed to organize the festival.

8. Although I did not hear explicit reference to *hora Americana* by the members of the cultural center, I was told by several informants that in Puerto Rico this phrase is used.

9. I recognize that this paragraph demonstrates an interpretation of Puerto Rican time from within a "popular American" conception of time. This is in part due to my researcher position, and in part due to the other norms that govern the "business" portion of both the Annual Dinner and the board meetings; as explicitly stated, these are governed not by Puerto Rican time but by "American" time.

10. The "official" end of the meeting is as stated, but on a few occasions those who could stay were invited to continue the conversation over coffee.

11. The topic in this instance was whether to have JM, a staff member, at board meetings to record minutes.

12. This reference is similar to the metaphor explained by Lakoff and Johnson (1980), "time is money."

13. This does not imply that business does not or cannot happen on Puerto Rican time.

14. The question of "whose" norm is a valid question when two cultural systems are intermingled. Within the "popular American" notion of norms as being tightly adhered to patterns of behavior, Puerto Rican time would seem to have low normative force, because there are no clear boundaries to demarcate beginnings and endings. Within a Puerto Rican conception of norms, time behavior seems to have higher normative force, for it helps to signify who is a member of this group and who is not.

15. This work was handed out during the 1994 Annual Dinner.

REFERENCES

Bellah, R. N., Madsen, R., Sullivan, W. M., Swidler, A., & Tipton, S. M. (1985). *Habits of the heart: Individualism and commitment in American life.* San Francisco: Harper & Row.

Carbaugh, D. (1989). *Talking American: Cultural discourses on "Donahue."* Norwood, NJ: Ablex.

Carbaugh, D. (Ed.). (1990). *Cultural communication and intercultural contact.* Hillsdale, NJ: Lawrence Erlbaum.

Carbaugh, D. (1994). Theory within the ethnography of communication. In D. Cushman & B. Kouacic (Eds.), *Watershed research traditions in human communication theory* (pp. 1-52). Albany: State University of New York Press.

Carey, J. (1975). A cultural approach to communication. *Communication, 2,* 1-22.

Clifford, J., & Marcus, G. E. (1986). *Writing culture: The poetics and politics of ethnography.* Berkeley: University of California Press.

Flores, J. (1993). *Divided borders: Essays on Puerto Rican identity.* Houston, TX: Arte Publico Press.

Geertz, C. (1973). *The interpretation of cultures.* Washington, DC: Basic Books.

Goodwin, M. H. (1990). *He-said-she-said: Talk as social organization among Black children.* Bloomington: Indiana University Press.

Hall, E. T. (1976). *Beyond culture.* New York: Doubleday.

Hilgers, T., Wunsch, M., & Chattergy, V. (Eds.). (1992). *Academic literacies in multicultural higher education: Selected essays.* Honolulu: Center for Studies of Multicultural Higher Education, University of Hawaii at Manoa.

Hymes, D. (1972). Models of the interaction of language and social life. In J. Gumperz & D. Hymes (Eds.), *Directions in sociolinguistics: The ethnography of communication* (pp. 35-71). New York: Holt, Rinehart & Winston.

Hymes, D. (1974). *Foundations in sociolinguistics: An ethnographic approach.* Philadelphia: University of Pennsylvania Press.

Hymes, D. H. (1980). *Language in education: Ethnolinguistic essays.* Washington, DC: Center for Applied Linguistics.

Irvine, J. T. (1979). Formality and informality in communicative events. *American Anthropologist, 81,* 773-790.

Lakoff, G., & Johnson, M. (1980). *Metaphors we live by.* Chicago: University of Chicago Press.

Lauria, A. (1964). *Respeto, relajo* and interpersonal relations in Puerto Rico. *Anthropological Quarterly, 37,* 53-67.

Lynch, J. (1989). *Multicultural education in a global society.* New York: Falman Press.

Mead, G. H. (1934). *Mind, self, and society: From the standpoint of a social behaviorist.* Chicago: University of Chicago Press.

Morris, M. (1981). *Saying and meaning in Puerto Rico: Some problems in the ethnography of discourse.* Oxford, UK: Pergamon Press.

Phelan, P., & Davidson, A. L. (Eds.). (1993). *Renegotiating cultural diversity in American schools.* New York: Teachers College Press.

Philipsen, G. (1987). The prospect for cultural communication. In L. Kincaid (Ed.), *Communication theories: Eastern and Western perspectives.* New York: Academic Press.

Philipsen, G. (1992). *Speaking culturally: Explorations in social communication.* Albany: State University of New York Press.

Rivera-Batiz, F. L., & Santiago, C. (1994). *Puerto Ricans in the United States: A changing reality.* Washington, DC: National Puerto Rican Coalition.

Sacks, H. (1992). *Lectures on conversation* (Vols. 1-2, G. Jefferson, Ed.). Oxford, UK: Blackwell.

Sacks, H., Schegloff, E. A., & Jefferson, G. (1974). A simplest systematics for the organization of turn-taking for conversation. *Language, 50,* 696-735.

Sapir, E. (1931). Communication. In E. R. A. Seligman & A. S. Johnson (Eds.), *Encyclopaedia of the social sciences* (Vol. 4, pp. 78-81). New York: Macmillan.

Schatzman, L., & Strauss, A. L. (1973). *Fieldwork research: Strategies for a natural sociology.* Englewood Cliffs, NJ: Prentice Hall.

Schneider, D. M. (1976). Notes toward a theory of culture. In K. Basso & H. Selby (Eds.), *Meaning in anthropology* (pp. 197-220). Albuquerque: University of New Mexico Press.

Shotter, J. (1993). *Conversational realities: Constructing life through language.* London: Sage.

Thompson, B. W., & Tyagi, S. (Eds.). (1993). *Beyond a dream deferred: Multicultural education and the politics of excellence.* Minneapolis: University of Minnesota Press.

Weider, D. L., & Pratt, S. (1990). On being a recognizable Indian among Indians. In D. Carbaugh (Ed.), *Cultural communication and intercultural contact* (pp. 45-64). Hillsdale, NJ: Lawrence Erlbaum.

4

When Rhetorical Theory and Practice Encounter Postcolonialism

Rethinking the Meaning of Farrakhan and the Million Man March Address

MAROUF HASIAN, JR. • *University of Utah*

> It is only when subaltern figures like women, Orientals, blacks, and other "natives" made enough noise that they were paid attention to.
>
> —Said, 1989, p. 210

For too many years communication scholars have assiduously avoided investigations of vernacular discourse and have focused attention on elite texts (Ono & Sloop, 1995).[1] This chapter invites critics to contemplate the possibility that researchers can begin a conversation between two of the many communities that are just beginning the enterprise of reaching out to "the Other"—the world of postcolonialism and the realm of rhetoric. As Lee (1998) has recently pointed out, intellectuals should now be in a position to critique the influence of "international imperialism" through their creation of alternative narratives and oppositional critiques of colonial power (p. 27). As I will argue throughout this chapter, both the rhetorical and postcolonial communities bring to the academy unique but related experiences and opportunities, and each of them can help us illuminate the ways in which discourse, power, and knowledge circulate within the halls of academia and in the broader rhetorical culture.

In order to carry out this task, this chapter is divided into three major sections. The first segment briefly discusses some of the communicative dimensions of postcolonial theorizing and criticism. The second section

---

AUTHOR'S NOTE: Marouf Hasian Jr. thanks the anonymous reviewers for their insights and suggestions.

provides a case study applying some of these insights by analyzing the discourse of Louis Farrakhan and the Nation of Islam. Finally, the third portion of the chapter provides a heuristic assessment of Farrakhan's brand of postcolonial inquiry.

POSTCOLONIAL THEORY: UNDERSTANDING THE "UNDISCIPLINED"

Throughout our journals, we continue to use Eurocentric models of communication that presuppose the existence of a rationalistic, Western (see Lucy & Frank, 1993) paradigm. In spite of the arguments espoused by critics like Crenshaw (1997, 1998), Lee (1998), Marvin (1994), McKerrow (1989), McGee (1975), Wander (1983, 1996), and Whitson and Poulakos (1993), for the most part we are content with investigations that search for the epistemic or intersubjective "meanings" that supposedly exist within the public sphere. This often entails focusing on the speeches of the great leaders rather than paying attention to the voices of the "other"—those subalterns who combat subordination by crafting their own texts and identities (Flores, 1996).

This valorization of elite discourse has its place, but when it becomes the exclusive or even primary mode of discussing rhetoric, we pay the high cost of denying a voice to the marginalized, the disempowered, and the colonized. For example, the subfield of rhetoric has been historically dominated by "public address" studies, and in the process of analysis, scholars employ Western standards of truth, beauty, and goodness in their assessment of salient texts. Ironically, as the rest of the academy has discovered the fruitfulness of taking the rhetorical turn, our anxieties as rhetoricians have brought forth forms of retrenchment that rely on the comforting search for new metanarratives. In other words, we replace one set of Platonic essences with another set of Aristotelian essences.[2]

In the idealized world of many rhetorical theorists, some audiences contain irrational members who are continually tempted by demagogues (e.g., Farrakhan), and it is up to the discipline to ensure that our politicians and other leaders use rational arguments within the technical and public spheres. Building on representational models of communication that reproduce the politics of classical liberalism and the economics of the marketplace, this reified view of rhetorical theory asks rhetors to emulate the "great" texts that are the productions of knowledgeable rhetors.

As Blair, Brown, and Baxter (1994) noted in a controversial article in *The Quarterly Journal of Speech,*

> works published in most of our academic journals display as little as possible the circumstances and activities of their production. Notably missing, or at least reduced to virtual silence, is the passion that obviously drives our choices to write about particular topics in particular ways. Our writings suppress our convictions, our enthusiasm, our anger, in the interest of achieving an impersonal "expert" distance and tone . . . issues of institutional or professional power are deemed superfluous to the substance and character of our scholarly efforts. (p. 383)

Many critics will admit that rhetorical theory and criticism are at their best when they are emancipatory, inclusive, and contextual, but frequently a stultifying orthodoxy is imposed by those who demand adherence to the canons of rhetoric. Although this may not be done intentionally, it nevertheless occurs frequently.

Granted, we have had movement studies and other approaches that have expanded the number of speakers that have to be considered, and we have encountered "critical" rhetorics (McKerrow, 1989) that have invited us to contemplate the need for critiques of emancipation. Some theorists have helped to shift our gaze beyond the confines of Anglo discourse (Delgado, 1993/1994; Flores, 1996; Lee, 1998). In their most libertine moments, rhetoricians have discussed the importance of decentered subjects, the role of deconstruction (Biesecker, 1992), and the need for empathic criticism (Condit, 1993). Yet for the most part, rhetorical theorizing is still an exercise in learning the tenets of "whiteness" (Nakayama and Krizek, 1995), and assimilation and accommodation are the prices paid for admission to the community.[3] Crenshaw (1997) remarked that these academic strictures circumscribe the ways that we talk about social relationships and individual experiences (pp. 253-254). Consciously or unconsciously, we have imbibed notions of civility and decorum that have domesticated rhetoric, and in the process we have reproduced and recirculated tales that treat as the foreigner anyone who may speak English yet think in un-American ways. There is the constant fear that in studying the vernacular, the cultural, and the popular, we have somehow forgotten the aesthetic power of the individual artist-genius who careful crafts his or her rhetorical text.

My necessarily impressionist view of the current state of rhetorical theory may perhaps be too skeptical for many communication scholars, but it nevertheless explains why rhetorical theorists have been some of the *last* scholars within the academy to seek a rapprochement with postcolonial theorizing.[4] Our ideographic prefigurations and cultural practices have made it extremely difficult for cultural studies advocates or postcolonial theorists to take seriously the belief that they have a place within the "field" of rhetoric. As Grossberg (1993) once observed, the disciplinary boundaries of a field sometimes ask us to leave behind the benefits that come from interdisciplinary perspectives. As a result, the foreign "other" can only speak in the native tongue of the master.

At the same time that rhetorical theorists grapple with the problem of maintaining a space within "communication," postcolonial theorists work collectively at explaining their own undisciplined agendas (Bhabha, 1990; Prakash, 1994; Said, 1978; Trinh, 1989). Like their colleagues in cultural studies who refuse totalizing labels (Grossberg, 1993, p. 89), postcolonial writers eschew any attempts to depoliticize their theories and practices.[5] Bringing together scholars from literary criticism, film studies, subaltern studies, cultural studies, and similar heterodox fields, postcolonialism remains an ambiguous yet unique approach to the academy. Yet in spite of this apparent inscrutability, it is possible to get some sense of the recurring themes of postcolonial discourse without disciplining the subject. As Dirlik explained in 1994,

> Postcolonialism is the most recent entrant to achieve prominent visibility in the ranks of those "post" marked words (seminal among them, postmodernism) that serve as signposts in (to) contemporary cultural criticism. Unlike other "post" marked words, postcolonialism claims as its special province the terrain that in an earlier day used to go by the name of Third World. It is intended, therefore, to achieve authentic globalization of cultural discourses by the extension globally of the intellectual concerns and orientations originating at the central sites of Euro-American cultural criticism and by the introduction into the latter of voices and subjectivities from the margins of earlier political and ideological colonialism that now demand a hearing at those sites at the center.[6] (p. 329)

Although postcolonial writers disagree on which specific analytic tool is most effective in this quest (deconstruction, neo-Marxism, poststructural theorizing, discourse analysis, audience reception theory, etc.), they often agree on the need to interrogate the taken-for-granteds of nationalistic and colonial discourse. In many ways, postcolonial theorizing is most illuminating when it works at the boundaries of the academy, refusing to be amalgamated into any single discipline such as communication, English, or political geography.[7] For the purposes of debate and discussion, I will focus attention in this section on three key issues for postcolonialism: representation, disciplinarity, and materiality.

Many postcolonial critics would agree with Said (1989) that one of the purposes of an academic is to "represent" the disempowered, the diasporic denizens of the planet.[8] This does not mean simply inverting the power relationships so that the dominant speakers are silenced while we hear the monologues of newly empowered subalterns. Nor does it mean that we uncritically celebrate all forms of vernacular discourse (Ono & Sloop, 1995). It simply means that as critics we sensitize ourselves to the ways that our canons and our communication habits silence those who would like to belong to the public sphere.

From the point of view of postcolonial critics, traditional academic practices sometimes engage in a form of "Orientalism" (Said, 1978) that hinders our ability to understand other cultures. This Orientalism influences the forms of deliberation that are considered rational, the behavior that is regarded as natural, and the standards that are used to decide what should be considered to be fact or mere opinion. Rather than seeing the polysemic nature of interpretations, we sometimes casually accept the univocal tales of dominance that influence the ways in which we think of issues like resource scarcity or human rights (Spivak, 1994). Regardless of whether this colonization takes the form of military occupation, economic exploitation, or political disempowerment, colonization in all of its manifestations creates situations that cannot be critiqued as long as we are committed to valorizing particular models of rhetoric. Consensus models may ask us to celebrate the joys of nationhood, but they also have the potential of helping us forget the foreign Other.

Although postcolonialism has been used as a critique of disparate power relationships on a number of continents, most of the early work in this area has focused attention on the abuses that have come from European colonialism and its lasting legacy in what used to be called "the Third World" (Fanon, 1966). For many postcolonial critics, grand metanarratives have been used as political capital in imperialistic cultural conflicts, and it is up to organic intellectuals to find a way to replace these constructs with local, situational knowledges that give voice to those who have suffered the ravages of modernity (Said, 1989). As Bhabha (1990) once argued, the "traditional authority of those national objects of knowledge—Tradition, People, the Reason of the State, High Culture, for instance," depends on the transformation of partial visions into larger representations that are in constant need of critical interrogation (p. 3). Said (1982) made a similar claim when he argued that "instead of noninterference and specialization," we need "interference, a crossing of borders and obstacles" in order to determine what discursive constructs have been effaced and forgotten (p. 24, quoted in Strine, 1991, p. 199). In many cases, this has brought calls for political intervention rather than simple engagement in description or ahistorical explanation. In the same way that some rhetoricians talk about the "social relevance" of rhetorical scholarship (Ivie, 1995), postcolonial advocates remind us of the need to give voice to the subalterns who live on the margins.

In order to provide some examples of the potential power of postcolonial criticism, I note the work of Said (1994a, 1994b), Spivak (1994), and Supriya (1996). Said, through his analyses of various novels, journals, music, and other texts, has attacked the alleged excesses of both the Israeli government and the Palestinian Authority. His writings have helped bring awareness to the plight of refugees living in both Gaza and on the West Bank. Spivak (1994), building on her earlier deconstructive work, has provided important information regarding the difficulties that surround development programs such as the Flood Action Plan in Bangladesh. Here in the United States, Supriya (1996) has used her research to publicize the problems facing immigrant women who must cope with the familial expectations of several different cultures.

Postcolonial theorizing thus radically alters the ways in which we read "texts," inviting us to no longer view nationalistic documents as objective and apolitical containers of knowledge. Unlike rhetorical theories, which sometimes privilege the great rhetor who creatively produces persuasive documents, postcolonial analyses focus on the areas of slippage, where various cultures have learned to misread, appropriate, and shape these same texts for their own purposes. Stories that used to be read as examples of violations of colonial norms and good manners are now read as acts of intransigence, where the disempowered create their own discursive spaces.[9] Reconstructed histories remind us that there are many Indias, many Israels, and many U.S. Americas, and orthodox canons are demystified as new idioms replace the old. In the same way that McGee (1990) talks about the ways that "fragments" circulate within the public sphere, postcolonial theorists discuss the importance of "imagined" communities (Anderson, 1986) and the malleability of national boundaries.[10]

This combined requirement—that theorists both "intervene" and at the same time "represent" the subaltern—brings with it unique challenges for the postcolonial writer. As Suleri (1992) recently warned,

> While alteritism begins as a critical and theoretical revision of a Eurocentric or Orientalist study of the literatures of colonialism, its indiscriminate reliance on the centrality of otherness tends to replicate what in the context of imperialist discourse was the familiar category of the exotic. . . . When . . . a twentieth-century Anglo-American critic turns exclusively to the question of alterity in its colonial context, he or she runs the risk of rendering otherness indistinguishable from exoticism, and of representing "difference" with no attention to the cultural nuances that differentiation implies. (p. 12)

How does one discuss material issues and facilitate social change without reinscribing and recirculating new forms of Orientalism? How can a critic represent the Other without herself/himself becoming an elite whose power of speech or representation is evidence of a power disparity? Many of these theorists believe that the best way to carry out the postcolonial project is to change rhetorical inscriptions, disrupt the binaries that are used in hegemonic signification processes, and highlight the material conditions of the oppressed. As I will note later, in my case example of Farrakhan, this is not always an easy task.

In the same way that McKerrow (1989) demands that "critical" rhetoric never cease questioning texts of domination and emancipation, postcolonial theorists are unwilling to limit themselves to illuminating the ways in which marginalized groups have been victimized or disempowered within dominant texts. Postcolonial theorists are thus constantly looking for ways to redeploy texts and to transgress traditional explanatory schemes in representing the Other. This is an act of reconstruction, of appropriating the work of dominant texts in acts of subversion. Gilroy (1992), for example, points out the ways in which our hermeneutics can be informed by studying the shared transatlantic ("the black Atlantic world") cultural experiences of African Americans on different continents. Prakash (1992) uses the concepts of hybrid identities to reformulate the ways in which we think about the relationship between Hindu, Muslim, and British notions of class, capitalism, and colonialism.

Unlike some rhetorical investigations, which have accepted uncritically the chronologies of modernity and the progressive tales of the West, postcolonial fabrications point out the contradictions in classical liberal narratives and possible sites of resistance and intransigence. These theorists look for the ways in which the undisciplined subalterns can nevertheless gain a voice, even if this means simply avoiding acquiescence in the occupation of prefigurations or the recognition of disparate power relationships. By uncovering points of colonial complicity, such theorists focus our gaze on the silencing of the "native," and they incessantly interrogate existing totalizing knowledge claims.

Although critics like Said (1994a, 1994b) recognize the influence of great speeches, texts, and literatures, they nevertheless read these texts against the grain, and they refuse to countenance romantic interpretations that privilege the Occidental over the Oriental. Reworking and renegotiating the languages of empire, postcolonialists take disciplinary texts and revise them, using new idioms to produce tales that reveal themes and myths that may not have been consciously planned or anticipated by either the text "author" or the canonical communities. As participants in undisciplined cultural practices, such theorists are able to openly form political alliances, admit emotional commitments, and articulate the need for radical epistemic changes within the academy. Perhaps Cherwitz and Darwin (1995) are correct in their assessment that "performance" alone may be impossible, but postcolonial theories have also shown us the politics involved in Western epistemologies that have hidden the presence of the Other.

One of the most frequent complaints leveled against postcolonialists is the claim that reliance on cultural artifacts, including music, film, autobiographies, literatures, and so forth, prevents them from focusing attention on the "real" material needs of those who have been colonized.[11] In the process of drawing our attention to the power of discourse and signification, such theorists are supposedly leaving behind important factors such as critiques of capitalism or economics. Neo-Marxists ridicule postcolonial analyses of talk that dissuade people from engaging in substantive material reforms. Ahmad (1994), for example, complained that an

> obvious consequence of repudiating Marxism was that one now sought to make sense of the world of colonies and empires much less in terms of classes, but much more in terms of nations and countries and races, and thought of imperialism itself not as a hierarchically structured system of global capitalism but as a relation, of governance and occupation, between richer and poorer countries, West and non-Western . . . with the colonial relationship broken, the

newly independent states were expected to combat imperialism with their nationalist *ideologies.* (p. 41)

Ahmad has not been alone in his lamentations. Dirlik (1994), noting the rising power of postcolonial critics within the academy, claimed that these theories are actually a description of the practices of academic intellectuals and can be distinguished from discussions of the conditions that have come from global capitalism (p. 331). To make matters worse, Dirlik (1994) observed that focusing on "discursive thematics" provides us little new information on the plights of vast numbers of "Third World" populations that exist on the margins of modernity (p. 337). Such critics contend that the move away from materiality has paved the way for conservative rhetorics that reinscribe colonial methodologies and epistemologies in ways that militate against emancipatory politicalization.

Although these materialist critiques have made important contributions to the postcolonial conversations, they underestimated the power of discursive "performativity" (Said, 1989, p. 222), where marginalized communities empower themselves by gaining an appreciation of the ways in which discourse codes can be used in order to formulate social change. Just how much advantage we gain from blending structural and material concerns together remains to be seen.

On first impression, then, the reader might get the notion that perhaps the amalgamation of rhetorical and postcolonial approaches to discourse is an inherently problematic venture. The history of public address, filled with hubris and triumph in its emulation of the greats, comes face to face with its foreign interlocutor. We cannot escape this confrontation by contemplating the possibility that we can add a few Others and then continue on with the same canons, the same genres, and the same epistemic assumptions. Nor can we ask postcolonial theorists to simply tone down their arguments in order to gain a hearing in the pantheons of rhetoric.

One fruitful approach could involve bringing together some of the best parts of rhetorical and postcolonial theorizing. This would mean the creation of a new space, one that builds on the advantages of both positions at this historical moment. Rather than introducing any grand new narrative, we could create informed communication studies that accept the limited epistemic insights that come from local knowledges that are coproduced by dominant and marginalized communities. We could follow the lead of critics who advocate the study of "vernacular" discourse (Ono & Sloop, 1995; Rafael, 1990; Sloop & Ono, 1997, p. 52). In place of uncritical celebrations of national bicentennials and foreign conquests, we would reformulate our studies of epideictic, forensic, and deliberative genres to include queries that focus our gaze on the cultural beliefs of the ordinary citizen who may never be a great speaker or even hear a "great" speech.

For those of us who are interested in critical rhetoric, the challenge is to find ways of replacing a totalizing vision of nationality with a lens that focuses on how the "people, the popular, the masses" have become that "unsurpassable matrix on which social formations are articulated, disarticulated and transformed" (Chen, 1988, p. 12). In a world filled with hate, venom, and racism, it behooves us to find ways of giving voice to those denizens of the world who will no longer acquiesce in the uncritical celebration of nationalism and empire building.[12] The recent events in "Bosnia," "Iraq," and "Germany" provide us with reminders of the enduring legacy and pervasiveness of colonialism in all of its manifestations.

In the next section, I provide a brief case example of some of the ways in which colonial rhetoric influences how some U.S. Americans today view the Other. More specifically, the concepts of representativeness, disciplinarity, and materiality are addressed.

DECODING FARRAKHAN'S MILLION MARCH ADDRESS

When most U.S. Americans hear the word *colony* associated with their nation, they have a tendency to genuflect to a discussion of the American War of Independence from Britain that began in the 1770s. Although this is an important chapter in the nation's collective memory, it is not the only time these issues of colonization have surfaced in our Anglo African rhetoric (Condit & Lucaites, 1993). As JanMohamed (1985) trenchantly observed, the political histories of colonialism contain a number of sedimented discourses, and many of these have been forgotten in our traditional tales of classical liberal democracy.[13] Those that we have retained are often domesticated so that ideological conflicts are resolved within "existing channels" (Murphy, 1992, p. 67).

Since the time of the founders, black writers and speakers have debated the relative merits of assimilation versus separatism, the meaning of Constitutional "equality," and liberty in the midst of slavery. During the first half of the 19th century, many African Americans expressed their anger and frustration as the U.S. government continued to defend the legality of slavery while emancipation took place in the British West Indies (Bowers, 1995). At the same time, many whites in America seriously contemplated the possibility that the best way to provide a haven for this Other was to provide for the emigration of the black "race" to another continent (Condit & Lucaites, 1993, pp. 68-100).

Faced with such racist ideologies, blacks in the 19th and 20th centuries created a number of oppositional rhetorics, but for the most part they adopted variants of two predominant ideologies—"emancipatory liberalism" or the "philosophy of global anti-imperialism" (Berman, 1994, p. 66). The first of these positions highlighted the importance of staying in the United States and using Constitutional reforms as a means of bringing about social change. This liberal stance has been advanced by jurists such as Thurgood Marshall, Christian activists such as Martin Luther King, Jr., and military leaders such as Colin Powell.

At the same time, there have been African Americans who have advocated a more global approach to racial problems. Audiences have been invited to listen to the separatist discourse of Marcus Garvey[14] or Malcolm X (Patterson, 1995, p. 43; Ware & Linkugel, 1982). Facing segregationist policies, this latter group of leaders adopted separatist positions that encouraged blacks to redefine themselves as members of a larger global community. Although these writers often disagreed among themselves on the importance of issues such as expatriation, immigration, or citizenship, they often shared a willingness to critique the colonial ambitions of both the U.S. American and European empires.

Such critics have left us a legacy of oppositional discourse, a collection of powerful commentaries that have been deployed by advocates attempting to alter the material conditions of underrepresented communities of subalterns. As Gardell noted in 1996,

> We see in the NOI [Nation of Islam] a combination of the notion of militant Islam and the legacy of classical black nationalism, and the movement produced some of the leading African American nationalists of the twentieth century: Elijah Muhammad, Malcolm X, and Louis Farrakhan. . . . The European superpowers incessantly forced their ways into "new" areas with their military and commercial spearheads. . . . The precolonial existence of Islam and Christianity in Africa was ignored, as was the content of various African religions, and so the inhabitants could be presented as living their life in barbarous fear and superstition. (pp. 5, 14, 15)

Until recently, it has been taken for granted in U.S. mythology that the majority of people of color have accepted assimilationist narratives that promise incremental freedoms and economic gains in the name of color blindness and equality. In spite of the occasional appearance of a popular "demagogue," the consensus of opinion seems to have been that African Americans of all classes would benefit from integrationist policies.

The rising power of Louis Farrakhan has brought to the surface the latent tensions that have existed in the ideological struggle between emancipatory liberalism and anti-imperial separatism. Although Farrakhan and the Nation of Islam have been around for decades (Alexander, 1998; Gardell, 1996; Levinsohn, 1997; Magida, 1996; Marshall, 1996; Singh, 1997), it was not until the historic Million Man March that this rhetor and his organization were taken seriously by mainstream U.S. America. On October 16, 1995, Louis Farrakhan addressed millions of Americans who were interested in hearing the views of a charismatic public figure. For more than two and a half hours, Farrakhan provided his immediate and television audiences with narratives that sounded very much like progressive tales of Anglo emancipation from British colonialism.

On the surface, Farrakhan's narrative was deceptively simple. He asserted that most of U.S. America was suffering from an assortment of maladies (malice, arrogance, power, wealth) that stemmed from "white supremacy" (Farrakhan, 1995, p. 14). This meant that the whites making plans in "a few smoke-filled rooms" did not understand the trials and tribulations of the masses (p. 10). For at least 400 years, Europeans and other whites had tried to "control" (p. 5) blacks and other people of color by putting them into slavery (or stealing their knowledge), and now these oppressed people needed to search for new ways of finding a more "perfect union." President Clinton and other leaders of the "mainstream" (p. 10) were "out of touch with reality" (p. 10). These politicians were not offering any real solutions to these conundrums, because the president's advisers did not understand the importance of Islam or the teachings of Master Fard Muhammad. Within this tale, there were "still two Americas," (p. 1), because the presence of menaces like Fuhrman, Helms, and Bilbo (p. 12) showed that "non-White people" were still considered to be the "burden bearers" of the nation (p. 2).[15] Farrakhan said that by setting people of color against each other through "narrow restrictions," empowered whites maintained their control over the divided communities of the world (p. 6). By establishing a "new covenant" based on the secrets of the ancient "Masonic Order," Farrakhan proposed to help the nations of the world cure the disease of racism (p. 12).

FARRAKHAN AND THE ISSUE
OF REPRESENTATIVENESS

Throughout his Million Man March address, Farrakhan tried to present himself as one of the world's leading Islamic leaders, one who truly represents the views of the multitudes. This Minister of the Nation of Islam claimed that his immediate audience was made up of almost 2 million blacks at the march and more than 10 million citizens who were watching from home. He proposed that his listeners pledge their lives to the goal of striving "toward a more perfect union" (Farrakhan, 1995, p. 4) by following an eight-step process that involved pointing out the "wrong in the society" (p. 6), acknowledging those problems (p. 7), confession, repentance, atonement, forgiveness (pp. 7-8), reconciliation, and restoration (pp. 8, 14).

Farrakhan's subject position was that of a mystic messenger of God, a "doctor" (Farrakhan, 1995, p. 9) who understood the importance of "atonement and reconciliation" (p. 1). Like Elijah, he had the job of "turning the hearts of the children back to their fathers" (p. 10). Farrakhan argued that he was being unfairly maligned by outsiders who did not understand his patriotism or his links to Martin Luther King, Jr., Malcolm X, and ancient biblical figures (pp. 4-7). These nonbelievers did not like the way he was speaking the truth about "governments," "principalities," "rulers," and "administrations" (p. 6). The Nation of Islam leader went on to imply that "the beautiful White House" may have been involved in conspiracies that brought trouble to King, Malcolm X, and W. E. B. Du Bois (pp. 9-10). By exposing these activities, he said the "descendants of the builders of the pyramids" could recover from their "amnesia" (p. 12).

At the beginning of the Million Man March address, Farrakhan brought together the sacred and the secular by reconfiguring the scene that served as a backdrop for this momentous event. In this Minister's periodicalization of historical events, the present occasion was linked to an Islamic past and a redemptive future (Farrakhan, 1995, pp. 1-3). In many ways, this part of the performance built on a variety of Judeo-Christian motifs, and Farrakhan also highlighted the lessons of Islam throughout his address.

Audiences were both edified and entertained by Farrakhan's ability to blend this theological discourse with political commentaries that reminded his audience that few changes had taken place since the time of the Kerner Commission in 1968. For example, the United States was still "two Americas, one black, one White, separate and unequal" (Farrakhan, 1995, p. 1). Unlike more patriotic leaders, who might have celebrated U.S. covenants and exceptionalism, Farrakhan went out of his way to create a picture of a nation that is still enduring the material pains of a colonial legacy of slavery. In the first few minutes of his speech, this Minister made a not-unexpected allusion to Abraham Lincoln, but it was not for the orthodox purpose of praising the crafting of the Emancipation Proclamation. In Farrakhan's confrontational rendition of the tale, Lincoln was considered to be a typical white leader who understood the importance of "separation" but not "equality." In the cultural memories of most U.S. Americans, Washington's mall and Lincoln's memorial were iconic reminders of freedom or liberty, but in Farrakhan's symbolic constructions such places were merely reminders that slaves were brought "on this Mall in chains to be sold up and down the Eastern seaboard" (p. 1).

Strategically, Farrakhan's first few minutes were used to set the tone for the rest of the speech, and in many ways the presentation seemed to be tailored for audience members who may have expected to hear a message of institutional racism, perhaps without his usual anti-Semitism. The speech became tactically important not only for its presence but also for its absences. For instance, we heard no narrative about Yacub and the diabolical invention of the white race.[16] Instead, we were offered a more moderate rhetoric of redemption for those who wanted improved conditions for all races.

FARRAKHAN, POSTCOLONIALISM, AND DISCIPLINARITY

In order to help bolster his credibility as one of the world's experts on racial problems, Farrakhan has to show his audience both his expertise and his detractors' ignorance on such controversial topics as the history of slavery, the true causes of racism in U.S. America, and the origins of poverty throughout the world. Pauley (1998) has explained that the Minister was trying to "enhance his ethos by reshaping his public persona" and that he needed to find some of the rhetorical forms that would resonate with a "widely heterogenous American audience" (p. 514). Yet limiting his audience to U.S. Americans would have meant that Farrakhan would have had to give up some of his self-defined international role as an Islamic leader. Said (1989) has mentioned that for postcolonial critics, the creation of this authenticity is no easy task, and the Nation of Islam's leader has to find a way of delegitimizing the status of his adversaries.

Like other anticolonial speakers, Farrakhan was trying to alter the disciplinary language that would be used in describing the past and present causes of the world's racial situation. As Fanon explains in Black Skin, White Masks (1967), the demand that "the other" learn the language of the colonizer brings the potential "death and burial" of local cultures (pp. 17-19). In his Million Man March address, Farrakhan adopts a populist form of discourse that is radically different from more orthodox— and academic—forms of argumentation and historical recollection. Throughout his performance, he portrays himself as a leader who is in possession of the mystic lexicons of the past, a humble messenger who has not forgotten the enduring Masonic power of ancient Egypt. Through his use of numerology, he demonstrates his ability to see things that are hidden from those who are blinded by the ignorance of white supremacy.17 Listen, for example, to his explanation of the continuing influence of the number 19:

> In the background is the Jefferson and Lincoln Memorial, each of these monuments is 19 feet high. . . . What is so deep about this number 19? . . . That number 19—when you have a nine you have a womb that is pregnant. And when you have a one standing by the nine, it means that there's something secret that has to be unfolded. . . . George Washington, who was a grand master of the Masonic order, laid the foundation, the cornerstone of this capitol building where we stand. George was a slave owner. Now, the President spoke today and he wanted to heal the great divide. But I respectfully suggest to the President, you did not dig deep enough at the malady that divides Black and White in order [to] effect a solution to the problem. (Farrakhan, 1995, p. 2)[18]

For many Moslems around the world, the importance of the number 19 comes from an interpretation of a chapter in the Holy Qur'an in which 19 guardians stand watch at the entrance of Hell (Pauley, 1998, p. 534, note 17). As Tynetta Muhammad explains, hidden in the language of the Qur'an are "the mathematical keys to deciphering God's hidden messages to the world" (quoted in Gardell, 1996, p. 179). Farrakhan thus implied that Clinton's surface learning prevented him from appreciating the deeper meanings that could come only from apprehending the links between Egypt, the founding Masons, and the historic Million Man March. In place of quotations from experts, we are offered a text that blends together strands from Biblical allusions, Islamic principles, and black nationalist rhetorics.

The Minister's brief discussion of Clinton and his focus on numerology therefore served several complementary discursive functions. It reminded his immediate and distant audiences that they too had the potential to learn Islamic tenets and learning, as long as they were open-minded enough to take seriously the study of numerology. If they took pride in acknowledging past accomplishments and went through the arduous task of progressing through the stages of atonement and reconciliation, they could break the chains of slavery and colonialism. Furthermore, the presence of millions at the march showed the world that not even the president of the United States could ignore Farrakhan and his followers. The focus on Masonic legends and key numbers provided Farrakhan with a disciplinary lexicon that shifted attention away from "mainstream" Constitutional claims and toward more allegedly global concerns.[19] This studied avoidance of more orthodox discussions of the civil rights creeds meant that Farrakhan could now chastise those politicians who believed in a truncated world history. For example, near the middle of his address, Farrakhan excoriated Clinton for not being able to "harmonize the dark people of the world" (Farrakhan, 1995, p. 15), and he contended,

> You've got Arabs here. You've got Hispanics here. I know you call them illegal aliens, but hell, you took Texas from them by flooding Texas with people that got your mind. . . . The Native American is suffering today. He's suffering almost complete extinction. Now, he learned about bingo. You taught him. . . . What makes you like this? See, you're like this because you're not well. And in the light of today's global village, you can never harmonize with the Asians. (Farrakhan, 1995, p. 15).

The implicit assumption here is that a knowledgeable Farrakhan has the antidote for the poison of "white supremacy." As Crenshaw (1998) opined, modern constructions of "colorblindness" present a "cultural ideal" that includes a "modern world without color prejudice" (p. 244), and it is this imaginative creation that is being interrogated by this Minister of the Nation of Islam.

By attempting to alter the yardsticks that measure U.S. standards of progress, Farrakhan is inviting his audience to become participants themselves in the search for the "truth" about racism. As Fisher (1984) once explained, human storytellers need to be able to provide different forms of rationality (p. 9), and Farrakhan's followers could gain a complex sense of pride, pleasure, and amusement by observing the befuddlement of those who belittle the importance of numerology. This mixture of satire, sarcasm, and deadly seriousness served as a commonsense form of discourse that interrogated the taken-for-granteds of more formalistic rhetorics. Leaders like Clinton may have treated racism as an individual or family problem, but this gathering brought together hundreds of thousands of people who might have thought differently.

During the first hour, Farrakhan augmented his discussions of numerology with history lessons that debunked much of U.S. civil religion. Within his chronological account, the national Seal and Constitution were no longer revered documents, but proof positive that Masons were still trying to emulate the Pharaohs in their "pursuit of the Israelites" (Farrakhan, 1995, p. 2). Defending his links to Jesus, Moses, Muhammad, Newton, and Einstein, he ridiculed those who would try to separate the message from the messenger (p. 3). In Farrakhan's selective histories, this day had been foreshadowed centuries ago:

> So today, whether you like it or not, God brought the idea through me and he didn't bring it through me because my heart was dark with hatred and anti-Semitism, he didn't bring it through me because my heart was dark and I'm filled with hatred for White people for the human family of the planet. If my heart were that dark, how is the message so bright, the message so clear, the response so magnificent? [Applause]. (Farrakhan, 1995, p. 3)

What is interesting here is that Farrakhan gives the impression that his advocacy of "truth" allows him to disdain rather than hate those who possess white power. Why would he resort to hatred when people of color can gain their own social agency by gathering under the banner of Islam?

Such reasoning may have appeared convoluted to his detractors, but his punctuation of time was filled with occasional allusions to historical practices that could not be easily dismissed. Listeners may not have accepted all of his ideas about numerology, but some of them could nevertheless sympathize with a speaker who shared their sense of racial injustice. Part of Farrakhan's postcolonial critique involved remembrances of things past—the "blood of our ancestors," the lynchings, and the other deaths overlooked by the traditional history books. In his self-described search for "truth," the Minister was merciless in his war on falsehoods. For example, the U.S. Constitution may have attempted to form a union, but it came at the cost of ignoring the need for a broader "more perfect union" (Farrakhan, 1995, p. 3).

Much of the second half of Farrakhan's presentation involved his explanation of how this "more perfect union" could be obtained. Before he outlined this redemptive plan, however, he wanted to make sure that no one missed his indictment of the status quo. One of the most intriguing parts of Farrakhan's oration involved his framing techniques, which invited audiences to think about their ideas concerning the representation of color in the United States. Perhaps anticipating that he could be called a racial separatist, he tried to present himself as a unifier fighting against the power of whiteness. Unnamed and omnipresent social agents were said to have "whitened up" the nation's institutions. "White supremacy," he averred, "has poisoned the bloodstream of religion, education, politics, jurisprudence, economics, social ethics, and morality" (Farrakhan, 1995, p. 16). In Farrakhan's postcolonial tale, the audience is presented with a vision of a country tearing itself apart—a world filled with "wasted cities," imperfect laws, and humans who don't believe in atonement (pp. 4-5).

What made Farrakhan's address so fascinating, and yet so maddening, was the way in which he used several narrative substructures to create a pastiche of arguments that illustrated the United States' shortcomings as a colonial empire. By decentering U.S. American history and placing it in a more global context, he appeared to be a leader who rises above the provincial concerns of a spoiled and tattered nation. His revisionist history contained texts that allowed the audiences to identify with claims about conspiracy themes, the need for moral regeneration, institutional racism, the spread of Islam, or the need for political independents in the U.S. American polity. For example, one portion of his public address contained an imaginary monologue that Farrakhan used to respond to the Clinton speech that had been presented earlier in the day in Texas. The Minister answered the administration's purported cultural amnesia by pointing out that,

> We are a wounded people but we're being healed. But President Clinton, America is also wounded. And there's hostility now in the great divide between the people. . . . And we can't gloss over it with nice speeches, my dear, Mr. President. . . . You honored the marchers and they are worthy of honor. But

of course, you spoke ill directly of me, as a purveyor of malice and hatred. I must hasten to tell you, Mr. President . . . that I come in the tradition of the doctor who has to point out, with truth, what's wrong. And the pain is that power that has made America arrogant. (Farrakhan, 1995, p. 8)

To buttress these claims, Farrakhan immediately moved his tale back to Egypt and the Pharaoh, and this shift in time and space allowed him the opportunity to show how the "great city of Washington is like Jerusalem" (Farrakhan, 1995, p. 9). Other observers liked to think of themselves as members of a "great America," but they were simply a small part of a much larger "sea of tranquility" (p. 9). In Farrakhan's apocalyptic visions, the "children of Israel prefigured our suffering here in America" (p. 10), and "a whole world is lost" without atonement.

Sloop and Ono (1997) have commented on the importance of vernacular discourse for marginalized cultures, and in this case, Farrakhan made it clear that he had reached the stage where he wanted his listeners to replace the arguments of "Gingrich," "Dole" and even the "Supreme Court" with "responsible" insights from Islam. Building on his earlier uses of Egyptology, Farrakhan amalgamated sarcasm with hope as he talked about one of his favorite Biblical stories:

> You know, pastors, I love that scripture where Jesus told his disciples, go there and you'll see an ass and a colt tied with her. Untie them and bring them to me. If anybody asks you what you're doing, because it may look like you're stealing and you know they are going to accuse you of stealing, tell them the Master got need of these. . . . The donkey is tied up. . . . But, hai [*sic*], the ass is now talking with a man's voice. And the ass wants to throw the rider off, because he got a new rider today. (Farrakhan, 1995, p. 12)

Although Farrakhan would quickly move on to other subjects, he had reassured his listeners that they would no longer live the life of the colonized donkey.

FARRAKHAN'S POSTCOLONIAL CRITIQUE AND THE ISSUE OF MATERIALISM

At the same time that Farrakhan dealt with the complexities of representativeness and disciplinarity, he faced the question of just how much material change was going to take place following his address. As Magida (1996) once noted, many people of color still saw Farrakhan as "an opportunist, a mere dilettante of black harmony" (p. 197). In his Million Man March address, the Minister tried to answer his critics by magnifying the healing powers of Islam while simultaneously ridiculing the Clinton administration's economic policies. Farrakhan implied that the squalor and poverty that existed in the United States could only have come from the presence of "white supremacy." In the middle portion of his address, he berated Clinton for remembering "those six European nations out of which this country was founded" while forgetting the "children of Africa," "Asians," "Hispanics," and "Native Americans." (Farrakhan, 1995, p. 13). Worse yet, "white America" was a land that

> can't harmonize with the dark people of the world who out number you 11 to one. . . . White supremacy has to die in order for humanity to live. [Applause] . . . now you've whitened up everything. Any great invention we made you put white on it, because you didn't want to admit that a Black person had the intelligence, that genius. . . . We had to be buried somewhere else, that is sick. Some of us died just to drink water out of a fountain marked White. That's sick. Isn't it sick? (Farrakhan, 1995, p. 14)

Farrakhan's allusions to the material conditions of a segregated U.S. America had the potential to resonate with audiences who confronted the power of whiteness daily.

These emotionally draining narratives gave listeners a way out of their dilemmas and a sense of denouement. In concluding passages of his oration, Farrakhan operationalized for his audience what they would have to do in order to engage in acts of "atonement and reconciliation." He indicated that the world could remove the "false idea of white supremacy" (Farrakhan, 1995, p. 15) by performing a variety of acts that involved self-help techniques. For blacks, this meant emulating the "Asians," who had mastered the sciences and the arts without bashing other people (pp. 15-16). It also meant performing acts of purity, such as following the Nation of Islam in avoiding the eating of swine or other activities that were related to the "filth of degenerate culture" (p. 16). Local organizations could be formed that would work for the "uplift and the liberation of our people" (p. 16). New adherents could also "rebuild the wasted cities" (p. 4), stop fratricidal conflict, prevent the selling of drugs (p. 12), and register millions of potential voters (pp. 16-17).

Unlike some of Farrakhan's other addresses, he ended this presentation by explaining that the search for atonement included the possibility that the "Black, the poor and the vulnerable in this Society" could be helped (Farrakhan, 1995, p. 17). Absent were any of the usual complaints about Jewish conspiracies or Arab ownership of local stores—this was a march of hope for all creeds, colors, and nationalities. With the millions of dollars collected by the leaders of the march, people of color around the world could now participate in an idyllic world filled with people who were willing to "clean up their acts" (p. 19). To emphasize the international flavor of his call, Farrakhan concluded his address by presenting an Arabic prayer and song, and he asked his listeners to turn to their neighbors and hug them.

ASSESSMENT

Judged by orthodox standards of public address, Farrakhan's presentation might be considered a failure. As Pauley (1998) insightfully observed, not all of Farrakhan's listeners accepted the messages presented in this ecumenical and prophetic style. Many commentators thought that Clinton's earlier address was a much more positive approach to dealing with the issue of racism. One of the predominant complaints heard in the weeks after the Million Man March was that Farrakhan's speech was a lengthy, rambling presentation. Other observers talked more about the behavior of the crowd and the unity of the marchers than they did about Farrakhan. One Brooklyn-based writer argued that in spite of the fact that Farrakhan's speech had "no coherent program," the

> marchers transformed the narrow religious theme of atonement into a more secular theme of universal brotherhood; they converted the Nation of Islam's patronizing exclusion of black women into a temporary division of assignments, and welcomed the few women who came; they overcame the lack of a program and the absence of protest by manifesting an overwhelming display of unity and pride. Above all, black men were presented as responsible individuals belonging to a cohesive ethnic group with specific group interests. (Roberson, 1996, p. 19)

While admitting the appeal of the presentation for hundreds of thousands of Farrakhan's listeners, some commentators still complained of the "obscure allusions" and "esoteric mix of numerology, Egyptology, secret Masonic mythology, biblical allegory and Muslim mysticism" (Wilgoren, 1995, p. A1). For one sociologist (Patterson, 1995), Farrakhan's address communicated little besides providing a call for "personal responsibility," and much of this black separatist rhetoric simply continued a discussion of "colonization" drives that had been in existence since the time of Martin Delaney and Bishop Henry Turner (p. 43). An editorial writer for *The New York Times* summarized the views of many whites when he argued that Farrakhan was still a "hate-filled demagogue with a divisive, separatist ideology and an appalling record of racism, sexism, anti-Semitism and homophobia" (Rich, 1995, p. A23).

Yet there were also millions of Americans who seemed to agree with at least part of what Farrakhan had to say. As Cooper (1997) recently observed, "[C]learly, many African Americans see a very different man and message in Louis Farrakhan and his aides than White Americans see" (p. 35). Gallup polls revealed that 2 years before the march, only about 3% of blacks mentioned Farrakhan as an important national leader, but after the march, more than 12% articulated a belief that he was the most important black leader in the United States (Moore, 1995, p. 20).[20] One participant in the march wrote a letter to the editor of *The Washington Post* arguing that Minister Farrakhan and the Nation of Islam were promoters of "individual responsibility and family" (Garrison, 1995, p. C6). Another supporter complained that the media left unreported the lack of "violence, rancor and dissension" at the march (Hadley, 1995, p. C6). Although Farrakhan lost some support following his infamous 20-nation "world friendship tour" (Holmes, 1996a, p. A1), he was considered by many to be a political force to be reckoned with in the future.

The more orthodox analysis of the speech provides us with important insights, but we need to widen our gaze to include criticisms that come from postcolonial perspectives. Rather than judging Farrakhan by assuming the existence of some universal public address yardstick, we could evaluate and assess Farrakhan's own claims regarding the issues of representation, disciplinarity, and materiality. As Lalvani (1995) explained, adopting a postcolonial stance means focusing attention on the binaries, the contradictions, and the ambivalences involved in the discursive constructions of difference.

First, are Farrakhan's views representative of the vast majority of blacks or other people of color? Can the adoption of Masonic rhetorics and an understanding of numerology emancipate those who on a daily basis face racial injustice? Farrakhan's apparent move to include all people of color in this discussion might be initially applauded by many postcolonialists. In spite of his conservative creeds, one could argue that at least Farrakhan is a critic who insists that there are still massive power disparities around the globe. Farrakhan's focus on the need for pride and self-help reminds us of the fragility of the identities of those who are constantly placed on the margins in U.S. society. Hundreds of thousands of individuals, who may not have shared all of Farrakhan's visions, nevertheless acknowledged by their presence at the march the power of a discourse that provided some hope for the Other who had been silenced in the name of progress, modernity, and rationality. As Allen (1998) averred, Farrakhan "speaks out forcefully against the incidents of African American oppression" (p. 87). Even some of Farrakhan's harshest critics are willing to concede that here was a person who understood "that the days of the colonized black mentality are over" (Kelley, 1996, p. 16).

On the other hand, Cha-Jua and Lang (1997) contend that following the Million Man March, "Farrakan's messianic convictions" meant that he seemed to be viewing himself as "*the* African American national leader" (p. 65). Angered feminists around the country had earlier complained vociferously about the important absence of women of color (Alexander, 1998), and now the Minister's brand of "atonement" seemed to create even more divisions. On the international scene, Farrakhan's world tour, which was "designed to win him international recognition," turned into a debate about his reactionary politics, his controversial visits to "anti-imperialistic post-colonial governments," his denial of slavery in Sudan and Mauritania, and his friendship with leaders of countries that allowed multinational oil conglomerates to continue exploitation overseas (Cha-Jua & Lang, 1997, pp. 65-66). We have little tangible proof of the emancipatory power of either Farrakhan's disciplinarity or his representativeness.

Although Farrakhan consistently claimed to be widening the discussion about race and class, he often undermined his own credibility by dogmatically assuming a position of superiority that obviated any need for meaningful dialogue between individuals or communities. Throughout his address, Farrakhan talked of many different constituencies that were supposed to be aided by the Nation of Islam, but few groups have been included in any subsequent political or economic negotiations with empowered decision makers. Farrakhan's postcolonial stance may appear constructive, but a deeper reading of these fragments reveals that many times his narrative simply *inverted* binaries. That is, in place of white supremacy is a variant of Islamic or black supremacy. At the same time, Farrakhan obscures class differences within the nation by making it appear that anyone who participates in "atonement" can automatically spiritually or economically benefit from his leadership. Farrakhan's weak form of postcolonial critique thus ends up as a defense of classical liberal forms of utopian capitalism.[21] Some postcolonial critics might applaud the ways in which Farrakhan echoes the remarks of scholars like Hacker (1992), who reminded us that we are still a nation that is "separate" and "unequal." The spotlight placed on the economic disparities in the United States by this Minister of the Nation of Islam helps us appreciate the contradictions that still exist in a society filled with both poverty and plenty. The efforts of millions of liberal supporters of the civil rights movement have clearly helped to create a black middle class with some upward mobility, but many U.S. Americans still face a variety of forms of racism. Those who see the wretchedness and privation around them can identify with a leader who associates these conditions with the persistence of "white supremacy."

However, diagnosing global problems and providing pragmatic cures are two different things. Postcolonial critics might point out that there has been little change in the material conditions of African Americans or any other community since the time of the march.[22] Ahmad (1994) observed that postcolonial rhetoric can only be productive if it helps facilitate substantive change. In the years since the Farrakhan address, there have been few indications of any revolutionary change in the distribution of income for millions of impoverished Americans. Some commentators claim that the Minister's conservative brand of self-help provides little guidance to those who are still dependent on government support in the form of affirmative action, government loans, or welfare payments. Kelley (1996), for example, remarked that

> Louis Farrakhan's "legitimation" as a black political leader via the Million Man March unmistakably spotlights the central paradox of black politics: integration has been a material success but an ideological and spiritual failure; black nationalism, on the other hand, has been an ideological success but a material failure. Although the general impetus toward integration appears to be moribund (if not dead), one cannot argue that it has been unsuccessful. (p. 13)

In sum, Farrakhan's call for separatism and privatization could potentially weaken black economic development.

Ono and Sloop (1995) argue that critics must not automatically think that all populist calls for liberation and freedom are emancipatory and productive. Farrakhan's seductive tales obfuscate as much as they illuminate, and even this relatively mild variant of the Minister's rhetoric must be placed within the context of other presentations that are filled with anti-Semitism and racial invective.[23] At the same time that the "contributions of the Nation of Islam" should be acknowledged, some of Farrakhan's "epistemological assumptions" reflect "the worst tendencies of the dominant culture" (McPhail, 1998, p. 426). Scholars who are sensitive to the plight of the Other may appreciate a scathing indictment of the class inequalities and remnants of colonialism that still exist in the United States, but these will not be remedied by conservative self-help programs. For substantive changes to take place, vernacular rhetorics that come from more than a single rhetor (Morris, 1993) and that provide us with a wide range of options in facing racial and class conundrums are needed. This is the real promise that may come from the merger of rhetorical and postcolonial theorizing.

NOTES

1. In spite of the influence of Foucault's (1980) work, the dominant rationalistic paradigm depoliticizes most rhetorical critiques.

2. For an important critique of the politics involved with some of these figurations, see Nakayama and Krizek (1995).

3. Feminist theorists have encountered similar difficulties. As Biesecker (1992) explained, many studies in rhetoric still take the approach that we simply need to expand the list of "great" works that can be taken as a sign of inclusion (p. 143). Biesecker pointed out that this does not change the "criteria" that are used to determine what goes into the list.

4. Any discussions of colonialism within the field of communication are few and far between. For some exceptions, see Bass (1995), Condit (1993, pp. 179-80), Conquergood (1991), Kray (1993), Lee (1998), and Shome (1996, 1998). For related critique of Canadian discourse, see Charland (1987).

5. Good introductions to the vast literature on postcolonialism can be found in Lazarus (1993) and Williams and Chrisman (1994).

6. For an analysis of the difficulties of defining *postcolonialism,* see Shohat (1992) and Lee (1998, p. 27).

7. Some critics take this even further and argue that members of "academic subspecialties" can be considered to be "colonized" (Said, 1989, p. 207). This perhaps goes too far, given the disparities between the power of academicians and that of other denizens of the planet.

8. For more commentary on this issue, see Chakrabarty (1992) and Said (1994a). Cultural studies theorists have also extensively discussed this issue (Grossberg, Nelson, & Treichler, 1992).

9. One of the best examples of the ways in which colonial discourse can be appropriated can be found in Chakrabarty (1992).

10. For specific discussions of the ways in which "fragments" are used in the creation of hybrid identities, see Shohat (1992, p. 109).

11. For the response of one advocate of cultural studies to similar Marxist or neo-Marxist attacks, see Grossberg (1995).

12. On the relationship between critical rhetoric and the "American Empire," see Owen and Ehrenhaus (1993).

13. Our own discipline has been engaged in some forms of cultural amnesia (Rigsby, 1993).

14. For example, Marcus Garvey tried to counter some of the prejudices of the early 20th century by creating a Pan-African association that would bring together the oppressed communities living in the United States, the West Indies, Central America, and other parts of the world (Clark & Garvey, 1974).

15. The use of the names of [Mark] Furhman, [Jesse] Helms, and [Theodore] Bilbo seemed to be an allusion to the Biblical architect Hiram, who died at the hands of Juelo, Jubela, and Jubelum (Shulevitz, 1995, p. 95).

16. In some of the narratives presented by the Nation of Islam rhetors, "Yacub" is the name of a mad scientist who purportedly created the white race through an evil genetic experiment (Crouch, 1985, p. 21).

17. Shulevitz (1995) explains that the idea of "hidden knowledge" is deeply rooted in "African-American popular culture" (p. 24). She goes on to claim that numerology has many adherents "among some Bible-reading black Christians" (p. 14).

18. Earlier in the day, President Clinton (1995) had given an address on the issue of racism and its relationship to family problems. Zarefsky (1996) has recently defended Clinton's address as a call for unity among various communities. For more detailed explanations of the importance of the number 19 in the discourse of the Nation of Islam, see Muhammad (1996) and Pauley (1998).

19. For an insightful discussion of Farrakhan's use of conspiratorial appeals in such situations, see Goldzwig (1989).

20. This poll was taken before Farrakhan went on his world tour. Much of his credibility may have been lost when human rights advocates pointed out that Farrakhan seemed to be supporting repressive regimes (like Sudan) that condoned forms of slavery (Holmes, 1996b, p. A18).

21. In the words of one commentator, Allen (1995), "what seemed at first glance to be the mounting of a protest against the powers and structures that be" was turned inward to place the burden on African Americans to "get their own house in order" (p. 28).

22. Cloud (1994) recently reminded critical rhetoricians of the need to take into account both the discursive and material components of rhetoric. Her analysis of the Iraqi war illustrates the dangers of focusing exclusively on the ideological aspects of social change.

23. Analyses of Farrakhan's rhetoric in prior decades can be found in Crouch (1985) and in Brackman (1994).

REFERENCES

Ahmad, A. (1994). *In theory: Classes, nations, literatures*. London: Verso.

Alexander, A. (Ed.). (1998). *The Farrakhan factor*. New York: Grove.

Allen, E., Jr. (1995). Toward a "more perfect union": A commingling of constitutional ideas and Christian precepts. *The Black Scholar, 25*, 27-34.

Allen, E., Jr. (1998). Minister Louis Farrakhan and the continuing evolution of the Nation of Islam. In A. Alexander (Ed.), *The Farrakhan factor* (pp. 52-102). New York: Grove.

Anderson, B. (1986). *Imagined communities: Reflections on the origin and spread of nationalism.* London: Verso.

Bass, J. D. (1995). The perversion of empire: Edmund Burke and the nature of imperial responsibility. *Quarterly Journal of Speech, 31,* 208-227.

Berman, P. (1994, February). Reflections: The other and the almost the same. *The New Yorker, 70,* 61-71.

Bhabha, H. K. (Ed.). (1990). *Nation and narration.* New York: Routledge.

Biesecker, B. (1992). Coming to terms with recent attempts to write women into the history of rhetoric. *Philosophy and Rhetoric, 25,* 140-161.

Blair, C., Brown, J. R., & Baxter, L. A. (1994). Disciplining the feminine. *Quarterly Journal of Speech, 80,* 383-409.

Bowers, D. L. (1995). A place to stand: African-Americans and the first of August platform. *The Southern Communication Journal, 60,* 348-361.

Brackman, H. (1994). *Ministry of lies: The truth behind the nation of Islam's "The secret relationship between blacks and Jews."* New York: Four Walls Eight Windows.

Cha-Jua, S. K., & Lang, C. (1997). Providence, patriarchy, pathology: Louis Farrakhan's rise and decline. *New Politics, 6,* 47-71.

Chakrabarty, D. (1992). Postcoloniality and the artifice of history: Who speaks for "Indian" pasts? *Representations, 37,* 1-26.

Charland, M. (1987). Constitutive rhetoric: The case of the *Peuple Québécois. Quarterly Journal of Speech, 73,* 133-150.

Chen, K. -H. (1988). *History, theory, and cultural politics: Towards a minor discourse of mass-media and postmodernity.* Unpublished doctoral dissertation, University of Iowa, Iowa City.

Cherwitz, R. A., & Darwin, T. J. (1995). Why the "epistemic" in epistemic rhetoric? The paradox of rhetoric as performance. *Text and Performance Quarterly, 15,* 189-205.

Clark, J. H., & Garvey, A. J. (1974). *Marcus Garvey and the vision of Africa.* New York: Vintage.

Clinton, W. J. (1995, October 23). Remarks at the University of Texas Austin. *Weekly Compilation of Presidential Documents, 31,* 1847-1853.

Cloud, D. (1994). The materiality of discourse as oxymoron: A challenge to critical rhetoric. *Western Journal of Communication, 58,* 141-163.

Condit, C. M. (1993). The critic as empath: Moving away from totalizing theory. *Western Journal of Communication, 57,* 178-190.

Condit, C. M., & Lucaites, J. L. (1993). *Crafting equality: America's Anglo-African word.* Chicago: University of Chicago Press.

Conquergood, D. (1991). Rethinking ethnography: Towards a critical cultural politics. *Communication Monographs, 158,* 179-194.

Cooper, B. (1997). "It's going to be a rough ride, buddy!": An analysis of the collision between "hate speech" and free expression in the Khallid Abdul Muhammad controversy. *Howard Journal of Communications, 8,* 15-39.

Crenshaw, C. (1997). Resisting whiteness' rhetorical silence. *Western Journal of Communication, 61,* 253-278.

Crenshaw, C. (1998). Colorblind rhetoric. *Southern Communication Journal, 63,* 244-256.

Crouch, S. (1985, October 29). Nationalism of fools: Farrakhan brings it all home. *The Village Voice,* pp. 21-24, 102.

Delgado, F. P. (1993/1994). Richard Rodriguez and the cultural wars: The politics of (mis)representation. *Howard Journal of Communication, 5,* 1-17.

Dirlik, A. (1994). The postcolonial aura: Third world criticism in the age of capitalism. *Critical Inquiry, 20,* 328-356.

Fanon, F. (1966). *The wretched of the earth* (C. Farrington, Trans.). New York: Grove.

Fanon, F. (1967). *Black skin, white masks.* New York: Grove.

Farrakhan, L. (1995, October 16). *Transcript from Minister Louis Farrakhan's remarks at the Million Man March* [On-line]. Available at http://www.cldc.howard.edu/bah/text/ Farrakhan_Speech.html

Fisher, W. R. (1984). Narration as a human communication paradigm: The case of public moral argument. *Communication Monographs, 51,* 1-22.

Flores, L. A. (1996). Creating discursive space through a rhetoric of difference: Chicana feminists craft a homeland. *Quarterly Journal of Speech, 82,* 142-156.

Foucault, M. (1980). *Power/knowledge: Selected interviews and other writings by Michel Foucault* (C. Gordon, Trans.). New York: Pantheon.

Gardell, M. (1996). *In the name of Elijah Muhammad: Louis Farrakhan and the Nation of Islam.* Durham, NC: Duke University Press.

Garrison, D. T. (1995, October 22). The million man march [Letter to the editor]. *The Washington Post,* p. C6.

Gilroy, P. (1992). Cultural studies and ethnic absolutism. In L. Grossberg, C. Nelson, & P. Treichler (Eds.), *Cultural studies* (pp. 187-198). New York: Routledge.

Goldzwig, S. R. (1989). A social movement perspective on demagoguery: Achieving symbolic alignment. *Communication Studies, 40,* 202-228.

Grossberg, L. (1993). Can cultural studies find true happiness in communication? *Journal of Communication, 43,* 89-97.

Grossberg, L. (1995). Cultural studies vs. political economy: Is anybody else bored with this debate? *Critical Studies in Mass Communication, 12,* 72-81.

Grossberg, L., Nelson, C., & Treichler, P. (Eds.). (1992). *Cultural studies.* New York: Routledge.

Hacker, A. (1992). *Two nations: Black and white, separate, hostile, unequal.* New York: Scribner.

Hadley, B. A. (1995, October 22). Letters to the editor: The million man march. *Washington Post,* p. C6.

Holmes, S. A. (1996a, February 22). Farrakhan's angry world tour brings harsh criticism at home. *The New York Times,* p. A1.

Holmes, S. A. (1996b, March 24). Slavery is an issue again as U.S. looks to Sudan. *The New York Times,* p. A18.

Ivie, R. (1995). The social relevance of rhetorical scholarship. *Quarterly Journal of Speech, 81,* i.

JanMohamed, A. R. (1985). The economy of Manichean allegory: The function of racial difference in colonialist literature. *Critical Inquiry, 12,* 59-87.

Kelley, N. (1996). The specter of nationalism. *New Politics, 6,* 13-18.

Kerner, O. (1968). *Report of the national advisory committee on civil disorders.* Washington, DC: U.S. Government Printing Office.

Kray, S. (1993). Orientalization of an "almost white" woman: The interlocking effects of race, class, gender, and ethnicity in American mass media. *Critical Studies in Mass Communication, 10,* 349-366.

Lalvani, S. (1995). Consuming the exotic other. *Critical Studies in Mass Communication, 12,* 263-286.

Lazarus, N. (1993). Postcolonialism and the dilemma of nationalism: Alijaz Ahmad's critique of third worldism. *Diaspora, 2*, 373-400.

Lee, W. S. (1998). Patriotic breeders or colonized converts: A postcolonial feminist approach to antifootbinding discourse in China. In D. V. Tanno & A. González (Eds.), *Communication and identity across cultures* (International and Intercultural Communication Annual, Vol. 21, pp. 11-33). Thousand Oaks, CA: Sage.

Levinsohn, F. H. (1997). *Looking for Farrakhan.* Chicago: Ivan R. Dee.

Lucy, X., & Frank, D. A. (1993). On the study of ancient Chinese rhetoric/Bain. *Western Journal of Communication, 57*, 445-463.

Magida, A. J. (1996). *Prophet of rage.* New York: Basic Books.

Marshall, A. (1996). *Louis Farrakhan: Made in America.* Rockford, IL: BSB Publishing.

Marvin, C. (1994). The body of the text: Literacy's corporeal. *Quarterly Journal of Speech, 80*, 129-149.

McGee, M. C. (1975). In search of "The People": A rhetorical alternative. *Quarterly Journal of Speech, 61*, 235-249.

McGee, M. C. (1990). Text, context, and the fragmentation of contemporary culture. *Western Journal of Speech Communication, 54*, 274-289.

McKerrow, R. (1989). Critical rhetoric: Theory and praxis. *Communication Monographs, 56*, 91-111.

McPhail, M. L. (1998). Passionate intensity: Louis Farrakhan and the fallacies of racial reasoning. *Quarterly Journal of Speech, 84*, 416-430.

Moore, D. W. (1995, November). Farrakhan gains support as national leader among black Americans. *Gallup Poll Monthly, 362*, 20-23.

Morris, R. (1993). Modernity's Prometheus. *Western Journal of Communication, 57*, 139-146.

Muhammad, T. (1996, April 3). Unveiling the number 19. *The Final Call,* p. 27.

Murphy, J. M. (1992). Domesticating dissent: The Kennedys and the freedom rides. *Communication Monographs, 59*, 61-78.

Nakayama, T. K., & Krizek, R. L. (1995). Whiteness: A strategic rhetoric. *Quarterly Journal of Speech, 81*, 291-309.

Ono, K. A., & Sloop, J. M. (1995). The critique of vernacular discourse. *Communication Monographs, 62*, 20-46.

Owen, A. S., & Ehrenhaus, P. (1993). Animating a critical rhetoric: On the feeding habits of American empire. *Western Journal of Communication, 57*, 169-177.

Patterson, O. (1995, October 30). Going separate ways: The history of an old idea. *Newsweek, 126*, 43.

Pauley, J. L. (1998). Reshaping public persona and the prophetic ethos: Louis Farrakhan at the Million Man March. *Western Journal of Communication, 62*, 512-536.

Prakash, G. (1992). Postcolonial criticism and Indian historiography. *Social Text, 31/32*, 8-19.

Prakash, G. (1994). Subaltern studies as postcolonial criticism. *American Historical Review, 99*, 1475-1490.

Rafael, V. L. (1990). Nationalism, imagery, and the Filipino intelligentsia in the nineteenth century. *Critical Inquiry, 16*, 591-611.

Rich, F. (1995, October 18). Fixation on Farrakhan. *The New York Times,* p. A23.

Rigsby, E. D. (1993). African American rhetoric and the "profession." *Western Journal of Communication, 57*, 191-199.

Roberson, P., Jr. (1996). The Million man march: Wrong message, wrong messenger. *New Politics, 6,* 19-21.

Said, E. (1978). *Orientalism.* New York: Vintage.

Said, E. (1982). Opponents, audiences, constituencies, and community. *Critical Inquiry, 9,* 1-26.

Said, E. (1989). Representing the colonized: Anthropology's interlocutors. *Critical Inquiry, 15,* 205-225.

Said, E. (1994a). *Culture and imperialism.* New York: Vintage.

Said, E. W. (1994b, January). Second thoughts on Arafat's deal. *Harper's Magazine, 288,* 15-18.

Shohat, E. (1992). Notes on the "post-colonial." *Social Text, 31/32,* 100-113.

Shome, R. (1996). Postcolonial interventions in the rhetorical canon: An "other" view. *Communication Theory, 6,* 40-59.

Shome, R. (1998). Caught in the term "post-colonial"—why the "post-colonial" still matters. *Critical Studies in Mass Communication, 15,* 203-212.

Shulevitz, J. (1995, November 6). Farrakhan's secrets. *New York, 28,* 24, 95.

Singh, R. (1997). *The Farrakhan phenomenon: Race, reaction, and the paranoid style in American politics.* Washington, DC: Georgetown University Press.

Sloop, J. M., & Ono, K. A. (1997). Out-law discourse: The critical politics of material judgment. *Philosophy and Rhetoric, 30,* 50-69.

Spivak, G. C. (1994). Responsibility. *Boundary 2, 21,* 19-64.

Strine, M. S. (1991). Critical theory and the "organic" intellectuals: Reframing the work of cultural critique. *Communication Monographs, 58,* 195-201.

Suleri, S. (1992). *The rhetoric of English India.* Chicago: University of Chicago Press.

Supriya, K. E. (1996). Confessionals, testimonials: Women's speech in/and contexts of violence. *Hypatia, 11,* 92-106.

Trinh, T. M. (1989). *Woman native other.* Bloomington: Indiana University Press.

Wander, P. (1983). The ideological turn in modern criticism. *Central States Speech Journal, 34,* 1-18.

Wander, P. (1996). Marxism, post-colonialism, and rhetorical contextualization. *Quarterly Journal of Speech, 82,* 402-435.

Ware, B. L., & Linkugel, W. A. (1982). The rhetorical *persona*: Marcus Garvey as black Moses. *Communication Monographs, 49,* 50-62.

Whitson, S., & Poulakos, J. (1993). Nietzsche and the aesthetics of rhetoric. *Quarterly Journal of Speech, 79,* 131-145.

Wilgoren, D. (1995, October 22). Farrakhan's speech: Masons, mysticism, more. *The Washington Post,* pp. A1, A18.

Williams, P., & Chrisman, L. (Eds.). (1994). *Colonial discourse and post-colonial theory: A reader.* New York: Columbia University Press.

Zarefsky, D. (1996). *The roots of American community.* Needham Heights, MA: Allyn & Bacon.

5

Negotiating Societal Stereotypes

Analyzing The Real World *Discourse by and About African American Men*

MARK P. ORBE • *Western Michigan University*
KIESHA T. WARREN • *Western Michigan University*
NANCY C. CORNWELL • *Western Michigan University*

> And just as nature was beginning to play cruel tricks with our bodies—the voice change, the hair growth in unusual places, the hormones reacting in mysterious ways—so, too, did the world begin to change all around us. Suddenly, we were no longer "cute little boys." The faces, especially the white ones that had once smiled at us as our mothers led us around Jersey City now looked away in fear. White people would react nervously when I got on elevators with them or when I stood next to them at bus stops . . . white boys would hold their girlfriends whenever I walked by them at school.
>
> —Powell, 1997, pp. 37-38

> It was [in college] that he learned the power of racial stereotypes. Tall and dark complexioned, Staples noticed he inspired a fear in whites when he approached them on the side walk. At first he sought to reassure them by whistling Vivaldi. Then he found malicious glee in frightening them in a game he called "scatter the pigeons."
>
> —White, 1994, p. 68

African American men have long recognized and written about the power of societal stereotypes on their everyday life experiences (e.g., Brown, 1965; Ellison, 1947; Wright, 1966). Although many European Americans might question the prevalence of these stereotypes in everyday discourse, recent literary works (e.g., Boyd & Allen, 1995; McCall, 1994; Staples, 1994) illustrate the saliency of a general societal stereotype of Black men in the United States today. Gibbs (1992) describes the

107

existing stereotype, especially for young African American men, as defining Black men as "deviant, dangerous, and dysfunctional" (p. 268). The focus of this chapter is on examining—and subsequently connecting—the discourse involving predominantly Black male stereotypes through two different scholarly lenses. First, a macroanalytic framework is used to critically examine how images of Black communicative behaviors across one mediated text, MTV's *The Real World,* constitute a source of public discourse that strengthens a societal fear of Black men. Second, we use a series of recent research projects on African American male communication to explore the ways in which societal stereotypes are negotiated within the context of everyday life experiences. In addition to contributing to the growing amount of work that critically examines stereotypical media images of African Americans in general (Bogle, 1994; Cooks & Orbe, 1993; hooks, 1992; MacDonald, 1983) and of African American men specifically (Berry, 1992; Elise & Umoja, 1992; Evoleocha & Ugbah, 1989; Smith, 1993), this line of inquiry works to incorporate both macro- and microlevel analyses in an attempt to provide a more broad perspective on public-private discourse by and about Black men.

Specifically, the focus of this chapter will be on *The Real World's* signification of Black men as "dangerous." Following a brief description of our analytical framework, we offer a critique of the overrepresentation of African American male characters in a MTV special entitled "Most Dangerous Real World Episodes." The final sections of the chapter draw from ongoing research on African American male communication to explore how the "dangerous" stigma is acknowledged and negotiated in the everyday interactions of Black men.

ETHNOSEMIOTIC ANALYSIS

Traditionally, semiotics has focused on the ways in which meaning is created and realized (Barthes, 1972). Meaning, according to Eco (1976), is created and maintained through an associative process of signification, whereby a signifier (a name, image, or discourse) is used to signify (stand for) a concept or idea (a stereotype or status). A semiotic analysis typically works to interpret how this signification process inherently communicates the themes and values of a society (Saussure, 1966) and ultimately affirms the ideological system of the status quo as natural and inevitable (Barthes, 1972). Existing research has established semiotics as a productive lens through which to explore mediated texts (Fry & Fry, 1984; Orbe & Strother, 1996; Robinson & Straw, 1984) as well as public-private discourse (Fiske, 1994; Hawkes, 1977). A distinctive feature of semiotic inquiry is its utility in revealing how meaning is socially produced and situated in power relations and struggles (O'Sullivan, Hartley, Saunders, Montgomery, & Fiske, 1994). Within this tradition, semiotics—as a theoretical approach and its associated methods of analysis—is an appropriate method for our work on discourse by and about African American men.

More specifically, the research presented here can best be described as an ethnosemiotic analysis. Fiske (1994) uses this conceptual advance to emphasize the centrality of personal/cultural/professional standpoints that researchers bring to their analyses. We believe, as does Fiske (1994), that the interpretations generated through a semiotic lens are most meaningful when researchers situate themselves as subjective participants in their analyses. In this regard, it is important for readers to understand that our analysis is informed by several critical elements. First, none of us is an African American man. The first two authors are members—by birth, marriage, or other associations—of various African American communities (residential, familial, social, religious, and professional). Therefore, our interpretations of the signification of Black men in public-private discourse are situated in past and present relationships with a diverse set of African American men (as family members, friends, significant others, and "brothers"—in terms of fraternal and religious relations).

The third author's life experiences have not included close ties to Black communities; however, her professional and political orientation is rooted in civil rights and feminist organizations. Each of our interpretive lenses is simultaneously similar and different. Despite various cultural differences (e.g., only one of us is African American, only one of us is male, and each of us comes from markedly different socioeconomic backgrounds), our similarities are grounded in a genuine desire to reveal the complex ways in which underrepresented groups' members are positioned in various social dimensions. In this regard, we view the diversity of our subjective positionalities as an inherent strength within the ethnosemiotic analytical framework used here to explore discourse by and about African American men.

Second, all three authors self-identify as "heavy users" of television, averaging between 4 and 8 hours of "time" daily. Although our viewing habits in terms of programming preferences are similar in some regards (i.e., two authors faithfully watch Black-oriented shows like UPN's *Moesha*), distinct differences do exist (i.e., one author regularly views prime-time sitcoms, dramas, and science fiction fare). In terms of our analysis of African American male representation on MTV's *Real World,* it is important to recognize that our interpretations are informed by countless interactions with other *Real World* fans prior to, as well as during, the research process. Most of our discussions about the Black male cast members on the show have involved African American women and men; however, a significant (albeit smaller) number of exchanges have involved non-African Americans. In short, an ethnosemiotic analytic framework appears appropriate here, especially because our analysis is directly informed by the complexity of our lived experiences.

BLACK MEN ON/IN *THE REAL WORLD*

In early 1992, the viewing public was introduced to MTV's newest form of innovative television programming: a series that promised to bring the real life experiences of a diverse group of young people (18 to 25 years old) into the homes of millions. *The Real World* is succinctly described by the creator-producer as a show about "real people, undirected, sharing their lives" (Huriash, 1996, p. C25). The premise of the show is simple: MTV chooses seven individuals, representing diverse backgrounds, to reside rent-free in a house for 3 months while every aspect of their lives is taped by a multitude of cameras. The result is a Generation X fishbowl of sorts, one that is viewed by 60 million people in 52 countries every week and that has become a cult hit for MTV (Sakurari, 1996).

For many viewers (and scholars), one of the most intriguing aspects of the show is the cultural diversity of each cast. In this regard, MTV's *The Real World* provides a glimpse into social relations based on race-ethnicity, gender, sexuality, class, and religion. For the purposes of the researchers interested in how cultural difference is negotiated through discourse, the show represents an interesting point of reflection in that it creates a publicly mediated text of the private discourse of a culturally diverse group of people. Like Ang (1985) and Fiske (1994), we situate ourselves as fans as well as critical researchers of the show. Because MTV has aired each season in its entirety, as well as in special formats (e.g., *Real World* marathons), we have had ample opportunity to view each episode individually (within the sequential context of that particular season), collectively (within and across specific seasons), and reflectively (viewing earlier episodes with knowledge of subsequent episodes and seasons). What makes the discourse by and about African American men on *The Real World* especially attractive to viewers—as well as researchers—is that it is not regulated by a predetermined script, as most televisual texts are. Instead, the show presumably represents "real people in real life situations."

The Dangerous Nature of Black Masculinity[1]

Over the course of the first six seasons, MTV viewers have been introduced to 45 different cast members, representing a cross section of the cultural diversity in the United States. Among these individuals were 4 African American men: (a) Kevin, a 25-year-old writer and part-time teacher from New Jersey, who appeared on the first season in New York City; (b) David, a 21-year-old stand-up comic from Washington, D.C., who was part of the second season, which was filmed in Los Angeles; (c) Mohammed, a cast member from the third season (San Francisco) who is a 24-year-old musician and singer; and (d) Syrus, a 25-year-old self-defined "playa" from Sacramento who appeared in the sixth season, which was located in Boston. Although this analysis of African American male representation on the show will draw from each of the episodes within each respective season, the focus will be on the discourse and images featured in the "Most Dangerous Real World Episodes" special, which aired on March 7, 1998. Of particular interest to the analysis provided here is that, although African American men constituted less than 9% of all cast members, they were featured in over 50% of the "most dangerous" segments presented in the 7-hour marathon special. The highlights of these shows reproduced a series of intense conflicts centered on three Black men: Kevin, David, and Syrus.[2] The collective re/framing of these most dangerous episodes created a packaged set of discourse texts involving African American men. The intensity of negative Black male images (signified as accused rapist, violent aggressor, etc.) within this special program crystallized for us a desire to make sense of how and why African American men were so prominently featured through such fear-evoking codes. In essence, the episodes provide insight into the ongoing process by which interactions involving African American men are inextricably linked to predominant societal stereotypes that regard

Black men as inherently angry, physically threatening, and sexually aggressive.[3]

Black Male as Inherently Angry. Throughout the course of the New York, Los Angeles, and Boston seasons, viewers are provided with a brief window into the worlds of Kevin, David, and Syrus. We learn that each has come from a tough inner-city life (Jersey City; Washington, DC; and Los Angeles; respectively) and are well versed in the harsh life lessons of racism. Although each of these young men has a different communication style, the discourse that each displays during the episodes signifies different manifestations of an angry Black male persona. Kevin confronts housemates with his "radical politics" and shares his "black revolutionary" poetry on stage. David surrounds himself in the images, lyrics, and symbols of "gangsta rap." The discourse of these Black men, as well as the descriptive/reflective/interactive discourse about them from their housemates, are made more powerful through the association of images from their life-worlds. In this regard, the discourse is situated within camera angles and footage that include posters of Malcolm X and gangsta rap artists and shots of inner-city life, as well as various Black and African artifacts. These signs are repeated and subsequently extended, in that viewers are shown these signs in relation to all African American male cast members. All wear clothing (i.e., baggy pants, gold chains, or earrings) associated with inner-city young Black men. Kevin's natural look, Syrus's shaved head, and Mohammed's dreadlocks present three versions of a similar antiestablishment code; the music associated with each person (frequently gangsta rap) also reflects this typification of Black male power and resistance.[4]

Through exposure to the African American men on MTV's *The Real World,* viewers are given some insight into the source that fuels Black male anger. Most often, this insight comes from instances when the African American male cast members strive to educate the others on "what it's like to be a Black man in America." In each season, we see attempts of the lone Black man in the house to enlighten his roommates (and consequently the television viewers) as to the various problems that Black men face on a daily basis. In this regard, other members of the house learn—some, for the first time—the impact that societal stereotypes have on the life experiences of Black men (i.e., being harassed by police in areas where they do not "belong"). We see these attempts to educate in different instances, taking a variety of forms. Kevin uses his poetry, confrontation of others, and other less volatile means, such as posting provocative thoughts on a bulletin board. David uses rap lyrics and his comic talents to drive home some issues. Finally, Syrus uses a number of "teachable moments" to enlighten his housemates. Although these interactions serve as a means to educate non-African Americans as to the experiences of African American men living in an inherently racist country, they also seem to contribute to the credibility of the angry Black male stereotype. These men's discourse, intended as a means to enlighten others, was negotiated by the cast members as additional evidence for existing stereotypical images of African American men. From a critical view/researcher's perspective, this appeared to be the case especially with non-African Americans as seen in their interactions with their Black male housemates. For instance, in one particularly intense conflict involving Kevin and Julie (an 18-year-old European American woman), she accuses him of "having a lot of misdirected anger." In another interaction, a twenty-something European American male housemate attests that "all [he] know[s] of Kevin is a pattern of aggressive behavior." David experiences similar responses from the Los Angeles cast. Irene, a 24-year-old woman of Latino descent who happens to be a Los Angeles deputy sheriff, articulates her fear of David by explaining that "he has something up inside of him that's building, and building, and building." The "something" that Irene and others seem to sense is the Black man's internal reaction to a history of racism in the United States.

Although a number of mechanisms of dealing with this inherent anger are given fleeting attention (i.e., Kevin's poetry and radical politics), what is foregrounded for the viewers are the violent ways that African American men express their "pent-up rage." Most often, cast members fear that the anger of Black men will be "misdirected" at "innocent" bystanders. This point is made apparent in a conversation between New York cast members Kevin and Andre (a twenty-something European male).

Andre: It seems like you're taking this out on us.

Kevin: It all came out yesterday. This country is racist as hell. That's the reality. Way that I was accused of spitting in someone's face, and picking up something that I don't even know what it is and threatening to hit somebody.

Andre: I don't think that had anything to do with you being Black, though.

Kevin: Andre . . .

Andre: No, seriously, do you think that that is cause for all of this?

Kevin: Listen, Andre. From my perspective, whenever a Black person, including myself, has an opinion, and is assertive about it, we become threatening to White people.

Andre: There is racism, but you can't go about it . . . by posting signs. You're telling the wrong people, man . . . who here is racist?

Clearly, Kevin's attempt to explain how most European Americans unconsciously tap into the racist stereotypes that pervade their thinking is met with visible resistance. As Andre says, racism is not constructed as a problem for most, only for those most overtly associated with the discourse of extremists (i.e., the Ku Klux Klan or Aryan Nation). This point is crystallized in one interaction between Kevin and Julie, an 18-year-old European American woman from Alabama who is experiencing big-city life for the first time. In one poignantly revealing exchange, she responds to his claim that "racism is everywhere" by shouting, "BECAUSE OF PEOPLE LIKE YOU, KEVIN, NOT PEOPLE LIKE ME!" Racism, therefore, is not only a problem most salient for African Americans; according to some, it is also a problem perpetuated by African Americans.

Black Males as Violent Threat. As seen thus far, discourse signifying a justified societal fear of Black men is clearly maintained in *The Real World.* The audience sees that Black men possess an inherent anger triggered by a past, present, and future of racism. Interposed with powerful images that signify this intrinsic tension is the discourse of other cast members that reveals their fear of potential violence stemming from Black men with so much internal rage. In fact, several non-African American cast members confidentially confess[5] their discomfort around Black men who, in their eyes, clearly have great "potential" for violence. Interestingly, comments taken from three of the four casts that featured an African American male group member are strikingly similar in the ways that this fear is expressed. In each case these perceptions are offered by non-African American women following a house conflict:

I really like Kevin . . . and could never deny that. I respect him a lot, and think that he is really intelligent and has a lot of important things. . . . That doesn't mean that I ever want to be alone with Kevin . . . in my life. I will never be comfortable, and don't really understand how I can be expected to be. (Julie, 18-year-old European American woman)

During the two days before we had our talk with David, what went through my mind was . . . how I was feeling. I had this unsafe feeling. . . . I had this threatening feeling. . . . (Irene, 24-year-old Latina)

I thought that [Syrus] came across a little strong last. . . . I got the idea that [he] was about to hit me. . . . He can apologize until the cows come home, and I can say, "fine, I accept your apology" . . . but I'm not going to forget what happened. In the back of my mind, that will always be there. (Montana, a 25-year-old European American woman)

These women's articulation of a general fear of Black men is particularly compelling because—with the exception of one incident involving David and another male housemate in Los Angeles—viewers never see any violent outbursts from the Black male cast members. This is especially telling given Montana's comments regarding Syrus, whose personality is extremely easy-going, nonconfrontational, and nonviolent. What appears to be happening, at least as it is deconstructed through this ethnosemiotic analysis, is that specific cast members unconsciously tap into long-established stereotypes of African American men in framing current perceptions of Kevin, David, and Syrus. Then, based on these underlying stereotypes, cast members—most often European American women—work to persuade others to adopt their interpretation of certain behaviors enacted by African American men. Regardless of the different personal characteristics of Kevin, David, and Syrus, a similar sign is invoked: Black men represent a threat.

Even when the possibility for violence is slim, cast members articulate that the perceived potential for violence remains a salient issue for them in their interactions with Black men. In two different instances, for example, Julie and Kevin (New York City cast) are involved in a conflict when Julie makes her fear of Kevin apparent by asking him if he was going to physically harm her. In one scene, Julie asks Kevin, "Why are you getting so close? Why are you getting so emotional? What are you going to do, hit me?" Kevin attempts to explain that proximity and emotional expressiveness are culture-specific; Julie's response is to emphatically assert her perception that "It's not a black-white thing." Kevin then gives expression to the larger question in the minds of those who recognize the subtle influence that stereotypes have on this interaction when he confronts Julie's perception by asking, "Do you assume that because I'm a Black man that I'm going to hit you?"

Black Male as Sexually Aggressive. The third interlocking signifier/ stereotype, one that solidifies a clear justification for societal concern and fear, involves the sexual aggressiveness associated with Black men. Whereas this signifier works more on an inferential level with Kevin and his New York City housemates (e.g., Kevin's disclosures about his sexual fantasies in response to a lighthearted discussion on issues prompted by a "book of questions"), it is foregrounded in the discourse surrounding Syrus and David.

From the outset, Syrus's persona is most clearly represented by his love for women; in fact, his life revolves around "his theory that women are like potato chips . . . [you can't have just one]." Within the first three Boston episodes, viewers witness a barrage of clips with Syrus "macking"—hugging, holding, flirting, and dancing with—several different European American women. In fact, his behaviors become a house issue when he continues to bring different women home into the wee hours of the morning. Syrus responds to others' complaints by invoking his (sexual) "freedom to do whatever he wants." "I feel like I'm in a damn prison," he contends.

Questions regarding Syrus's sexual freedom to pursue a variety of women are juxtaposed with a more problematic context during the third episode, when cast members (and viewers) learn that Syrus was accused of rape while in college. Syrus adamantly denies the charge; he describes the woman as being the aggressor ("she took my clothes off") on the night in question. Whereas he appears to convince some of his housemates that, in fact, some women do "cry rape," others remain unmoved by his emotional arguments. Regardless of Syrus's guilt or innocence, the producers of the show choose to highlight discourse that signifies him as sexually aggressive. Syrus becomes a Black man who potentially may use rape to satisfy his sexual needs.

Whereas Syrus's sexual appetite is foregrounded in the creation of his *Real World* persona, David's sexuality is signified in a subtler yet equally powerful manner. First and foremost, David is a comedian, always joking and "playing the fool" for the camera. Through his comedy, however, signs of his sexual aggression are alluded to as he jokingly discusses his love of masturbation and as he finds amusement in pulling his pants down in front of the cameras. His playful joking with housemates becomes increasingly problematic during one episode, when a prank between him and Tami, a 24-year-old African American woman, escalates into a heated conflict. In the most replayed Los Angeles episode, David playfully attempts to pull the blanket off of Tami, who is in her bed for the night wearing only her underwear and bra. For a couple of minutes, there is a lighthearted struggle; the mood changes drastically when David continues to try to pull the blanket off of Tami as she gets up to take a phone call. The latter part of the interaction is filled with screams of "Stop! Don't! David, stop!" from both Tami and Beth (a twenty-something European American woman). A line has clearly been crossed when Tami escapes to the bathroom, throws on a robe, and immediately begins to retaliate against David. The following exchange is excerpted from the ensuing conversation:

David: You guys were laughing, giggling, playing—

Tami: You can take off your pants in front of the camera, but I am not like that. It was NOT funny, okay?

David: Here, hey, here you go. . . . I'll take off my clothes [drop his pants to his ankles, exposing himself]

Irene: [calls from the bedroom, where she is still in bed] I'll call the police and scream rape!

Beth: We should file charges against him.

During this exchange, John (a young European American man from a small town in Kentucky) theorizes, "It's all about rap music, and the violence and tension that builds up . . . and this is what happens."

Two salient issues are signified during this exchange. First, John associates David's aggression with the violence portrayed in rap music. In essence, his comments enact a sense-making mechanism for understanding the violent nature of Black masculinity. Second, and even more central to the fear of Black men, is Irene's threat to accuse David of rape. Interestingly, Irene's discourse, contextualized within her identity as a deputy sheriff for the Los Angeles police department, invokes another powerful code from an African American male perspective. Accusations of rape, however, become more intense as Beth confronts David directly:

David: You're going to press charges for me pulling a cover off of her??? For playing??? You guys were on the floor screaming [mocking their playful tone] "Stop . . . stop."

Beth: Yeah, and that is what a rapist says too—

David: Rape??? This hasn't anything to do with rape!

Beth: [Imitating a rapist] Yeah, you wanted it baby.

David: I didn't try to rape—this hasn't nothing to do with rape!

Beth: No means no, okay?

David: Wait a minute . . . who? . . . when? You're taking this too far; I wasn't going to rape the girl. . . . I was playing. . . . I was just pulling the blanket.

The power of a European American woman's conjuring up metaphors of the Black male rapist is not lost on David, who obviously recognizes the power of such accusations. "In the old days," he tells the group, "I would be hung. Because a woman said rape . . . not rationally hung, just hung."

When David confronts Beth about her use of the term, she readily "takes it back." However, the signification of David as a sexually aggressive potential rapist cannot be easily erased from the minds of the female housemates. As was accomplished with Syrus, signifiers maintained through the discourse of others have successfully invoked the image of Black man as rapist. Consequently, this stereotype appears to remain in the consciousness of others as they contextualize David's other behaviors (i.e., joking about masturbation and pulling his pants down). Without a doubt, David—regardless of his small physical stature and joking persona—is a person to be feared. This characterization is reinforced further when, based on the women's fears, he is asked to leave the house and subsequently is replaced on the show.

THE SALIENCY OF MEDIATED
IMAGES IN EVERYDAY DISCOURSE

According to the creators and producers of the show, the characterizations of African American men (as well as others) on MTV's *Real World* are based on real-life discourse. One point central to this analysis, however, is the manipulation of discourse that occurs through the process by which real-life experiences are transformed into a mediated text (Campbell, 1995). In terms of docudramas like *The Real World,* questions regarding the accuracy and authenticity of the show are often raised (Orbe, 1998). How real can the show be when a multitude of cameras and microphones surround each interaction? Don't the creators-producers choose individuals who reflect "characters" who promise to provide the most drama? Is what we see "reality," or is it the producers' vision—manipulated through cast selection and editing—of what will attract viewers?

Scholars connect the existence of stereotypical images in the media with our everyday interactions (Essed, 1991; van Dijk, 1987). According to Kellner (1995), media images, such as those perpetuated on *The Real*

World, are a central beginning in how "many people construct their sense of... 'us' and 'them'" (p. 1); such images therefore become an important source of exploration for those interested in the impact that mediated images have on the substance of our everyday lives (Brooks & Jacob, 1996). According to Omi (1989),

> Popular culture has been an important realm within which racial ideologies have been created, reproduced, and sustained. Such ideologies provide a framework of symbols, concepts, and images through which we understand, interpret, and represent aspects of our "racial" existence. (p. 114)

Because of the power of mediated images, characterizations of African Americans are never neutral; instead, each portrayal either "advances or retards the struggle for self-determination and empowerment" (Elise & Umoja, 1992, p. 83). MTV's *Real World* inherently has great potential to provide representations of Black men that, instead of stereotyping such a large, heterogeneous group, reflect the rich diversity of their life experiences. However, instead of reaching this potential, the first six seasons of the show, overall, work simply to reinforce existing societal stereotypes that regard Black men as dangerous creatures who deservedly invoke fear in others.

In addition, what makes this mediated text even more problematic is the claim that the show reflects "real-life experiences of real people." In essence, the show captures the interactional nature of discourse informed by stereotypes; everyday discourse of real people (which is consciously or unconsciously affected by media images) is used to create a media text that works to reinforce existing personal stereotypes that the media helped to cultivate in the first place. The issue here is not to debate which came first, personal stereotypes or media stereotypes; instead, the focus is to present an analysis of discourse that seeks to illustrate the powerful connection of mediated stereotypes of African American men to their everyday interactions.

Societal Stereotypes and Everyday Interactions

To further explore the impact of such stereotypes on African American men, two specific questions guide the subsequent analysis: (a) What level of consciousness do African American men have in terms of the effects that stereotypes have on their everyday interactions? and (b) How do African American men negotiate the existence of such stereotypes in their interactions with others? A series of recent research projects on African American male communication provides a rich source of data to explore these questions. Over a 3-year period (1992-1995), 41 African American men residing in two different Midwestern states participated in a program of research that inductively gathered insight into how they perceived their communication with non-African Americans. Most respondents were between the ages of 23 and 33 years, and a few were in their late teens or early 50s. Beyond diversity in chronological age, the participants involved in this ongoing research represented a diverse set of circumstances, personal histories, and lived experiences. In this regard, the participants included high school and college students, blue-collar workers, community activists, radio personalities, university faculty and administrators, corporate professionals, and community clergymen. This research, conducted by the first author, used different methodological tools (critical incidents, in-depth interviews, and focus group discussions)[6] to explore how African American men give voice to the cultural mores that inform their communicative experience (Orbe, 1994b, 1996a). These initial analyses were based on phenomenological methodology to reveal the general communication patterns of African American men. The existence of societal stereotypes and the ways in which they affect the everyday life experiences of African American men were not focal aspects of these studies, but these issues emerged in responses.

As a means to reveal insight into the process by which societal stereotypes inform everyday discourse, the following analysis was conducted. Thirteen critical incident responses, eight in-depth interviews, and five group discussions that included references to societal stereotypes were transcribed. The initial analysis, conducted independently by each researcher, revealed a number of signifiers directly or indirectly related to how African American men perceived the impact of stereotypes on their everyday interactions. A collaborative reexamination of these issues, coupled with another review of transcripts, generated the emergence of three central themes that appeared to capture the essence of the participants' experiences.[7] Descriptions of these thematic revelations are provided below.

In order to feature the voices of African American men, we illustrate how each theme emerged in the responses as well as the discourse in the interviews and focus group discussions. We have chosen to focus our analysis on the practices described by the African American men that related to the stereotypes reinforced in the *Real World* discourse. Thus we narrowed our attention to the interrelated signifiers (inherently angry, potentially violent, and sexually aggressive) that speak to the perception of African American men as dangerous.[8] A distinct consciousness of the various effects of societal stereotypes, such as those that permeate mediated texts such as MTV's *Real World,* was evident throughout the description of lived experiences offered by African American men.

Acknowledging Societal Stereotypes. Several African American men shared examples of their interaction with European Americans in authority positions who assumed the African Americans were inherently dangerous. These examples include descriptions of comments from European Americans, college professors, retail store employees, and immediate supervisors who appear fearful of Black men—even those with whom they have had some continued contact. This presumption is also inherent in the recalled and predicted actions of police officers, as reflected in the comments of one 20-year-old African American man during his interview:

> [I've had] conversations with people; particularly one professor and a couple of students telling [me] about incidents of being followed by the police down here. It's probably happened to almost every Black man. If not in [this small university town] it's happened to them in their home town . . . just followed because you are Black. It happens all the time and everywhere. (Orbe, 1994a)

This practice has become so prevalent that, in the Black community, it is commonly referred to as "DWB"—Driving While Black. In recognition of the role that this societal stereotype plays in the lives of Black men, many parents provide their sons with specific instructions on how to respond to being confronted for this "offense."

A similar pattern underscoring the stereotype of Blacks as "dangerous" is played out in their interactions with acquaintances, colleagues, and strangers, even in situations where the danger of potential harm is minimal. For some African American men, this involves seeing European Americans crossing the street, presumably to avoid close contact, or hearing car door locks clicking as they walk by in broad daylight. For one 21-year-old African American man who supported himself through college delivering pizzas, evidence for the stereotype involved his experience in elevators, with "White girls crunching over in the corner of an elevator" in response to his presence. In other instances, even the security of a male companion did not alter the European Americans' "natural reaction" to Black men:

> I am on the elevator and a stack of pizzas in my hand, and there's this girl and her boyfriend on the elevator. . . . The guy's right next to the door. . . . I'm on this side and she's kind of right in the middle. . . . She had the nerve—with her boyfriend right there—to take her purse and put it on the other side. (Orbe, 1994a)

A number of the African American men involved in this project offered possible explanations for European Americans' general reactions to them. "I think a lot of it has to do with many people just feeling uncomfortable being around Black people . . . they are paranoid," explained one 17-year-old participant in his interview (Orbe, 1994a). "They don't know what we are capable of, because they have never been around us," rationalized another African American man who was part of a focus group (Orbe, 1994a). The connection between societal stereotypes—most often accumulated with no real contact with African Americans—and quality of interracial interaction was made apparent. In some instances, stereotypes of African American men were fueled by outsiders' perception of specific communities that stood as representations for Black life in general. One middle-aged African American man shared the following example as part of a focus group discussion:

> We had one friend from Indiana—not too far from Gary. And I don't know if any of you know Gary, Indiana, but it is a depressed place. It is a sad situation. And her whole idea of Black people, having come from a predominantly White area, was Gary, Indiana. (Orbe, 1994a)

For some participants, mediated images of African Americans were directly associated with the discourse of European Americans. Such was the case when non-African Americans attempted to use their knowledge of African American culture—gained through mass-mediated images—in order to break down communication barriers. One 19-year-old African American man described instances when Whites "use words they picked up from MTV Raps or BET" (Orbe, 1994a). Another participant, in his late 30s, who was in the same focus group, shared what happens whenever colleagues congratulate him on any accomplishment: "I just don't get a handshake—you know I get the 'Fresh Prince of Bel-Air' handshake!" (Orbe, 1994a).

Being Cautious. Because of a heightened awareness of how others might unconsciously adopt the fallacy that all Black men are "dangerous," many of the African American men who participated in interviews and focus groups described how this served as a backdrop to their everyday life experiences. Most Black men shared specific instances in which stereotypical thinking appeared to be directly manifested in public-private discourse and in the nonverbal behaviors of others. The African American men who shared their experiences with us also described how they perceived that societal stereotypes overtly or covertly affected all of their interactions. A mindfulness as to the impact of societal stereotypes was maintained by African American men in lieu of past experiences and the perpetual existence of stereotypes (on or just below the surface). Therefore, interpretations of their everyday interactions must be understood in this context.

Many Black men describe their interactions with European Americans as "cautious," "superficial," "selective," or "filled with a lot of skepticism." These characteristics reflect the distinct consciousness that informs how African American men communicate with non-African Americans. One African American man, who works as a university administrator on a predominantly European American campus, shared,

> I am inclined to be very cautious dealing with White Americans based on their socialization process. There's a tremendous amount of skepticism that I feel with Whites. And while I try to not allow that to dictate my behavior and actions, it's unconsciously or subconsciously there. (Orbe, 1996b)

Similar sentiments were shared by a number of African American men in their interviews or focus group discussions. Even when interacting with European Americans whose communicative behaviors did not reflect any adherence to societal stereotypes, African American men's discourses were enacted with a clear recognition of the potential effects of such negative images. One 26-year-old man, who had worked in the northeast for a state department in which he was the only African American man, shared how he remained cautious despite friendly social invitations:

> Every Monday they would come in laughing [about their after-work socializing on Friday] . . . and they would say, "Why don't you come?" But I knew that I tolerated [them] all during the week and [they] tolerated me. But get some liquor up in [them] and have them call me a nigger and we are going to fight. And I would go to jail and be fired. And be called a violent, radical Black man. (Orbe, 1994a)

Clearly, the impact of social stereotypes on the everyday discourse of African American men was evident, regardless of whether the effects were actual, perceived, or potentially present. In this regard, some Black men noted that their communicative behaviors appeared to be decoded by others through a perceptual filter composed of stereotypes that signified Black men as inherently angry, potentially violent, and sexually aggressive. Our transcripts were filled with instances of African American men sharing how intimidated European Americans were by their mere presence.

Respondents also said that whenever African American men were "expressive" about their opinions, they were perceived by others as being "radical." Assertive discourse, processed through a stereotype-laden perceptual filter, was viewed as aggressive, threatening, and hostile. This very scenario was played out when one 18-year-old African American man appeared on a community-access television program and voiced his concerns about local racism. Although other African Americans praised his courage, a few European American acquaintances confided in him that some of their friends viewed his discourse as intimidating:

> I told them [White acquaintances] that I don't mean to make people scared of me, that is far from what I'm trying to do. I want people to respect me, first of all. And respect the cause that I am out for... If that is making people scared of me, then I'm sorry. (Orbe, 1994a)

A cautious state of mind is revealed in the following example, from a 19-year-old African American man who had adapted successfully through the "culture shock" of leaving inner-city Philadelphia for a small Midwestern college town. His interactions with Whites on campus, however, were filled with "a lot of stress" because he believed that Whites were always second-guessing what he was saying and searching for subtle hints that would reinforce their stereotypes of young Black men from the inner city. He anticipated that they would selectively attend to certain aspects of his communication and conclude, "I knew it! I knew it! I knew that he is really *that way*" (Orbe, 1994a).

Countering Societal Stereotypes. For African American men, being cautious typically leads to discourse that attempts to manage the existence of societal stereotypes in a variety of ways. Although our review of the transcripts revealed a multitude of specific communication tactics in response to negative stereotypes characterizing Black men as dangerous, a distinct pattern emerged that provided some structural insight into their responses. We saw the African American male respondents as strategically using discourse to counter the societal stereotypes. The strategies were either direct (naming stereotypes as such and then dealing with them) or indirect (avoiding direct confrontation but subtly refuting stereotypes), and, depending on the interaction, strategies reflected a proactive or reactive manner.

As with the discourse of the Black men on *The Real World,* most of the examples of African American men directly confronting the existence of stereotypes occurred after the stereotype emerged in interactions with others. In some instances, this involved "calling out"—assertively pointing out overt or covert examples of prejudiced thinking—those European Americans who consciously or unconsciously allowed their preconceived notions of Black men to inform their discourse. One 18-year-old African American man shared in his interview that, as part of a pre-job training workshop, he took the opportunity to point out the subtle ways that stereotypes of African Americans hinder effective communication. Hopeful about the possible effects of his attempts, he described how meaningful his comments appeared to be for others: "We talk[ed] about different stereotypes that we have about each other and different things like how we are going to have to deal with lots of different people" (Orbe, 1994a).

The mindfulness that governs the communication of African American men foregrounds the distinct possibility that others will perceive them within the boundaries of societal stereotypes. In many instances, Black men's increased attention to verbal and nonverbal codes allows them to immediately recognize European Americans' misperceptions and simultaneously react in ways to counter existing stereotypes. The discourse of one 22-year-old African American man, who attempted to ease the discomfort of European American women with whom he often shares an elevator, illustrates how his increased sensitivity led him to a specific tactic:

If I see that they feel uncomfortable, then I'll say, "Hi, how are you all doing tonight?," "What are you all doing tonight?," this, that, or the other. Usually, I get some feedback, but they still stay on the other side of the elevator . . . I really try to alleviate the problem by making an effort. (Orbe, 1994a)

As discussed in the previous section, African American men perceive societal stereotypes as potentially having a negative effect on their interactions with non-African Americans. Because of this, they often proactively enact discourse that refutes the legitimacy of any stereotypes—prior to any indication that negative stereotyping might occur. Although this type of strategic discourse is usually offered in more indirect ways, sometimes it takes a direct form. For instance, African American men appear more likely to deal with stereotypes directly and proactively when they perceive others as having few or no past interactions with African Americans. These persons, it is assumed, are more likely to be influenced by societal stereotypes fueled by various mediated texts that characterize the dangerous nature of Black men. Part of the process of attributing the potential effects of stereotyping involves, in the words of one African American man who participated in a focus group, "watching people, watching how people interact, listening to what they say to other people." Other times it involves "asking certain questions that would yield certain responses" (Orbe, 1994a). In any case, the rationale behind efforts to dispel existing myths about African American men very early on in relationships with others is clear, as articulated by one 18-year-old participant:

> Everyone in the office was from a suburb . . . and never really experienced a Black person . . . I knew that people thought that I was just another Black kid from the streets that the company was trying to help. . . . My idea was to change their attitudes, so that they couldn't look at all Blacks the same. (Orbe, 1996b)

On the other hand, dealing with societal stereotypes in a more indirect manner allows African American men to counter the problematic nature of being characterized as a dangerous threat to others more subtly. This strategic response by African Americans to negative stereotyping allows European Americans to negotiate their perceptions of Black men without the pressure of direct confrontation. In some instances, African American men might enact this type of discourse in order to avoid the "walls of defensiveness" that are instantaneously constructed by European Americans accused of prejudiced thinking.

Within the transcripts that described the communicative experiences of African American men, we found numerous examples of the indirect ways in which they negotiate societal stereotypes in everyday discourse. The most common strategy for indirectly negotiating the existence of negative stereotyping is to "play the part." This communication tactic refers to the multiple ways that African American men may choose to manipulate their discourse, as well as their nonverbal mannerisms, in order to appear more acceptable to White society. In essence, this includes avoiding any communication behaviors that are associated with the stereotypical image of the angry, potentially violent Black man. Most of the participants discussed how they assume a different communication stance when communicating with European Americans; instead of using their "natural voices," they "avoid slang words" and "talk like Whites." Other African American men shared how they monitor their nonverbal codes (dress, use of space, eye contact, touch) in order to reduce the likelihood that their actions might be perceived as threatening. One focus group of young and middle-aged professional men even discussed how they learned that shaving off all of their facial hair apparently presents a less dangerous persona.

What ties all of these communication behaviors together is that they attempt to refute existing negative stereotypes of Black men without directly confronting the existence of stereotypical thinking by Whites. Strategic discourse, like that used to "play the part," was used as an attempt to put others at ease during interactions. Other attempts include the following from a 20-year-old male student about his experience in a group of undergraduate engineering students, who, for example, work together to make sure that none of them is the lone African American in any of their classes:

Since we are all taking the [same] classes . . . every quarter we get together and ask, "What classes are you taking?" . . . So, usually, it will be three or four of us from the Summer [program for minority students in engineering] in the same class. We rigged it that way so that the first year, we wouldn't be the only ones in the class. (Orbe, 1994a)

In addition to ensuring that an internal support group exists for each class, these students are attempting to use "increased diverse numbers," among other conscious strategies (such as sitting in the front row), to counter existing stereotypes that often inform interactions with professors.

In addition to offering indirect challenges, the African American men in other situations subtly use discourse to refute societal stereotypes that become evident during interracial interactions. For example, one man in his late 30s (who also self-identified as having both African and Native American ancestry) shared how he countered the preconceived notions of several persons without ever bringing attention to how pervading stereotypes filtered Whites' initial perceptions of him:

When I came out, they immediately perceived me as one thing . . . because of the way that I look. [So], I showed them that I was vulnerable. I sort of opened up and stripped away all of that exterior stuff and let them see what's inside. (Orbe, 1994a)

In this specific instance—a public social gathering—the participant talked about how his willingness to "be real" with others helped to expose the "soft side" of African American men.

Still other alternative communication tactics were apparent in the case of one 28-year-old African American man who, sitting in his own office, was publicly belittled by a European American male colleague. The colleague then left the man's office without providing any opportunity to respond. The man describes his reaction:

And so, I sat in my office. My first response was to get up . . . or should I say that I thought about getting up and going behind him and giving him a piece of my mind. But something kept me there . . . something kept me in the seat. (Orbe, 1996b)

That "something," as was later articulated in the interview, was a clear recognition of how others in the office thought he would respond to this incident. Based on the pervasiveness of stereotypes that regard Black men as inherently angry and potentially violent, coworkers were assumed to be anticipating explosive retaliation that was sure to follow such an altercation. Instead, the African American respondent wrote a detailed memo to the colleague's supervisor that outlined the inappropriateness of his actions. Although the memo did not directly confront the stereotypes that were the basis of the interaction (accusations that the African American man was incompetent), his actions helped to counter the stereotype of Black men as explosively dangerous.

REFLECTION(S)

The ethnosemiotic investigation presented here sought to examine the discourse by and about African American men in two different texts. First, our analysis revealed the pervasiveness of a significant system that defined Black men on MTV's *Real World* as dangerous threats to members of mainstream society. This stereotype was maintained through three closely related signifiers: the Black man as inherently angry, potentially violent, and sexually aggressive. Second, we found that African

American men's discourse about everyday experiences reflected the existence of negative societal stereotypes. Three themes captured the essence of the responses: (a) acknowledging societal stereotypes, (b) being cautious, and (c) countering societal stereotypes. One of the major strengths of this analysis is the ways in which an ethnosemiotic framework was used to identify, and subsequently provide insight into, the prevalence of existing negative stereotypes attributed to and experienced by African American men.

Stereotypes, as a crucial aspect of intergroup identity formation (e.g., Hecht, Collier, & Ribeau, 1993), are perpetuated through discourse enacted in a variety of communication contexts: mass media, as well as organizational, small-group, interpersonal, and intrapersonal settings. The strength of a societal stereotype is based on its pervasiveness in each context and on the discourse within each that serves as reinforcement for constructs enacted in other contexts. In this regard, it appears to be of little use to try to decipher whether mass media stereotypes primarily inform interpersonal interactions or if stereotypes gained through interpersonal encounters are the mechanism that fuels the construction of mass media images. Of more significance to the arguments presented in our analysis is the recognition of the inextricable ways in which our communication can work to create a perceptual filter that informs our perceptions in all contexts. These perceptual filters, such as the prevalence of existing stereotypes that signify Black men as dangerous, function as unconscious mechanisms to ensure that stereotypical thinking persists even when discourse is encountered that contradicts one's preconceived ideas. For example, even when European Americans interact with an African American man who may defy the legitimacy of existing societal stereotypes, the strength of their perceptual filter may encourage the perpetuation of the stereotype while leaving room for possibilities of "exceptions."

According to Fiske (1994), ethnosemiotic analyses recognize "that what is absent from a text is as significant as what is present" (p. 422). What was absent from the discourse on MTV's *Real World,* an absence that also persists in the everyday life experiences of our African American male respondents, is any substantial evidence of meaningful relationships between European Americans and African American men. According to the texts examined here, interracial relationships that advance beyond superficial discourse appear to be very small in number.

We contend that two major barriers disrupt the process of establishing meaningful relationships between African American men and European

Americans: (a) a pervasiveness of negative societal stereotypes consciously or unconsciously acquired and maintained by European Americans, and (b) the tendency for African American men to feel compelled to "play the part" when communicating with European Americans. In most cases, the perceived dangerous nature of African American men (as inherently angry, potentially violent, and sexually aggressive) is maintained through the proliferation of mass media images amidst the absence of any meaningful interpersonal interaction. The depictions of inner-city life in the printed or visual media and the images on MTV's *Real World* do have a significant impact on how non-African Americans perceive Black men. This is especially true for members of societies such as the United States, which is one that largely functions within racially separated realities. In order for existing societal stereotypes of African American men to be contested, individuals must participate in discourse that interrupts the cyclical nature of communication systems that perpetuate such problematic constructs. A productive site of contestation can occur within everyday interactions. An important first step is to acknowledge the ways in which existing societal stereotypes are manifested within our daily communication. We believe that the insights provided in this analysis serve as a clear indication of how existing negative stereotypes attributed to Black men in the United States are evident in various communication contexts, including everyday interactions.

The ethnosemiotic analysis presented here—one that sought to connect the discourse by and about African American men in mediated and interpersonal contexts—begs for additional scholarly attention. This is especially true in regard to representations of Black masculinity in mass media outlets that provide a context for examining how mediating factors such as class, age, sexuality, and national origin are negotiated within the formation of the black masculine subject.

Furthermore, additional insight can be gained from other research endeavors that seek to listen to the voices of "everyday" African American men who face the effects of stereotypes in a society where mass media influences are inescapable.

In a larger sense, however, the research described here also has implications for scholarship that seeks to explore the relationship between culture and communication. Our attention has been on the ways in which cultural stereotypes are negotiated by one historically marginalized segment of the U.S. population. However, during this process, we have implicated the ways in which these stereotypes are created, maintained, or transformed within dominant group identity. Societal stereotypes of African American men, in this regard, can be seen as centrally relevant to how European Americans negotiate their own identities. This implication is aptly captured by African American writer James Baldwin, who understood that "If I'm not who you say I am, then you're not who you think you are" (quoted in Dates & Barlow, 1990, p. 5). In other words, we argue that maintaining (false) societal stereotypes of out-group members facilitates the development of in-group identity frameworks that are problematic.

A primary space where this particular point of inquiry might develop is within emerging research on the social construction of "Whiteness" (Frankenberg, 1993; Nakayama & Martin, 1999). The literature on Whiteness—especially in terms of research that works to articulate the process by which White cultural identity is constructed, has largely been uninterrogated, privileged, and unacknowledged (Jackson, 1999). Such research can extend our understanding of race and identity. It is our contention that exploring the influences of prevalent stereotypes of out-group members on how dominant (in-group) identity is negotiated can provide communication researchers with yet another small piece to the larger intercultural communication puzzle.

NOTES

1. See Akbar (1990) and Jackson (1997) for in-depth discussions on the importance of deconstructing Western hegemonic representations of Black masculinity. These scholars argue for an Afrocentric conception of Black masculinity that is enacted differently in terms of that which is reflective of being a male, boy, man, or masculine subject. Our criticisms of the images of Black masculinity in the media are consistent with this emerging framework, in that both analyses critique the ways in which most representations and discussions ignore such distinctions. In fact, we hope that this ethnosemiotic analysis will help illuminate the role the media play in hindering a more complete understanding of Black masculinity (see, for example, criticisms articulated in Jackson, 1997, pp. 743-477).

2. Mohammed maintains a marginal presence (at best) within these "most dangerous" episodes. This came as no surprise to *Real World* fans who watched the San Francisco season and noticed the lack of attention given to his role in the house. In fact, although Mohammed was part of the cast throughout the entire season, his prominence within the final (edited) footage is reminiscent of the invisibility of Black men described in Ralph Ellison's *Invisible Man* (1947).

3. The initial conceptualization of how these three images were signified within *The Real World* was the result of a preliminary semiotic analysis performed by and published by the first author (Orbe, 1998). Through the ethnosemiotic analysis presented here, these stereotypes were fine-tuned, clarified, and subsequently examined to determine how they were negotiated in the everyday lives of African American men.

4. For a more substantial treatment of how the Black masculine subject is characterized by a distinctive physiognomy, see Dyson (1993).

5. One of the features of *The Real World* is the confessional room. Over the 3 months of their stay in the house, cast members are required to spend time alone in this room self-disclosing (only to a camera) their personal reflections on the events happening with others. Frequently, footage from the confessional is edited into footage of actual interactions, so that viewers gain insight into how each person perceives the interaction as it unfolds.

6. Critical incidents asked each person to provide a detailed description of a past incident when he interacted with a non-African American. In-depth interviews and focus group discussions (ranging from 3 to 6 persons) lasted 45 to 75 min and used similarly open-ended questions (e.g., "What is one word that could describe how you view your interactions with non-African Americans?") to generate an inductive exchange between the researcher and participants. For a more detailed description of the methodological procedures used in data collection (e.g., explanation of participant selection, diversity of participants, and the Topical Protocol used in interviews and focus groups), see Orbe (1994b, 1996a).

7. Two of these ideas (*acknowledging* and *negotiating societal stereotypes*) emerged from the independent analyses of transcripts. The third, being cautious, developed from a variety of ways that African American men had described their interaction with non-African Americans. In this regard, *being cautious* was chosen because it appeared to capture the essence of these men's general interracial communication experiences (i.e., "superficial," "selective," or "filled with a lot of skepticism").

8. In addition to finding instances where Black men negotiated stereotypes that rendered them as dangerous (i.e., inherently angry, potentially violent, and sexually aggressive), the transcripts spoke to the prevalence of another societal stereotype: Black man as ignorant or stupid. For those in professional positions, this stereotype was revealed in the ways that coworkers and supervisors interacted with them. Many European Americans perceived them as "affirmative action hires" who did not necessarily have the proper qualifications for the job. Because of this perception, African American men are often on the receiving end of condescending talk, remedial instructions, and genuine surprise when their performance exceeds others' low expectations. The discourse of others used when interacting with African American male students resembles a similar signifier. On campus, however, Black men are seen as "affirmative action cases" or an uneducated/ ineducable athlete. In either case, the general societal stereotype of Black men as ignorant or stupid permeates their interactions with others.

9. One mass media text, *The Color of Fear,* a 1994 film by Lee Mun Wah, offers exceptional insight into how African American men, as well as men from various racial-ethnic backgrounds, negotiate masculinities within the context of multiple cultural markers.

REFERENCES

Akbar, N. (1990). *Vision for Black men.* Tallahassee, FL: Mind Productions.
Ang, I. (1985). *Watching "Dallas."* London: Methuen.
Barthes, R. (1972). *Mythologies* (A. Lavers, Trans.). New York: Hill and Wang.

Berry, V. T. (1992). From *Good Times* to *The Cosby Show*: Perceptions of changing televised images among Black fathers and sons. In S. Craig (Ed.), *Men, masculinity and the media* (pp. 111-123). Newbury Park, CA: Sage.

Bogle, D. (1994). *Toms, coons, mulattoes, mammies, and bucks: An interpretive history of Blacks in American films.* New York: Viking.

Boyd, H., & Allen, R. L. (1995). *Brotherman: The odyssey of Black men in America—An anthology.* New York: One World/Ballantine.

Brooks, D. E., & Jacob, W. R. (1996). Black men in the margins: Space traders and the interpositional strategy against b(l)acklash. *Communication Studies, 47,* 289-302.

Brown, C. (1965). *Manchild in the promised land.* New York: Macmillan.

Campbell, C. P. (1995). *Race, myth and the news.* Thousand Oaks, CA: Sage.

Cooks, L. M., & Orbe, M. (1993). Beyond the satire: Selective exposure and selective perception in *In Living Color. Howard Journal of Communications, 4,* 217-233.

Dates, J. L., & Barlow, W. (Eds.). (1990). *Split image.* Washington, DC: Howard University Press.

Dyson, M. (1993). *Reflecting Black: African American cultural criticism.* Minneapolis: University of Minnesota Press.

Eco, U. (1976). *A theory of semiotics.* Bloomington: Indiana University Press.

Elise, S., & Umoja, A. (1992). Spike Lee constructs the new Black man: Mo' better. *Western Journal of Black Studies, 6,* 82-89.

Ellison, R. (1947). *Invisible man.* New York: Vintage.

Essed, P. (1991). *Understanding everyday racism: An interdisciplinary theory.* Newbury Park, CA: Sage.

Evoleocha, S. U., & Ugbah, S. D. (1989). Stereotypes, counter-stereotypes, and Black television images in the 1990s. *Western Journal of Black Studies, 12,* 197-205.

Fiske, J. (1994). Ethnosemiotics: Some personal and theoretical reflections. In H. Newcomb (Ed.), *Television: The critical view* (pp. 411-425). New York: Oxford University Press.

Frankenberg, R. (1993). *White women, race matters: The social construction of whiteness.* Minneapolis: University of Minnesota Press.

Fry, D., & Fry, V. (1984). Semiotic model for the study of mass communication. In M. McLaughlin (Ed.), *Communication yearbook* (Vol. 9, pp. 443-462). Beverly Hills, CA: Sage.

Gibbs, J. T. (1992). Young Black males in America: Endangered, embittered, and embattled. In M. L. Andersen & P. H. Collins (Eds.), *Race, class and gender: An anthology* (pp. 267-276). Belmont, CA: Wadsworth.

Hawkes, T. (1977). *Structuralism and semiotics.* London: Methuen.

Hecht, M. L., Collier, M. J., & Ribeau, S. (1993). *African American communication: Identity and cultural interpretations.* Newbury Park, CA: Sage.

hooks, b. (1992). *Black looks: Race and representation.* Boston: South End.

Huriash, L. J. (1996, July 10). Surreal world. *Fort Lauderdale (FL) Sun-Sentinel,* p. C25.

Jackson, R. L. (1997). Black "manhood" as xenophobe: An ontological exploration of the Hegelian dialectic. *Journal of Black Studies, 27,* 731-750.

Jackson, R. L. (1999). White space, white privilege: Mapping discursive inquiry into the self. *Quarterly Journal of Speech, 85,* 38-54.

Kellner, D. L. (1995). *Media culture.* New York: Routledge.

MacDonald, J. F. (1983). *Black and white TV: Afro-Americans in television since 1948.* Chicago: Nelson-Hall.

McCall, N. (1994). *Makes me wanna holler: A young Black man in America.* New York: Random House.

Nakayama, T. K., & Martin, J. N. (1999). *Whiteness: The communication of social identity.* Thousand Oaks, CA: Sage.

Omi, M. (1989). In living color: Race and American culture. In I. Angus & S. Jhally (Eds.), *Cultural politics in contemporary America* (pp. 111-122). New York: Routledge.

Orbe, M. (1994a). [African American male communication]. Unpublished raw data.

Orbe, M. (1994b). "Remembering it's always Whites' ball": Descriptions of African American male communication. *Communication Quarterly, 42,* 287-300.

Orbe, M. (1996a). Laying the foundation for co-cultural communication theory: An inductive approach to studying non-dominant communication strategies and the factors that influence them. *Communication Studies, 47,* 157-176.

Orbe, M. (1996b). [Nondominant communication strategies and their influencing factors]. Unpublished raw data.

Orbe, M. (1998). Construction of reality of MTV's *Real World*: An analysis of the restrictive coding of Black masculinity. *Southern Communication Journal, 64,* 32-47.

Orbe, M., & Strother, K. (1996). Signifying the tragic mulatto: A semiotic analysis of *Alex Haley's Queen. Howard Journal of Communications, 7,* 113-126.

O'Sullivan, T., Hartley, J., Saunders, D., Montgomery, M., & Fiske, J. (1994). *Key concepts in communication and cultural studies.* New York: Routledge.

Powell, K. (1997). *Keepin' it real: Post-MTV reflection on race, sex, and politics.* New York: Ballantine.

Robinson, G., & Straw, O. (1984). Semiotics and communication studies: Points of contact. In B. Dervin & M. Voight (Eds.), *Progress in communication sciences IV* (pp. 91-114). Norwood, NJ: Ablex.

Saussure, R. (1966). *A course in general linguistics.* New York: McGraw-Hill.

Sakurari, S. H. (1996, July 17). The Real World is hell. *Salon,* 16-19.

Smith, S. (1993, November). *From the junkman to the garbage man: The evolution of the African American male in the Black situation comedy.* Paper presented at the annual meeting of the Speech Communication Association, Miami, FL.

Staples, B. (1994). *Parallel time: Growing up in the Black and White.* New York: Pantheon.

van Dijk, T. A. (1987). *Communicating racism.* Newbury Park, CA: Sage.

Wah, L. M. (Producer). (1994). *The color of fear* [Film]. (Available from Stir-Fry Productions, 1904 Virginia Street, Berkeley, CA 94709)

White, J. E. (1994, March 7). Between two worlds. *Time,* 68.

Wright, R. (1966). *Black boy.* New York: Harper & Row.

6

Media and Colonialism

Race, Rape, and "Englishness" in The Jewel in the Crown

RAKA SHOME • Arizona State University, West Campus

> Nationalism is constituted, from its origins, as a highly gendered relationship, dependent upon the marking on women's and men's bodies and in their identities, of the ideologies of national difference.
>
> —Radcliffe and Westwood, 1996, p. 135

The importance of the media in shaping and reinforcing dominant meanings of a nation and national identity has been noted by several scholars (Jeffords, 1994; Shohat & Stam, 1994). In today's postmodern culture, characterized by wide accessibility and circulation of images, the media influence how audiences perceive the nation space and how they think of themselves as a national community. Shohat and Stam (1994) note,

> In today's postmodern age, all political struggles necessarily pass through the simulcral realm of the mass media . . . contemporary media shape identity . . . [i]n a transnational world typified by global circulation of images and sounds . . . media spectatorship impacts complexly on national identity and communal belonging. (p. 7)

Because a nation and its national identity are constituted through cultural narratives (for example, sets of stories, myths, icons) that a group of people sharing the same geopolitical space use to conceive of a "Self" and to distinguish that Self from "Others," the media become a significant channel for the constitution of this national sense. Indeed, the perennial question that haunts a national space—"who are we as a people and society?"—is significantly influenced by visual images of society from the past, present, and future that are offered simultaneously to millions of viewers through various media representations of society.

135

In this chapter, I focus on the English national context of the 1980s to provide a case study of how the media shape and contribute to struggles over the meaning of a sense of nationalism. I examine the critically acclaimed 1984 British television serial *The Jewel in the Crown* (hereafter, *The Jewel*), which is set in India in the colonial British period of the early 1940s. Situating this text against the historical backdrop of the English New Right rhetoric of race and nation in the 1980s, I demonstrate how, through specific representations of the colonial period in India, *The Jewel* constructs a position of "Englishness" that reinforces the New Right's racialized rhetoric of the nation, a rhetoric in which an authentic Englishness was seen as being defiled by the penetration of "black and brown hordes" into a virginal national space.

By engaging in such an analysis, I hope to extend critical communication studies in the following ways. First, although much critical work has been done by communication scholars on the relationship between media and the rhetorical construction of race, there exists very little work that has examined cultural narratives of the media as national narratives. Thus, I argue in this chapter that popular media narratives are always national narratives, because they provide viewers with lenses for "making meaning" out of a geopolitical space that people inhabit together. Along these lines, such narratives enable us to imagine various kinds of people with whom we may never have personal contact who also reside in that space. This argument was first made by Anderson (1983, 1991), whose classic text *Imagined Communities* demonstrated the connection between print media capitalism and the emergence of an "imagined" national consciousness in the 19th century. Today, however, it is popular cultural discourses, such as television and cinema, that have become the site through which dominant meanings of nationhood are negotiated and reworked. By engaging in a critical analysis of *The Jewel,* I illustrate the cultural role media narratives play in the construction of a hegemonic national imagination and the ways in which narratives of gender, race, and imperialism intersect in this process.

Second, I attempt to further extend the emerging critical space of postcolonial scholarship in our discipline. Broadly put, postcolonial criticism is a methodological perspective that attempts to examine the power-laden ways in which narratives of imperialism and nationalism are both enabled and sustained, as well as resisted. In many of my recent works, I have argued on the importance of recognizing the role that communication discourses play in the production of colonialism and neocolonialism (Shome, 1996a, 1996b, 1999). In this chapter, I reinforce this argument by offering a postcolonial analysis of the role that media and intercultural discourses play in producing colonialist and nationalist ideologies.

The important issue to recognize in relation to media and nationalist ideologies is that the media allow for visibility. Through various visual depictions of society, the media provide visible markers for imagining a national self, and consequently the media also offer markers for "otherness" against which such self-recognition is, or is not, invited. As Jeffords (1994) notes, the nation "exists as something to be *seen* . . . [for] it is how citizens *see* themselves and how they *see* those against whom they define themselves that determines national self-perception" (p. 6).

In offering this argument, I do not deny the possibility of polysemic readings of media texts. After abundant debates in the field of cultural studies on the politics of polysemy, we now know that there is never a homogeneous reading of cultural texts. Cultural texts are polysemic. But that does not mean, as Condit (1991) has so cogently argued, that there are no limits to that polysemy. Because of the political economy of production and distribution of images, because the image-making apparatus is still largely owned by elites, and because "the people" are inscribed into certain dominant modes of consensus and meaning formation, polysemic readings are themselves constrained by the hegemonic power relations within which they occur. There can be only so much polysemy. To argue otherwise is to overlook the power of cultural domination that the media still have as an apparatus imbricated in a network of material and cultural relations; it would also mean that "the people" could exist as a separate enclave outside of dominant cultural power and relations of force.

ABOUT THE TEXT

The central narrative of *The Jewel* is framed by a discourse of interracial rape. The serial was promoted with the line, "This is a story of rape." Although the rape occurs in the second episode, its narrative presence informs the plot for the remaining 12 episodes. The plot is set in the preindependence British Raj period in India, spanning the historical years between 1942 and 1947. The serial is a narrative about an upperclass Indian-English man, Hari Kumar, who returns to India after the death of his father. In India, he falls in love with a white Englishwoman, Daphne Manners. The central action on which the plot rests is Daphne's rape by local natives on a night of intense anti-British riots by Indians. As a consequence of this event, Hari finds himself wrongly accused of the rape, and he is thrown into prison, where he is treated brutally. The rest of the story centers around the rape, as various characters over the next few years try to figure out what happened and the implications of the rape of a white woman in colonial society.

The Jewel is part of a media phenomenon that occurred in the English entertainment culture in the early 1980s. Between 1980 and 1984, a spate of films emerged that had the colonial "British Raj" period in India for their subject matter. Films such as *Passage to India* (1984), *Gandhi* (1982), *Far Pavilions* (1984), and *Heat and Dust* (1983) followed each other in quick succession. Although all of these films were highly successful, *The Jewel* in particular became a smashing hit, far surpassing the others in popularity. The popularity of this film was clearly manifested during its first broadcast by Granada Television, when the serial reached an average viewership of 8,050,000 people for each of its 14 episodes (Brandt, 1993). The following year the series was repeated on British Television's Channel Four, where it again reached a high viewership (at least for this time in England) of 1,732,000 viewers (Brandt, 1993). The serial's immense popularity was not confined just to England's shores but spread well beyond to numerous countries, including Canada, Australia, New Zealand, the United States, France, Belgium, Italy, Greece, Sweden, Iceland, and the Netherlands. Commenting on its phenomenal success, *Newsweek* magazine declared,

> the first thing you should know about *The Jewel in the Crown* is that it absolutely blew the British away . . . [I]t emptied streets to the extent reminiscent of the blitz. Dinner engagements were canceled, phone receivers hung off their hooks, and newspaper mail columns sprouted with impassioned historical dissertations. Inevitably, advertising copywriters seized upon the words "jewel" and "crown" to connote anything superlative . . . while among the high fashion and trendy, membership became all the rage. (Waters, 1994, p. 102)

The English newspaper *The Observer* (January 22, 1984, p. A4) called it "one of the best dramas ever made." *The Telegraph* (February 15, 1984, p. B2) hailed it as not just the "series of the decade but the richest drama of all." In 1984, director Ken Taylor won the National Award for Best Screenplay Adaptation. In 1985, *The Jewel* won the Golden Globe as well as the National Board of Review Award.

The overwhelming success of *The Jewel* was indeed significant. Although the British Raj period in India had been the subject matter of many English novels during the colonial era (and at the beginning of the English postcolonial era) such as *Kim, Passage to India,* and *The Raj Quartet* (on which *The Jewel* is based), never in postcolonial England had the British Raj subject matter been resurrected in popular culture with such intensity and received with such popularity.

Equally striking is the fact that despite the uniqueness of this media phenomenon, the films, especially *The Jewel,* that mesmerized the audience for days have not received much systematic attention in cultural criticism. The only significant interpretations of *The Jewel* that exist are film reviews. Film critics attempting to "make sense" of the popularity of this serial interpreted it as expressing a "colonialist nostalgia." They argued that the film allowed a postcolonial England, reeling under economic crisis and loss of imperial greatness, to peek into its colonial past for a particular vision of an empire now lost.

For example, Salman Rushdie, in a controversial review, contended that "the continuing decline, the growing poverty, and the meanness of the spirit of much of Thatcherite Britain encourages many Britons to turn their eyes nostalgically to the lost hour of its precedence . . . the jewel in the crown these days is made up of paste" (Rushdie, 1991, pp. 91-92). Employing a similar colonialist nostalgia argument, Gita Mehta (1985) claimed that "Britain's imperial connection with India was the grand moment of Britain's imperial history, and once again, in a veritable orgy of nostalgia, the British are asserting their right to package India for the rest of the world" (p. 188). In a similar vein, Higson (1993), in his recent study of Thatcherism and British cinema, defined these films as "heritage films" and suggested, like the other critics, that these representational resurrections of British colonialism in India were an effect of a postcolonial economic crisis in English society.

Although these readings are arguably justifiable, given England's decline in economic power in the postcolonial period, they nonetheless remain simplistic. They do not support *The Jewel* adequately within the political culture of the times. They do not explain why *The Jewel* was able to emerge at this particular time in England's history and what rhetorical functions it might be serving. If cultural texts are sites of power that are produced by and reflective of their political surroundings, then the colonialist nostalgia argument remains unsatisfactory. If *The Jewel* is simply about colonialist nostalgia brought about by a weak postimperial economy, then the space for such a nostalgic rendition of the empire had also existed in the 1950s and 1960s, and perhaps more so then, because that was the time when England first lapsed into an economic crisis when the existing Labor government was unable to manage its postcolonial economic predicaments. Thus, why was the Raj actively revived on celluloid in the early 1980s and not earlier? What was it about the larger play of forces in England at this time that created the space for the sudden appearance of a series of films that enacted certain representations of British colonialism in India?

These questions warrant a more nuanced and situated reading of *The Jewel* than has been attempted. If popular culture works as a barometer that enables us to gauge dominant cultural struggles and shifts of social forces, then the hyperpopularity of *The Jewel* provides us with case material through which to examine the ideological functions these resurrections of England's colonial past might have been serving in this significant historical moment. Thus, I argue that *The Jewel* constitutes a larger ideological struggle of the New Right, in which narratives of race, nation, and gender intersect in the process of defining a national self and setting up discursive boundaries of "us" and "them." An important feature informing this struggle was the way in which white womanhood came to function as a "sign" for the defilement of a seemingly authentic English body in the face of "unrestrained" migration of "colored" people into England.

In the following argument, I first offer a brief historical background of the English New Right's rhetoric of race and nation. This historical framework is necessary to adequately contextualize *The Jewel* and to provide the reader with a sense of the larger racialized struggle over "Englishness" that was occurring during this time. Next, I read *The Jewel* against this background to illustrate how the rape narrative within it works intertextually with other public narratives of the times—such as commercials, newspaper reports, and speeches—that also used the trope of a violated white woman to articulate a sense of the defilement of "Englishness." I focus particularly on the rape narrative in *The Jewel* because my argument is that the popularity of *The Jewel* had much to do with the way in which the metaphor of interracial rape played out in relation to the larger political culture of the times. As a result, British culture became obsessed with the notion of a loss of a "pure" English identity. In the process of offering this analysis, I address larger issues about the patriarchal implications of the discursive deployment of the female body as a sign for the nation, a deployment that often surfaces in national narratives in which the "penetration" of a nation by "others" is equated with the rape of a female body.

NEW RIGHT RHETORIC OF RACE AND NATION

The New Right emerged in the 1970s and was strengthened during Margaret Thatcher's administration in the 1980s. The New Right initially emerged as a reaction to the failed social-democratic consensus of the Labor government that had prevailed in the 1950s and 1960s. Thatcherism was the most populist arm of the New Right. Gordon and Klug (1986) note that "the new right set itself the task of saving Britain from what it regards as a state of economic and moral decline" (p. 6) in the postimperial period. A severe balance-of-payments problem—coupled with rising inflation, unemployment, the breakdown of the Keynesian welfare state, continuing immigration, the birth of various social movements that challenged the earlier materialism of England, Labor's alienation from the masses, and its failure to rework the economic apparatus sufficiently to secure the conditions necessary for a stable production of capital—resulted in a crisis in the nation's notion of its "Self."[1]

This crisis in national confidence began manifesting itself on several cultural fronts. Law and order broke down; youth crimes intensified; and a permissive culture of drugs, sex, and rock 'n' roll capturing the skepticism of the times appeared. Popular countercultural icons such as The Beatles and Mick Jagger reflected the mood of the times through songs such as "Help" and "I Can't Get No Satisfaction." In addition, countercultural ideologies generated by the cross-Atlantic waves of the Black Power movement, the civil rights movement, and Vietnam protests; the student movements in France and their failure in 1968; and the sexual revolutions sweeping the Western world—all of which in various ways expressed a "power to the people" theme—further contributed to this emerging sense of cultural insecurity and an antistatist mood.

Britons who were unable to psychologically reconcile themselves to England's postcolonial crisis in light of its imperial glory only a few years before began raising questions about "who are we as a people and society" as they desperately sought reasons for the decline in English society. It was at this point that the crisis began identifying what was wrong in society. That is, the source of the crisis became displaced onto what were soon regarded as subversive elements of society (Hall, 1988). "It is as if each surge of social anxiety f[ound] a temporary respite in the projection of fears onto and into . . . the discovery of demons, the identification of folk devils" (Hall, 1988, p. 36). It was in this process of struggle over national self-definition that the New Right stepped in and skillfully utilized people's anxieties to offer a new and racialized vision of Englishness. Because people were too eager to find demons and enemies to be able to name and fix what was wrong, race—one of the most visible signs of otherness—became a convenient force toward which the New Right directed people's frustrations. For example, Margaret Thatcher, in her famous "swamping" speech, noted that "people are rather afraid that this country might be swamped with a different culture. And you know, the *British character* has done so much . . . throughout the world, that if there is any fear that it might be swamped, people are going to be rather hostile to those coming in" (aired on Granada Television, January 30, 1978). And Alfred Sherman, a key right-wing ideologue, argued that "[nationhood] includes national character reflected in the way of life . . . a passport or residence permit does not automatically implant national values or patriotism" (quoted in Gilroy, 1987, p. 59).[2]

Such rhetorics, wherein the British nation and the British way of life were seen to be crumbling because of the presence of immigrants, became notably significant during the famous racial "riots" of the 1980s. Discourses about the riots in popular presses and newspapers used metaphors of violence and siege and of war on English society by blacks and immigrants in order to evoke a larger picture of a nation under attack from what Member of Parliament Cordle referred to as "coffee colored people" or "backward" societies (Hall, Critcher, Jefferson, Clarke, & Roberts, 1978, p. 240).[3]

It is against this background of race and nation, in which "nationalism and racism became so closely identified that to speak of the nation [was] to speak automatically in racially exclusive terms" (Gilroy, 1993, p. 27), that I situate *The Jewel* in order to demonstrate how its rhetoric constructs a hegemonic notion of Englishness that reinforces this larger New Right rhetoric of the nation. As mentioned earlier, my focus will be on the narrative of interracial rape within the serial.

FEMALE BODY AND IMPERIAL VIOLENCE: THE NARRATIVE OF INTERRACIAL RAPE

A central thrust in current feminist analyses of nationalism has been to demonstrate how rape narratives have often been used by nationalist discourses to justify racial and sexual oppression. For example, in a famous essay, Hall (1983) has cogently theorized, through her analysis of the discourse of lynching in the southern United States, how narratives about rapes of white women by nonwhite others have frequently emerged in colonial landscapes when there has been a fear of reversal of racial power relations. Indeed, as Layoun (1994) has further noted, "the recasting, the renegotiation of the order and boundaries of a dominant national narrative is [often] underwritten by what might seem a familiar obsession with the body of violated [. . .] woman" (p. 65). This is not to dispute the possibility that such rapes do occur. Rather, it is to make a larger suggestion that stories about rapes of white women have often been employed by patriarchal imperial discourses to regulate interactions between races and to maintain racial hierarchies.[4] The crucial question is this: In what ways do stories about attacks and rapes of white women by nonwhite others in an Anglo imperial culture reflect larger racial/cultural/sexual stories that the culture tells (and does not tell) about itself in a particular moment of crisis? For the English context of the New Right, what remains critical in light of this question is to explore what power-laden narrations were being enabled at this time through the rhetorical deployment of the trope of a raped white woman in media texts such as *The Jewel*. When we recall that this was a time in which the English nation was consumed with a fear about a loss of an "authentic" English identity in the face of "colored" migration, this exploration becomes especially salient.

To fully underscore the rhetorical import of the rape narrative in *The Jewel,* it is important to intertwine it with some other public narratives of the times in order to draw attention to how central the trope of a defiled white woman actually was in the public imagination. Against the background of anti-immigrant discourses, cultural narratives emerged in which arguments about the defilement of the national body were frequently made through the symbol of a violated and attacked white woman. For instance, on March 30, 1983, *The Sun* published a front-page column by a university professor that stated: "There are two crimes that haunt those living in British cities today. One is mugging, the other rape. . . . It is a woman's question and it is a question of race." It is especially interesting to note that such a comment from a figure of intellectual authority in a relatively moderate newspaper was not that far removed from reports in extreme fascist magazines.

An advertisement in a fascist magazine published in 1981 showed a close-up shot of two faces juxtaposed—one of an ape, the other of a black man. The headline read: "Ape, Rape." The text stated: "Look at these two creatures, they look the same, don't they, but they are not. . . . One is behind bars, one is not. The other however attacks, mugs, rapes, and kills (ask the police) . . . The sad conclusion is that the wrong one is behind bars" (Ware, 1983/1984, p. 25).

Political spokespersons such as Enoch Powell used a similar trope of a violated, attacked white woman to advance the notion of cultural contamination of England. In his famous "Rivers of Blood" speech delivered in 1968 (a speech that was crucial in swaying the national tide against immigration), Powell narrated the story of an old white widow, who lived in a seven-roomed house and who "worked hard and did well" until immigrants began moving into her neighborhood and her "quiet street became a place of noise and confusion." Gradually almost all of the white tenants left the neighborhood, and she ended up living alone in "growing fear," "afraid to go out [as] her windows [were] broken, excreta pushed through her letterbox," and she was followed everywhere by "wide grinning picannanies" (Powell, 1969, pp. 217-218). The white widow living alone, scared, and harassed, in her (now) "colored" neighborhood comes to function as a metaphor for the current situation in England and the seeming reversal of racial power relations within the English space.

In 1986 a repeated political broadcast by the Labor Party on "law and order" used a narrative about a fearful white woman to make a point about the lawless conditions in England brought about by immigrants. A young white woman in school uniform is seen hurriedly walking down a dark deserted road on the south side of London, an area heavily populated by immigrants. Heavy footsteps are heard, conveying the fact that she is being followed. The tension increases as she begins to walk faster. Just when we think she will be attacked we are relieved to find her in the arms of a man, a *white* policeman. This particular commercial, too, equates a white woman's safety with the safety of English society. The possible threat to her life is connected to immigrants, because the neighborhood through which she walks so nervously is one populated by blacks and immigrants.[5]

When placed against such a background, the importance of *The Jewel* as a television serial that has interracial rape as its central metaphor and that mesmerized the audience for months becomes clear. If, as Volosinov (1973) reminds us, every ideological sign acquires rhetorical power "through the process of social intercourse [and] is defined by the social purview of the given time period and given social group" (p. 21), then the rape narrative of *The Jewel* needs to be read as part of this larger intertextual phenomenon in which the figure of a violated white woman comes to function as a "sign" for a "raped" and "defiled" nation.

There are several significant rhetorical techniques through which the rape narrative is played out in *The Jewel.* Especially noteworthy is the way in which the story about the rape of Daphne Manners is delivered through rhetorical frameworks that rely on the ideological language of race in the present (that is, in the 1980s in England). A language is used by which blacks and immigrants, at the height of racial "riots" and anti-immigrant sentiments, are constituted through tropes of violence and savagery. I focus here on two significant rhetorical techniques through which the interracial rape is represented in the serial: the visual absence of the rape and the juxtaposition of the rape narrative against a framework of riots.

The first striking aspect about the rape narrative in *The Jewel* is the complete absence of any visual representation of it. This point is especially significant in light of the film's promotion line, that "this is a story about rape." If interracial rape is the fulcrum on which the film turns and organizes its plot, it becomes especially noteworthy that the rape is not shown but is left to the audience's imagination. Indeed, the similarity between *The Jewel* and *Passage to India* on this point is striking. The plot of both *The Jewel* and *Passage to India* hinge on the presence of an absence, the visual absence of an interracial rape of a white woman framed against the turbulent last few years of British rule in India.

Both films use strikingly similar ways of representing the site in which the absent rape is situated. The sites are ancient sites, liminal spaces on the borders of "civilization." In *The Jewel,* the site is an abandoned, unkempt historic garden littered with ruined buildings and statues. In *Passage,* the site is the dark caves on the high mountains of Marabar Hills, which resonate with the sounds of a savage echo, the carnal reverberations of which disrupt the very "civilized" language of English society. Both these sites are outside the civilized boundaries of English society— boundaries that the two white women, Daphne Manners and Adela Quested, dare to cross, for which they are punished.

Much like Powell's old widow, who is left behind by her white ex-neighbors and harassed by Others on the fringes of a civilized space, and much like the young white woman in the political commercial whose journey through South London is a journey beyond the civilized spaces of London, Daphne Manners and Adela Quested become subject to violence only when they abandon the sanctioned, civilized limits of English culture. In all these narratives, the distinction between a safe and wholesome society and an unsafe and violent society is underwritten through a spatial marking of a white woman's body and movement.

When these narratives are read intertextually with the larger political culture of the times, Daphne Manners, Adela Quested, Powell's widow, and the young white woman in the commercial all become signs for an English nation that has crossed over the limits of civilized space and is now being raped by colored people. Indeed, the fact that all of the rapes and attacks occur in borderland, in-between regions is additionally significant, because borders are intimately tied to immigrant flows and are the spaces where a nation is first seen to be "penetrated" by Others.

In the case of *The Jewel* the visual absence of the rape, and hence, the erasure of the rape scene from the narrative, is even more significant because of its difference from the original novel of 1966. In Paul Scott's (1966) novel *The Raj Quartet,* the rape scene is not delineated in an extended fashion. It is described in Daphne Manners's narrative where she talks of "that awful animal thrusting and the motion of love without one saving split-second of emotion" (p. 406), using a phrase that connects race to bestiality. But in the film there is no corresponding visual description. The "awful animal thrusting" on the body of a white woman in an interracial situation at a site abandoned by civilization is left to the imagination of an audience, at a time when racial riots were raging and public narratives were suffused with stories about threats to white women's safety.

There are two points in the film at which we, the audience, think we will be shown the rape and the rapists. But each time, the camera wrenches us away from the rape scene, teases us to imagine the rape and the rapists of a white woman, and refuses to provide any actual visual description. The first instance occurs during the narrative progression of the film toward the scene of the rape. We see Daphne Manners entering the Bibighar gardens on a night of intense riots by Indians. It is dark. Daphne is depicted through an extreme long shot that strategically reduces her figure and draws our attention to the eerie scenario that circumscribes her: the ruins, the unkempt garden, and the uncanny night filmed through a fluid blue filter. We alternately hear the distant cries of the rioters and an ominous music playing in the background. Daphne sees her Indian lover, Hari. We see Hari through an extreme long shot wearing white clothes, standing like a ghost at a remote distance, while a whiff of smoke from his cigarette wafts over the image. In a moment, as they begin to make love, the camera, refusing to let us see this interracial intercourse of love, abruptly cuts away to a hazy shot of native men lurking in the bushes at a distance. Their heads are covered and their features hardly distinguishable (we are given only a quick medium close-up shot of a pair of wild dark eyes).

At this point, when enough foreshadowing has been created through such editing techniques and we have been gradually prepared to see the rape that we know will occur at any moment, the camera suddenly switches to a long-distance shot of riots and the outbreak of lawlessness in the streets. The next time we see Daphne, we know from her visual appearance that she has been raped, but we don't know by whom. We can only speculate and make connections, based on the hints provided in the film—was it those native men hazily shown earlier, or was it any of the rioters on the streets, or was it Daphne's Indian lover Hari? However, it should be noted that this last possibility is canceled out very soon in the subsequent events.

The second instance in which we are again not presented with the rape occurs when Daphne recalls the rape a few days later; in this scene, through a flashback sequence, we are taken back to the scene of the rape. However, again, we are not presented with the rape. This time the camera builds up our curiosity but ultimately refuses to present the rape and the rapists. Just when we think we will be shown the actual rape and the rapists, the screen blanks out for a few seconds at the very moment the camera was beginning to show us incoherent shapes of five or six men in loose native clothes, filmed from the shoulders down (so we don't see their faces), covering Daphne's head. A chilling scream pierces the blank screen. And then we are jolted back to the present.

To adequately grasp the rhetorical force of this mode of representing the rape, this discursive feature needs to be seen in conjunction with yet another rhetorical feature: that of the constant framing of the rape against a narrative of riots. It is significant that throughout the film, references to the rape remain juxtaposed with references to the 1942 "riots" by Indians in India, which had generated intense anti-British feelings. For instance, the entire first scene at the Bibighar Gardens (which is also the locale where Daphne is raped) is narratively positioned against a background of riots. Daphne enters the gardens on the night of the riots. Just prior to this scene, we were shown footage of Indian rioters in the streets. As Daphne enters the Bibighar gardens, we hear faraway cries of rioters in the background. When the camera leaves this scene, where the rape takes place, it does so against the shots of angry Indian rioters marching in the streets carrying "Quit India" placards, providing images of the breakdown of law and order in the streets.

Such a framing of the rape against a background of riots is also seen in other instances in the film. For example, at the MacGregor house, when Daphne is lying on her bed recalling the rape, her recollections are accompanied by background sounds of gunshots, suggesting the ongoing riots in the streets. In the scene in which Daphne is asked by the English Deputy Commissioner, Robin Williams, whether she could provide a description of the rapists, she replies that they were "five or six men of that kind . . . hooligans, laborers, smelling of the awful smell that you get in third class compartments of Indian trains." This brief scene is again juxtaposed with footage of rioters in the streets carrying banners screaming anti-British slogans. One year later in Kashmir, when we are first introduced to Sarah Layton and her family, around whom the next 11 episodes of the serial are centered, one of the first exchanges that we hear between Sarah and her mother is about the rape of the now-dead Daphne and the riots of Mayapore. Thus, throughout the film, the rape and the riots are constantly linked together. We are not allowed to think of the rape without also being reminded of the riots.

I suggest that these two rhetorical aspects through which the rape functions in the film—the visual absence of the rape and its discursive framing by a narrative of riots—work together to reinforce the national imagery of the present (1980s), in which blacks and immigrants were seen as threatening to what Alfred Sherman (1979) once called "all that is English and wholesome." An English audience watching this serial at the height of racial riots in 1984 is not allowed to see the rape or to identify the rapists, but is instead teased into speculating about both through a framework of riots. This creates a rhetorical situation in which the audience, in lieu of any alternative information about the rape and rapists within the film, is rhetorically invited to pick from the current repertoire of ideologically charged images of blacks and Asians rioting in the streets of England in order to imagine the kind of men who might have violated a white woman on a night of intense riots in England's colonial past. The unseen rape that takes place against a night of violence in England's imperial past now acquires a localized significance in the present. The unidentified rapists in the film can now be easily imagined through racist images of the present. These are images so familiar and so easily available to the audience at this time. As Daphne Manners reminds the audience in her vague testimony of the rape: "I can't remember who they were. Their faces were covered. But what does it matter, *they all look alike, don't they?*" [emphasis added].

Indeed, in this colonial imagination, it does not matter who they were. The generic nonwhite male in the colonial imagination can occupy only one position in relation to a white woman, that is, the "always already" position of the hypersexual savage. The above comment by Manners is reinforced through the visual rhetoric of the serial. Because the audience is never able to identify the rapists, but can see them only through fragmented shots in which they all wear similar clothes or hazy shots that show them from the back and as interchangeable with each other, it does not matter who they were. Their individuality is not important. What is important in this narrative logic is that their bodies are collectively marked as a source and site of violence and savagery.

This rhetorical linkage between the rape in the serial and the situation in England in the 1980s works precisely because of the visual absence of the rape in the narrative. Instead of particularizing the rape as one specific instance that occurred in the past, the visual absence of the rape reinforces a normative memory about violence, white womanhood, and interracial relationships—a universal language in Anglo-Western culture about the fear of black male sexuality and its lust for the white female—the symbol of civilization.

The "Raj Revival" films such as *The Jewel* cogently illustrate the following. First, how colonial memory, that is, how one imagines the colonial past and what one chooses to remember of that past, is informed by the ideological forces of the present. In the imagining of the colonial past, the lines between colonialism and neocolonialism become blurred, for the ex-colonizer's remembrance of colonialism is always informed by her or his particular historical positioning in the present. Thus, the fact that the British Raj period in India is being remembered in the 1980s through the narrative of a white woman's rape and through a framework of riots is significant. Indeed, the framework through which the colonial past is remembered in *The Jewel* is reminiscent of a crucial point once made by Walter Benjamin about historical representations of the past in the present: "to articulate the past historically does not mean to recognize it 'the way it was.' It means to seize hold of a memory as it flashes up at a moment of danger" (quoted in Lowe, 1996, p. 97).

Second, a text such as *The Jewel* amply demonstrates one important rhetorical process that frequently surfaces during nationalist crises: the disarticulation of a group of meanings and symbols from a particular set of historical associations and its rearticulation to the present. It demonstrates how the language of the nation is always a cultural construction in which narratives of the past meet the needs of the present and forge new narratives, while often retaining in the process the larger rhetorical framework of the past through which the new narrative is delivered in the present. In this case, the fact that the language of the rape of a white woman in the colonial past of 1942 is resurrected in the present and is able to acquire such a grip on the viewing audience's imagination is significant.

Third, the serial underscores the centrality of the figure of the white woman in colonial imagination. It is significant that in *The Jewel*, the colonial conflict between the British and the Indians seems to be remembered through, and reduced to, a battle over the figure of the white woman, that is, who gets to "possess" her. Of course, colonial conflicts between Indians and British were much more that. The possession of the white woman and the struggle to "protect" her from dark savages seem to be central strands through which colonial times and the battle between the colonizer and colonized are envisioned in these films. The white female body is the property of colonial patriarchy and is the site through which racial hierarchy is battled over. For a white woman to be penetrated by Others (resulting in the possibility of the birth of mixed racial groups) is the beginning of the loss of a "pure" white identity.[6]

In *The Jewel*, Daphne Manners reverses and challenges racial rules in her relationship with the Other in the person of Hari Kumar. Hence, she has to be punished. She is raped. We are shown what kind of violence can be enacted on white women's bodies when they disrupt the racial norms set up by colonial logic about their movements and sexual desires. As one of the characters in the serial notes, "that Manners girl was warned that she was heading for it [the rape]." Daphne is narratively disciplined because she dared to cross the limits of civilized Englishness. We are left with the sense that if she had not crossed the spatial and cultural borders within which the English resided, her body would have been protected and her identity would have remained intact. For example, after the rape, she is portrayed as going crazy. This is significant, for it reminds one of the madness metaphors used by Enoch Powell in his famous "Rivers of Blood" speech to argue about the loss of an English essence in the face of "foreign" penetration. Daphne becomes a reminder to white women viewing this serial in the 1980s about what can happen when they dare to cross the racial logic that defines and circumscribes an essential English space and that simultaneously coconstructs and marks the limits of their racial movements.

Cultural narratives such as *The Jewel,* as well as other reports that deployed the figure of the violated white woman in England at this time, are reminiscent of a point once made by the notable cultural theorist of nationalism, Chatterjee (1990). Chatterjee argues that during a crisis in national identity or during the rearticulation of a national hegemony, issues of nationhood often end up being discursively inscribed on the body of the woman. Woman becomes a symbolic site through which cultural and political struggles are waged in the name of her defense and protection. Yet, in such struggles, woman's agency becomes bracketed as she becomes bound to yet another form of subordination. Her body and social space are subjected to various forms of discursive control, carried out in the name of preserving a national essence. Central to this control is the containment and policing of women's sexual desires, because the breeding and preserving of a dominant ethnic collective is reliant on the control of woman's sexual agency, especially when such sexuality dares to cross the lines of social acceptability.

By using the trope of a violated female body, national narratives such as *The Jewel* perform a double articulation wherein the discursive construction and disciplining of racial Others rest on a simultaneous regulation of women's sexual behavior and agency. To successfully breed the dominant ethnic collective in the face of a threatening multicultural landscape, women's sexual desires have to be disciplined and conditioned through regimes of discourse and representations that engender fear of interracial sexual relationships and that prevent voluntary interracial unions. In the colonial logic represented in *The Jewel,* the containment of a foreign body (Hari Kumar) becomes coterminous with the containment of a female body (Daphne Manners), and both find oppressive and obsessive expression in the figure of a raped woman. The biopolitics enacted over Daphne's body ultimately express a microphysics of racist power. Daphne's desire for the racial Other (Hari Kumar) becomes interrupted by the Nationalist "Law of the Father." Sexual desire is disciplined by colonial desire, and viewers are invited to imagine a sexual relation between a white woman and a nonwhite man through fear, violence, and death, because Daphne dies soon after her rape.

What is problematic about the symbolic usage of Daphne's body in *The Jewel* is that it is deployed to foreground rape and violence as markers of interracial relationships when it could very well have been employed to signify the possibility of interracial love, desire, and harmony (since the love between Daphne and Hari is a key element in the narrative). By positioning and promoting the narrative as a "story of rape" when it could also have been positioned as a "story of love," the film foregrounds a vision of multicultural relations that is to be primarily understood through a rhetoric of violence and failure. No matter how attractive the relationship between Daphne and Hari is, we are assured from the beginning that it will not work. Rape is the primary way in which we are invited to conceptualize the relationship between nonwhite males and white females, because its discursive presence dominates the entire narrative.

Although the film does allow some interracial romance between Daphne and Hari to flourish, ultimately colonial logic takes over. Daphne dies, and Hari is thrown into prison (which is itself a space for containing unwanted bodies). All that remains is a tiny transnationalism: Daphne's "bastard" (brown, *female*) child is kept hidden from (and hence denied to) English society, and her originating identity is never clarified. We never know whether the child was a product of rape or love, suggesting that where the entry of a nonwhite person into a white world is concerned, they mean one and the same. The future of race relations becomes interpreted only through violence, and the potential of positive race relations is denied to English society (much like Daphne's bastard child, the future of black and white is suppressed in the text).

PATRIARCHAL IMPLICATIONS
OF THE RAPE NARRATIVE

When we situate the rape narrative of *The Jewel* with numerous other public narratives of the times in which stories about attacks and rapes of white women were being used to contribute to a cultural imagination about the defilement of the English nation, the centrality of a defiled white female body in this imagination becomes clear. The white female body becomes a trope through which the logic of recuperating an essential Englishness by eliminating the penetration of Others is perpetuated. Indeed, such a discursive utilization of a (raped or defiled) female body by cultural narratives as they deal with the threat of foreign penetration is not unique to the English context but has also surfaced in the cultural language of numerous other nations.[7]

Such discursive use of a raped female body to symbolize a defiled national or cultural body is problematic for various reasons and needs to be severely countered by feminist critiques of nationalism. First, such rape scripts sustain a patriarchal narrative that reduces woman's body to the status of property and frames the racial and national struggle against Others in terms of ownership of that body. In such an equation, woman's sexuality becomes recoded as violable property (and seemingly violable only by racial Others), because the notion of woman as property lies at the root of rape.

Second, in this equation of a raped female body with an invaded nation, the female body ends up functioning as a signifier for the failure and powerlessness of the nation. On the other hand, national narratives often code moments of success, such as winning a war or going to war, through masculine tropes. For example, during the Falklands War (which was fought in this same time period), the English nation in Thatcher's war rhetoric was metaphorically coded as a tough, masculine adventurer battling rough, distant seas to save a tiny island from bandit-like aggressors. Thatcher claimed in her victory speech that "we fought to show that aggression does not pay and that the robber cannot be allowed to get away with his swag" (McFadyean & Renn, 1984, p. 108). In contrast to this very heroic and masculine image of England fighting battles against robbers in distant seas, public narratives at this time, as I have demonstrated, were coding the nation's internal crisis of "lawlessness" by immigrants through the trope of a violated, defiled female body. This is problematic, because the subtext implies that just as a nation is "raped" when it lacks the strength to defend itself, similarly, a woman is violated when *she* is unable to protect herself. The onus of rape in such a logic rests on the woman.

In addition, such a logic also reenacts a narrative in which the female body continues to be coded as the "second sex." That is, her body is weak, powerless, and frail, and hence it is appropriated to signify loss, death, and erosion of a national essence. Thus, woman and the female body become pejorative in such a script; they become a sign of the nation "unmanned."

Third, such rape scripts deployed by national narratives, however oppressive, are primarily about the nation's recognition only of women of the dominant ethnicity. The protection of the nation is usually not framed in terms of the protection of minority women. For example, whereas in the English national context at this time, the figure of a violated and attacked white woman was being used to rewrite a national narrative about a defiled English body, such rewriting had little to do with the violations and abuse that numerous black women suffered at the hands of neofascist groups such as the National Front and with the systemic racism of police violence in their everyday existence. In a survey (Hall, 1985) of 1,236 women (white and nonwhite) in London at this time by the feminist organization Women Against Rape, or WAR, 28% of all immigrant and black women noted that they had actually been physically assaulted because of their race, nationality, or both; 12% noted that they had been sexually assaulted because of their race; and 62% noted that they had been verbally assaulted because of their race. The point here is not that nonwhite women were the *only* targets of sexual violence, but that they were *also* targets of numerous violent acts, a point that seems to have been covered up in the New Right script of perpetuating a nationalist agenda through a discourse of a violated white woman.[8] Indeed, the nationalist appropriation of the rape script performs a double violence against the figure of the woman; not only does it discursively appropriate the female body to enact racist and masculinist hopes, it also renders invisible to the national imagination the bodies of numerous minority women who are subjected to all forms of violence during national unrest.

The "Raj Revival" films such as *The Jewel,* then, were much more than a simple expression of "colonialist nostalgia." They were a crucial part of the New Right discourse of race and nation in the 1980s in England, in which Englishness was seen as being defiled in the face of a threatening multiculturalism. *The Jewel* told a certain story about British history in India. Significant to that story was the way in which the past was delivered and imagined in the present through the trope of a violated white female body. In her groundbreaking book *Fictions of Feminist Ethnography* (1994), Kamla Visweswaran asks the question, if history or a historical representation is "ultimately the telling of a nation, what, then are the mnemonics of that history?" (p. 68). She continues, "[How] are identities of self related to the mechanics of memory, and the relevance of the past?" (p. 68).

If we understand that media narratives are national narratives, then in the case of *The Jewel* these become important questions. *The Jewel* cogently illustrates how the cultural mechanics of colonial memory in the 1980s in England were informed by the trope of a violated white female body. The fact that this articulation and linkage between the past and present was being made through the trope of a raped white female body illustrates yet again how central the metaphor of rape is in nationalist narratives as they define a national space against the invasion of Others. The centrality of the race-sex link is demonstrated in the imperial redrawing and reinforcement of racialized national boundaries, as well as

in the discursive containment of the female body to perpetuate and preserve notions of a racialized national essence. The link is inherently patriarchal in its hopes, desires, and enactments. In enacting racialized national hopes through and over the female body, *The Jewel* illustrates
convincingly that the language of nationalism is a language that springs
from "masculinized memory, masculinized humiliation, and masculinized hopes" (Enloe, 1990, p. 44).

NOTES

1. For a fuller description of these issues, see Hall et al. (1978) and Hall (1988).

2. The New Right rhetoric was scattered in various other places and not just confined to
political speeches. Peregrine Worthstone, a leading national writer of the Right Wing
Sunday Telegraph, wrote that "birds that are not of a same feather, do not flock together at
all easily" (quoted in Gordon & Klug, 1986, p. 18). The *Daily Express,* a right-wing
newspaper, in one of its representative editorials contended that "it is equally wrong not to
recognize that racial selectivity—a natural human preference for one's own kind—is
deeply ingrained in ALL peoples" (April 18, 1984, p. A5). Enoch Powell, the person whose
rhetoric laid the seeds for much of Thatcher's rhetoric, used metaphors of death and
madness to argue that "those whom the gods wish to destroy, they first make mad. We must
be mad, literally mad, as a nation to be permitting the annual flow of 50,000 dependents. . . .
It is like watching a nation busily engaged in heaping up its own funeral pyre" (Powell,
1969, p. 215).

3. In England the term *black* is used broadly to connote all nonwhite people.

4. Consider, for example, how stories about rapes and fear of rapes of white women by
Native Americans were also used during the "civilizing" of the West in the United States to
monitor racial interaction between "natives" and whites and to reinforce a racial hierarchy
by curtailing the possibility of the emergence of mixed racial groups.

5. Other examples abound of this use of the trope of white womanhood. For example, an
October 1981 issue of *The Times* ran a story about a "wolf pack" comprised of "black
muggers" that "hunted the streets of South London" and lurked in shadows "before
pouncing on women" walking alone. We are told that "when victims put up a fight, they
[are] punched, beaten, and kicked into submission." This story was placed only two
columns away from another story about a rape: the rape of a young white girl by a doctor,
whose foreign status is confirmed by his name, Ashby de la Zouch. In between these two
stories was strategically positioned a long debate about the "fairness" of the 1981
Nationality Act.

> In January 1982, the rape of a white woman in Glasgow and the alleged rapists'
> being set free took over the public imagination, and stories about it flashed across
> several newspapers. Jack Ashley, MP Labor, wrote a strong letter to the prime
> minister in which he linked these rapes of women to the failure of the "Crown"
> (therefore nation) to protect women and to prevent the breakdown of English
> civilization. This letter was printed in the front page of several newspapers,
> including *The Times.*

6. Even though in *Passage to India,* it is ultimately determined that Aziz did not actually rape Adela Quested, for my purpose that does not matter. What does matter is that the narrative of the film centers on a discourse of interracial rape.

7. See also Hall's (1983) classic essay on this point.

8. For example, in India, Nehru used the trope of a raped-violated female body to describe the British invasion. In Uganda, Idi Amin, in his desire to reconstitute the "authentic Ugandan woman," targeted a group of women who were discovered to be providing sexual services to European men. These women were coded as "violated" and were used as symbols for a nation space that was seen as being violated by Europeans. During the Gulf War, George Bush deployed the rape metaphor to describe the "penetration" of Kuwait by the "savage" Saddam. Journalistic narratives, such as Mascernhas's (1979) *Rape of Bangladesh,* a narrative about Bangladesh's penetration by West Pakistan, have also often invoked the rape metaphor to describe the invasions of nations. Indeed, again and again in the cultural language of the nation, we find that a rape script is employed to perpetuate and describe a sense of national defilement.

9. In much the same way, while discussing the "rape" of Kuwait and enacting a "protection" narrative, the Bush government ignored the numerous rapes of Sri Lankan and Filipino workers, for that would certainly have implicated many Kuwaiti men and would have interfered in the enactment of the United States' war rhetoric of protecting Kuwait, which was coded as having been "feminized" by Saddam's savage penetration.

REFERENCES

Anderson, B. (1991). *Imagined communities: Reflections on the origin and spread of nationalism.* New York: Verso. (Original work published 1983)

Brandt, G. W. (1993). *The Jewel in the Crown:* The literary serial; or the art of adaptation. In G. W. Brandt (Ed.), *British television drama in the 1980s.* Cambridge, UK: Cambridge University Press.

Chatterjee, P. (1990). The nationalist resolution of the woman's question. In K. Sangari & S. Vaid (Eds.), *Recasting women: Essays in Indian colonial history* (pp. 233-253). New Delhi: Kali Press.

Condit, C. (1991). Rhetorical limits of polysemy. *Critical Studies in Mass Communication, 6,* 103-122.

Enloe, C. (1990). *Bananas, beaches, bases: Making feminist sense of international politics.* Berkeley: University of California Press.

Gilroy, P. (1987). *There ain't no black in the Union Jack.* London: Hutchinson.

Gilroy, P. (1993). *Small acts.* London: Serpent's Tail.

Gordon, P., & Klug, F. (1986). *New right, new racism.* London: Searchlight.

Hall, J. D. (1983). The mind that burns in each body: Women, rape, and racial violence. In A. Snitow, C. Stansell, & S. Thompson (Eds.), *Powers of desire: The Politics of Sexuality* (pp. 328-349). New York: Monthly Review Press.

Hall, R. E. (1985). *Ask any woman: A London inquiry into rape and sexual assault.* Bristol, UK: Falling Wall Press.

Hall, S. (1988). *The hard road to renewal.* London: Verso.

Hall, S., Critcher, C., Jefferson, T., Clarke, J., & Roberts, B. (1978). *Policing the crisis: Mugging, the state, and law and order.* London: Macmillan.

Higson, A. (1993). Re-presenting the national past: Nostalgia and pastiche in the heritage films. In L. Friedman (Ed.), *Fires were started: British cinema and Thatcherism* (pp. 109-129). Minneapolis: University of Minnesota Press.

Jeffords, S. (1994). *Hard bodies: Hollywood masculinity in the Reagan era.* New Brunswick, NJ: Rutgers University Press.

Layoun, M. (1994). The female body and transnational reproduction. In C. Kaplan & I. Grewal (Eds.), *Scattered hegemonies* (pp. 63-75). Minneapolis: University of Minnesota Press.

Lowe, L. (1996). *Immigrant acts.* Durham, NC: Duke University Press.

Mascernhas, S. (1979). *Rape of Bangladesh.* Bombay: Kali Press.

McFadyean, M., & Renn, M. (1984). *Thatcher's reign: A bad case of blues.* London: Hogarth Press.

Mehta, G. (1985, April). All the raj. *Vogue,* 188-193.

Powell, E. (1969). *Freedom and reality.* New York: Arlington House.

Radcliffe, S., & Westwood, S. (1996). Remaking the nation: Place, identity, and politics in Latin America. New York: Routledge.

Rushdie, S. (1991). *Imaginary homelands: Essays and criticism, 1981-1991.* London: Penguin.

Scott, P. (1966). *The Raj Quartet.* New York: Avon.

Sherman, A. (1979, September 9). Britain's urge to self-destruction. *The Daily Telegraph,* p. A5.

Shohat, E., & Stam, R. (1994). *Unthinking eurocentrism: Multiculturalism and the media.* New York: Routledge.

Shome, R. (1996a). Postcolonial interventions in the rhetorical canon: An "other" view. *Communication Theory, 6,* 40-59.

Shome, R. (1996b). Race and popular cinema: The rhetorical strategies of whiteness. *Communication Quarterly, 44,* 502-518.

Shome, R. (1999). Whiteness and the politics of location: Postcolonial reflections. In T. K. Nakayama & J. Martin (Eds.), *Whiteness: The communication of social identity* (pp. 107-128). Thousand Oaks, CA: Sage.

Visweswaran, K. (1994). *Fictions of feminist ethnography.* Minneapolis: University of Minnesota Press.

Volosinov, V. N. (1973). *Marxism and the philosophy of language.* London: Seminar Press.

Ware, V. (1983/1984, Winter). Imperialism, racism, and violence against women. *Emergency,* 25-30.

Waters, H. (1994, December). Television: The season's transcultural gem. *Newsweek,* 102-104.

7

Similar or Different?

The Chinese Experience of Japanese Culture

YOKO NADAMITSU • *Josai International University*
LING CHEN • *Hong Kong Baptist University*
GUSTAV FRIEDRICH • *Rutgers University*

INTRODUCTION

Japan and China are close geographically, and much of their philosophical and cultural heritage is a shared legacy. It is natural, therefore, for people unfamiliar with the Eastern world to overlook differences between these two cultures. This is clearly reflected in cross-cultural communication studies, which focus on comparisons and contrasts of Eastern and Western perspectives. Typically, Asian cultures (such as Japanese, Chinese, and Korean) are studied with reference to, or in contrast to, Western cultures such as the United States (e.g., Yum, 1987). The tendency to consider Chinese and Japanese cultures as very similar to each other is also found in major intercultural communication textbooks, where maximal cultural differences are presented, implicitly or explicitly, between Asian and U.S. American cultures (e.g., Dodd, 1991; Gudykunst & Kim, 1992; Samovar & Porter, 1995).

Much cross-cultural communication research has explored the relation between culture and various types of communication behavior using the construct of individualism and collectivism. Hofstede's work (1980, 1983), and that of others since, concludes that Eastern cultures are more collectivistic than European and North American cultures. A large number of cross-cultural and intercultural communication studies have assumed this East-West difference as a starting point for investigation of cultural influence on a range of communication practices, from in-group and out-group relationships (Gudykunst, Yoon, & Nishida, 1987), to conflict styles (Trubisky, Ting-Toomey, & Lin, 1991), to communica-

158

tion goals (Kim, 1993). Furthermore, past cross-cultural research has suggested that a collectivistic orientation is closely related to a high-context communication style (Gudykunst & Ting-Toomey, 1988). This view has often led to an assumption that Japanese and Chinese cultures employ high-context communication styles, that is, a mode of communication in which most of the information is conveyed by context, and little is expressed in explicit verbal messages (Hall, 1976).

This focus on the East-West contrast, together with a reliance on one dimension for comparison, has emphasized similarities between Japan and China. In the past, cross-cultural communication studies have classified both Japanese and Chinese as collectivistic cultures, and thus, by comparison to Western cultures, both Japanese and Chinese are presumed to employ high-context communication. As a result, differences between these two Eastern cultures, as is true for all non-Western cultures, have been largely overlooked. Moreover, research in the past has largely taken a positivistic approach, with operational definitions of the concepts in the studies based on Western thinking. This approach is inadequate for identifying subtle nuances or underlying differences in the diverse cultures classified as collectivistic, because from a Western perspective these subtle differences are often regarded as unimportant.

Several scholars have challenged the positivistic approach to understanding intercultural communication—an approach that often labels cultures using essentialist assumptions. In a study on the role of communication for Chinese interpersonal relations, for example, Chang and Holt (1991) let Chinese informants talk, interpret, and define their own interpersonal relations instead of imposing etic, universal constructs on the information informants provided. The findings of this study challenge the commonly held perception that the Chinese, being collectivistic, use an indirect communication style. Based on similar assumptions, Lee, Wang, Chung, and Hertel (1995) call for multivocality, or different voices, within broad groups (e.g., women, people of color, Asians) in contextualized settings.[1] Collier (1998) also points out that binary and dualistic assumptions about cultural orientation (e.g., collectivistic vs. individualistic, high- vs. low-context) misrepresent within-group differences. She asserts that cultural identity is constructed in relation to one another and that "people enact identity to distinguish themselves, the 'insiders,' from others, the 'outsiders'" (Collier, 1998, p. 132).

Martin and Nakayama (1999) propose a dialectical approach to studying intercultural interaction to transcend dichotomy and its inherent mutual exclusivity. This approach entertains the notion that two contradictory ideas can coexist simultaneously and that multiple realities do exist. An objective of our research, then, should be to explore how differences and similarities emerge and work in various contexts. Although we approach cross-cultural communication from different angles, we share the general view that culture is social and relational, not objective or empirically independent.

To recognize that culture is a social reality is akin to accepting that it is socially constructed, which is a broad methodological perspective adopted in this study. The social construction perspective is premised on the assumption that cultural norms and practices are not fixed properties but rather are constituted in members' daily activities and social interactions. It acknowledges that "people categorize the world the way they do because they have participated in social practices, institutions, and other forms of symbolic action (for example, language) that presuppose or in some way make salient those categorizations" (Miller, 1991, p. 156). People construct and sustain reality in terms of their own cultural assumptions and cultural mandates, which in turn are made real in members' communication and interactions (Mumby, 1998). Thus, cultural identity emerges from the stories and talks that people share in their day-to-day activities (Cronen & Lang, 1994). People come to know who they are in relation to others and by their understanding of coherent cultural patterns that are constantly configured and shaped by context and that are reflected in their episodes of lived experience.

Within a general theoretical framework of the social construction perspective, our research program examines how insiders of Asian cultures labeled as collectivistic, namely Japanese and Chinese, perceive their differences and similarities. It is understood that, in the process of understanding social and cultural phenomena, multiple meanings can be provided and expressed by different voices. That is, different realities can simultaneously be constructed, coexist, and be made sense of, depending on how the phenomenon is interpreted and talked about. Because the current study looks at how Chinese perceive and interpret Japanese communicative behaviors,[2] Chinese cultural values and social norms inevitably form the frame of reference in which Japanese persons and Japanese behaviors are described and explained. Chinese informants' descriptions and interpretations of their experiences with Japanese, as part of their cultural practice, also reveal information about themselves.

Because this project is an initial exploration of similarities and differences as seen in communication within and between the two cultures, we opt for listening carefully to what cultural members say and letting them define the phenomena in their own terms. For this purpose, intensive one-on-one interviewing was considered the most appropriate methodology.[3] Our research question here is, "How do Chinese perceive Japanese as different in their cultural practices and communication behaviors?"

PROCEDURES

Informants

A total of 33 ethnic Chinese informants participated in the interviews.[4] The selection of Chinese informants was based on the criteria that they be from the People's Republic of China and have extensive experience with both Japanese and Chinese cultures. All Chinese informants were fluent in Japanese language. Also, the informants had regular and frequent interaction with members of the Japanese society.

There were 18 men and 15 women. The average age of male informants was 32.1 years, with a range from 25 to 40 years; the average age of the female informants was 33 years, with a range from 27 to 42 years. All participants except one had lived in Japan.[5] The length of time participants had lived in Japan varied from 1.5 years to 10 years. All participants were college educated. While in Japan, their occupations were as graduate students, company employees, college students, and university professors; there was also a kindergarten teacher and a freelance interpreter. Their occupations in China before arriving in Japan included high school student, college student, graduate student, college lecturer, medical doctor, government official, and company employee.

Data Collection

The first author contacted 33 individuals by letter and telephone to solicit their participation. Confidentiality of the informants' identities and the information provided was guaranteed orally over the telephone and in writing at the beginning of the interviews. Interviews were conducted in Japanese.[6] The length of interviews ranged from 1 to 3 hours, depending on the amount of information the interviewee was willing to share. The interview location was selected for the informants' convenience (e.g., a meeting room at a university, a facility for international students, or an informant's residence).

Informants were asked to describe their experiences in Japan and China. The informants were encouraged to elaborate and to provide detailed descriptions of their lived experience and their understanding of the incidents they described. The interviewer probed for stories that might not be revealed spontaneously.[7] The interviewer took notes of key concepts and expressions in the interview, and interviews were tape-recorded with the informant's permission. For two informants who were unwilling to be tape-recorded, detailed field notes were used for analysis.[8] The recorded interviews were fully transcribed as data and were analyzed and categorized using the coding procedure described below.

Data Analysis

In analysis, a major goal was to identify important underlying themes in the stories by the informants that would delineate differences between Japanese and Chinese. There were two stages in analysis. First, primary themes underlying the descriptions of Japanese and Chinese were identified. Then, the themes of these two data sets were compared and contrasted for further analysis.

For the purpose of the first stage, raw recorded stories were divided into elements that might be counted and compared using a "coding procedure" described by Strauss and Corbin (1990). Their technique consists of three stages: open coding, axial coding, and selective coding.

Open coding consists of "the process of breaking down, examining, comparing, conceptualizing, and categorizing data" (Strauss & Corbin, 1990, p. 61). This initial coding required the researcher to repeatedly review the record of the interviews (written transcripts and recordings). Each interview had categories of discrete instances of phenomena onto which different conceptual labels were placed. For instance, categories of Japanese characteristics might be "compliance with peer pressure" and "obedience to superiors."

Axial coding attempted to compare and contrast individual interview data. This involved an attempt to analyze the data into fundamental recurrent units across the interviews while simultaneously synthesizing categories into which those units fit. For example, a category that was repeatedly identified as "compliance with peer pressure" and as a Japanese characteristic was synthesized with another category, "avoidance of sticking out," which also often appeared in the primary category "Conformity." There was an effort to divorce the identification of elements and categories from the process of drawing general conclusions. In other words, the concepts that were drawn from open coding were reorganized as subcategories of primary conceptual categories.

In selective coding, core categories, which were the most important and encompassing concepts, were selected. A core category reflects "the central phenomenon around which all the other categories are integrated" (Strauss & Corbin, 1990, p. 116). For example, the category of "Conformity" was related to another primary category, "Strong In-Group and Out-Group Distinction." Thus, two primary categories that were drawn from axial coding, "Conformity" and "Strong In-Group and Out-Group Distinction," were integrated into a core category labeled "Strong Group Collectivity." By examining primary categories that were established during axial coding, a network of conceptual relationships of these categories was refined, and primary categories were integrated into core categories.

In the first stage of analysis, Japanese and Chinese data sets were independently analyzed using Strauss and Corbin's (1990) coding procedure. In the second stage of analysis, the themes of these two data sets were compared and contrasted. Some themes were found for descriptions of both Japanese and Chinese societies and could be paired as polar contrasts or antitheses with the two societies at opposite ends. Other themes described the presence or absence of a feature from the informants' accounts for one or the other society. The absence or presence of a theme then took one of two forms: (a) the difference between perceptions of the two cultures regarding that feature is one of degree, or (b) the differences lie in the absence of that feature for descriptions of one culture.

RESULTS AND DISCUSSION

The social construction approach assumes that one's reality is socially constructed and thus that multiple interpretations and explanations of a social phenomenon can exist, depending on the observers' historical backgrounds and cultural orientations. In other words, cultural and social expectations shape and regulate one's reality in addition to giving meaning to one's experience. Thus, Chinese informants' descriptions and explanations of Japanese behaviors are reflections of their view of cultural realities and, to a large extent, of their understanding based on their own cultural patterns and values. The raw data are observations and reflections of Chinese informants, with Chinese natives as the frame of reference. No attempt is made to generalize beyond that. Ultimately, we can interpret this data set on the basis of what Chinese think they are, in contrast to Japanese, and how their experience of Japanese culture is understood, constructed, and communicated.

Careful examination of the interview data uncovers several underlying themes that describe what the informants see as distinctly Japanese characteristics, which they do not share. In general, the informants perceive Japanese in this way:

> I picture Japanese as a school of fish. They look pretty. They have a unique communicating style. They don't have to use words to understand one another. Also, relationships within the school of fish are cold. They don't touch one another like other animals do—there is water between them. . . . Japanese feel safe as long as they are in a group, but out of a group, they can't survive—just like fish in a school. For example, one fish leads the school, and the other fish in the school follow the lead fish unquestioningly. If the leader dies, another will take over the position. But any fish can take the lead position, or rather, the school of fish can function even without a leader. . . . A group of Japanese moves smoothly and gracefully just like a school of fish. They work days and nights. . . . It is said that Japanese work like bees, but I don't think that's so. Bees are noisy. Japanese are quiet just like fish. (14M)[9]

Several themes emerged relating to the notion of self and others (both groups and individuals) and were grouped into two core categories: (a) sense of the collective and of the individual, and (b) social and personal relationship maintenance. There are several primary themes in each core category. Primary themes included in the category of the collective and of the individual are conformity, cohesiveness, group boundaries and membership, and person-to-person linkage (i.e., interpersonal bonding). For the category of social and personal relationship maintenance, primary themes include a sense of hierarchy, the level of formality, and the relationship among family and friends.[10] The two core categories and related primary themes are described and examined in the next section.

A Sense of the Collective and of the Individual

The Japanese word *gaman* (self-sacrifice, patient cooperation) occurred frequently in interviews, as informants attempted to describe uniquely Japanese characteristics that contrast with Chinese characteristics. Words that Chinese informants used to characterize themselves included *kojin* (individual) and *kojinshugi* (individualistic). All Chinese informants agreed that the collectivity or group consciousness of the Japanese, as reflected in social groups and organizations, was in sharp contrast to their own casual attitude toward social groups in general. Several Chinese informants used the following Chinese saying to characterize the unattached disposition of individuals in their society: "One Chinese is worth a dragon, but three Chinese are just as good as three bugs."

Primary themes that enhance the concepts of collectivity and individuality as the difference between the two societies include: (a) conformity, (b) group cohesiveness, (c) group boundaries and membership, and (d) person-to-person linkage as the base of human relations.

Conformity. This is a theme applied only to Japanese. Conformity describes a general tendency to "do what others do" or "be like everybody else," with emphasis on group uniformity and pressure to conform to group norms (Lebra, 1976). Conformity was seen as a reflection of a "strong sense of collectivity"; this view of conformity is seen in a typically straightforward expression of this opinion:

> What struck me most was Japanese group consciousness. That is very strong. They judge people by their group affiliation. Chinese are quite individualistic. (15M)

Many informants reported the peer pressure they observed in such cases as social gatherings of Japanese companies, where people do what others do, even if they may wish to take another course of action:

> There is a company year-end party that everyone is expected to attend. I don't like to go. But I have no choice. It doesn't look good if I don't go. I go to such a party, say, three times out of five. I will come up with some good excuses so that I don't have to go at least a couple of times. (4M)

The strong norm of "Do as others do" was reported for after-work socialization as well as for routines at work. Strong group conformity obviously affects the members' behaviors. One informant described her Japanese college classmates as being part of a culture where everyone "act[s] almost all alike." Many said that they had adjusted to the Japanese way and stopped doing things differently. Sticking out in a group (e.g., by initiating changes in a group, expressing one's opinion openly, competing with other members, or acting differently from the majority), participants explained, is regarded so negatively by the Japanese that few were willing to act out of line.

The Japanese tendency to adjust behavior to others for the sake of group unity and good interpersonal relations was described by Chinese informants as a nonconfrontational communication style.

> When they have to decide something in a group, first they wait and see what the majority opinion is, and then decide what they should say. So what they say may not be what they really think. (32F)

> In Japan, they don't express their opinions much. I feel that if I say something, they will follow what I said without much debating. That makes it rather uncomfortable for me to tell them my opinions. (1M)

These stories illustrate that Japanese are seen as following the majority instead of expressing individual preferences and are seen as quickly conforming to what everybody else seems to be doing. Informants did not discuss explicitly how Chinese act with regard to conformity. However, they expressed a reluctance to conform in the way the Japanese do and explained the change in their own behaviors in Japan to accommodate Japanese social conformity. By relating observations of Japanese conformity, especially their own adjustments to it, the informants presented the conformity as a practice that was unfamiliar to the Chinese. Informants stressed that Chinese would make personal decisions as to whether to attend a social event or not, whether to speak out in class or not, or to do a job in a way one sees fit.

To complete the picture, ostracism is also identified as a means of sanctioning members who violate group norms. Chinese informants reported that in Japan, those who do not conform are ostracized. Ostracism, by definition, is the act of expelling a member from a group and excluding the person from interaction with other members. The Chinese informants regarded the use of ostracism as a characteristically Japanese practice and a common deterrent to nonconformity. Informants shared what they described as the "horrifying" experience of being themselves ostracized or witnessing others being ostracized by social or work groups.

> One day I had a bitter confrontation with my professor. The next day, everybody in the lab ignored me. Nobody said anything to me anymore. I couldn't understand what was happening. It was so sudden. I was shocked. Now I know how hard it is to be ostracized. (19F)

At a company I worked for in Osaka, I saw a girl being ostracized by other female workers. They ignored her. They acted as if they didn't hear her. It seems to me that if the leader of a female group doesn't like a particular person, others in the same group ignore her as the leader did. (28F)

This is one aspect of the Japanese culture that shocked many Chinese informants. For them, the practice of ostracism explained a lot about the strong group consciousness of the Japanese; the fear of this treatment effectively prevented any attempts to not conform. According to 2M, "Japanese want to be a part of a group. What they fear most is not belonging to a group." Although informants did not mention anything about ostracism in China, the intensity of their reaction to this practice indicates that they probably had not experienced similar practices in Chinese culture.[11] To make sense of this strange phenomenon, Chinese informants seemed to piece together sequential occurrences of the incident to reach a reasonable conclusion: ostracism is understood as a horrifying alternative to conformity that few Chinese would opt for, and it is seen as a powerful collective tool leading toward conformity.

Group Cohesiveness. Whereas strong conformity, often accompanied with ostracism, is regarded as a negative aspect of Japanese group consciousness, the Chinese informants see Japanese group cohesion in organizations in a more positive light. Group cohesiveness reflects the degree to which a group is organized to function as a single unit—the degree to which all members, each doing his or her own part, work together with a shared sense of belonging to a team—cooperation, teamwork, and dedication to the group goal. Many Chinese informants were intrigued by the cohesiveness of Japanese groups and organizations.

As is often said, Japanese work in a team. In my case, I observed this in a work environment. They cooperate with one another in a group. In general, a shortcoming of person A is compensated by person B's strength, and their cooperation make the organization strong. . . . For example, when we worked with computers, there were only a couple of workers who knew the operation well. Others didn't know how to use the keyboard properly. The ones who knew willingly taught those who needed some help whenever they needed it. This was not just once. This would never happen in China. (2M)

Devotion to work or a strong work ethic was mentioned frequently.

> There was a thing that puzzled me at first. In Japan, even part-timers work conscientiously and honestly, just like ordinary full-time workers. Their movements are quick and efficient. They don't even make small talk while they are working. They are hard workers, and yet they seem cheerful. I couldn't understand why part-time workers would work just as hard as full-time workers. I couldn't help asking them how they could work like that. They said that everybody, including their parents, works like that, so it is nothing special. (2M)

High group cohesiveness was also interpreted as members' dependence on their affiliated group or organization for achievement.

> Japanese work for their companies. The company is just like their parents' home. If the company collapsed, they would feel as if they would also collapse. (10M)

> Japanese don't accomplish much alone. . . . Once they are in a group, they cooperate for a group goal and achieve something. (2M)

It seemed that Chinese view the cohesiveness of Japanese groups as a reflection of employees' giving priority to the benefit of the organization over their own advancement. Refusal to cooperate with the team or to work toward team goals may put one in a difficult position, as it amounts to nonconformity.

> My professor suggested that I teach my fellow group members a method which I had found successful for a given research project. I wanted to work by myself and write a paper on it. But he insisted that the project should be done in a team. I confronted him and said this was my research theme and I wanted to write my own paper. Then he threatened that if I wouldn't teach the method to the group, he would have me kicked out of the institute. (19F)

As seen in the last excerpt, Chinese informants expressed their own reluctance to be part of a group just for the sake of the group. They characterized themselves this way.

> One Chinese can do well, if the person is capable. But once Chinese get together, we speak up and push our opinions and, as a result, we can't function well as a group. . . . In fact, Chinese are aware of this as their weakness. (10M)

The lower level of group cohesion in Chinese is also depicted in their verbal communication mannerisms. A common expression used by many

Chinese to describe their own communication is *jikoshucho ga tsuyoi* (strong self-expression, forthright). The following illustrate how expressive Chinese are:

> It is often said that Chinese have 20 different opinions, we express ourselves too much. (1M)

> Chinese express [our]selves. When we have new ideas, we don't hesitate to speak up. In a way, we aren't careful when we speak. That is, when we speak, we often don't give much thought to the consequences. (2M)

Lower group cohesiveness is also suggested by a lack of commitment to the survival of the group.

> Chinese work together not for a group goal, but for someone they respect as a leader. (28F)

> Chinese often act individually. We are on our own. The Chinese Student Association at school is poorly organized as compared to other associations on campus. Suppose we plan a group trip. We can't reach consensus. One says that he has been to this place already, another says this place seems more interesting than that place . . . and so on. We won't easily compromise for the sake of group goals—to go somewhere for fun in a group, in this case. We don't depend on an organization that we belong to, and we don't care what others say about us. There are times we do things together with a few friends. But even so, there is always a possibility that we go separate ways. (7M)

This is a cultural characteristic long recognized by the Chinese themselves, as seen in the remarks of a late Chinese leader on the subject of group loyalty in the context of nation building. The Western-educated Sun Yat-Sen lamented early in the 20th century, "The Chinese people . . . they are just a heap of loose sand" (quoted in Bary, 1960, p. 769). Experience of the Japanese team spirit is understood to be in contrast to Chinese behavior in similar situations; Japanese are characterized as engaging in cooperative actions, characterized by an absence of self-expression, and an emotional commitment to the concept of group. In the mind of the Chinese informant, these are all properties of group cohesiveness that Japanese enact and display and that Chinese do not.

A Chinese preference to live as a "lone wolf" was noted, and informants express distrust of influences on individuals by a group.

Chinese think they know best. We [Chinese] don't like to work under someone else's instructions. (8M)

In China, everyone wants to be a boss. In Japan, a boss emerges and others strive to please the boss. (2M)

Informants' remarks suggest that Chinese are not directly hostile to groups but rather are less interested in cooperating or are not socialized to work voluntarily in a group. On the other hand, a few informants commented that the ability to cooperate is a positive and good trait, and that the unwillingness of some people to be in a group is due to a reluctance to follow orders rather than to an abhorrence of groups. In the context of larger groups and organizations, distrust of groups and the lack of interest in help explain individualistic behavior.

Although what we suggest here is tentative and awaits further validation, one thing seems to be clear: Chinese group cohesiveness is perceived by Chinese to be weak in comparison with Japanese cohesiveness. This lower level of group cohesiveness is manifested in a number of ways. One important feature of Chinese group interaction is a flexible sense of group membership.

Group Boundaries and Membership. For Japanese, it is assumed, a strong sense of shared membership enhances work cooperation and teamwork in groups and organizations. However, as informants pointed out, this often means that group members give up their own interests for the sake of the group and remain with the group no matter what. Stable and fixed group membership may tend to promote an exclusive attitude toward nonmembers. Informants repeatedly noted, in contrast to the Chinese practice, the sharply defined group boundaries and distinctions based on group membership in Japanese society.

Japanese students have a strong sense of group membership. . . . You can easily tell who belongs to which group, for example, at an athletic meeting for graduate students and faculty. They always sit together with only their lab members. It is just like a family. In China, the relationships among students are on a person-to-person basis. Students in different labs can be good friends. (3M)

Japanese exclusiveness, in terms of their group affiliation, is seen in all kinds of formal and informal situations.

At college[s] in Japan, there are a lot of sports clubs. A member of a group goes to a cafeteria a little before noon to secure seats for other members at lunch time. He puts things on a table as a marker of territory so that his group can sit together. It is a strange scene. Things are on a table, but nobody is there. It is crowded around noon, you know, but I often can't find a space to sit and eat because of such groups and clubs. (21F)

I was told by one of the senior professors in my lab team not to be close to professors of other labs. It's OK to exchange simple greetings, but speaking with other professors was discouraged. . . . I asked why. The answer was that they are not in our group. He also said, "You may not understand why, but if you speak to professors of other labs, I would be in trouble." (19F)

Even in the same group, respondents said that in university settings it seems difficult to maintain a similarly close relationship to two seniors at the same time. Several mentioned the exclusive atmosphere in Japanese academia and attributed it to academic cliques in school; participants also related this exclusivity to a similar phenomenon in business working environments. These examples also illustrate the benefits and predictable outcomes of having shared group membership in Japanese society.

The top management of a Hiroden company is taken by the X University graduates. Graduates of Y University have power in Hiroshima Gas. If a graduate of Z University went to work for Hiroshima Gas, I doubt he could be promoted as high as president. (13M)

In contrast, informants reminisced about more flexible group membership in China: Groups were open for members to come and go. What may lead one to join a group or not is the relative "costs and benefits" associated with membership. If costs outweigh benefits, in a member's assessment, that member will leave the group and move on to another that better meets his or her needs and interests. The Chinese rationale for the necessity of groups and organizations focuses on self-protection. Chinese informants commented that issues of loyalty and commitment to the group are much less prominent.

I join groups only because they provide the means of maintaining my life. I have no emotional attachment to any groups. For instance, I left my previous company and I can leave the university anytime which I currently belong to. I think most Chinese would feel the same way. (1M)

> I wouldn't hesitate to leave a group today if I didn't share its opinions, and it is no problem for me to join another group on the following day. If later I find it beneficial to me to be with the previous group, I will rejoin that group. (23F)

As seen from the remarks above, the differences perceived between Japanese and Chinese regarding group membership and boundaries may be a matter of degree. However, Chinese informants presented a shared view of themselves that contrasts with their view of the Japanese: Chinese depict themselves as independent of and unattached to social groups in general, with the important exception of family and close friends. Their self-proclaimed individualistic attitude is also demonstrated in their way of creating personal support networks through friendship.

Person-to-Person Linkage as a Base of Human Relations (Interpersonal Bonding). This is a theme describing the notion of interpersonal bonds on a personal level. Chinese participants elaborated on the importance of this theme in the Chinese practice, in contrast to its absence in Japan. Chinese friendship ties are often as close as those of a family. In China, the circle of friends is not bound to existing (role-related) social groups. Chinese informants explained that their friendships are based on a person-to-person connection rather than on shared group memberships.

> When my family needed to have a telephone installed, we had a little problem. So, I asked my friend to help us. . . . She asked her friend. . . . I don't know who eventually arranged the phone installation. (26F)

A Chinese explanation of this single-link network is this:

> Networks of friends are more important than such groups [as work organizations]. As long as I have my network of friends, I can survive anywhere in China. (1M)

Networks of friends include both horizontal relations (relationships between friends of equal status) and vertical relations (personal connections to those in a position of authority).

> After all, one who has strong connections wins. I mean that personal connections link you to higher authority. Those who have strong connections with higher authority win the game. I'm not saying having horizontal connections

won't help. But ultimately, having connections with someone in high status makes things work. (2M)

Informants' stories tell us much about how Chinese build a network of friendships, each established through personal connections, that are linked together in a relay fashion. Eventually, one of these connections may lead to someone who can help. This particular fashion of informal relationships seems to play an important role in Chinese society.

The four themes of conformity, group cohesiveness, group boundaries and membership, and interpersonal bonding demonstrate how the Japanese sense of collectivity and individuality looks unique, or quite different, through the eyes of Chinese informants. These Japanese characteristics (higher conformity, higher group cohesiveness, and more distinct group boundaries and membership) generally coincide with the conceptualization of collectivism in which group goals are more important than individual goals, in which "people belong to in-groups or collectivities which are supposed to look after them in exchange for loyalty" (Hofstede & Bond, 1984, p. 419), and in which a higher degree of group cohesiveness is a logical product. Conformity demands a priority on group goals over personal interests, and ostracism penalizes nonconforming members. These two behaviors correspond to the reported location of the Japanese on a Collectivism Scale measuring the need for individual uniqueness and reward/punishment from in-group members: Japanese were found to be low in the former and high in the latter (Yamaguchi, 1994). A sharp distinction of group boundaries is presupposed in another major characteristic of collectivism, that is, particularism, the application of differential standards based on shared membership to create a distinctive sense of group exclusiveness (Gudykunst & Ting-Toomey, 1988).

On the other hand, descriptions of the Chinese characteristics (lower conformity, lower group cohesiveness, flexible group boundaries and membership, and relationships based on person-to-person influence) allow for questioning the common practice of assuming that the Chinese, with an orientation to collectivism, are similar to the Japanese. The Chinese respondents were consistent in their perceptions of the collectivistic characteristics of the Japanese as strikingly different from their own preferences.

Social and Personal Relationship Maintenance

The second core category is maintenance of social relationships as the fabric of society. Here, the perceived strict sense of hierarchy in Japanese interpersonal relationships is contrasted with the more informal Chinese relationships. Whereas informal relationships, built on personal connections, are described as prominent in Chinese society and as overriding social hierarchies of status, age, or official role, the Japanese interpersonal relationships are formal and role based. Related primary themes include: (a) the sense of hierarchy, (b) the level of formality, and (c) the relationship among family and friends.

The Sense of Hierarchy. This theme occurred frequently in the interviews. That is, the Japanese are seen as having a stronger sense of hierarchy in interpersonal relationships within a group or organization than Chinese have. Informants repeatedly noted the rigid distinction Japanese make between *senpai* (senior or mentor) and *kohai* (junior) in the hierarchy. To illustrate,

> In Japan, you can't say no to your *senpai,* even if he or she is only a year senior to you. (19F)

> For instance, among PhD students, third-year students are higher in status than second-year students. Within the group of third-year PhD students, hierarchy is determined by age. (3M)

Informants suggest that a strong sense of hierarchy encourages subordinates' reliance on the higher authority.

> I don't think a lone wolf type of person can do well in a society like Japan. . . . Even in academia, you get a job through your *senpai* in the same school. You are a part of such a hierarchical structure. Whether you like it or not, you are under his control. (6M)

Superiors' strong control over subordinates was reported as the complementary side of subordinates' submissive attitude toward those in authority. These two sides represent another aspect of hierarchy: complementary roles of a superior's dominance and a subordinate's submission. Many Chinese informants reported stories and comments that focused on reciprocity and submission between persons of unequal status in Japanese society. Informants also noted a strong sense of hierarchy among the Japanese in the way they communicate with people of different status. The informants' stories emphasize the nonconfrontational style employed by the Japanese.

Suppose you started working at a company only six months ago. If you were to express your opinions to your superiors or *senpai,* they would think you were presumptuous. (5M)

In contrast, informants reported that open and direct expression occur even between superiors and subordinates in Chinese work environments, although subordinates' opinions are not necessarily accepted by their superiors.

Chinese say what they think, even though their boss doesn't adopt their opinions. As a matter of fact, their opinions are turned down in many cases. But Chinese express their opinions anyway even after they are turned down repeatedly. (2M)

To Chinese informants, hierarchy seems to be imprinted in the minds of people in Japanese society. They described experiencing a society where a status difference is implied by and attached to every formal social role, and they noted that people were extremely sensitive about these differences. Informants gave accounts of the Japanese people's strong sense of hierarchy between people of different status, describing this sense in terms of its impact on them:

When I speak to my Japanese professor on the phone, I get nervous, even though I have known him for a long time and he is kind and takes very good care of me. I still get nervous. This does not happen in China. . . . When I visit him at school, I cannot feel relaxed while speaking to him. Something is different here. (4M)

In relation to the above comment, the perceived priority given by Japanese to formally assigned status over the personal relationship was noted.

When I was working part-time for a company, I became good friends with a couple of Japanese. Even those whom I thought were my friends at work were strict about mistakes. For example, I am working for a mannequin company. We occasionally go to department stores to set up a display. . . . We sometimes make mistakes—breaking glass or accessories, or jumbling the proper order in assembling a display set, or something like that. Say I break some glass; my superior would scold me. For the eventual improvement of work efficiency, nothing is wrong with that. But emotionally I feel somewhat betrayed. (8M)

The respect that Chinese accord their elders is perceived to differ from the kind of deference to superiors described in Japanese organizations. This might be related to the value Chinese place on family as the archetypal in-group.

> In China, people of different status can become as close as family . . . once we get close, we become really close. We feel protective of subordinates, and to someone in higher status we have loyalty, probably more so than Japanese. Well, what makes us different from Japanese in hierarchy is how close we can be like family. (4M)

In general, Japanese interpersonal relationships were perceived by the informants to be hierarchical, as relationships in which formal roles and status are taken more seriously than they are by Chinese. In comparison, Chinese described their own interpersonal relationships as family-like (measured by personal closeness), and other considerations, such as status and age, became secondary. This seems to be a feature that Chinese consider a major difference between the two cultural groups. Chinese seem to be able to establish and maintain friendships more easily than Japanese, without as much concern about age, status, and occupation. On the other hand, it is implied that unless people maintain human relationships, life can be difficult in China.

Formality. Formality is a way to reinforce the structure of hierarchy by infusing responsibilities into the incumbent's role. Adherence to procedures prevents deviation and leads to maintenance of the status quo. It discourages subordinates from taking on more responsibilities. Informants characterized the Japanese as valuing a strict compliance to rules and routine procedures to maintain the hierarchical structure—they also saw Japanese as having a relative lack of initiative.

> There are several ways to accomplish the same goal. But once a rule of procedure is set, Japanese follow the same old routine, even if they are aware of better ways to do things. For example, when I was working at a kindergarten in Japan, all kindergarten teachers repeated the same old routine every day from morning till evening. Nobody tried something different. Nobody complained. (30F)

In addition, rules for social interactions were reported. For example, the order and the right of speaking in a meeting seem to be governed by unwritten rules and reflect the hierarchical structure.

At the meeting, a full professor, an associate professor, and an assistant give their opinions, but students barely say anything. . . . The professor states his opinion last. . . . First, the associate professor is given a chance to speak up, and then the assistant, which is followed by a technician. (3M)

The formality of Japanese norms stands in contrast to Chinese informants' accounts on the Chinese emphasis on achieving practical goals rather than the formality of procedure. One informant cited a statement by Chinese leader Deng Xiaoping to illustrate how practical Chinese are:

There are no set rules in China. Do you know Deng Xiaoping's statement? "Whatever it is, white cat or black cat, if it catches a mouse, it is a good cat." That's a typical Chinese attitude. (30F)

This preference for practicality is also shown in the Chinese style of business management. Informants offered their observations in comparing Chinese to Japanese management.

[A Chinese] upper administrator decides on a work objective and leaves it to his subordinates to decide how to do it. As long as you succeed in the project, nobody says anything, even if you work on the project entirely on your own. (28F)

In China, where for decades, regulations and rules have been part of the ever-changing political and societal climate, going through formal procedures is often futile and ineffective for achieving goals. On the other hand, personal relationships have been reliable. To illustrate,

When I do research on the Chinese economy, I use informal channels to get information, such as former classmates, friends, *senpai,* and *kohai.* Because, unlike Japan, China doesn't have clear laws and regulations to restrict the availability of confidential government data to the public. I use my personal connections to collect data, which may or may not be confidential. (4M)

In Chinese society, efforts to establish a legal system are a recent and ongoing occurrence. Thus, it seems that being practical is the result of unique social circumstances. In fact, informants presented practicality as a unique Chinese characteristic.[12] The binary category of formality/practicality is reflected in the descriptions that mark the practices of two cultures as different.

Relationships Among Family and Friends. Although Chinese informants characterized Japanese interpersonal relationships within a social group or an organization as hierarchical and formal, another aspect of contrast between Japanese and Chinese was related to (close) interpersonal relationships with friends and family members. All Chinese informants who commented on Japanese friendships and family ties remarked on how different Japanese are from Chinese in this respect. In general, Chinese informants perceived a lack of closeness in most Japanese interpersonal relationships, in contrast to the great value that Chinese place on close ties among family members and friends.

> Chinese friends are equivalent to what Japanese would call best friends. Japanese friends are mere acquaintances from the Chinese perspective. (8M)

> I don't know any Chinese who have no friends. But I know there are some Japanese who don't have any friends at all. . . . In Japan, so-called friends means someone you have fun with. (31F)

Chinese informants reported what seemed to be a lack of personal attachment in Japanese interpersonal relationships, where an individual takes an impersonal approach to friends, especially in matters involving personal contribution and sacrifice.

> Chinese friends frankly tell me what is wrong with me if I have some problems. They give me suggestions and advice because they think it will help me. Japanese friends don't say anything that might possibly hurt my feelings. . . . It costs energy to be with Japanese friends because I have to be extra careful not to disagree with them. (24F)

This Japanese attitude is interpreted as the Japanese not wanting to face any confrontations that may cause emotional friction. To the Chinese respondents, the nonconfrontational attitude of Japanese to their friends is an indication of their low involvement with their friends.

To illustrate how close friendship manifests itself and fuses into the concept of family among Chinese, informants shared their perceptions and personal stories.

> In China, once we become good friends, we are just like brothers and sisters. My things are theirs, and their things are mine, too. (10M)

I have this female friend who is just like my sister. We have been friends since we were little. Her family even let me live with them for a year when I was a junior-high student. (30F)

When it concerns family and friends, informants reported that Chinese displayed a total commitment and involvement with friends that implied friends were a part of their holistic identity.

My family is a part of me. Close friends are just like my family, so they become part of me too. (15M)

Like the old Chinese saying "I am willing to stab myself on both sides of the belly if it is for the sake my friends." Chinese think that they are willing to die for their good friends. . . . I don't have such good friends. But I know I can die for my family. . . . Yeah, kinship is special. (2M)

By contrast, family relationships in Japan appear to be less interdependent and helpful than those in Chinese families, particularly when it comes to the relationships between elderly parents and their children. Some Chinese informants stressed that filial piety was not practiced in Japan.

Japanese children don't take good care of their parents once they get married. In China, one of the children in a family lives with their parents and takes care of them. . . . I call my brothers and parents back in China at least once a month. . . . If I neglect my parents, I will be criticized by people around. (5M)

In Japanese home dramas on TV, I often hear old parents saying that they want to go to nursing homes rather than cause trouble for their children. They also say that they feel less indebted that way. Such a parent-child relationship just doesn't occur to the Chinese mind. (4M)

The above examples may suggest that Japanese parent-child relationships are more individualistic, rather than being interdependent as would be expected in collectivistic cultures. Although Japanese parents were perceived to be individualistic, however, their intentions or motivations may not be the same as those in members of individualistic cultures such as the United States, whose members value self-sufficiency and their independence. Japanese elderly parents say they do not want to depend on their children because they do not want to be a burden to their children. They may volunteer to go to nursing homes because they do not want to feel indebted to their children, rather than because they want to keep their independent stance.[13]

Our Chinese informants can only make sense of unfamiliar practices of Japanese friendship and caring for elderly parents based on their own social and family values. From their point of view, "Japanese relationship among family and friends is cold," and, though perhaps based on obligation, Chinese informants stressed altruism in family and friendship among Chinese, which seemed to be the ideal that informants were striving for in practice. This ideal is seen implicitly, for example, in an informant's report that the closeness of a friend was judged by the fact that the friend performed a favor without expecting a return (13M). Several informants further specified what they saw as the difference of psychology between Chinese and Japanese on this point.

> In Chinese society, we don't regard family and friends as a burden. We rather think that we can be related by helping one another. We still believe strongly that being interdependent is a good thing. On the contrary, Japanese try not to burden anybody as much as they can. (4M)

> Nothing is wrong with giving trouble to your own children. That's what the parent-children relationship is meant to be. (25F)[14]

The form of traditional relationships in Chinese society has been influenced by economic causes; poverty and insufficient welfare support contributed to the need for close ties among friends. However, the Chinese respondents' ideas about close human relationships are built around and modeled after the family as a whole. Traditional Chinese values (such as filial piety and *guanxi*-ism[15]) are manifested in the interviewees' intensifying their sense of belonging to a family and in their inclusion of friends as quasi-family members. In contrast to their strong ties and collectivity within the family, however, the Chinese attitude toward other social groups outside of the family circle is depicted as matter-of-fact or cold.

Informants related their perceptions of a general lack of concern or consideration among Chinese for people one does not know.

> I have to sacrifice myself for my friends. But if they were not my friends, I wouldn't share anything with those people even if I have plenty. . . . Japanese are not very nice to their friends, but not very cold to strangers either. In China, we can select our customers. It is perfectly acceptable to sell our products to someone we like, but not to someone we dislike. In Japan, everyone is your

customer. If you find a customer disgusting, as long as he buys your products, you have to treat him as a god. (5M)

Informants' shared stories suggest that social status and group affiliation alone cannot earn respect or consideration from Chinese. Instead, these Chinese implied that the credibility of an outsider must be established through personal contacts and interactions leading to personal relationships. Unfriendly public behavior of Chinese to strangers was described as somewhat common and was described negatively by some of the Chinese informants. They mentioned that passengers in China were "aggressive" (21F), and that people fight in a bus for stepping on someone's foot and "never apologize" (9M).

For the category of social and personal relationship maintenance, three themes have emerged: the sense of hierarchy, the level of formality, and the relationship among family and friends. Informants' comments clearly show how Japanese and Chinese differ in development and maintenance of familial and nonfamilial interpersonal relationships. Reportedly, Japanese have a much stronger sense of hierarchy and high formality, whereas Chinese have a weaker sense of status difference and high practicality. The notion of social hierarchy is conceptually similar to one of Hofstede's cultural variability dimensions—power distance. Power distance in a hierarchy is defined as "the difference between the extent to which B (boss) can determine the behavior of S (subordinate) and the extent to which S can determine the behavior of B" (Hofstede, 1980, p. 72). In other words, in large power-distance cultures, superiors exert control over their subordinates, and subordinates accept the controlling power as a fact of life. Power distance is positively related to the degree of conformity and negatively related to the degree of independence (Hofstede, 1980). In general, people in collectivistic cultures are thought to accept status (and power) differences more readily than do those in individualistic cultures (Triandis, Brislin, & Hui, 1988). The Chinese respondents perceive the Japanese to be a group with large power distance. High power distance was accompanied by a perception of high collectivism, which is also consistent with past research.

For the Chinese self-perceptions, however, the findings are not consistent with past research. It is interesting that Chinese, who are also regarded as collectivistic, see the high degree of hierarchy in Japanese society as one of the major features distinguishing it from their own culture. Informants note that Chinese have a weaker sense of formal status difference and lower formality than do Japanese. Chinese are, however, highly collectivistic in the circle of family and friends, as illustrated by the informants' stories. Chinese enjoy strong ties with family and friends, but at the same time, they show more flexible attitudes toward social hierarchy. In view of the reported positive correlation between collectivism and power distance mentioned above, the issue is the appropriateness of the cross-cultural communication literature's characterization of both Chinese and Japanese as collectivistic and similar.

The results suggest that formality-informality is an important aspect in the construction of cultural communication norms. Our Chinese respondents placed utmost importance on family and considered familylike informal communication as a model for interpersonal relationships, whereas Japanese were described as respecting affiliation with social groups and preferring formal manners of communication with role hierarchy. Formality-informality is seen in two aspects of culture-specific communication: (a) procedures for goal achievement, and (b) psychological distance in interpersonal relationship.

For Japanese, adherence to formality was perceived to maintain group harmony for effective achievement of group goals. Japanese group members feel safe and protected by acting according to the instructions of procedures. In contrast, Chinese were described as not caring much about group solidarity. When formal procedures do not enhance effectiveness or when they stand in the way of a task, Chinese reportedly were ready to go around them. Chinese value practicality, rather than formality, for goal achievement. Instead of being guided by formulated procedures and regulations, Chinese tended to prefer to use personal links or informal personal connections, which they trusted the most, even when this could lead to the violation of organization rules.

Another component of formality-informality is interpersonal distance; a difference was observed in this aspect of relationship building and maintenance between Japanese and Chinese. Chinese respondents noted that, for both Japanese and Chinese, such factors as age, status, and occupation can determine one's roles and can form hierarchy in human relationships. The difference lies in whether one is able or willing to establish interpersonal relationships beyond the formal roles that one assumes in society. Chinese informants claimed that differences of age, status, and occupation can be secondary once they become close friends or a pseudofamily. Stories in this study suggest that informal interpersonal relationships are essential even in the work environment for Chinese. In other words, Chinese prefer and even pursue an informal, and thus personal, relationship in social interaction, which can become so influential that it may override structural rules. In comparison, Japanese interpersonal relationships are described as more hierarchical, and personal relationships are often overshadowed by social roles such as *senpai-kohai* and teacher-student.

Although described as collectivistic within socially affiliated groups, Japanese are viewed in this study as independent and as not sharing much with their friends and family. This makes an interesting contrast to Japanese group collectivity, which the Chinese informants also identified as a uniquely Japanese characteristic. Given that Japanese were perceived to display a higher degree of group collectivity, their lack of attachment to and involvement with family and friends, who are supposed to be the closest group for Chinese, made our informants question what it means to be part of a group for Japanese. This brings out an interesting issue for further investigation: the basis for (primary) in-groups and out-groups in the two cultures.

CONCLUSION

Cross-cultural communication research that uses broad dimensions such as individualism-collectivism to study East-West comparison may overemphasize similarities and overlook differences between cultural groups within Eastern traditions. The ultimate objective of this research project is to examine both differences and similarities perceived by Chinese between two Eastern cultures—Japanese and Chinese.

The findings raise important issues and implications for the development of cross-cultural communication studies. Taking a social construction approach, the current study starts with Chinese observations and interpretation of their encounters with Japanese and has found evidence partly supporting and partly contradicting previous research of these two cultures. Contrary to generalizations from past research about Eastern cultures and communication, the Chinese informants perceived considerable differences between themselves and the Japanese. Examination of their experience has produced findings on areas that past communication research has obscured. To the Chinese informants, Japanese family relationships and friendships were perceived as less intimate and more distant than those of the Chinese. Japanese group consciousness (other than that of the family) appeared strikingly strong in contrast to their weak interpersonal bonds (even for their family). Japanese social structures were described as distinctly hierarchical—with rigid role relations—as well as highly cohesive. Further, Japanese society was perceived as demanding strict social conformity and as being higher in procedural rigidity and formality than Chinese society. Japanese modes of communication were reportedly nonconfrontational and were more high context than Chinese modes. These descriptions of Japanese through the eyes of Chinese, in turn, tell us much about what Chinese are like.

Chinese cultural characteristics are reflected and displayed in the way Chinese perceive and understand Japanese behaviors. They present who they are in the way they describe and explain Japanese behaviors. In comparison with Japanese, Chinese described themselves as more practical and informal in social interactions. Chinese viewed themselves as quite independent outside of the family, with flexible group affiliations and a rather weak sense of social hierarchy. Their stories tell us that what is of paramount importance to Chinese is their families and friends, who are, for all practical purposes, quasi-family bonded through personal contacts.

The social construction approach provides an alternative understanding of "the sense of the collective and the individual" and "social and personal relationship," with new insights into the making of cultural characteristics as well as the comparison between cultures. Membership is constituted in behaving, feeling, and thinking like Chinese or Japanese. It is defined, understood, and constituted in interaction as social discourse.

For Chinese informants, Japanese group consciousness appeared strong when compared to their own cultural orientations and practices. It is noteworthy that Chinese informants did not describe themselves as "collectivistic" in their strong bonds with family and close friends. Although Chinese respondents described themselves as being "individualistic" and took a critical stance toward the Japanese strong sense of group in the context of social affiliations outside of family circle, they expressed quite unfavorable opinions about the seemingly more distant and less intimate, and thus more individualistic, relationships among Japanese family and friends. This demonstrates multiple ways in which different self-identified groups create and respond to concepts such as *individualistic* and *collectivistic* and how they are enacted, perceived, and defined. Concerning the differences of communication styles, Chinese informants frequently pointed out the Japanese nonconfrontational, indirect manner in contrast to their own confrontational, direct style. Given that their comments focused on interpersonal communication, it is intriguing to note that the issue of freedom of public speech in China did not come out explicitly in the series of interviews. This may be because the Chinese informants simply did not want to talk about it or because they may be in a habit of not thinking about it.

Through the stories and reflections that Chinese share about their intercultural experience with Japanese, we learn what constitutes "Japanese-ness" and "Chinese-ness" in the eyes of Chinese. Based on descriptions reported by Chinese informants who reside in or are frequent visitors in Japan, this study not only reveals differences between Japanese and Chinese that a comparison with a Western culture could not have captured, but also highlights the dynamic and constructive nature of culture and communication.

NOTES

1. These authors and others (e.g., Chen, 1997; Lee, 1998; Lu, 1993/1994; Lum, 1996) are part of a recent development in studies of Chinese communication to critically examine a Western view of East Asian communication that has become rigidly dichotomous and insensitive to regional diversity. The authors wish to thank an anonymous reviewer for bringing some of this work to our attention.

2. The limited space here does not allow a discussion of the concept of and labels for particular culture(s) from a social construction perspective. It is necessary to mention, however, that labels as a means to identify, describe, discuss, and talk about something are part of the social construction process. In particular, the groups under study here, Chinese and Japanese, are defined by the way they are discussed. What is meant by *Chinese* or *Japanese* only makes sense as they are developed within a discourse.

3. Tanno and Jandt (1994) advocate the redefinition of the "other"; they argue that researchers in multicultural studies need to understand informants as "co-creators" of knowledge instead of regarding the "other" as a separate objective entity. Similarly, we consider Chinese informants not as objects of research, but rather as participants or coproducers, (together) with whom we learn what it means to be "Japanese" or "Chinese" from their perspective and how "Japanese-ness" and "Chinese-ness" are perceived and constructed through their discourse. Chinese respondents describe and explain as the "outsider" how they perceive Japanese through their interactions with Japanese. Simultaneously, they provide the "insiders' view," as both groups are Asian.

4. Informants were identified using a snowball technique based on individual contacts.

5. Although one informant never lived in Japan, he was well versed in the Japanese language and had a number of personal encounters with the Japanese through his work and frequent visits to Japan. He had intensive Japanese language education for 4 years at a college in China. His work responsibilities as a government official entailed oral translation between the Chinese and Japanese languages, and the translation topics ranged from diplomatic relations to business negotiations.

6. Although the researchers were aware of the possibility that the validity of the data might be affected by interviewing Chinese in their second language, we chose to use the Japanese language for two reasons. First, the high language proficiency of the Chinese

informants was judged by several factors: many informants were taking university courses taught in Japanese; several were graduates of Japanese courses taught in Japanese; some were working at Japanese organizations; and others had intensive Japanese language training in China. The researcher who interviewed these informants never had difficulty in communicating with them during the interviews. In fact, a total of 35 Chinese were originally interviewed, but 2 interviewees were excluded because of their inadequate Japanese language ability. Second, the common language between interviewees and the researcher who interviewed them was Japanese, and a direct person-to-person interview was considered to be a better way of establishing rapport and probing for detailed information than being assisted by a translator as a communication mediator. In addition, although the interviewer was Japanese, acknowledging the fact that the interviewer was then living in the United States helped the informants to situate her in a rather neutral position, neither on the Chinese nor the Japanese side.

7. We borrowed the "coat hanger" technique suggested by Garfinkel, Livingston, Lynch, MacBeth, and Robillard (1988) as an interview strategy.

8. The data presented in this chapter as "interview excerpts" are from tape-recorded interviews only. The information provided by the two respondents who declined to have their interviews recorded was not included among the examples of discourse but was useful in corroborating the generalizations about Japanese and Chinese against the specific stories told. Their stories were consistent with those of the others.

9. Each informant is identified here by a number for anonymity; the sex is indicated by M (male) or F (female).

10. It is in the nature of qualitative data that the stories or observations can be relevant to more than one primary theme and that a comment may not fall precisely within a theme.

11. Because the Chinese informants reside in a foreign country, they might be more sensitive to "being excluded" than if they were in their own country.

12. Chinese coordinate their activities through constructing norms that are appropriate to the situation and relationship. For the Chinese we interviewed, sometimes the formal, regulative rules have little to do with the acts and moves they made, and respondents said that they tended to follow ways that work.

13. A public-opinion poll on Japanese marriage and family conducted by *Asahi Shimbun* (Asahi Newspaper) was reported in its March 29 issue ("Kazoku-zou," 1999). A table of detailed survey statistics was also included as an appendix to an article about Japanese marriage in *Asahi Soken Report*—a journal issued by Asahi Shimbun Sougou Kenkyu Center ("Zenkoku seron," 1999). The poll found that over 70% of the survey participants say they feel most comfortable when they are with their family. However, when it comes to the issue of who is responsible for parents in their old age, 52% think that children do not necessarily have to take care of their elderly parents. Although 60% think that they can rely on family in their old age, 61% do not want to depend on family if there are alternatives. Whether such attitudes to family are perceived to be cold, and thus unfavorable, or independent so as not to be anyone's burden, and thus considerate, depends on one's cultural values.

14. Including elderly parents in the single family living unit is a "moral and constitutional requirement" for adult children in China, which suggests that adult children's taking care of parents has the status of a formal legal obligation (Buruma, Faison, & Zakaria, 1996).

15. *Guanxi* (connection) implies a particularistic tie or relationship that helps an in-group member not only to achieve his or her personal goals, but also to receive privileges

and special treatment. *Guanxi*-ism is a key concept for understanding the relation-oriented character of Chinese behavior in various contexts, with their emphasis on family and quasi-family members. *Guanxi*-ism is thus an important guiding principle of interpersonal relationships in Chinese society.

REFERENCES

Bary, W. T. (1960). *Sources of Chinese tradition: Vol. 2.* New York: Columbia University Press.

Buruma, I., Faison, S., & Zakaria, F. (1996, February 18). Class climbing. *New York Times Magazine,* 38.

Chang, H. C., & Holt, G. R. (1991). The concept of yuan and Chinese interpersonal relationships. In S. Ting-Toomey & F. Korzenny (Eds.), *Cross-cultural intercultural communication* (pp. 28-57). Newbury Park, CA: Sage.

Chen, L. (1997). How we know what we know about Americans: Chinese sojourners talking about their experience. In A. González, M. Houston, & V. Chen (Eds.), *Our voices: Essays in culture, ethnicity, and communication* (2nd ed., pp. 177-186). Los Angeles: Roxbury Press.

Collier, M. J. (1998). Researching cultural identity: Reconciling interpretive and postcolonial perspectives. In D. V. Tanno & A. Gonzalez (Eds.), *Communication and identity across cultures* (International and Intercultural Communication Annual, Vol. 21, pp. 122-147). Thousand Oaks, CA: Sage.

Cronen, V., & Lang, P. (1994). Language and action: Wittgenstein and Dewey in the practice of therapy and consultation. *Human Systems: The Journal of Systematic Consultation & Management, 5,* 5-43.

Dodd, C. H. (1991). *Dynamics of intercultural communication* (3rd ed.). Madison, WI: Brown & Benchmark.

Garfinkel, H., Livingston, E., Lynch, M., MacBeth, D., & Robillard, A. (1988). *Respecifying the natural sciences as discovering sciences of practical action, I & II: Doing so ethnographically by administering a schedule of contingencies in discussions with laboratory scientists and by hanging around their laboratories.* Unpublished manuscript.

Gudykunst, W. B., & Kim, Y. Y. (1992). *Communicating with strangers: An approach to intercultural communication* (2nd ed.). New York: McGraw-Hill.

Gudykunst, W. B., & Ting-Toomey, S. (1988). *Culture and interpersonal communication.* Newbury Park, CA: Sage.

Gudykunst, W. B., Yoon, Y., & Nishida, T. (1987). The influence of individualism-collectivism on perceptions of communication in ingroup and outgroup relationships. *Communication Monographs, 54,* 295-306.

Hall, E. T. (1976). *Beyond culture.* Garden City, NY: Doubleday.

Hofstede, G. (1980). *Culture's consequences: International differences in work-related values.* Beverly Hills, CA: Sage.

Hofstede, G. (1983). Dimensions of national cultures in fifty countries and three regions. In J. Deregowski, S. Dzuirawiec, & R. Annis (Eds.), *Explications in cross-cultural psychology* (pp. 335-355). Liss, The Netherlands: Swets & Zeitlinger.

Hofstede, G., & Bond, M. (1984). Hosftede's culture dimensions: An independent validation using Rokeach's value survey. *Journal of Cross-Cultural Psychology, 15,* 417-433.

Kazoku-zou 50-sai ga wakareme—Kizuna-ishiki ni henka no me [Image of family changing: Poll shows generation gap—Those under 50 have a different view of family ties]. (1999, March 29). *Asahi Shimbun* [Asahi Newspaper], pp. 10-11.

Kim, M. (1993, May). *Individual differences in communication goals in Korean and American speakers.* Paper presented at the Intercultural Communication Association convention, Washington, DC.

Lebra, T. S. (1976). *Japanese patterns of behavior.* Honolulu: University of Hawaii Press.

Lee, W. S. (1998). Patriotic breeders or colonized converts: A postcolonial feminist approach to antifootbinding discourse in China. In D. V. Tanno & A. González (Eds.), *Communication and identity across cultures* (International and Intercultural Communication Annual, Vol. 21, pp. 11-33). Thousand Oaks, CA: Sage.

Lee, W. S., Wang, J., Chung, J., & Hertel, E. (1995). A sociohistorical approach to intercultural communication. *Howard Journal of Communications, 6,* 262-291.

Lu, X. (1993/1994). The theory of persuasion in Han Fei Tzu and its impact on Chinese communication behaviors. *Howard Journal of Communications, 5,* 108-122.

Lum, C. M. K. (1996). *In search of a voice: Karaoke and the construction of identity in Chinese Americans.* Mahwah, NJ: Lawrence Erlbaum.

Martin, J. N., & Nakayama, T. K. (1999). Thinking dialectically about culture and communication. *Communication Theory, 9,* 1-25.

Miller, J. G. (1991). The social construction of the person: How is it possible? In R. A. Shweder (Ed.), *Thinking through cultures* (pp. 156-185). Cambridge, MA: Harvard University Press.

Mumby, D. K. (1998). Organizing man: Power, discourse and the social construction of masculinity(s) in the workplace. *Communication Theories, 8,* 164-182.

Samovar, L. A., & Porter, R. E. (1995). *Communication between cultures* (2nd ed.). Belmont, CA: Wadsworth.

Strauss, A., & Corbin, J. (1990). *Basics of qualitative research: Grounded theory procedures and techniques.* Newbury Park, CA: Sage.

Tanno, D. V., & Jandt, F. E. (1994). Redefining the "other" in multicultural research. *Howard Journal of Communications, 5,* 36-45.

Triandis, H. C., Brislin, R., & Hui, C. H. (1988). Cross-cultural training across the individualism-collectivism divide. *International Journal of Intercultural Relations, 12,* 269-289.

Trubisky, P., Ting-Toomey, S., & Lin, S. (1991). The influence of individualism-collectivism and self-monitoring on conflict styles. *International Journal of Intercultural Relations, 15,* 65-84.

Yamaguchi, S. (1994). Collectivism among the Japanese: A perspective from the self. In U. Kim, H. C. Triandis, Ç. Kâgitçibasi, S. Choi, & G. Yoon (Eds.), *Individualism and collectivism: Theory, method, and applications* (pp. 175-188). Thousand Oaks, CA: Sage.

Yum, J. O. (1987). Korean philosophy and communication. In D. L. Kincaid (Ed.), *Communication theory: Eastern and Western perspectives* (pp. 71-86). San Diego, CA: Academic Press.

Zenkoku seron chousa shouhou [Table of a Japanese public-opinion poll]. (1999). In *Asahi Soken Report: No. 138* (pp. 104-135). Tokyo: Asahi Shimbun Sougou Kenkyu Center.

8

Exploring the Communication/ Culture Connection

A Comparison of Japanese and American Discourse

YUMIKO YOKOCHI • *Nikko Securities Company International*
BRADFORD 'J' HALL • *University of New Mexico*

One of the common sayings we have heard in the field of intercultural communication is Edward Hall's (1959) claim that "Culture is Communication and Communication is Culture." This statement has rung true with many different scholars over the years and justified a variety of research endeavors. We argue that the value of this metaphorical statement is that it makes explicit the inescapable relation between these two basic components of our lives. Traditionally, these two concepts are treated in a way that suggests a clear linear connection between culture and communication, with culture essentially dictating what one's communication will be. Even when the possibility of communication's influencing culture is noted in principle, it is generally ignored in practice (e.g., see Gudykunst & Ting-Toomey, 1988). The overall purpose of this chapter is to explore the culture/communication connection, while being particularly sensitive to how communication constitutes culture.

Although the connections between culture and communication can be considered at a purely philosophical level, we find that these concepts become much more clear when specific examples are considered. We will apply our concerns to two communities, Japan and the United States, which are frequently considered to be culturally quite distinct. Certainly within each of these communities there are multiple cultures. However, there seem to be enough consistent differences across the two communities to justify them as starting points for our research. Thus, an additional purpose of this chapter is to discover and compare differences between Japanese and U.S. American conversational patterns in a given context and to show how these mundane conversations create and recreate culture.

CULTURE AND COMMUNICATION:
TWO PERSPECTIVES

Most research in the social sciences may be seen to be grounded in the four-pronged question "How can we best describe, understand, predict, and change human interaction?" Of course, not all four of these goals are a part of every research endeavor. Our study is primarily focused on description and understanding. There are many ways in which the four parts of this question are answered, including examinations of personality traits, social structure, historical relations, and so forth. One major effort at answering this multifaceted question involves using the concept of culture. When differences or challenges in human interaction arise, we often hear the cry, from a variety of different disciplines, that culture is the culprit.

Two major perspectives in the social sciences on how culture and communication are connected may be described as the *traditional force* perspective and the *reflexive force* perspective.[1] Both perspectives privilege culture in their efforts to meet their goals. Furthermore, on the surface, both of these perspectives define culture in similar ways. Scholars committed to these perspectives agree that culture involves values, norms, and basic premises for producing and understanding communication (Carbaugh, 1990b; Samovar & Porter, 1995). However, their assumptions regarding how culture, in terms of values and norms, helps to explain human interaction (or communication) are quite different. Each perspective has two different key assumptions regarding the link between values/norms and communication. These assumptions provide a foundation from which to begin researching and answering the broader question: How may culture be used to describe, explain, and predict communication?

The traditional force perspective makes two assumptions:

1. The connection between culture and communication is essentially one in which norms and values assimilated over time determine communication (causal connection).
2. These values and norms may be said to have force for specific groups of people, such as different nationalities or ethnicities (local application).

The *causal connection* assumption implies that the world is made up of social effects produced by independent causes. The independent causes in this case are the norms and values of a particular group of people, and the dependent causes are the specific communicative behaviors in which members engage. The second assumption, *local application,* limits the generalizability of the causal connections claimed in this perspective to specific *groups* of people. These groups of people are considered to basically agree about what the important norms and values are.

One type of traditional force perspective can be found in Ting-Toomey's (1988) theory of intercultural conflict. Take, for example, her proposition that "Members of individualistic, LC [low-context] cultures would tend to use more autonomy-preserving strategies (negative-face need) in managing conflict than would members of collectivistic, HC [high-context] cultures" (p. 227). In this case the values of individualism or collectivism, or the norms for high- or low-context speech, are posited as causing particular communicative behaviors (ones that are oriented toward negative face). These norms and values are used to describe, explain, and predict communicative behaviors of groups of people. Thus, in terms of norms and values, culture is seen as causally connected to communication, and finding out if a specific culture shares these ideas of collectivism, of low-context norms, and so forth would be crucial in making further predictions.

One of the concerns with this perspective is illustrated in Bilmes's (1976) classic work on negotiation within a Thai village. Bilmes (1976) details the decision process that occurred in a Thai village regarding the building of a village temple. One of the points of disagreement centered around whether to follow through on an earlier agreement to have everyone contribute money to the building project before asking those who had previously contributed for more money. One person argued for his position using the value of equity, whereas another argued for his stance based on the values of freedom and individual choice. In another case, people argued for opposing practices based on the norms of expressing trust and requiring accountability. In each of these cases, the values and norms used to justify a position were seen by the village members as having great worth.

The fact that these values and norms were acknowledged as important within the Thai village yet were positioned in opposition to each other is problematic for the assumption that action is causally connected to strongly held norms and values. I may feel that equity and freedom of choice are both very important, but in a particular case I may have to choose an action that does not fit one of the values or norms. This choice will not always be the same. Based on traditional force research, Sitaram and Cogdell (1976) found that U.S. Americans greatly value efficiency over hospitality. It is not hard to find an example in which this is indeed the case; however, it is also not very hard to find examples in which U.S. Americans have chosen not to do the most efficient thing in order to be hospitable. The choice of which value to act on seems to be more connected to specific situations than to the group membership implied by the local application assumption.

The fact that a value or norm is strongly held by community members does not necessarily mean that it has a causal connection to behavior. In the example noted earlier, Ting-Toomey (1988) demonstrated an awareness of the problems inherent in causal claims about human interaction in her use of the phrase "tends to" in her proposition. This phrasing allows for a way out if the researcher does not find the causal connection to hold true. However, the basic "culture causes communication" idea is still assumed. These efforts to cover for the fact that the causal connection assumption does not hold up have been going on for some time. For example, Swartz (1984) predicted certain patterns of parent-child interaction based on the norms and values that Swahili parents and children professed. When observation showed that these expected patterns did not occur, he decided that there are norms that are guides (causal) and norms that are tokens (not causal). Swartz (1984) still argued that some values and norms are causal, but his research could only support the token type.

The second perspective, the reflexive force position, also has two key assumptions:

1. The connection between culture and communication is essentially one of a resource for managing meaning (*sense-making connection*).
2. The application of these resources depends on the perceived situation (*contextual application*).

The sense-making assumption implies that norms and values are used as communicative resources through which people may understand what happened in the past, interpret the present, and try to influence the future. This perspective suggests a world that is shaped by human choices for which individuals are held responsible. The values and norms discussed by Bilmes (1976), such as freedom of choice, equity, trust, and accountability, are not independent variables but are rather part of the way people make sense of what has happened and make plans for what they want to have happen. For example, while growing up, one of the authors was familiar with two common sayings, "He who hesitates is lost" and "Look before you leap." Both of these sayings were regarded as valid, and both expressed accepted and important wisdom in his culture, yet they would not serve as good predictors of what may happen or even as a good explanation of why certain actions occurred. These two sayings could be used to praise or blame someone regardless of the specific actions she or he may have taken. Cultures provide the resources for people to make sense of what happens around them, but they do not force a single interpretation. This fact has played havoc with researchers' efforts to create simple recipes for intercultural success.

The contextual application assumption also highlights the fact that it is possible for a person to "value honesty" or "believe that he or she should respect his or her parents" yet still feel fine about acting in ways that violate these ideals in given situations. For example, Hall (1998) found that even though people felt that acting in prejudicial ways was wrong, they still felt that prejudiced acts were acceptable in certain situations and at times were even seen as the correct way to act.

We refer to this perspective as the reflexive force because it highlights the fact that culture and communication work back on themselves, allowing for a dynamic change that is grounded in what has come before. Our interest in showing how communication and culture have this reflexive relationship underlies our acceptance of the sense-making connection and contextual application assumptions noted above.

CULTURAL SYSTEMS: JAPAN AND THE UNITED STATES

Our specific case involves a comparison of Japanese and U.S. American conversational patterns. Our interest is in demonstrating how mundane talk creates and recreates culture. We have chosen to do this in a comparison format to better highlight the cultural differences in the talk. One standard way to compare cultures is to begin with etic variables and see how people from the two groups compare. Some examples of this type of approach using the United States and Japan can be found in work by Barnlund (1975), Gudykunst (1993), and Klopf (1991). This sort of work fits best with the traditional force perspective. Instead, we will review the Japanese and American cultures by briefly explaining some key emic concepts for each community. These concepts (and others) make up systems of common sense through which people understand and produce action (e.g., culture). We use the terms *Japan* and *United States* to connote the cultural entity (the shared system for producing and interpreting action), not the political or geographical entity. We also realize that in the political entities known as the United States and Japan, there are many different cultures. However, we will base our present discussion on what are typically discussed as the mainstream or dominant cultures within these countries. We recognize that our review is not exhaustive, but we hope to give the reader a feel for each culture by highlighting important 'native' concepts.

Core Concepts

For purposes of comparison, the Japanese and U.S. American cultures will be viewed as different "solar systems," each with a number of related values, norms, and assumptions that are held in orbit by a "sun" or core concept. To be *held in orbit* does not refer here to a causal connection that implies that all behavior is determined by the concept; instead, the term refers to an interpretive connection in which various norms, values, and behaviors can be made sense of in light of the core concept. For Japan, this core concept is *wa,* and for the United States, this concept is the *self.*

Wa may be loosely translated into English as unity or the desire to be one with those of your group. Wierzbicka (1991) explains *wa* as a concept that, while recognizing that people are not one thing, highlights the desire to be like one thing. In other words, although people have differences, at the deepest level it is best when people want the same thing. This deep level of sharing underlies the desire for harmony in interpersonal relations and a consideration of others within the group. *Wa* is both a source of power and a point of praise. Through the unity that is *wa,* people can accomplish much, and the recognition of *wa* among a group of people is a great honor.

The notion of *self* in the United States highlights the dignity and value of each unique person. In the end, it is the individual that matters. Much of U.S. American culture has its roots in Christianity, and the importance of the individual can be seen in Jesus's parable about leaving the ninety and nine, going to search for the one, and then rejoicing more in the recovery of the one than in the other ninety-nine (Matt. 18:12-13). Each person is assumed to be special in his or her own right.

Given these core concepts, it is easy to see why one of the most common explanations for Japanese and U.S. American difficulties is the idea that Japan is collectivist in orientation and the United States is individualistic (Brislin, 1993). Does this mean that in Japan there is no concern for the individual or individual goals? Or that in the United States there is no group loyalty or team spirit? Obviously the answer is no in both cases. However, it does mean that these concepts dominate and make sensible other important concepts in the cultures. In the United States, for example, groups, including the government, exist to protect individual rights, whereas in Japan individuals are expected to act in ways that protect the unity or *wa* of the group.

Orbiting each of these cultural suns are nine "planets" or emic values and norms that provide a gross overview of the Japanese and U.S. American cultural systems. We will present each of the Japanese and U.S. American planets together in hopes that the comparison of the two cultural solar systems will be more clear. However, in doing so, we do not wish to imply that these pairs are direct opposites or polar contrasts. They are, rather, values or norms important within each community that may or may not directly contrast with each other.

Assertiveness and Enryo. A quick look around the self-help section of most U.S. American bookstores will quickly demonstrate how popular the idea of being assertive is in the United States. *Assertiveness* is defined as the practice of behaviors that enable individuals to act in their own best interest or to stand up for themselves without undue anxiety (Alberti & Emmons, 1986). Thus, assertiveness focuses on how the self can fulfill its own needs without hurting others. *Enryo,* on the other hand, involves an effort to avoid explicit opinions, assessments, or other displays of personal feelings (Hall & Noguchi, 1995; Lebra, 1976). *Enryo* is a form of self-restraint that proscribes the bringing of attention to oneself and one's personal desires in order that others will not think badly of one (Wierzbicka, 1991). When people avoid these expressions of personal desires, they are showing a reverence for the value of unity encompassed in *wa.*

Tatemae *and Honesty. Tatemae* refers literally to the outward surface of a building and is often used to indicate a concern for what can be seen by others (Condon, 1984). This concern for the surface is manifested in the Japanese desire for gifts, food, and other products to be aesthetically pleasing, regardless of functionality (Hamada, 1991). *Tatemae* is often contrasted to *honne,* or what is on the inside, when it is applied to communication. Thus, although there are particular times when speaking with one's true voice is appropriate, manifesting the appropriate *tatemae* or outward display is generally the preferred mode of communication. The *honne* is devalued, because it is seen as a threat to the *wa* of the group. In contrast, the U.S. American value of honesty is found within one's self, and people are supposed to be true to it. Although there are certainly times and places where this is not the case, by and large people are urged to be completely honest with others, and those who are able to do so in difficult circumstances are valorized. Regardless of whether or not they themselves are always honest, U.S. Americans value personal honesty in others (Stewart & Bennett, 1991).

Clarity and Sasshi. Closely related to the notion of honesty is the U.S. American concern for clarity. Writing within the U.S. American tradition of public speaking, Osborn and Osborn (1988) argue that "clarity is important to every language function" (p. 250). The United States has been characterized as a "low-context" culture because U.S. Americans often want everything spelled out in the verbal code and strive to take the guesswork away from what is meant (Hall, 1983). The focus in the United States is on the speaker or self and the clarity with which he or she presents the message, unlike with *sasshi,* in which the detection of meaning relies on the listener. The concept of *sasshi* is more focused on the listener and his or her ability to understand inexplicit messages (Okabe, 1983). *Sasshi* refers to the ability to guess or intuit another person's meaning without that person having to express it directly in the verbal code. Ishii (1984) describes it as the listener's sensitivity or the ability to engage in sharp guesswork. Miike (1997) notes that, although *sasshi* can lead to communication difficulties in Japan, it is still viewed as an ideal. We maintain that this is because successful *sasshi* depends upon a certain degree of *wa* and is also taken to be a manifestation of *wa.*

Amae *and Merit. Amae* is a form of mutual dependency (Doi, 1973). It is somewhat similar to bittersweet forms of dependency between a mother and a child. *Amae* points toward a relationship in which one person is in a protective stance toward another (Wierzbicka, 1991). Maynard (1997) maintains that the desire for *amae* motivates one to belong to a group and to depend on another's love. The emphasis on a protective relationship and mutual dependency is in keeping with the importance of *wa.* Although *amae* and merit are not directly related, the underlying sense of dependence (*amae*) versus independence (merit) highlights a cultural difference. U.S. Americans believe that people should work for what they get and avoid dependence on others. The idea that "it is not what you know, but who you know" in reference to certain rewards is often spoken as a negative sign of the times. The U.S. American "work ethic" strongly supports the idea of people earning their own way based on merit, not on relational ties. Children in the United States quickly learn that being considered the teacher's "pet" is not a socially favorable position. The self earns respect through individual merit.

Equality and Jouge Kankei. U.S. Americans stress equality or an "even playing field" in all that they do. Built into the Constitution of the United States is the idea that everyone should have an equal chance; the notion that one person is naturally more worthy than another is abhorrent. Philipsen (1992) discusses how mainstream U.S. America advocates a "code of dignity" that stresses the underlying worth of each individual. This focus on equality is strongly oriented to the starting point, though, not the ending point. U.S. Americans need to have a winner, but they also like the idea that everyone started at the same level. Nakane (1970) describes Japan as a vertical society, because one can find vertical relationships that are viewed as good and natural in almost every facet of Japanese life, for example, in the *sempai/kohai* relationship. The *sempai* demands respect and honor, and it is very difficult for someone in a *kohai* position to disagree with or contradict what is said or desired by the *sempai*. To do so would threaten the *wa* of the group.

Giri *and Freedom.* Giri is a type of obligation felt toward others who have done something good for the person (Benedict, 1947). This is a much stronger sense of obligation than is typical in the United States. Befu (1986) describes it as a "moral imperative to perform one's duties toward members of one's group" (p. 162). It also implies a much longer-term relationship and a sense that one will be forever in the other's debt (Cathcart & Cathcart, 1997). This sense of obligation is natural in a community that stresses *wa*. Each person must be closely tied—socially, emotionally, and so forth—to the others. U.S. Americans, on the other hand, value personal freedom and strongly resist any constraints and obligations to others. Carbaugh (1990a) shows that U.S. Americans prefer to say just what they want and to allow others to do the same, as long as what is said does not infringe on the freedom of others. Efforts to restrict freedom in any way are typically vilified in the U.S. press.

Communication and Awase. U.S. Americans are great believers in the power of communication. It is often felt that if people would just "communicate," they could solve any problem. Communication is different than just talking. It implies a close, supportive, and flexible approach to the other person (Katriel & Philipsen, 1990). Katriel and Philipsen (1990) describe a ritual of communication that is informally espoused in many settings, from U.S. talk shows to interpersonal advice giving. This ritual of sharing of self must end with a sense of "I'm okay, you're okay." If it does not, then there is what is called a perceived communication breakdown or a lack of communication. Thus, real communication is supportive of each person's self. *Awase* refers to the ability to always adjust to the situation or circumstances (Condon, 1984; Tezuka, 1992). This value emphasizes that a person is constantly changing as needs demand. There is little concern for a consistent self that is built on solid ground. The self is something that moves with the situation. The group is what is solid and needs to be maintained, not the self. Thus, maintaining *wa* is based on being flexible in situations, not on consistently following principles.

Kenson and Pride. Kenson involves discounting one's abilities in order to maintain the status quo of a relationship and to avoid standing out or appearing to think too highly of one's self (Hall & Noguchi, 1995). It is sometimes manifested in a verbal apology, and it demonstrates a desire not to disturb the nature of the relationship. In this way, *kenson* helps to maintain *wa,* whereas a boasting or assertive attitude about one's abilities would threaten the group harmony. For example, a speaker may begin a speech by apologizing to the audience for her or his low status or insufficient knowledge on the topic; such an apology is perceived as adequate humility. However, U.S. Americans want people to feel pride in their work. To apologize is to admit that one is not proud of one's work and is often seen as a sign of weakness. U.S. Americans strive to become the very best. U.S. Americans are concerned about winning and feel that it is important to have a winner.

Creativity and Kata. U.S. Americans value what is new and different. The nonconformist or person who can break the mold and act creatively is seen as a hero. *Kata* refers to the way something is done (De Mente, 1993). In Japan, there is a *kata* or form for almost everything, from the way one swings a baseball bat to the way one performs a tea ceremony (Whiting, 1977). This valuing of form over function and process over outcome is again related back to the concept of *wa.* When people do things in the same way and one knows what to expect, it is much easier to develop *wa.*

There is no claim that these values exist in some unchanging way in either of these cultures. The values or concepts discussed above are interpretive ideals that are used to make sense of behaviors, not rigid standards that dictate every behavior, and their application will vary across time and space. However, our cultural experiences lead us to believe that these values and norms have been shown to be meaningful, such that if people are seen as violating these values, they are open to blame and criticism. Our goal in this study is to identify and then describe the emergence of patterned conduct that can be understood and interpreted based on these concepts.

Research Questions

1. What, if any, differences exist between U.S. American and Japanese nationally identified group members' ways of speaking within a comparable context?
2. Given the answer to the first question, what is the connection between the participants' discourse and the broad values and "solar systems" of the Japanese and U.S. American cultures?

METHODS

The material for our particular study comes from 20 role plays. All of the role plays were audiotaped and transcribed by the researchers. Ten of the role plays were engaged in by U.S. Americans, and 10 were performed by Japanese. All of the role plays were done in the native language of the speakers. For the sake of presentation and comparison, the Japanese role plays have been translated into English. The translation was done by the first author, who is a "native" Japanese speaker and has had considerable experience in translating between Japanese and English. However, during the analysis, both the Japanese and English versions were considered.

For many, the study of discourse or conversation demands only naturally occurring talk. However, Jackson (1986) argues that the purpose of the research and the argument to be made determine the appropriate form of data and that even hypothetical examples have their role in research. We adopted role plays for two reasons. First, we were able to compile, within a reasonable period of time, multiple examples of talk in similar circumstances. Second, the patterns of talk we were looking for in the connection between culture and communication can occur in a role play as well as in other kinds of natural conversations. Although we did determine the initial setup, we provided no scripting in terms of what should be said, how it should be said, or what the outcome should be. Therefore, the interactants were left on their own to discuss, as they saw fit, a scenario that could occur. Based on the authors' backgrounds in both communities, the role play was felt to be something that could occur in every-day life.

The role play information that the members received was as follows:

Person 1: You want to borrow the class notes from last week because you were absent. You want to study tonight for the missed class. The other person is your classmate, but you haven't talked with him or her much.

Person 2: One of your classmates with whom you have not talked much asks you to lend her or him your class notes from last week. You wanted to use your notes right after the class tonight.

The role play was written by the first author with Japanese students in mind, but it was also felt to be appropriate for U.S. American students. In no instance did any of the participants indicate that the role play was an atypical or abnormal situation. This situation was chosen in part because it presents a potentially awkward or face-threatening situation. It was hoped that such a situation would more clearly demonstrate cultural differences.

All of the role plays were engaged in by individuals associated with a large university in the Southwestern United States. Some of the Japanese participants were not regularly enrolled students but were part of a special and intensive language program for international students recently arrived in the United States who were trying to improve their English. The average age of the Japanese participants was 28 years, and the average age of the American participants was 26 years.

Both the U.S. and Japanese role plays were primarily done by women. Only 2 of the 10 Japanese and 2 of the 10 American role plays involved men. This gender difference emerged because of our desire to match the participants based on gender and age; the Japanese students were recruited first, on a volunteer basis, and then U.S. American volunteers who closely matched the gender and age of the Japanese participants were selected. Although this difference in the numbers of women and men should be considered when interpreting discourse examples, our initial review of the role plays with gender in mind revealed no substantive differences between male and female discourse.

Given our research interests, we adopted a discourse analytical perspective for exploring and comparing the two sets of conversations. Pomerantz and Fehr (1997) introduce five steps or tools for analyzing conversation. They are: (a) select a bounded sequence, (b) characterize the nature of actions in the sequence, (c) consider how the speakers' packaging of actions provides for certain understandings of the actions performed and the matters talked about, (d) consider how the timing and taking of turns provide for certain understandings of the actions and the matters talked about, and (e) consider how the ways the actions were accomplished implicate certain identities, roles, or relationships for the interactants.

All of these steps were followed in our analysis. We ensured a bounded sequence because of our use of the same role play. We carefully mapped out each utterance within each of the 20 conversations in terms of the utterance's meaning and role within the dialogue. Then we looked for patterns across the conversations and sought to understand why we were hearing the conversations the way we were. Next, we considered timing, turn taking, and other packaging elements and their roles in the conversations. Finally, we considered the relational identities that were created within the talk itself. Each step was done by examining the utterances both individually and together. Any differences of opinion between authors were discussed and worked out to the mutual satisfaction of both researchers, recognizing the native expertise of the first author in regards to Japanese culture and the native expertise of the second author with U.S. American culture.

We also showed transcripts of these conversations to 12 other individuals (6 Japanese and 6 U.S. American) from within the same larger university setting. We asked these individuals if they could identify whether the conversations had taken place between Japanese or U.S. American participants. In addition, these individuals were asked to explain their choices. Each of these 12 people received six conversations (three from each group) to identify, and each received conversations that were systematically chosen to ensure equal coverage. Given that the Japanese individuals in our study were currently living in the United States, the 6 U.S. Americans for this part of the study were recruited because of their past experience living with Japanese.

DISCUSSION OF FINDINGS

The first two research questions focus on what differences, if any, exist between the talk of Japanese and U.S. Americans within a given situation as well as what the relationship is between these differences and the Japanese and U.S. American values and cultural systems.

Based on close and repeated examination as well as discussion, we found a variety of differences and similarities between the U.S. American and Japanese interactions. The differences centered around two main issues, time and orientation.

Time

The Japanese conversations on average were over 10 seconds longer than those of the U.S. Americans. In part this was because the Japanese conversations were filled with short responses known in Japan as "aizuchi." These responses often consisted of just one word and displayed active participation in the conversation. *Aizuchi* have been found in other studies to be a common feature of Japanese conversation patterns (Goddard & Wierzbicka, 1997; Lebra, 1993). Examples of *aizuchi* can be seen in the two excerpts below:

Japanese 3

    1 J: Ah = K = hi hhh
    2 K: Oh = hi.
    3 J: How are you?
    4 K: I am all right
    5 J: Is your class going OK?
    6 K: Yeah = somehow (.) it is a lot of work = but
    7 J: I agree this class
    8 K: Hyou think so, too?
    9 J: is a little demanding, isn't it?:::
    10 K: Yeah:
    11 J: But for me = I was absent (hhh) last week and it became even
    12 K: Yeah.
    13 J: tougher I feel:
    14 K: Is that so
    15 J: Yes = and I would like to borrow your notes. Is that possible?

Japanese 9

    1N: Excuse me. Um::::: we haven=t
    2Q: Yes.
    3N: really talked much yet, but =
    4Q: =Yes.

5N: I was absent last week and::

6Q: Yes.

7N: I don't have notes from the last week. I would like to borrow your notes. Would it be possible?

In both of these examples, there is frequent interaction and verbal attentiveness from both people in the conversation. This contrasts sharply with what we observed in the American conversations. In general, the Americans spent much more time on any given turn of talk. For example,

American 8

1 X: Z, ah, I missed last week class, and I'd, really would like to get your notes. I realize it is late. You, know, it is dark. But I still would like to get a copy of ah the notes because I really need to study tonight for the test coming up. Would you mind?

2 Z: Uh, is there any way you can follow me to like a copy center or something? And maybe you can make them?=because I don't (.) I really needed them tonight, but I realize, I would like to give them to you if possible. Or maybe you can copy 'em right now?

In the above example, we can see that the U.S. Americans spent more individual time with each turn of talk, developing an idea without verbal assistance from the other. In addition, the U.S. Americans did not make the same effort to interject short comments into the speech of the other when it was the other's turn. This difference can be connected to the notions of self and *wa* discussed earlier. The longer turns of the Americans allow the individual speaker to star without any outside help. The speaker expects and is expected to say what is on her or his mind in a clear and complete way. This style of speech encourages self-assertion and may easily be interpreted as self-centered by those who do not value this way of speaking.

The Japanese *aizuchi,* however, may demonstrate a much greater interdependency. By mutually creating the flow of the conversation, both parties are better able to demonstrate and build *wa.* The constant interaction allows the individual to practice *awase,* whereas the more incomplete utterances provide training for developing *sasshi,* situational adjustment. Further, the mutual dependency formed in the interaction is reminiscent of *amae*-style relationships.

The examples above also illustrate another consistent difference related to timing. The Japanese took longer than the U.S. Americans to build up to the actual request to borrow the notes. Even though individual Americans tended to take longer in a given turn of talk, they tended to get to their request more quickly in the conversation than did the Japanese. As was seen previously, the U.S. American made her request in the first turn of talk (this was true of 60% of the American interactions, and another 30% of Americans made the request by the third turn), whereas 60% of the Japanese did not make their request until the fifth turn or later. It should be noted, however, that the other 40% of the Japanese made their request in the first utterance. Thus, simply because a request is made quickly does not mean that it is un-Japanese. Overall, however, the Japanese as a group gave the impression of being much less direct than the Americans. Given the contrasting values of assertion and *enryo,* this type of difference is not surprising.

Orientation Toward Self, Other, and Task

The second major distinction we found dealt with the orientation expressed by the speakers. The Americans' talk focused on the self or the task that the self needed to accomplish, whereas the Japanese displayed more of an orientation toward the other person. For example, the four U.S. American interactions that did not have the request in the first turn of talk had four qualifying questions that directly led to the request.

American 10

1 B: Ah, and I wasn't in class last week and I was wondering if you were there?
2 C: Yeah, I was.

American 1

1 A: B? (1.0) Did you take..ah..notes from last class?
2 B: Yeah, I did?

Each of these questions by the Americans qualified the other person as someone who could help the speaker with his or her problem. The single instance of what may be seen as a qualifying question setting up the request in the Japanese conversations is shown below:

Japanese 1

> 1 I: J, umm, excuse me, can I talk to you now?
> 2 J: Well, sure. What is it?

This qualifying question is clearly less direct than those used by the U.S. Americans, in the sense that it does not narrow the field of inquiry to class attendance or notes for the class as the U.S. American examples do. In addition, the question comes across as more of a concern about potentially bothering the other person, rather than a simple check to see if the other is qualified to grant the request. Thus, its status as a qualifying question is somewhat in doubt.

Although the Japanese did not ask the type of qualifying questions the Americans did before making their request, they frequently (60% of the time) asked a type of question after the request had seemingly been granted that the U.S. Americans never did. We call these confirmation checks. For example,

Japanese 9

> 15 N: or well maybe I could copy them and. (1)
> 16 Q: Oh that would be
> 17 N: I can take the copy home=
> 18 Q: =Yes. That would be fine, too.
> 19 N: Is that okay?

Japanese 7

> 1 Q: Um P, I was absent last week (1) I would like to study tonight for last week so could I borrow your notes?
> 2 P: Ah:: (1.5) I am going to study that notes myself: (1) Am::::: well then:::: what about copying them?
> 3 Q: Oh is that good for you?

These types of checks imply an explicit concern for the other person's feelings and a desire to make sure that everything is mutually agreed upon. To U.S. Americans, this practice may appear as though the requester is almost searching for a "no" answer. For example,

Japanese 5

1 M: Umm, I was absent last week::: Well:: (1) I would like to see your notes: Do you have time now?

2 N: =Oh sure.(2)

3 M: Today::: (1) I suppose you need to take the notes home tonight to study::?

4 N: Well, I could use another notebook so that=s fine.

5 M: Oh, but it is too much to ask::

Confirmation checks evident in our data function as a way to build *wa,* just as qualifying questions help clarify if the other person can help meet the needs of the self.

Another way in which the Japanese orientation toward other is displayed is in utterances that express apology or concern over bothering the other person. In 90% of the Japanese conversations, there were at least one or more expressions that explicitly communicated some variation of "excuse me" or "sorry to have to bother you." This sort of expression happened in only 10% of the American conversations.

These apologetic expressions about having to bother the other person and the confirmation checks that show an explicit concern for not imposing one's will over the other are all examples of what is referred to as negative face (Brown & Levinson, 1978). Negative face, which demonstrates a concern for the other's needs and autonomy, was manifested in every Japanese conversation, but in only one of the U.S. conversations. Positive face strategies, which show explicit support and praise of the other person, were only found in one U.S. conversation.

American 3

1 E: Hi F (.) I was wondering(.) I was absent last week in class=and I know you take really good notes so I was wondering if I could borrow them.

The U.S. American explicitly praises the other person in this request. However, because it is presented as part of the reason why the request is made, the praise still comes across more as concern with the self's accomplishing her task than as an expression of concern and support for the other.

Both the Americans and the Japanese did express self concerns when asked to borrow the notes; for example,

American 1

1 A: B? (1.0) Did you take..ah..notes from last class?

3 B: Yeah, I did?

4 A: The test's coming up, I, I haven't had a chance to talk to him, and I really need those notes, could I, xerox them? Can I borrow tonight (.) take, and copy'em?

5 B: Tonight doesn't work for me, cause I wanted to look'em over since the test is coming up, but maybe tomorrow or something you can stop by=

Japanese 8

7 P: I am sorry to bother you but could I borrow your notes?

8 R: Well I wanted to use them tonight:: (1) Do you need them tonight? If it is okay for you to borrow them tomorrow (.5) I can give them to you tomorrow.

The Japanese person (R) and the U.S. American (B) say almost the same thing. The Japanese person, however, includes a question to see if it is okay to borrow the notes the next day, thus showing more of a concern for the other, whereas the U.S. American maintains more of a focus on self. This question by the Japanese person verbally demonstrates a willingness to restrain one's personal desires (*enryo*) even when these desires are raised. It also allows for more *awase* and adjustment than what is demonstrated in the American example. However, the U.S. American's omission of this question subtly grants her more individual freedom from the needs of the other person.

The Japanese occasionally (in 20% of the conversations) demonstrated a deprecating attitude toward the self that was not found in any of the U.S. American conversations:

Japanese 3

15 J: Yes=and I would like to borrow your notes. Is that possible?

16 K: Oh my notes are very bad, but if it is OK with you=

17 J: Yeah, sure.

18 K: Hplease use them.

Japanese 4

5 L: Um, then, I would like to borrow your notes. Would it be possible?

6 J: Well, my notes are very messy.

7 L: Oh, mine are just as bad.

8 J: Hwith everything mixed up and it is hard to read

9 L: (laugh) Oh, no, I don't think so

10 J: Maybe it is better than nothing, huh?

These self-deprecatory comments are examples of the Japanese concept of *kenson* discussed earlier and serve to maintain the status quo of a relationship.

Differences in orientation between the two communities may be summarized in the following ways. The Japanese, through their discourse, conveyed the stance that "we will be together, so how can we take care of this need while maintaining the relationship?" The U.S. Americans displayed a stance of, "I have a need that brings me in contact with you, so let's work out how this need may be met." These two stances again seem to fit with the organizing cultural concepts of *wa* and self.

The explicit care with which the Japanese participants spoke with indirectness, displayed concern for the other's face, used confirmation checks, and slowly built up to the request suggest to us that talk is seen as very powerful and perhaps potentially dangerous in Japanese discourse. The power of talk is so great that it is not easily controlled, and the individual must buffer what she or he says to the other so as not to create overwhelming obligations that disturb the *wa* of the group. In the United States, talk is viewed as being powerful only if used correctly, so one needs to use more direct talk to clearly create the obligations among people that are necessary for the self to satisfy his or her wants and for the society to survive. Thus, for the U.S. American, talk has power that can be controlled, and to make use of its power, one must use it directly and forcibly, or else the needed impact will not be felt.

SUMMARY AND IMPLICATIONS

The differences discussed in this section are not meant to exhaust all the differences that may exist between patterns of American and Japanese speech; these differences should also not be treated as inviolable standards of talk upon which to base sweeping generalizations. Rather, the differences we discuss are those that emerged in the patterns of speech between members of different communities who were respondents in our study.

The patterns we note were neither exhaustive of nor exclusive to each group. For example, even though the Japanese generally took longer to build to the request than did the U.S. Americans, 40% of them nevertheless made the request in the first turn of talk. Even though the Japanese used negative face moves much more often, these could also be found in U.S. American conversations.

It is noteworthy that in addition to the differences we found, the respondents in the second part of our study could identify differences between groups. They were able to correctly identify over 85% of the conversations (62 of the 72 total). The U.S. American respondents identified 89% correctly and the Japanese respondents 83%. The fact that these respondents were able to reasonably identify which conversations were between Americans and which were between Japanese suggests that the differences found here were not unique occurrences; these correct identifications also hint at the importance of talk in constituting culture and cultural identity. However, the second part of this study more directly highlights that culture, when approached as community-specific norms and values, tends both to produce distinctive patterns of talk and to be produced by that talk.

Noticeable differences in the discourse have important implications for scholars focusing on the relationship between culture and communication and how communication may constitute culture. From a traditional force perspective, an initial response to the results above is to note that culture, as an independent variable, must be causing the patterns of communication that became evident. Thus, culture provides an explanation of the differences found.

A problematic observation within the traditional force perspective is that our second group of participants consistently used the same norms and values to identify which group was doing the talking, regardless of whether or not they were accurate in their identification. In general, the rationale used to identify Japanese conversations was that the Japanese were expected to be more polite, apologetic, and concerned with the other person than U.S. Americans were expected to be. Thus, even when one of the U.S. American or Japanese participants thought that a U.S. American conversation was a conversation among Japanese, this assumption was based on the same reasons that were used for identifying all conversations among Japanese. The same norms and values were used to attribute correct and incorrect group identity.

A direct causal connection interpretation is not easy to maintain. For example, two different respondents in the second part of the study noted the phrase "I was wondering" as a key in deciding what identity the person had. One claimed that the person who used the phrase was Japanese, because she was being indirect in her beginning comments; the other felt she was U.S. American, because she focused on herself. The exact meanings of the behavior or words are not as important as the fact that different sets of values and norms were being applied consistently. Indeed, after being informed of wrong answers, the respondents showed their "expertise" by explaining how they had been confused and what it was about the correct answer that made even more sense based on values and norms associated with the different communities.

We believe that our own interpretations (like all interpretations) of the conversations were inherently influenced by our understandings of these two cultures. For example, the negative face focus on the other, which we relate to creating *wa,* could also be interpreted as showing deference to the self of the other person. It could be argued that the positive face move of the other shows a desire to build group unity. Our interpretations, however, do make sense of the patterns of behavior.

At the same time, these findings may encourage others to go beyond the causal traditional force assumptions. For example, Ting-Toomey's (1988) proposition, cited earlier, was that "Members of individualistic, LC [low-context] cultures [such as the United States] would tend to use more autonomy-preserving strategies (negative-face need) in managing conflict than would members of collectivistic, HC [high-context] cultures [such as Japan]" (p. 227). Although our data may raise questions about this claim, these data do not so much refute Ting-Toomey's (1988) particular claim, which may hold true in many circumstances, as call for a close examination of conversational contexts in which the claim may hold true and, because of variations across contexts, call for the questioning of the worth of causal claims in general.

Based on our observations, we claim that culture influences communication by providing resources through which we all make sense of the world around us. These resources create a pathway for people to connect with other people and with their environment. Both the Japanese cultural system, centered around *wa,* and the U.S. American one, centered around the concept of *self,* allow people to share meaning and coordinate action. Although there were differences in dealing with the situation presented in the role play, there was no noticeable difference in community members' ability to handle the situation successfully. The cultures that were evident were different, but each provided a reasonable path for successfully navigating the needs of those involved.

The idea that culture as interpretive system indeed has an impact on the way we speak is certainly supported in our research. However, our data also indicate that we believe that communication affects culture. We argue that communication and patterns of discourse influence a culture by constituting and confirming it as well as by challenging and changing it.

Concrete examples of successful communication give the culture life. Conversations that emerged in our study provide examples of this influence. For example, confirmation checks not only demonstrate *wa* but actually help to build or constitute the value of *wa* while also confirming its importance in the culture of the Japanese. Communication thus constitutes culture, because culture would not have form or meaning without it; to the extent that communication reinforces the culture, it confirms the importance and power of culture.

Communication and patterns of discourse that do not reinforce accepted patterns of sense because of creative communication with a group expand both the material that must be made sense of and the ways we study how members of groups may make sense. This expansion recognizes the challenge to those using the cultural system, requiring the creation of new methods of sense making that modify what has existed before. For example, the response below includes an initial reference to a personal desire or need; this is not consistent with some values and with what makes sense within the Japanese community, even though the rest of the utterance does reinforce these patterns.

Japanese 8

8 R: Well I wanted to use them tonight:: (1) Do you need them tonight? If it is okay for you to borrow them tomorrow (.5) I can give them to you tomorrow.

There are many ways in which this message could be expressed within any given cultural system. If the notion of personal desire found in the above message becomes more prevalent or is noticed as an acceptable way to respond to a request among Japanese, then some explanation is likely to be made, and the system of sense may be modified. In doing so, certain norms and values will also need to be modified. In the United States the notions of "If it feels good, do it" and "Do your own thing" would likely shock many early settlers, who valued individual work and self-reliance, yet these notions can be traced back to talk in the formative years of the United States that stressed the individual (see Swidler,

1986). Although change is typically a slow and complex process, the creative nature of human communication may modify culture.

The connection between culture and communication is complex, because the two concepts are so closely interwoven in the fabric of our lives. We have tried to illustrate both sides of this connection through our analysis of Japanese and American talk in a given context. Hopefully, we can use this understanding of the relationship between communication and culture to deal with the challenges of intercultural communication in more complete and effective ways.

NOTE

1. Although modified for our present purposes, the identification and discussion of these two perspectives is inspired and guided by lectures given by Gerry Philipsen (1987).

REFERENCES

Alberti, R., & Emmons, M. (1986). *Your perfect right: A guide to assertive listening* (5th ed.). San Luis Obispo, CA: Impact Publishing.

Barnlund, D. (1975). *The public and private self in Japan and the United States.* Tokyo: Simul Press.

Befu, H. (1986). Gift-giving in a modernizing Japan. In T. Lebra & W. Lebra (Eds.), *Japanese culture and behavior* (Rev. ed., pp. 158-170). Honolulu: University Press of Hawaii.

Benedict, R. (1947). *The chrysanthemum and the sword.* London: Secker and Warburg.

Bilmes, J. (1976). Rules and rhetoric: Negotiating the social order in a Thai village. *Journal of Anthropological Research, 32,* 44-57.

Brislin, R. (1993). *Understanding culture's influence on behavior.* Fort Worth, TX: Harcourt Brace.

Brown, P., & Levinson, S. (1978). Universals in language usage: Politeness phenomenon. In E. Goody (Ed.), *Questions and politeness: Strategies in social interaction* (pp. 56-289). Cambridge, UK: Cambridge University Press.

Carbaugh, D. (1990a). Communication rules in *Donahue* discourse. In D. Carbaugh (Ed.), *Cultural communication and intercultural contact* (pp. 119-149). Hillsdale, NJ: Lawrence Erlbaum.

Carbaugh, D. (1990b). Toward a perspective on cultural communication and intercultural contact. *Semiotica, 80,* 15-35.

Cathcart, D., & Cathcart, R. (1997). The group: A Japanese context. In L. Samovar & R. Porter (Eds.), *Intercultural communication* (8th ed., pp. 329-339). Belmont, CA: Wadsworth.

Condon, J. (1984). *With respect to the Japanese.* Yarmouth, ME: Intercultural Press.

De Mente, B. L. (1993). *Behind the Japanese bow.* Lincolnwood, IL: Passport Books.

Doi, T. (1973). The Japanese patterns of communication and the concept of *amae*. *Quarterly Journal of Speech, 59,* 180-185.

Goddard, C., & Wierzbicka, A. (1997). Discourse and culture. In T. A. van Dijk (Ed.), *Discourse as social interaction* (pp. 231-257). London: Sage.

Gudykunst, W. B. (1993). *Communication in Japan and the United States.* Albany: State University of New York Press.

Gudykunst, W. B., & Ting-Toomey, S. (1988). *Culture and interpersonal communication.* Newbury Park, CA: Sage.

Hall, B. J. (1998). Narratives of prejudice. *Howard Journal of Communication, 9,* 137-156.

Hall, B. J., & Noguchi, M. (1995). Engaging in *kenson*: An extended case study of one form of "common" sense. *Human Relations, 48,* 1129-1147.

Hall, E. (1959). *The silent language.* New York: Doubleday.

Hall, E. (1983). *Dance of life: The other dimension of time.* Garden City, NY: Anchor.

Hamada, T. (1991). *American enterprise in Japan.* Albany: State University of New York Press.

Ishii, S. (1984). *Enryo-Sasshi* communication: A key to understanding Japanese interpersonal relations. *Cross Currents, 11,* 49-58.

Jackson, S. (1986). Building a case for claims about discourse structure. In D. Ellis & W. Donahue (Eds.), *Contemporary issues in language and discourse processes* (pp. 129-147). Hillsdale, NJ: Lawrence Erlbaum.

Katriel, T., & Philipsen, G. (1990). "What we need is communication": "Communication" as a cultural category in some American speech. In D. Carbaugh (Ed.), *Cultural communication and intercultural contact* (pp. 119-149). Hillsdale, NJ: Lawrence Erlbaum.

Klopf, D. W. (1991). Japanese communication practices: Recent comparative research. *Communication Quarterly, 39,* 130-143.

Lebra, T. (1976). *Japanese patterns of behavior.* Honolulu: University Press of Hawaii.

Lebra, T. S. (1993). Culture, self, and communication in Japan and the United States. In W. B. Gudykunst (Ed.), *Communication in Japan and the United States* (pp. 51-87). Albany: State University of New York Press.

Maynard, S. K. (1997). *Japanese communication: Language and thought in context.* Honolulu: University Press of Hawaii.

Miike, Y. (1997). Japanese *Enryo-Sasshi* communication revisited: A critical review of literature and suggestions for future research. *Dokkyo Working Papers in Communication, 15,* 77-99.

Nakane, C. (1970). *Japanese society.* Berkeley: University of California Press.

Okabe, R. (1983). Cultural assumptions of East and West: Japan and the United States. In W. Gudykunst (Ed.), *Intercultural communication theory: Current perspectives* (pp. 21-44). Beverly Hills, CA: Sage.

Osborn, M., & Osborn, S. (1988). *Public speaking.* Boston: Houghton Mifflin.

Philipsen, G. (1987). Lecture presented for Speech Communication 590 class, University of Washington, Seattle.

Philipsen, G. (1992). *Speaking culturally: Exploration in social communication.* Albany: State University of New York Press.

Pomerantz, A., & Fehr, B. (1997). Conversation analysis: An approach to the study of social action as sense making practices. In T. A. van Dijk (Ed.), *Discourse as social interaction* (pp. 64-91). London: Sage.

Samovar, L., & Porter, R. (1995). *Communication between cultures* (2nd ed.). Belmont, CA: Wadsworth.

Sitaram, K. S., & Cogdell, R. T. (1976). *Foundations of intercultural communication*. Columbus, Ohio: Merrill.

Stewart, E., & Bennett, M. (1991). *American cultural patterns: A cross-cultural perspective* (Rev. ed.). Yarmouth, ME: Intercultural Press.

Swartz, M. J. (1984). Culture as "tokens" and as "guides": Swahili statements, beliefs, and behavior concerning generational differences. *Journal of Anthropological Research, 40*, 78-89.

Swidler, A. (1986). Culture in action: Symbols and strategies. *American Sociological Review, 51*, 273-286.

Tezuka, C. (1992). *Awase* and *sunao* in Japanese communication and their implications for cross cultural communication. *Keio Communication Review, 14*, 37-50.

Ting-Toomey, S. (1988). Intercultural conflict styles: A face-negotiation theory. In Y. Y. Kim & W. B. Gudykunst (Eds.), *Theories in intercultural communication* (pp. 213-235). Newbury Park, CA: Sage.

Wierzbicka, A. (1991). Japanese key words and core cultural values. *Language in Society, 20*, 333-385.

Whiting, R. (1977). *The chrysanthemum and the bat: Baseball samurai style*. New York: Dodd.

9

Interclass Travel, Cultural Adaptation, and "Passing" as a Disjunctive Inter/Cultural Practice

DREAMA MOON • *California State University, San Marcos*

[T]o what extent [do] neocolonial forces, whether they be representations of "others" or representations of self, underwrite cultural, political, and academic discursive practices?

—Shome, 1996, p. 51

In her exploration of the possibility of a postcolonial rhetorical practice, Shome (1996) challenges communication scholars to analyze their own academic discourses and to situate them within larger political practices. In particular, she suggests that we must reflect on difficult questions, such as: To what extent do our scholarly practices serve the interests of existent relations of domination and hegemony within a society? As Shome suggests, it behooves us to reflect on our choices about the kind of issues we explore in our research and on how we choose to frame particular social topics. Issues such as these are currently being pursued by critical inter/cultural[1] scholars in a variety of ways.[2]

Part of the critical project within inter/cultural inquiry is to interrogate and potentially rework foundational concepts that seem to support business as usual. In particular, many critical scholars argue that inter/cultural inquiry could be broadened in useful ways via an engagement with the politics of power and domination. As part of the critical project, this

AUTHOR'S NOTE: An earlier draft of this work appeared as a chapter in my dissertation (directed by Thomas K. Nakayama, cochaired by Michael L. Hecht). A revised draft was presented at the 1999 conference of the Western States Communication Association. I extend my appreciation to Mary Jane Collier and the reviewers for their insightful comments on an earlier version of this chapter.

chapter takes up the concept of adaptation traditionally used in inter/cultural scholarship and rearticulates it within poststructuralist notions of identity and resistance. Specifically, I reframe adaptation in terms of passing as inter/cultural practice and argue that studying passing practices enables us to situate cultural adaptation, transitions, and cultural traveling within a framework of cultural politics. I do so by examining class passing practices identified in the discourses of women of working-class origin who are employed as office workers, adjunct faculty, and tenured and nontenured professors in the class-privileged academy.[3]

One of the most sustained critiques leveled by critical inter/cultural scholars has been concerned with the fragmentation of traditional ideas of "culture as nation-state" predominantly employed in mainstream inter/cultural inquiry (Flores, 1996; Moon, 1996; Ono, 1998; Nakayama, 1997; Nakayama & Krizek, 1995; Yep, 1998). With some limited exceptions (e.g., Butsch, 1992; Cloud, 1996; Moon & Rolison, 1998; Wander, 1979), the idea of social class as an important social and cultural marker has been ignored. This chapter adds to the critical project around culture by broadening it to include social class as an important aspect of cultural identity. Explicitly, I address the link between communication and social class, specifically how communicative processes such as adaptation work in the production and expression of class, classism, class privilege, and class resistance.

Following Bullock (1995), I recognize both the objective (i.e., educational attainment, occupation, income) and subjective (i.e., felt identity) elements involved in defining social class. Separating objective and subjective measures of class can be confusing, in that it distracts our attention from what joins these elements, their cultural situatedness. In this study, I take social class to be constituted in ways similar to the constitution of other cultural identities: group membership (both ascribed and avowed), dress, interests, everyday practices, speech patterns, tastes, and so forth, all occurring within historical, social, and political contexts (Foley, 1989). During the enculturation process, we learn the ways of our own class of origin, the ways of other classes, and the social value or lack thereof attached to them. In this way, our social class of origin—like race, sexual orientation, and gender—is integral to our sense of who we are, how the world works, and our place within that social world. Although later in life we might acculturate to other class realities, the effects of enculturation into our social class of origin are not obliterated. In this study, I ascertained the women's perceptions of their social class membership in two ways.[4] First, I posed this initial question to all interviewees:

> People talk about social classes such as the upper class, the poor, the middle class, the working class, and so forth. Do you consider yourself a member of a social class, and if so, what class would that be?

In addition, after the interview, each woman completed a short demographic questionnaire that asked them to identify both their current social class and their class of origin.

Although class analyses in communication research tend to be focused on deconstructing mediated texts (e.g., Cloud, 1996; Wander, 1979), I focus here on everyday communication practices. Raymond Williams (1980) cautions us against ignoring the "natural, everyday, and the ordinary" as sites of social reproduction as well as of contestation and struggle (p. 51). Thus, I conceptualize everyday communication as a primary means through which culture is expressed, patterns of interaction are shaped, and resistance and acquiescence to dominant class relations are levied. These everyday forms of interaction can reflect, produce, disrupt, and reinscribe dominant social relations around class. Thus, culture and cultural change are implicated in the communicative process in both constitutive and reactive ways.

This chapter proceeds in three sections. First, I provide a brief overview of traditional understandings of adaptation in the inter/cultural communication literature and discuss the methodological strategies I employed in this study. Then I present the notion of passing as a disjunctive inter/cultural practice deployed by women of working-class origin in the academy, explore three forms of passing practices identified in their narratives, and examine intersections among class passing and racial privilege. I end by suggesting how inter/cultural scholars might reconfigure adaptation and related foundational concepts in ways that are more reflective of the struggle and contestation that take place within and between cultural groups.

POLITICIZING ADAPTATION

Within inter/cultural research, the challenge presented by cultural transitions has received a fair amount of attention, accompanied by a substantial body of literature dealing with the process of adaptation (Anderson, 1994; Berry, 1992; Church, 1982; Jun, 1980; Keasley, 1989; Kim, 1995, 1996). Although this body of work is too extensive to cover in detail here, for the most part, these scholars seem to conceive of cultural travelers in nationalist terms (i.e., a U.S. American, a Japanese), and they conceive of adaptation as a linear, positive, and individualistic change process (Hegde, 1998).[5] In addition, these works often take an assimilationist tone, with the traveler expected to "take on the characteristics of the dominant group" (Subervi-Velez, 1986, p. 71). The linearity of adaptive processes as frequently conceived is illustrated in descriptions of movement from cultural outsider to insider (Kim, 1995). This evolutionary view is further exemplified in the work of Kim (1996) when she describes the successful adaptive outcome in this manner: "As the old 'person' breaks up, new cultural knowledge, attitudes, and behavioral elements are assimilated into an enactment of growth—an emergent 'new' person at a higher level of integration" (p. 357). Implied in this perspective is a free agent engaged actively in a process of evolution and growth.

Whereas Kim (1995, 1996) and others do attend to the fluid nature of identity, the focus remains on the migrant's efforts to adapt, his or her resiliency, and his or her ability to rise to the challenge that is passed by cultural difference (Hegde, 1998). Little is said about the effects of the dominant culture's attitudes toward various forms of difference, which, of course, have a great deal to do with travelers' adaptive experiences. As Anderson (1994) notes, "the stranger-host relationship is often an insider *versus* outsider relationship" (p. 306). Thus, it would seem that travelers' adaptive strategies must take into account the responses, real and imagined, of the dominant/host culture. For example, we have seen historically in the United States that some groups' efforts to assimilate or integrate have been impeded or simply denied, and other groups have experienced segregation and separation seemingly at the whim of the dominant/host culture. Although Berry (1992) and others have identified various types and modes of adaptation, they do not theorize the implications of power, either in terms of the choices travelers can and do make regarding these modes or in terms of the role of the dominant/host culture in migrants' choices and adaptive outcomes. In other words, although travelers do exercise power within the adaptive process, the dominant/host culture is in a position to thwart, or at least to complicate, adaptation processes. As a result, travelers who are members of subordinated groups may develop local tactical methods of survival when they must move among the majority culture (Gramsci, 1971; Shuter, 1982; Wolf, 1971).

One set of localized tactics that travelers may draw upon are passing practices. The articulation of such practices may help us capture the complexity of adaptive processes. Passing, as an inter/cultural practice, allows for shifting among identities and competencies and takes into account the power relations that usually undergird inter/cultural interactions. As a liminal practice, passing disrupts binary views of self/other and us/them and calls our attention to the politics of identity that play out within adaptive processes and inter/cultural travel (Fine, 1994; Hall, 1991).

In light of this, adaptation may fruitfully be seen as a dynamic process that plays out within prevailing relations of power operations. In this view, adaptation is a process composed of moves and countermoves as individuals and groups jockey for the most favorable positions available within the social structure. As a result, adaptation often incorporates elements of both resistance and acquiescence to the hegemonic social structural order. In short, adaptation is posited as a process of negotiation, in which identities (and, by association, resources attached to those identity positions) are struggled over and contested rather than simply retained or relinquished.

In the next section, I explore passing as a tactic of cultural players who are embroiled in situations within which judgments about inter/cultural competence have material effects. Drawing on interviews with nine women of working-class origin employed by a major university, I explore the ways in which these interclass travelers acquiesce to, navigate, and resist class-privileged notions of cultural competency. Moving in the elite context of the academy, these women articulate their tactics for navigating an often less than friendly environment. Though passing is a practice intelligible and accessible to all of these women, they differ in how they conceptualize passing, view its effects, and make choices about engaging it. The disagreement among them lends evidence to both the complexity of passing and the difficult decisions cultural travelers face in making use of adaptive strategies.

THE POLITICS OF CLASS PASSING

Having spent most of my life as a member of the lower class, my experiences within the university, and in particular graduate school, were fraught with culture shock. Quite often, I found myself filled with anxiety and doubt about my personal worth, my speech patterns, my style of dress, my intellectual abilities, and just about everything else that contributed to my sense of efficacy. I felt that I did not belong; however, when I visited home, the fit was no longer comfortable there either.

My personal experiences as a class traveler provided the impetus to develop a dissertation project that addressed class practices within the academy. As part of my research interests in race and gender, I chose to limit my study to white women. I conducted and audiotaped in-depth interviews with 13 white women employed in faculty and professional staff positions at a major U.S. University; 9 of these women are of working-class origin, and their narratives provide the data for this chapter. Some of the participants were women I knew and invited to participate, and others were referred to me by other participants. At the time of this study, all of these women occupied positions higher in the academic hierarchy than I did. As I worked with the transcripts using a variety of analytic strategies (Hurtado & Stewart, 1997; Scott, 1991; Strauss & Corbin, 1990), a number of themes emerged.[6] One such recurring theme was that of *class passing*. Although passing has been touted as a viable tactic of various marginalized groups (Daniel, 1992; Tyler, 1994), not everyone who can pass chooses to do so. For five of the women in this study, the deployment of passing was seen as a viable political response to class oppression, but for the others, passing was viewed as a form of acquiescence to the social implications of structural class systems.

The four women who opposed the use of passing often framed their opposition within an ideological commitment to the working class. Class and class identity were configured in distinctly political terms and were situated within larger structural and social relations. For these women, to pass was to acquiesce to the limits determined by, and the assumptions underlying, these relations. As Frankie,[7] a tenured professor, illustrated,

> I think how you theorize, how you think about being a poor kid, influences whether or not you feel it is necessary to pass, and also how you explain how you got where you are. I think we're so ingrained in individualistic ideology: I am where I am because of my work and my abilities. It's not an adequate explanation. It has a lot to do with structure. It has a lot to do with chance. And by that, I really mean "structured random chance" for kids from the lower class. I mean, we have structured into this society, chances for *some* kids from the lower class.

Women who situate social class in these terms are highly aware of its links to, and intersections with, other structures of privilege and penalty, such as race and sex. For them, the deployment of passing as an adaptive tactic is viewed as an individualist response to a structural issue, one that disrupts the connection between theory and practice. In their view, how one conceptualizes this theory-practice link frames and informs the kinds of decisions one makes regarding passing. As Bonnie, another tenured professor, observed,

> We have real hierarchies in this society that say that class membership makes you worthy, and that's what I oppose. Just as we have those divisions that say membership in a particular gender makes you worthy, or *worthier* to put a finer point on it. In terms of sexual orientation, in terms of race, it's the same thing.

Among these women, passing is sometimes positioned as a form of denial and disengagement with historical and structural realities and as a rejection of a historically informed cultural identity. Although identity is not posited as a presocial essence, the historical, social, and structural implications of one's class position and class identity are recognized. In this view, passing is configured as "not being true to who you are." Contrary to what a surface reading of this position might suggest, this picture of passing does not signify the existence of an essentialized identity but instead positions identification as an inherently political act—one that resists hegemonic ascriptions of identity and the meanings embedded in identification labels. Betty, a secretary, articulated this oppositional stance:

> When I think of *lower class,* I don't think of a person who is "lower" in terms of "worse," but I do think of it in terms of someone who maybe isn't interested in participating in consumer culture and who has different philosophical views. Like [the idea], "let's give all the corporations lots of money and the biggest tax cuts." That to me is totally reversed to my [way of] thinking.

Her viewpoint illustrates the complexity of passing as an adaptive strategy. Here, identification is seen as a political act. One behaves "true to who one is" by enacting behaviors that are seen as politically aligned with progressive leftist politics. Thus, identification is not about essences but about positions that one takes up in response to oppressive structural conditions. In this view, to pass is to reinscribe these conditions both implicitly and explicitly.

Class Passing and White Privilege

The women who refused to pass presented the most detailed analyses of the interlocking nature of systems of privilege based on race, sex, class, and so forth. These women described the ways that privilege works and explored their own individual relationships to, and participation in, these systems. Alice, a tenured professor, outlined this position:

> I recognize three major divisions of power [race, class, and gender] in this society. I don't want to be a part of perpetuating them, but at the same time, I refuse to ignore them, and pretend they don't exist. I think that one of the many places that we might start in terms of coming to grips with all of this is to acknowledge the divisions and talk about the depths to which they affect us as human beings.

This respondent echoes my belief that people can use the social penalties that they experience in a particular arena as a means of engaging with their privilege in other arenas. Collins (1990) spends a great deal of time explaining how one might utilize this strategy as a means of gaining greater personal insights and of developing more nuanced social analyses. She does, however, note that there is no necessary correspondence between one's experience of subordination and the development of critical abilities. Such connections must be forged consciously over time.

These four women seem to have used their subordinate class status to reflect on race and white privilege. Following Wildman (1996), they position privilege as a form of social entitlement to which privileged persons often seem oblivious. For instance, in their observations of the apparent invisibility of class privilege to the middle class, they expressed amazement that middle-class people often seem to feel a sense of entitlement that they themselves did not. Frankie specified this point when she noted,

> Like if you would go to a restaurant or something, people with a privileged background have an expectation that if the service isn't right or something, they would complain. I'm happy if *anybody* is waiting on me at all, and I don't

have to cook and wash up afterwards! It is sort of a different orientation towards privilege that I don't feel I share.

Similarly, Alice expresses her frustration that the middle class seems to expect, as a matter of course, treatment and resources that she sees as privilege. She related a story about a man of middle-class origin she had once dated:

> We were talking about welfare, and he goes, "Well, no one ever gave me anything. I did it all myself." I just went ballistic on him! I said, "Yeah! You grew up in a home where it is *expected* that you go to college and you always *knew* you would go to college. You had dental care, which I certainly didn't have. You had good health care, which I didn't have growing up. Your college was paid for! You were given everything!" One of his complaints was that his parents didn't give him an allowance when he got into college, and he had to actually earn his own spending money. At that moment I thought, this crystallizes the difference between us. I grew up with none of that. He did, and so he expected it. To him, all of that was a given. It was not something he got. In fact, like he said, he got "nothing."

One cannot help noticing that middle-class persons may perceive the privileges attached to their class status as "nothing," just as many whites fail to perceive the social benefits attached to their racial membership (Nakayama & Krizek, 1995).

Moving beyond merely observing that they possess white privilege, the women tended to focus on how best to participate politically and personally. For instance, Betty, a secretary, posed the following:

> The issue of race is very important to me. At the same time, what's the potential of white people? That's real important too. In terms of what is our potential to be supportive and to play a supportive role as opposed to the dominant role. And in those instances where you're asked to participate and to contribute, how do you do that without dominating? And I think that's a real important question for me.

Here is where these women bring to light more clearly the basis for their rejection of passing. In their analyses, class passing is viewed as a form of internalized oppression, confirmation that one has accepted the view of self constructed by others. Bonnie most clearly articulated this:

I think the whole notion of internalized oppression has become very important to me in terms of the real structural and institutional potential to cause individuals to become complicitous in their own oppression. Part of that complicity is fleeing who you are. Of *not* being from the lower class, of *not* being a woman, of *not* being a white person, of not being a person of color. So for me, the acknowledgment of one's structural and historical identity is extremely important and that's one step on to saying "What do we do about this?"

In this view, to pass is to comply, to participate freely in one's oppression. In addition, passing may impede the sorts of careful investigation required to dismantle systems of privilege. In short, these women saw passing as a reactionary, rather than an oppositional, adaptive tactic. In the next section, I examine the narratives of the women who employed passing practices.

VARIETIES OF PASSING PRACTICES

I now turn to the five women for whom passing was a viable response to interclass relations within the academy. Using a traditional cultural adaptation lens, their behavior might be viewed as merely assimilative, and without potentially disruptive tensions. However, rereading passing as a strategy of the socially disenfranchised, which is chosen as a way of making use of imposed systems within which one is situated, enables a more nuanced reading (de Certeau, 1984). Although compulsion may be a privilege of the powerful, as de Certeau suggests, the weak can exercise power and perhaps avoid compulsion to some degree by using tactically chosen adaptive strategies such as passing. Passing as a transformative practice can upend class relations, and, like any other social behavior, passing can also cement those relations. From our conversations, I identified three forms of passing practices, each having a different emphasis. The first form was used to lay claim to privileges often reserved for the middle and upper classes. Here, women were interested in gaining material rewards and resources otherwise denied them. The second passing practice was seen as an attempt to achieve acceptability within groups perceived as desirable. The last practice, oppositional inter/cultural competence, was perhaps the most varied tactic described by the women. Here, women used oppositional forms of competence to parody the elite class, to investigate the class politics of the middle class, to code-switch with their class peers, and to resist being positioned by the middle class in ways they did not like or choose.

Laying Claim, Playing the Game

In this form of passing, the women's focus is on appropriating whatever material resources and rewards they can within a hierarchically ranked class system not designed to benefit them. They work hard, although they comprehend that hard work and individual effort are insufficient to become what Cora calls "a player in the game." For instance, Cora acknowledges that although there are some successful people "who have done it on their own," she perceives that "these are exceptions rather than the rule." Cora's story best exemplifies this passing practice. It is important to note that she positions this adaptive tactic as a "game," suggesting that, although she is aware of the game's real material rewards and penalties, she is quite clear on the constructed rather than natural nature of the game.

Cora works as an administrative assistant in her office. She works two jobs in order to make ends meet and to maintain some of the outer trappings of class privilege. As she stated,

> Sometimes it [working two jobs] means sacrificing things like days off, like vacation time, like just any free time for me. I have to sacrifice these things because I have to work extra hard to maintain the lifestyle that I want. I have to have more than one job to make enough money to be more than lower class.

Cora said that she can get at least some of what she wants by learning and playing by what she calls "the rules of the game." For example, one of the rules she learned is that education is monetarily rewarded within university employment, so she obtained a master's degree, which gave her "some more money." She stated, "If I had not have completed my master's degree, I would not have gotten that little extra every year." Earning a "little extra" not only benefits her personally, but more important, it puts her in a position to assist family members and friends who lack material resources. In turn, some family members are able to acquire more cultural capital in terms of higher education, which allows them to better position themselves within the class rewards system and assist still other members of the family. In this way, playing the game is a tactic that allows for communal as well as individual benefits.

Becoming a player is not without risks. One can quickly lose sight of the notion of play and develop a possessive investment in the game (Lipsitz, 1998). When the game—be it classism, racism, or sexism—has a "cash value," people often invest in identities and behaviors that provide them with "resources, power, and opportunity" (Lipsitz, 1998, p. vii). If this occurs, one may become a cultural enforcer, imposing and re-producing, rather than disrupting, oppressive cultural rules. Women of working-class origin who have found playing the game beneficial may become frustrated with those of their class who eschew passing.

Again, Cora offers a pertinent example. Cora expressed a great deal of annoyance with one of her supervisees. The offending situation revolves around the employee's refusal to take college courses, despite the fact that by doing so, she is likely to obtain the promotion and raise she has pursued for some time. The employee, who did not complete high school, isn't interested in pursuing additional education, and the position she wants does not require it. Although the job description indicates that job experience may be substituted for education, Cora astutely noted,

> It [the job description] says "so many years experience OR a degree." If you don't have that degree, that "so many years" doesn't matter. I don't care WHAT that job description says over in Human Resources. They will NOT ap-prove a promotion for her because she doesn't have a degree.

Despite the employee's many years of experience and satisfactory per-formance, the university consistently refuses to approve her promotion. Cora's advice is to "take classes and play the game." As Cora puts it, "The rule says you got to have that college education to quote unquote 'get ahead.'"

Although Cora's intent is to be helpful, she begins to impose the game on the supervisee. When Cora's employee resists, she, rather than the university, becomes the target of Cora's frustration and anger. In this way, instead of becoming an advocate for the employee's promotion, Cora becomes a gatekeeper for the game, a role that functions to keep the rules, and the social relations enabled by them, in place. When asked if she saw the University's treatment of this woman as fair, Cora replied,

> As soon as you learn the rules of the game and you play the game, then you're one of the players. If you fight it, if you don't want to play the game by their rules, then you're not accepted as one of them.

Cora may be astute in her observation that being a dedicated and de-pendable employee does not get you what you want if you buck the sys-tem; however, she does not interrogate her own role in maintaining that system. In our conversation, I pointed out that, even if this woman took classes, it would literally take years for her to obtain a degree. Cora responded, "Yeah, but it would *look* like she was making some progress." Here, Cora exhibits her awareness of the link between visibility cues and material effects of social categories. In other words, she emphasizes that if one *looks* like a player, one will be *treated* like a player.

Two issues seem important here. The first is Cora's emphasis on *performative* aspects of passing, and the second is her seeming lack of empathy with the plight of her employee. In terms of the first issue, Cora situates playing the game within a politics of visibility that involves not simply playing by the rules but, perhaps more important, *appearing* to play by them—a more nuanced tactic. For Cora, appearing to play the game functions effectively in assisting the class passer in achieving her objectives. Also, despite the unfair treatment experienced by her employee, Cora does not seem to empathize with her struggle. Although one of the functions of written job descriptions is to prevent the sort of arbitrariness present in this situation from occurring, Cora seems to view the employee's refusal to use the rules to her advantage as more problematic than the lack of fairness or justice contained within the university rules system.

Garnering In-Group Acceptance

Passing practices may also be used to gain entry into neighborhoods of desirability, cultural spaces inhabited by those with greater amounts of privilege. These spaces are not necessarily geographic; instead, they are frequently metaphorical locations in which one may feel at home and safe. Whereas Cora employs passing as a tactic for gaining material rewards, Flo, a secretary, appears to be more concerned with garnering reference group acceptance. Bradshaw (1992) articulates this use of passing as "an attempt to achieve acceptability by claiming membership in some desired group" (p. 79) and to avoid the psychic pain often associated with out-group membership. Here, social rather than material benefits seem to be prioritized.

The social penalties of being ascribed a lower-class identity often include ridicule, social exclusion, and loss of self-esteem (Ehrenreich, 1989; Gardner, 1993; Langston, 1993). Such penalties encourage coming to see oneself and one's class through the middle-class gaze. For instance, when Kelly, an adjunct faculty member, brought friends from college to her parents' home, they made fun of her parents' working-class tastes and activities. She says, "For the first time I [felt] shame about where I came from." Her response was to stop talking about her parents and her childhood and to never bring friends from college home in the future.

In Flo's case, although in-group acceptance is important to her view of self as a secretary, she has few material resources available with which to construct a middle-class persona. As a mother almost completely responsible for the financial support of her family because of her husband's physical disability, Flo must call on other resources in order to develop an effective passing practice. The persona that she constructs relies on a complex mix of education, tastes, and practices. For example, Flo admits that "it is very important" to her that people know that she has a master's degree; prefers the "finer" things in life, such as classical music, literature, and intellectual conversation; and is "erudite."

The class pass in Flo's case is complicated by the dissonance created by conflicts around the reality of what she does (i.e., her occupation as a secretary), what being a secretary signifies to her, and the manner in which she desires to be perceived. Reminiscent of Bonnie's view of passing as a way of minimizing contradiction, Flo lives in/out the contradiction between who she appears to be and who she is. Flo explained the meanings surrounding the sign of secretary:

> When I think "secretary," I think of this woman I worked with in Oklahoma when I was a work study student—Shirley. Horrible dyed hair, home dye job, always had huge roots. Really awful blue eye shadow, too much of it. Chewed gum all the time and would always tell me about these meals she was making with "ham-berger" meat [said with a twang]. She could type like a demon—96 words a minute after mistakes! She was phenomenal, but she was *so,* just *so,* she epitomized "secretary!" which is lower class to me. And I'm a secretary now. That's all I am. And it's important to me for people to know that I *did* go to school. Especially in an academic setting. See, I told you: SNOB! It's kind of like I *have* to do this [work as a secretary]. I have a degree in vocal performance and there's not a lot of call for wanna-be opera singers.

In an extremely complex reversal, the self that Flo constructs for the consumption of others is that of an opera-singer-passing-as-a-secretary. In our discussion, she persisted in positioning herself as a "snob," another element of the middle-class persona as she conceives it. The disjunctures in her presentation cause Flo to doubt whether her constructed class self is convincing to the people around her, especially to the faculty, for whom, she says, "class seems more of an issue." For example, Flo observes that students are "less quick to look down on you if you just wear jeans all the time and don't have a new outfit every day of the week and a zillion pairs of shoes!"

In addition, many of the faculty with whom Flo works are self-identified feminists, which further complicates matters for her. When she first came to the department, she thought that "feminism was kind of like a real equalizer" and that status hierarchy would give way to what she calls "a flat thing instead of a pyramid." She was quite disappointed to find that "some feminists are more equal than others." Flo further reflected,

> It's just that it was surprising to me, and sometimes things go on here that I think "But you're a feminist! How could you possibly do this?!" You know, I thought feminism was kind of like a real equalizer, but it's not.

Thus, Flo learned a painful lesson about how class loyalties can interfere with gender solidarity. Flo's story points to the ways in which gender and social class identities often intersect to create status hierarchies and to highlight differences among women as a group. In short, gender solidarity may be a rather naive expectation in a multistructured society in which race and class interests often intersect with gender to create different alliances among people.

Despite Flo's attempts to pass, the ways in which some faculty members communicate with her serve as painful reminders of her out-group status. She recollected moments in which she experienced feeling like an outsider:

> I guess I feel more of that when a lot of name dropping goes on. I'm only thinking of a couple of the professors, but it's like "When I was talking to so-and-so" or "when I was in such-and-such a place." Invariably, it's like they're basically saying "Well, I'm really cool cause I did this or I've been there and you haven't." I'm not particularly well-traveled because I've never had the opportunity or the money. Our professors get to go to really exciting and fun places and I think that's cool, but when they start using it as a means of drawing attention to themselves, then I think "Wait a minute here! There are other people here who have experiences that are just as valuable!"

Flo particularly experiences feelings of not belonging when asked to perform what she views as "menial tasks." She sees such requests as communicating status and power in a way that positions her outside the realm of the in-group:

I don't find people treating us, the staff, as lackeys necessarily. Sometimes they [faculty] get to be a bit. . . . Well, alright, when I'm given an envelope and they say "Would you type this?" I think "Type it yourself!" To me, it's like this, "type my envelope." And I think, I'm in the middle of doing something here and you want me to stop and type your envelope! Or fax something. When you could do it yourself. Just little incidents now and then. There's a general feeling that their time is more valuable than mine which, I suppose, is defined by society. If I quit, there's always somebody willing to step right in, because there are always people who need work and a job.

Flo's closing comments demonstrate an awareness of the structural dimensions of the class hierarchy and of her place within it, reminding her of the temporary and conditional nature of whatever in-group acceptance that she is able to garner.

Oppositional Inter/Cultural Competence

The third form of passing practices is grounded in notions of inter/cultural competence. In general, the traditional inter/cultural scholarship defines competence in terms of two dimensions, effectiveness and appropriateness (Collier, 1988, 1989, 1998; Hecht, 1978; Koester, Wiseman, & Sanders, 1993; Martin, 1993; Spitzberg & Brunner, 1991; Spitzberg & Cupach, 1984; Spitzberg & Hecht, 1984). Effectiveness involves making judgments about communicative performances and outcomes, whereas appropriateness constitutes what is considered proper and suitable (Koester et al., 1993). The role of cultural identity is also emphasized, in that judgments of inter/cultural communication competence are predicated on the extent to which interactants' cultural identities are mutually avowed and confirmed in inter/cultural interactions (Collier, 1988; Hecht, Collier, & Ribeau, 1993).

Because judgments of competence seem to be social rather than simply personal, such determinations constitute another arena of contestation and struggle, as marginalized groups seek to resist, subvert, and make use of dominant perceptions of competency. When passing practices are developed as tactics for enacting oppositional inter/cultural competence, the notion of competence referenced is of a different form. Although inter/cultural scholars seem to agree that different cultural groups (i.e., based on race, nation, or ethnicity) do competence differently, variations in competence among class groups have seldom been considered (Collier, 1988; Hecht, Collier, & Ribeau, 1993; Martin, 1993; Spitzberg & Brunner, 1991).[8] In addition, within the context of cultural transitions, it is often the migrant's competence that is at issue rather than that of the host culture. Though we can think of historical examples in which migrants successfully opposed incompetent responses by the host culture to their adaptation attempts (e.g., racial segregation, internment camps), judgments of competency made by hosts, who tend to exercise more power within the social milieu, are likely to carry more social weight.

In oppositional forms of class competence, the elements of parody, play, opposition, and resistance are often incorporated in order to situate competence within a frame of cultural politics. This use of passing practices is highly complex, because middle-class competence rules may sometimes be used to subvert the social relations available within a particular context, whereas in other situations, exaggerated displays of inter/cultural competence and strategic (in)competence are deployed as forms of mimicry. In other words, in oppositional inter/cultural competence, the goal is not to be appropriate, but to deploy cultural knowledge about middle-class competence as a way of disrupting or parodying its hegemony or of protecting one's sense of self-worth.

Tanya's story provides us with an example of oppositional class competence that involves a constant working back and forth between class identity positions and perceptions of competence. Tanya is a newly tenured professor. She experiences a great deal of anger and annoyance with what she calls the "self-promotional demands of being a professor." In terms of working-class practices, talking about oneself and one's accomplishments is neither valued nor encouraged, particularly if one is a woman (Gardner, 1993). In addition, self-aggrandizement, according to Hurtado (1996), is frequently a norm within dominant groups that functions to keep people in their proper places. Confronted with academic pressure to self-promote, Tanya experiences a dilemma. Her response is predicated on the context of the interaction. For instance, she employs a sort of strategic ambiguity in dealing with working-class persons. Her comment highlights the context-dependent aspect of identity, inter/cultural competence, and passing.

Tanya said that, in the academy, "I never feel like I belong, like a professor-person." Her feelings reflect those of many working-class women in academe, who often feel that they straddle two class cultures without fully belonging to either one (Langston, 1993). In professional situations, Tanya seeks out people for interaction whom she describes as "normal, everyday people who are not taken with the fact that they are professors." In dealing with those whom she views as class peers, Tanya employs a kind of strategic ambiguity about her occupation in order to minimize distance between herself and these persons:

> I don't even usually tell people what I do. Some people ask me what I do and I tell them "I teach." Like this group that I go to. I haven't told them what I do. They know that I am the cook [in the group] and that's about all they know. When I go to Santa Fe, I don't tell the people out there what I do. In fact, a lot of people have said, "you don't seem like a professor and you don't act like one." Well, how are you supposed to act? You know, they're supposed to be snobby and intellectual. I don't want to give off that aura. I think that it shouldn't matter. I think it sounds pretentious, like I'm brighter than I am.

In elaborating on her tendency to downplay her university position, she expresses trepidation that people will assume that she believes that she is superior to them because of her educational status. She also seems to be concerned that the channels of communication between herself and others would be negatively affected:

> It's just that I have more education than other people. That's all it means. I don't want people to feel like they can't talk to me. So, that's why I don't like to talk about what I do because I think it impedes conversation with people.

Thus, in Tanya's view, class privilege, or the ascription of such privilege, disrupts competent communication, in that privilege is always already a reflection of the social disavowal of the identity of the other. In short, the interaction never begins at the same starting line for interactants but is always already imbued with cultural politics. Strategic ambiguity can be used in this way as a tactic for equalizing the interpersonal relations between self and others.

On the other hand, Tanya depends on the tactics of exaggerating middle-class competence or using very aggressive forms of it when dealing with arrogant professors or other class elite. Although Tanya seems to experience a degree of discomfort with the privilege implied by her occupational class position, she does not hesitate to invoke this privilege when her sense of self is threatened:

> There are times when someone is being obnoxious that I will tell them that I'm on the faculty and I have a doctorate and I will say it exactly in that [uppity] tone. You know, there are times when I think that if someone's trying to be superior to me that I'll do that because I know that will shut them up in a hurry. If

I were talking to a blue blood from Philadelphia, I would be sure to tell them exactly who I was!

In this context, Tanya invokes an aggressive form of middle-class competence. Her communicative goal here is quite different than it was in her previous story. Whereas with "everyday people," she exercises a strategically ambiguous form of competence in order to make connections and to encourage communication, this desire is absent in the latter context. Tanya's enactments of inter/cultural competence appear to be context-dependent and, more important, power-sensitive. For instance, because self-promotion seems to be a valued cultural practice within academic and other class-privileged groups, to invoke this norm aggressively with "blue-bloods" or arrogant professors can be seen as an appropriate and effective response, whereas to do so with people closer to her working-class roots is not. In addition, Tanya's disapproval of self-promotion norms suggests the presence of another view of inter/cultural communication competence that stands in opposition to the communication competency rules of the privileged class.

A second form of oppositional competence noted in the women's discourses involves the employment of mimicry or parody. Mimicry entails deliberately taking on a subordinate role, in an exaggerated way, and donning, in a performative sense, the identity one has already been assigned (Irigaray, 1985). However, the performance is intended to display the ascribed identity as a "fake rather than the natural or real thing" (Tyler, 1994, p. 235). Mimicry can also involve the performance of a sort of hyperincompetence or a strategic form of (in)competence deployed as an "in-your-face" tactic within class-privileged environments. Alice, an office worker, related a story about her middle/upper-class colleagues that illustrates these ideas:

> Nothing gives me greater pleasure than going to dinner with my hoity-toity friends and I'll take my napkin and put it in my shirt collar and sit there with my knife and fork on the table in both hands and it just appalls them!

Drawing on her cultural knowledge of middle-class norms, tastes, and notions of competence, Alice rather enjoys parodying what she might describe as the "hoity-toityness" of the class privilege. In performing hyperstereotypical perceptions of the lower class for the viewing pleasure of middle-class audiences, she makes fun of class distinctions and of negative attributions regarding the lower class. However, it is unclear in her account if her friends ever get the joke. This lack of clarity highlights the problematic nature of parody and mimicry. As Tyler (1994) points out, mimicry is a highly nuanced tactic in that it is extremely audience centered; that is, one assumes that the other will be able to get the joke. When others do not get it, negative stereotypes often become more deeply entrenched within the minds of the audience, thus shoring up oppressive class relations rather than disrupting them in any substantial way.

The last form of oppositional class competence identified in our conversations centered around a strategic form of class (in)competence that must be distinguished from the preceding discussion on parody. In this form of oppositional class competence, the class passer may employ strategic violations of middle-class competence rules in order to ascertain the class politics of others. In other words, this is a means of discovering "where people are coming from." Alice described a work situation in which she used this tactic:

> I'd go to these meetings on campus and the women would be dressed in their suits and stuff like that. And I might go in my Levis because I want[ed] to see what their reaction [would be]. I want[ed] to see if they're looking beyond what the outside of people is.

More than simply identifying the class alliances of others, Alice expressed that this tactic also helped her make decisions about developing potential allies. Clearly, she is seeking out those individuals who are able to look beyond mere appearances to other aspects of the person. Whereas parody depends on others' ability to get the joke, strategic (in)competence is a passing practice aimed at acquiring information in order to form alliances that might aid one in navigating the class-privileged academic culture.

PASSING AS INTER/CULTURAL PRACTICE

> [P]assing is about identities: their creation or imposition, their adoption or rejection, their accompanying rewards or penalties. Passing is also about the boundaries established between identity categories and about the individual and cultural anxieties induced by boundary crossing. Finally, passing is about specularity: the visible and the invisible, the seen and the unseen. (Ginsberg, 1996, p. 2)

Ginsberg's comments suggest that one of the assumed effects of living in a racist, sexist, and classist society is the internalization by members of subordinated groups of the dominant culture's definitions and characterizations of them. Passing as an inter/cultural practice indicates that the relation between dominant definitions and their internalization by cultural travelers is more complex than traditional treatments of adaptation reveal. Cultural actors deploy passing practices in ways that may reinscribe dominant class caricatures but that also call them into question, play with them, and deconstruct them; furthermore, all of these often occur simultaneously.

Passing as a disjunctive practice threatens the security of dominant identities by creating category crisis, defined by Garber (1992) as "a failure of definitional distinction, a borderline that becomes permeable, that permits border crossings from one (apparently distinct) category to another" (p. 16). In foregrounding the liminal, passing practices call into question fixed concepts of identity and move us beyond nostalgic visions of originary identities (Rust, 1996). This link between essence and enactment is a crucial one for inter/cultural communication scholars. As Rust (1996) points out, passing practices "ridicule essentialist notions of a 'true' self" (p. 23). This insight is particularly relevant to inter/cultural communication inquiry in retheorizing adaptation as a process that produces identities rather than one that is entered into by prediscursive subjects.

The study of passing practices not only highlights the politicized aspect of identification processes, but also further complicates other significant inter/cultural concepts, such as cultural adaptation and inter/cultural competence. Passing offers an alternative to traditional ways of conceptualizing modes of adaptation by situating cultural transition processes within prevailing relations of power. Although the impacts of situational and social elements are sometimes remarked upon in the inter/cultural literature on cultural transitions, the majority of research addresses the issue of adaptation at the psychological level, thus deflecting the power relations implicated in the transition experience and placing the onus for failure to adjust or adapt primarily on the shoulders of the individual migrant. Within a passing framework, adaptation can be reenvisioned as a process of negotiation within which identities are contested and struggled over rather than simply retained or relinquished.

Finally, the traditional inter/cultural literature treats the concept of cultural travel (i.e., sojourning) within primarily international contexts, obscuring how transition processes are experienced in other venues, such as that of interclass travel. By making links to these other venues, conceptual and theoretical concepts may be broadened to include other contexts, and connections between multiple layers of identification can be made more easily.

In conclusion, the differences between scholars' attention to more traditional modes of adaptation and passing appear to be located in the focus on the inherently political nature of passing, attendance to power dynamics, and play with essentialized views of identity. Passing practices offer an alternative vision of adaptation by situating transition processes within current structural and political relations. Passing practices necessitate recognition of the wider social relations within which one moves, of one's place within them, and of one's willingness to move to or go beyond borders. In these ways, passing as a disjunctive inter/cultural communicative practice highlights the problematic nature of identification processes as well as the way these processes play out within cultural transitions.

NOTES

1. The term *inter/cultural* is used to denote a stance that acknowledges the dialectical tensions between and among cultural and intercultural elements present in all inter/cultural encounters. It also points to the arbitrariness of the borders that inter/cultural scholars construct, and often police, to separate and distinguish the "intra-" from the "inter-" cultural, the emic from the etic, and so forth.

2. For example, see Chang and Holt (1997); Collier (1998); Dace and McPhail (1997); Halualani (1997); Hegde (1998); Leeds-Hurwitz (1997); Martin and Nakayama (1999); Martin, Nakayama, and Flores (1998); Moon (1996, 1998, 1999); Moon and Rolison (1998); Ono (1998); and Yep (1998).

3. As part of my dissertation project, I interviewed nine white women of working-class origin. My research questions revolved around how these women constructed their gender, class, and racial identities and how they came to understand themselves as "woman," as white, and as classed. Although for the purposes of this chapter I am highlighting the class aspects of their narratives, gender and whiteness also play out in these class enactments in myriad ways. In other places, I highlight other cultural aspects (for example, for a more focused discussion of the interactions of gender, race, and class within these narratives, see Moon (1999).

4. The strategies I used to ascertain the social class memberships of the women in this study were developed from the ideas generated by Jackman and Jackman's (1983) national study on social class in the United States.

5. For an excellent review of cross-cultural adaptation literature, see Anderson (1994).

6. Drawing from researchers such as Hurtado and Stewart (1997), Scott (1991), and Strauss and Corbin (1990), I developed what I call a "critical qualitative" analysis of the data. The primary differences between traditional and critical qualitative analyses as I see

them are twofold: (a) an emphasis on "thick" analysis rather than thick description; and (b) an attempt to link individual experience to collective realities, such as historical and political contexts, power relations, structural implications, and so forth. In other words, the interest is not simply in letting participants speak for themselves, but also in "connect[ing] their experiences to a broader social framework" (Hurtado, 1996, p. viii).

7. The names of the women, cities, and other identifying information have been changed to protect the participants' confidentiality.

8. For examples that do address notions of class competency within communication, see Huspek (1993, 1994).

REFERENCES

Anderson, L. E. (1994). A new look at an old construct: Cross-cultural adaptation. *International Journal of Intercultural Relations, 18,* 293-328.

Berry, J. W. (1992). Psychology of acculturation: Understanding individuals moving between two cultures. In R. W. Brislin (Ed.), *Applied cross-cultural psychology* (pp. 232-253). Newbury Park, CA: Sage.

Bradshaw, C. K. (1992). Beauty and the beast: On racial ambiguity. In M. P. P. Root (Ed.), *Racially mixed people in America* (pp. 79-88). Newbury Park, CA: Sage.

Bullock, H. E. (1995). Class acts: Middle-class responses to the poor. In B. Lott & D. Maluso (Eds.), *The social psychology of interpersonal discrimination* (pp. 118-159). New York: Guilford.

Butsch, R. (1992). Class and gender in four decades of television situation comedy: Plus ça change . . . *Critical Studies in Mass Communication, 9,* 387-399.

Chang, H. C., & Holt, G. R. (1997). Intercultural training for expatriates: Reconsidering power and politics. In A. González & D. V. Tanno (Eds.), *Communication and identity across cultures* (International and Intercultural Communication Annual, Vol. 20, pp. 207-230). Thousand Oaks, CA: Sage.

Church, A. (1982). Sojourner adjustment. *Psychological Bulletin, 91,* 540-575.

Cloud, D. L. (1996). Hegemony or concordance? The rhetoric of tokenism in "Oprah" Winfrey's rags-to-riches biography. *Critical Studies in Mass Communication, 13,* 115-137.

Collier, M. J. (1988). A comparison of intracultural and intercultural communication among acquaintances: How intra- and intercultural competencies vary. *Communication Quarterly, 36,* 122-144.

Collier, M. J. (1989). Cultural and intercultural communication competence: Current approaches and directions for future research. *International Journal of Intercultural Relations, 13,* 287-302.

Collier, M. J. (1998). Researching cultural identity: Reconciling interpretive and postcolonial perspectives. In D. V. Tanno & A. González (Eds.), *Communication and identity across cultures* (International and Intercultural Communication Annual, Vol. 21, pp. 122-147). Thousand Oaks, CA: Sage.

Collins, P. H. (1990). *Black feminist thought: Knowledge, consciousness, and the politics of empowerment.* New York: Routledge.

Dace, K. L., & McPhail, M. L. (1997). Complicity and coherence in intra/intercultural communication: A dialogue. In A. González & D. V. Tanno (Eds.), *Communication and identity across cultures* (International and Intercultural Communication Annual, Vol. 20, pp. 27-47). Thousand Oaks, CA: Sage.

Daniel, G. R. (1992). Passers and pluralists: Subverting the racial divide. In M. P. P. Root (Ed.), *Racially mixed people in America* (pp. 91-107). Newbury Park, CA: Sage.

de Certeau, M. (1984). *The practice of everyday life* (S. Rendall, Trans.). Berkeley: University of California Press.

Ehrenreich, B. (1989). *Fear of falling: The inner life of the middle class.* New York: HarperPerennial.

Fine, M. (1994). Working the hyphens: Reinventing self and other in qualitative research. In N. K. Denzin & Y. S. Lincoln (Eds.), *Handbook of qualitative research* (pp. 70-82). Thousand Oaks, CA: Sage.

Flores, L. A. (1996). Creating discursive space through a rhetoric of difference: Chicana feminists craft a homeland. *Quarterly Journal of Speech, 82,* 142-156.

Foley, D. E. (1989). Does the working class have a culture in the anthropological sense? *Cultural Anthropology, 4,* 137-162.

Garber, M. (1992). *Vested interest: Cross-dressing and cultural anxiety.* New York: Routledge.

Gardner, S. (1993). "What's a nice working-class girl like you doing in a place like this?" In M. M. Tokarczyk & E. A. Fay (Eds.), *Working-class women in the academy: Laborers in the knowledge factory* (pp. 49-59). Amherst: University of Massachusetts Press.

Ginsberg, E. K. (1996). Introduction. In E. K. Ginsberg (Ed.), *Passing and the fictions of identity* (pp. 1-18). Durham, NC: Duke University Press.

Gramsci, A. (1971). *Selections from the prison notebooks of Antonio Gramsci* (Q. Hoare & G. N. Novell-Smith, Eds. & Trans.). New York: International.

Hall, S. (1991). Ethnicity, identity, and difference. *Radical America, 3,* 9-22.

Halualani, R. T. (1997). A sovereign nation's functional mythic discourses. In A. González & D. V. Tanno (Eds.), *Communication and identity across cultures* (International and Intercultural Communication Annual, Vol. 20, pp. 89-121). Thousand Oaks, CA: Sage.

Hecht, M. L. (1978). Toward a conceptualization of interpersonal communication satisfaction. *Quarterly Journal of Speech, 64,* 47-62.

Hecht, M. L., Collier, M. J., & Ribeau, S. A. (1993). *African American communication: Ethnic identity and cultural interpretation.* Newbury Park, CA: Sage.

Hegde, R. S. (1998). Swinging the trapeze: The negotiation of identity among Asian Indian immigrant women in the United States. In D. V. Tanno & A. González (Eds.), *Communication and identity across cultures* (International and Intercultural Communication Annual, Vol. 21, pp. 34-55). Thousand Oaks, CA: Sage.

Hurtado, A. (1996). *The color of privilege: Three blasphemies on race and feminism.* Ann Arbor: University of Michigan Press.

Hurtado, A., & Stewart, A. J. (1997). Through the looking glass: Implications of studying whiteness for feminist methods. In M. Fine, L. Weis, L. C. Powell, & L. M. Wong (Eds.), *Off white: Readings on race, power, and society* (pp. 297-311). New York: Routledge.

Huspek, M. (1993). Dueling structures: The theory of resistance in discourse. *Communication Theory, 3,* 1-25.

Huspek, M. (1994). Oppositional codes and social class relations. *British Journal of Sociology, 45,* 79-102.

Irigaray, L. (1985). *This sex which is not one* (C. Porter with C. Burke, Trans.). Ithaca, NY: Cornell University Press.

Jackman, M. R., & Jackman, R. W. (1983). *Social class awareness in the United States.* Berkeley: University of California Press.

Jun, J. -K. (1980). Explaining acculturation in a communication framework. *Communication Monographs, 47,* 155-179.

Keasley, D. J. (1989). A study of cross-cultural effectiveness: Theoretical issues, practical applications. *International Journal of Intercultural Relations, 13,* 387-417.

Kim, Y. Y. (1995). Cross-cultural adaptation: An integrative theory. In R. L. Wiseman (Ed.), *Intercultural communication theory* (International and Intercultural Communication Annual, Vol. 19, pp. 170-193). Newbury Park, CA: Sage.

Kim, Y. Y. (1996). Identity development: From culture to intercultural. In H. B. Mokros (Ed.), *Interaction and identity* (pp. 347-369). New Brunswick, NJ: Transaction.

Koester, J., Wiseman, R. L., & Sanders, J. A. (1993). Multiple perspectives of intercultural communication competency. In R. L. Wiseman & J. Koester (Eds.), *Intercultural communication competence* (International and Intercultural Communication Annual, Vol. 17, pp. 3-15). Newbury Park, CA: Sage.

Langston, D. (1993). Who am I now? The politics of class identity. In M. M. Tokarczyk & E. A. Fay (Eds.), *Working-class women in the academy: Laborers in the knowledge factory* (pp. 60-72). Amherst: The University of Massachusetts Press.

Leeds-Hurwitz, W. (1997). Introducing power, context, and theory to intercultural training: A response to Chang and Holt. In A. González & D. V. Tanno (Eds.), *Communication and identity across cultures* (International and Intercultural Communication Annual, Vol. 20, pp. 231-236). Thousand Oaks, CA: Sage.

Lipsitz, G. (1998). *The possessive investment in whiteness.* Philadelphia: Temple University Press.

Martin, J. N. (1993). Intercultural communication competence: A review. In R. L. Wiseman & J. Koester (Eds.), *Intercultural communication competence* (International and Intercultural Communication Annual, Vol. 17, pp. 16-29). Newbury Park, CA: Sage.

Martin, J. N., & Nakayama, T. K. (1999). Thinking dialectically about culture and communication. *Communication Theory, 9,* 1-25.

Martin, J. N., Nakayama, T. K., & Flores, L. A. (1998). A dialectical approach to intercultural communication. In J. N. Martin, T. K. Nakayama, & L. A. Flores (Eds.), *Readings in cultural contexts* (pp. 5-14). Mountain View, CA: Mayfield.

Moon, D. G. (1996). Concepts of "culture": Implications for intercultural communication research. *Communication Quarterly, 44,* 70-84.

Moon, D. G. (1998). Performed identities: "Passing" as an intercultural discourse. In J. N. Martin, T. K. Nakayama, & L. A. Flores (Eds.), *Readings in cultural contexts* (pp. 322-330). Mountain View, CA: Mayfield.

Moon, D. G. (1999). White enculturation and bourgeois ideology: The discursive production of "good (white) girls." In T. K. Nakayama & J. N. Martin (Eds.), *Whiteness: The communication of social identity* (pp. 177-197). Thousand Oaks, CA: Sage.

Moon, D. G., & Rolison, G. L. (1998). The communication of classism. In M. L. Hecht (Ed.), *Communicating prejudice* (pp. 122-135). Thousand Oaks, CA: Sage.

Nakayama, T. K. (1997). Dis/orienting identities: Asian American, history, and intercultural communication. In A. González, D. V. Tanno, & V. Chen (Eds.), *Our voices: Essays in culture, ethnicity, and communication* (pp. 14-20). Los Angeles: Roxbury.

Nakayama, T. K., & Krizek, R. L. (1995). Whiteness: A strategic rhetoric. *Quarterly Journal of Speech, 81,* 291-309.

Ono, K. A. (1998). Problematizing "nation" in intercultural communication research. In D. V. Tanno & A. González (Eds.), *Communication and identity across cultures* (International and Intercultural Communication Annual, Vol. 21, pp. 193-202). Thousand Oaks, CA: Sage.

Rust, M. (1996). The subaltern as imperialist: Speaking of Olaudah Equiano. In E. K. Ginsberg (Ed.), *Passing and the fictions of identity* (pp. 21-36). Durham, NC: Duke University Press.

Scott, J. (1991). The evidence of experience. *Critical Inquiry, 17,* 773-779.

Shome, R. (1996). Postcolonial interventions in the rhetorical canon: An "other" view. *Communication Theory, 6,* 40-59.

Shuter, R. (1982). Initial interactions of American blacks and whites in interracial and intraracial dyads. *Journal of Social Psychology, 117,* 45-52.

Spitzberg, B. H., & Brunner, C. (1991). Toward a theoretical integration of context and competence inference research. *Western Journal of Speech Communication, 55,* 28-46.

Spitzberg, B. H., & Cupach, W. R. (1984). *Interpersonal communication competence.* Beverly Hills, CA: Sage.

Spitzberg, B. H., & Hecht, M. L. (1984). A component model of relational competence. *Human Communication Research, 10,* 575-599.

Strauss, A. L., & Corbin, J. (1990). *Basics of qualitative research: Grounded theory procedures and techniques.* Newbury Park, CA: Sage.

Subervi-Velez, F. (1986). The mass media and ethnic assimilation and pluralism: A review and research proposal with special focus on Hispanics. *Communication Research, 13,* 71-96.

Tyler, C. A. (1994). Passing: Narcissism, identity, and difference. *Differences: A Journal of Feminist Cultural Studies, 6*(2/3), 212-248.

Wander, P. (1979). The angst of the upper class. *Journal of Communication, 29*(4), 85-88.

Wildman, S. M. (1996). *Privilege revealed: How invisible preference undermines America.* New York: New York University Press.

Williams, R. (1980). *Problems in materialism and culture.* London: Verso.

Wolf, T. (1971). *Radical chic and maumauing the flak catchers.* New York: Bantam.

Yep, G. (1998). My three cultures: Navigating the multicultural identity landscape. In J. N. Martin, T. K. Nakayama, & L. A. Flores (Eds.), *Readings in cultural context* (pp. 79-84). Mountain View, CA: Mayfield.

10

Discursive Construction of Differences

Ethnic Immigrant Identities and Distinctions

JOLANTA A. DRZEWIECKA • *Washington State University*

Ethnicity provides a sense of self and a sense of place in a society. The meanings of ethnicity as an identity category are not homogeneous; instead, they are constantly redefined and struggled over by heterogeneous groups who claim the same ethnic label but whose experiences, practices, and positions in social structures vary. Immigrants in particular struggle to define themselves, to establish both commonality and difference from others. Because immigrants are situated in multiple and heterogeneous positions, they attempt to recreate meanings and practices that reflect their particular experiences and cultural memories as authentic. In these struggles, ethnicity acquires a symbolic value.

In this chapter, I use Bourdieu's concept of *habitus* to argue that in the immigrant context, ethnicity becomes cultural capital, and that both practices of and struggles over ethnicity are generated by differences between immigrant cohorts, clashes between preemigration class positions, and differing patterns of cultural incorporation. Ethnicity provides an embodied sense of one's place and should be understood as constructed across the differences in habitus that engender distinctions within an ethnic immigrant group. Simultaneously, I am extending the notion of habitus, developed by Bourdieu on the basis of intracultural analysis, in order to explain how immigrant repositioning between two social structures generates struggles between immigrant groups over ethnic meanings and practices. I focus on social distinctions that emerge in discursive presentations of self and its relations with others.

AUTHOR'S NOTE: Jolanta Drzewiecka thanks Thomas Nakayama, Jess Albers, the editor of this volume, and the anonymous reviewers for their helpful comments on the earlier drafts.

This study investigates distinctions within the Polish immigrant group in Phoenix, Arizona. The focus on Polish immigrants in the United States, in Bourdieu's terms, is an act of *classification.* The term *Polish* functions here as a significant social label and category. By focusing on Poles living in the United States, I do not mean to suggest that all Poles necessarily have more in common with each other than with various others. What they do have in common are differences and struggles over their ethnic identities. In the context of this study, I chose this classification in order to demonstrate how ethnicity becomes a complex and heterogeneous social category constituted differently by different social groups. Polish immigrants create social fields that are fraught with tensions over how "Polishness" should be defined and tensions over who and what is authentically Polish. Polishness becomes a symbolic capital struggled over by different "Polish" groups situated differently within and between social structures. I begin by reviewing discussions of ethnicity in intercultural communication. Next, I explain how concepts of habitus and heterogeneity, multiplicity, and hybridity enable us to rethink ethnicity in the immigrant context. Finally, I move to the analysis of interview data.

ETHNICITY

Theoretical concerns with ethnicity in the United States emerged in the 1950s in the context of immigrant adaptation (Hutchinson & Smith, 1996). Since then, the study of ethnicity has developed in many different and complex directions. The word *ethnicity* has its roots in the ancient Greek word *ethnos,* which translates as "people" or "nation" (Jenkins, 1997). Hutchinson and Smith (1996) point out that the term was used by ancient Greeks as "a synonym of *gentile,* that is, non-Christian and non-Jewish pagan (itself a rendering of Hebrew *goy*) in New Testament Greek" (p. 4). Although the term denoted a group of people living together and sharing cultural or biological characteristics, it was used by Greeks to refer to "other" people, and this sense still dominates popular usage as well as some scholarly interrogations of ethnicity.

The interpretive approach to understanding cultural identity and the more recent critical approaches have opened possibilities of intricate and contextual theorizing of ethnicity. First, Collier and Thomas (1988) argued that cultural identity is dynamic and fluid and is constituted in interactions. Continuing in this direction, Hecht, Collier, and Ribeau (1993) developed a sophisticated view of ethnicity within the layered theory of identity. Hecht et al. (1993) argue that identity and ethnicity are cocreated in communication. That is, they are enacted in the exchange of messages. Building on Philipsen's work, the authors argue that conversation, code, and community are central to cultural communication and are the means of constructing ethnic identity and culture. As a set of personal characteristics, identity is enacted in social interactions with and in relationship to others, and, finally, it becomes a basis of group bonding. Hence, identity is situated in four frames: personal, enacted, relational, and communal (Hecht, 1993). Hecht et al. (1993) define ethnic identity as "perceived membership in an ethnic culture that is enacted in the appropriate and effective set of symbols, cultural narratives, similar interpretations and meanings, and common ancestry and traditions" (p. 30). The focus is placed on investigating the content of ethnic identity through relevant frames. This approach presented a multidimensional and dynamic view of ethnicity. Such views were later challenged by critical scholars.

Critics in other fields warn against essentializing ethnicity through heritage or fixing it as "something that people 'have,'" or, indeed, to which they "belong" (Jenkins, 1997, p. 14). Hall (1990/1994) contends that shared heritage as a basis for identity implies "stable, unchanging and continuous frames of reference and meaning, an essence" (p. 393) that imposes "an imaginary coherence on the experience of dispersal and fragmentation" (p. 394). Similarly, Balibar (1991) argues that ethnicity is fictive, in that it is not natural but is represented *as if* it were a natural base of "community, possessing of itself an identity of origins, culture, and interests which transcends individual and social conditions " (p. 27).

Critical communication scholars focus on understanding ideological struggles, economic and historical contexts, difference, and representation. The main focus is on identity and its multiple construction in political, historical, and cultural contexts, and discursive articulation through such critical predicates as race, class, ethnicity, gender, and nationality (e.g., Collier, 1998; Delgado, 1998; Hegde, 1998a, 1998b; Houston, 1992; Lee, 1998; Martin, Krizek, Nakayama, & Bradford, 1996; Nakayama, 1994; Tanno, 1994). Although ethnicity is only one of the identity sites discussed, some studies have specifically focused on ethnicity. For example, Tanno (1994) stressed that naming is a crucial process to ethnic identity, which is multiple and historically constructed. Delgado (1998) argued that Chicano rappers articulate Chicano ideology and empower Mexican American audiences. Hegde (1998a) began her interrogation of immigrant identity by arguing, "Ethnicity is a discourse created to invite a common system of meanings for a group" reproduced by immigrants to make sense of their contradictory surroundings (p. 34). For Hegde, ethnicity is always gendered and must be understood in relation to specific material and discursive locations. This critical turn in communication challenges us to theorize ethnicity in relationship to culture and social structures and as a contested set of fragmented social positions and symbolic values.

This study presses further in this direction by linking ethnicity to social, economic, and cultural structures. I focus on differences and struggles as processes forming ethnicity and on the relations between these processes and social structures in the immigrant context. I understand ethnicity as an ongoing and political phenomenon rather than as a static attribute or an essence fixed through a shared heritage. Ethnicity is conceived as "complex repertoires which people experience, use, learn and 'do' in their daily lives, within which they construct an ongoing sense of themselves and an understanding of their fellows" (Jenkins, 1997, p. 14). As Hall (1991) contends, although "ethnicity is the necessary place or space from which people speak" (p. 36), it is recreated as both a knowable and imaginary place. Ethnicity is contested and heterogeneous, because it is a place within a specific history, a specific set of power relations and tradition. As such, ethnicity changes as the relations change, transforming and giving expression to different groups' desires and needs for their place in the world. Ethnicity is articulated through and across identity and differences.

ETHNICITY, CULTURE, AND DIFFERENCE

Examination of differences as formative elements of ethnicity requires that we understand culture as not simply the sum of historically transmitted patterns. As Hall (1986) paraphrases E. P. Thompson, "no 'whole way of life' is without its dimension of struggle and confrontation between opposed *ways* of life" (p. 37). Culture is best understood as

> *both* the meanings and values which arise amongst distinctive social groups and classes, on the basis of their given historical conditions and relationships, through which they "handle" and respond to the conditions of existence; *and* as the lived traditions and practices through which those "understandings" are expressed and in which they are embodied. (Hall, 1986, p. 39)

Culture is a constitutive process that can "arise from, express, and constitute a range of social relations, including those based on gender, class, and region of origin, or religion, as well as ethnicity" (Bottomley, 1991, p. 305). Ethnicity is constituted differently and differentially within different cultural systems of meanings, values, traditions, and practices, as well as social divisions.

In her examination of material conditions of Asians and Asian Americans in the United States, Lowe (1996) provides three concepts that are very powerful in addressing differential constitution of ethnic, cultural, and racial groups. She argues that cultural and ethnic categories are marked by heterogeneity, hybridity, and multiplicity. These notions refer to material contradictions created by histories of differential power relations and different positions within social structures. Heterogeneity, according to Lowe, "indicates the existence of differences and differential relationships within a bounded category—that is among Asian Americans, there are differences of national origin, of generational relation to immigration exclusion laws, of class backgrounds in Asia and economic conditions within the United States, and of gender" (p. 67). The term *hybridity* refers to the creation of cultural practices and objects in the context of uneven and asymmetric power relations. Finally, *multiplicity* refers to the positioning of subjects along several different axes of power in the context of capitalism, patriarchy, and race relations.

Lowe's argument is particularly potent in reference to a very large and dynamic category: Asian Americans. However, the concepts she puts forth point to the necessity to rethink and examine how differences in material conditions affect articulation of cultural and ethnic meanings from within and without a given group. Lowe makes it possible to focus on a particular group—as defined by common history of immigration and political situation, as well as by the perceptions of others—and to analyze it as a site of fragmentation and differences. Although Polish immigrants and Polish Americans are, as a group, very different from Asian Americans in respect to race relations and in respect to their singular rather than plural national origins, an understanding of this group can benefit from a cautious application of Lowe's concepts. Immigrant ethnic identities formed on the basis of common "place of origin" are fraught with differences between class positions, immigration cohorts, and generational groups, as well as political affiliations. "Otherness," as an identity relation, is not defined simply through racial or ethnic distinctions between "us" and "them"; rather, as Ganguly (1992) paraphrases Suleri, "otherness is to be found where you are sitting" (p. 28). The relationship between ethnicity and culture is further complicated by the interrelationship with social structure and class. Bourdieu's (1977) notions of habitus, symbolic capital, and social fields address the interrelationships between these concepts.

HABITUS

Bourdieu's notion of habitus provides a concept that is useful for examining how ethnicity provides one with an embodied sense of one's place in the midst of power struggles over cultural expressions and over the definition of ethnicity itself. Bourdieu (1977) views the social world as social space, a topology, which consists of multiple fields and their relations to one another. The field consists of partially autonomous forces as well as struggles for positions within the field. Positions within the field are based on the allocation of symbolic and economic capital to social actors. Symbolic capital refers to material forms that are not recognized as capital, for example, dress, accent, style, and so forth. The symbolic capital legitimizes certain definitions of the social world, whereby "the struggle between symbolic systems to impose a view of the social world defines the social space within which people construct their daily lives, and carry on . . . the symbolic conflicts of everyday life in the use of symbolic power of the dominant over dominated, i.e., education, relationships in the workplace, social organizations" (Harker, Mahar, & Wilkes, 1990, p. 5). Theoretical classes may be constructed by researchers to specify "objective similarities and real connections" (Harker et al., 1990, p. 10) among people occupying the same position within social space. Classes may include gender, age groups, social classes, and other groupings to which cultural capital is allocated (Bourdieu, 1984).

The concept of habitus enables Bourdieu to reformulate the notion of class in terms of cultural capital at a time when the significance of economic capital is diminishing (Eder, 1993). According to Bourdieu, "habitus is a system of durable, transposable dispositions which functions as the generative basis of structured, objectively unified practices" (Bourdieu, 1977, p. vii). Habitus generates a social world by its capacity to produce practices and works and by its capacity to distinguish between them on the basis of taste (Bourdieu, 1984). It mediates between a social structure and the actions of agents (LiPuma, 1993). Habitus is developed and shared by those who occupy similar positions in the social field. It is important to stress that these dispositions, although conditioned by objective conditions, are not conscious but unconscious and habitual. They are self-evident in the sense that they lead "one to exclude oneself from the goods, persons, places, and so forth from which one is excluded" (Bourdieu, 1984, p. 471).

Habitus represents an embodied knowledge about one's place in the world, a knowledge of that which can be taken for granted. Habitus is "a past which survives in the present and tends to perpetuate itself into the future by making itself present in practices structured according to its principles" (Bourdieu, 1977, p. 82). It is not a static product. Rather, it is a set of principles that regulate not only practices and perceptions but also its own structure and development into the future, as well as transformations and revolutions. Habitus is developed in social positions within a field, and it exhibits people's adjustment to their positions.

HABITUS AND ETHNICITY

The usefulness of the concept of habitus to the understanding of ethnicity has been recognized by scholars. Jenkins (1997) argues that habitus is "the embodied and unreflexive everyday practical mastery of culture" where the sense of self is located (p. 77). Habitus is implicated in the practice of ethnicity, including practices, material objects, perceptions, and judgments. Bentley (1987) argues that "sensations of ethnic affinity are founded on common life experiences that generate similar habitual dispositions. . . . It is the commonality of experience and of the preconscious habitus it generates that gives members of an ethnic cohort their sense of being both familiar and familial with each other" (pp. 32-33). Ethnic identity is derived from a shared habitus, which enables people to recognize their commonalities.

Yelvington (1991) aptly challenges Bentley (1991), arguing that when habitus is made synonymous with ethnicity, it can neither account for shifts in ethnic boundaries leading to reinventions of ethnicity nor explain differences in "ways of living" within ethnic groups. The critical function of habitus, the generation of social distinctions, is lost. In his response, Bentley (1991) asserts that habitus, as a "structuring structure" that incorporates new experiences, not only can explain what binds members of ethnic groups together through multiple surface expressions but also can explicate feelings of ambivalence that come from differences in habitus within ethnic groups. Bentley, however, does not account for the relationship between habitus and ethnicity. Differences in cultural schemata cannot be accounted for when habitus is equated with ethnicity; in addition, equating the two erases the notion of social distinctions, which in Bourdieu's conceptualization are central to habitus.

I argue that ethnicity should be understood as constructed across differences in habitus and that differences in habitus engender distinctions in cultural capital. Ethnicity is not simply habitus, however; rather, it is symbolic capital as well as a repertoire of daily practices that are conditioned and structured by habitus. That is, ethnic positions (different ethnicities, e.g., Polish ethnicity) and their location in social and cultural structures, as well as how a particular ethnicity is practiced by individuals situated differentially in a social structure, condition one's habitus. Furthermore, the production, perception, and appreciation of ethnic practices and works are generated by habitus. This complex relationship between ethnicity and habitus can explain differences within ethnic groups as well as struggles over the meaning of ethnicity and ethnic identity in the immigrant context.

ETHNICITY, IMMIGRATION, AND HABITUS

This notion of habitus enables scholars both to examine relations between ethnicity and to study differently and differentially constituted immigrant groups in terms of cultural capital. For many groups, ethnic identification becomes salient upon migratory resettlement. Migration provides a host of new experiences and activities in daily life and, even more important, situates individuals within new sets of cultural and economic politics. The identities of Poles living in Poland are shaped more significantly by culture, religion, and nationality. Ethnicity or ethnic differences have not been important elements in constructions of commonality and difference, because the socialist system was legitimized by the imposition of national and cultural homogeneity. Although Polish Jews were a significant exception to the ideology of homogeneity, their difference was defined through religious and political terms.

In the United States, Polish immigrants become identified as an ethnic group and enter into ethnic, cultural, and racial politics as white ethnic immigrants. Ethnicity becomes relevant as a position within the social structure, because ethnic positions are endowed with symbolic capital in the United States. As Miller (1990) argues, ethnic identity is the result of the dynamic conjunctions of social structures, class conflicts, and cultural patterns in the old country and the new. Ethnicity evolves from a complex dialectic that exists between an immigrant group and a host society. (p. 98)

Who is Polish and the correct way to be Polish matter because the label "Polish" names the whole social group and differentiates this group from other groups. Ethnicity is struggled over because of the social value it acquires in this specific social order, in which being Polish can no longer be taken for granted, because Poles are surrounded by others.

Prior to immigration, people live within specific social locations and share habitus with others who occupy similar positions. Their habitus includes social principles, opinions, and understanding of both their own location and their economic capital. All these elements are called into question when people cross national and cultural borders. The habitus they bring with them serves as a lens that allows them to make sense of their experiences and to position themselves in relation to others. Habitus also incorporates into its structure changes that occur because of immigrant experiences, cultural adaptation, and changes in economic conditions. Those who share the same ethnic label do not necessarily share the same cultural expressions or the same habitus. Upon migration, habitus is restructured; it is no longer the same habitus immigrants had in Poland, and it changes differently from the habitus of those who stayed in Poland. Most important, ethnicity becomes a contested cultural capital through which habitus distinctions are articulated. Neither Poles in Poland nor Polish immigrants in the United States are homogeneous in terms of class, religion, social background, or gender; however, in the United States, these differences are articulated through struggles over ethnic identification.

Inevitably, these changes and interactions lead to clashes, as being "Polish" becomes one of the most important types of symbolic capital. Polish identity is negotiated and contested on the basis of habitual social dispositions. According to Bourdieu (1977, 1984), fields identify specific areas of struggle. In this study, the social space occupied by Polonia is a social field composed of Polish immigrants' struggles over the definition of their social world. Bourdieu's theory transcends distinctions between objective and subjective structures in a dialectic. His theory is firmly grounded in qualitative research. According to Bourdieu, a field can be described only based on a study of particular practices. For these reasons, Bourdieu's work is particularly useful for this study because it allows a mapping out of the field of Polonia and the struggles within the field. The meaning of Polishness, and thus of identity, is the main object of these struggles carried out on the basis of class, generation, and other distinctions.

METHODS

I analyze discursive constructions of differences within one Polish immigrant group. I use a broad definition of *discourse* as a system of expressions that are produced by and indicate habitual dispositions (Bourdieu, 1991). Bourdieu argues that social distinctions function below the level of consciousness and discourse; however, they are manifested in discourse through vocabulary that indicates oppositions and antagonisms within imposed systems of hierarchies. For Bourdieu, discourse is always habitual and reflects relations of power. In this case, I focus on distinctions in group members' descriptions of each other. To this end, I conducted interviews with Polish immigrants. Interviews provide texts of identity; in these texts, social relations and distinctions become visible as interviewees locate themselves in relationship to cultures, communities, and others (Ganguly, 1992; Hegde, 1998a; Holmer-Nadesan, 1996; Preston, 1997).

I interviewed 33 Polish immigrants. The pool of participants drawn for this study represents the following groups: (a) 7 male and 4 female post-World War II immigrants who came to the United States following displacement by the war; they ranged in age between 60 and 70 years; (b) 13 immigrants (12 women and 1 man) who came to the United States between 15 and 30 years ago; their ages ranged from roughly 40 to 70, with most participants being in their 40s and 50s; and (c) 9 immigrants (7 men and 2 women) who were born in the United States of Polish immigrant parents and who maintain identification with Poland; their ages ranged between 24 and 60, with most participants being in their 30s, 40s, and 50s. Two thirds of the participants were highly educated professionals, and one third were of working-class backgrounds.

Initially, I developed some contacts in the Polish community in Phoenix by attending community events and visiting the Polish bakery. The gatekeepers I met on these occasions introduced me to the participants of this study. I also met some of the participants through U.S. American acquaintances. On average, interviews lasted about an hour and a half. On several occasions, I met with participants for two sessions. Most often I traveled to participants' homes, but I also met them at the Polish church, on school grounds, or in a restaurant. Interviews were in-depth and unstructured. Although I had an interview guide prepared, each interview was different, because I followed up on particular stories told by the interviewees (Lincoln & Guba, 1985; Lofland & Lofland, 1995). I was interested in participants' positions, experiences, and interpretations. Each interview was recorded and transcribed. The issues analyzed in this study were not anticipated; they emerged in the context of a qualitative study of more general issues of cultural identity and adaptation to the United States.

My own identity marks my interests in this project. I came to the United States 9 years ago and became sensitive to distinctions made by myself as well as by other Polish immigrants. My relationship with other Poles living in the United States is not an easy one. Often, I do not identify with other Poles; our cultures and our political and religious views differ. Sometimes we are willing to overlook these differences, overwhelmed by nostalgia and longing for "home"; at other times, the differences become barriers. I am a marginal member of the core community centered around the church, although in this sense I am probably very typical of many others who feel ambivalent about religion. I visit the bakery and, occasionally, the church, primarily to learn about the community.

Polish identity is a site of divisions and conflicts. There were times during my ethnographic observations when I felt quite different from Poles around me, not fitting in or belonging to the community and culture they transported and re-created. I had to struggle to keep my "Polish" hierarchies and prejudices in check. I took up this project in part as an opportunity to understand the problematics of identification including its discontinuities and differences.

My position as an academic at a U.S. university was salient in these interviews. Most participants perceived me as a relative newcomer and were willing to share their experiences with me. Most of them readily agreed to being interviewed and traveled in the intense Arizona summer heat to meet me, often after work, or they received me in their homes. Some of them wanted to make sure that I would write this study in English for U.S. Americans, because they thought that Poles have written enough about Poles for Poles. A few participants expressed interest in copies of the finished product. There were only two incidents when potential respondents rejected my request for an interview. In one case, someone who initially consented informed me that her work schedule changed and that because she had very little free time, she wanted to spend it running her own errands. In another case, someone I met at a party agreed to be interviewed but later refused to grant me an interview because, as she said, she did not consider herself Polish and she could not say good things about Poles, especially the ones in the United States. She felt uncomfortable saying negative things, and that was why she did not want to participate in an interview. Interestingly, she said that she would have granted an interview to a U.S. journalist and discussed Poland with her, but she would not talk with me because I was Polish and would therefore judge her based on her negative comments. This is also a very important source of data. It shows that "Polish" is indeed a sign of conflict. Unfortunately, this also indicates a gap in my data, because people with those feelings—and based on my personal experiences, there are many of them—would either not express them to me or could not be identified for an interview, as they were probably not active members of the community.

THE FIELD AND HABITUS OF POLONIA

The field of Polonia is a field of struggles, including struggles between different immigrant generations, different political groups, social classes, and groups with differing ways of cultural integration. Although some of the struggles are specific to the dynamics of Polonia, others are carried out based on distinctions that have been transferred and transformed from Poland. These struggles have long roots in the history of Polish immigration to the United States and in differences between groups immigrating at different times. I start by examining the historical context. Next, I move to the analysis of how habitus distinctions are articulated in the interview material. The analysis suggests that the symbolic struggles for positions within the field of Polonia center on positions of differentially situated immigrant cohorts, preemigration class positions, and different patterns of cultural integration.

Habitus and Immigrant Cohorts: Historical Context

Struggles between different cohorts of immigrants have historically formed the field of Polonia. Historically, Polish immigration to the United States has been significant in numbers and continuous since the first immigrants started arriving in the 17th century. Polish immigration may be categorized into the following main waves: colonial immigration

(1608-1776), political immigration (1776-1854), economic immigration (1884 until World War II), exile immigration (post-World War II: 1945-1969), and contemporary Polish immigration (Lopata, 1994; Pienkos, 1984; Polzin, 1982; Pula, 1995). This grouping is very general; however, although it is possible to distinguish other immigration groups differing in backgrounds and reasons for immigration (Jaroszynska-Kirchmann, 1996), this grouping provides a useful class of distinctions. The economic immigration, also referred to as mass immigration, was the first large group of Polish immigration to the United States. Those who came before 1929 were mostly from rural backgrounds, very poor, and with few skills beyond farming. Immigrants coming after 1929 were better educated, of urban backgrounds, and more affluent. World War II refugees were admitted between 1945 and 1969. Many of them found themselves outside of Poland during or after the war, when they were forced out or left voluntarily on ideological grounds. In all cases, they did not want to go back because of their anti-Communist sentiments or war experiences. There were also groups of political refugees who came from socialist Poland after October 1956 and groups of Polish Jews who left Poland following "a government-induced anti-Semitic campaign" in 1968 (Jaroszynska-Kirchmann, 1996, p. 166).

Most recent immigrants came in two main groups: post-1970 and post-1984 (Jaroszynska-Kirchmann, 1996; Lopata, 1994). Most of them identified themselves as "political immigrants," although 50% came at the invitation of relatives. Lopata (1994) cites sources estimating that about half a million Poles have left Poland for the United States since 1984. This phenomenon has been described in Poland as a "brain drain" and represents a huge problem for the struggling country, which is unable to provide the material rewards to retain badly needed intellectual resources. Although many immigrants in this cohort were reportedly educated and under 40 years of age, they were emigrating to improve their careers and standard of living. As Jaroszynska-Kirchmann (1996) argues, even those who had the goal of bettering their economic conditions were "to a certain extent, victims of the prevailing political system in Poland," and their claims to the "political immigrant" label are justified (p. 167). However, the choice of a "political" rather than "economic" immigrant label reflects strategic positioning within international politics as well as in the field of Polonia. Many immigrants leaving Poland chose this label because it enabled them legal entry to the United States as asylees at the time when immigration policies were motivated by the political goal of undermining Communism. The preemigration class position of these different groups of immigrants described above greatly contributed to the conflicts that have ensued and that have formed the field of Polonia.

The notion of habitus is useful in interpreting these conflicts. Bourdieu (1984) argues that "different conditions of existence produce different habitus" and that "habitus organizes practices and perceptions of practices" (p. 170). Preemigration class status as well as the economic and political changes in Poland taking place as different groups were emigrating are combined with adjustments to the U.S. Economic and cultural system in the production of the structures of habitus. The different cohorts in the United States operate on the basis of different symbolic capitals. Each immigrant group had to establish its identity in relation to the U.S. Social structures as well as in relation to the already existing Polonia, which often led to many conflicts and social negotiations incited by "the history, degree of assimilation, life goals, education, relations to the homeland and so on" (Jaroszynska-Kirchmann, 1996, p. 152). Preemigration class positions therefore have been some of the most important sources of conflicts within and across waves of immigration.

The class structure in Poland changed in the postwar period. Whereas before the war, the "class system was polarized between the various strata of peasants and the *szlachta* or gentry" (Lopata, 1994, p. 26), after the war, education became a class marker in a socialist "classless" system and the intelligentsia emerged as a "higher" class. Polish class structures were transferred as well as combined with U.S. classifications.

One of the conflicts occurred between post-World War II displaced persons and members of the "old" Polonia (economic immigrants). As Jaroszynska-Kirchmann (1996) explains, post-World War II immigrants were not familiar with the historical, cultural, and political context of American Polonia, and "[t]hey tended to consider Polonia 'the fourth province of Poland,' according to popular nineteenth-century concepts" (p. 163). For this group, being from Poland signified a higher cultural status in relation to "the fourth province." In addition, Polish class structures continued to generate "old" distinctions. The older economic immigrants found that their "new" money did not erase their premigration peasant class position in the eyes of more educated and more recent newcomers. They were not considered to be knowledgeable about Poland and were thus seen as unable to represent it. The newcomers of middle-class background "detested the older immigrants' lack of Polish language skills, their Americanization, low educational level, and 'peasant' ways of life" (Jaroszynska-Kirchmann, 1996, p. 164).

These distinctions were not readily accepted by old Polonia, because their habitus had been restructured by incorporating U.S. classifications, which included the idea that a greater length of residency in the United States conferred a position higher than that of newcomers. Members of the older groups claimed the exclusive right to represent Poland and considered their cultural experiences from Poland as more authentic. They adopted a patronizing stance toward the newcomers, who often did not know the economic and cultural realities in the United States. Additionally, the more recent, educated groups of immigrants were able to move up the ladder faster, angering older groups, who had had to work harder to accomplish what the newcomers gained quickly.

Although the conflicts take place between groups that are situated differentially in terms of objective conditions, they are articulated through ethnicity as a cultural capital that each group claims as exclusively its own. The earlier cohort is invested in their length of stay in the United States, their earned economic status, and their prior experiences in Poland. The more recent groups are invested in their education, which gives them a higher status position in Poland over the "peasant class," as well as in their cultural experiences in Poland, which were markedly urban. Not only is "the way of life" in Poland different for different economic groups, but it has also changed as Poland quickly moved from a barely begun capitalist system during the interwar period to the Soviet-style socialist system after the war, which eased access to education for many. Both groups are invested in the symbolic capital of "being Polish," but in a different way and in a different context. In this case, both the pre- and postemigrant positions and habitus clash as different immigrant groups encounter differences not only in positions in the immigrant context, but also in continued and changed Polish social and economic structures as well. These groups have different ideas about how being Polish should be expressed. The perception is that the fact of a peasant background is not covered up by living many years in the United States; however, this perception is contested by those so described. That is, although these distinctions might be accepted in Poland as self-evident, the older immigrant cohort claims a higher position within the field in relationship to the newcomers on the basis of conditions that are not accepted by the more recent generation, including longevity of residence and access to material resources.

This historical context has provided an overview of general conditions that lead to struggles over the symbolic capital. The analysis of interviews with immigrants that follows focuses on discursive articulations of habitual dispositions and distinctions. The struggle between immigrant groups situated differentially in terms of cohorts and class positions continues. The analysis of the present context allows for examination of how differing positions and habitual distinctions are articulated discursively. The analysis focuses on articulated differences between immigrant cohorts, pre- and postimmigration class distinctions, and different patterns of cultural integration.

Habitus, Immigrant Cohorts, and Adjustments

Within the field of Polonia in Phoenix, one set of struggles emerges between the different immigrant cohorts and adjustments to new social and economic positions. The earliest cohort in the specific field examined here consists of people who came to the United States following World War II; this group went to Chicago first and much later moved to Phoenix, often to retire. The next immigrant group consists of the 1970s political and professional immigrants. Finally, there are those who were born in the United States whose parents immigrated right after World War II. The most pronounced conflict takes place between these three cohorts and the Solidarity-era immigrants, who came to the United States, often directly to Phoenix, in the 1980s. The heterogeneity of these groups is established through different experiences, different reasons for immigration, and different perceptions of each other conditioned by their material positions and socialization in different economic systems.

These cohorts left Poland at different times, had different experiences both in Poland and in the United States, and had very different expectations of the United States and of each other. Immigrants in the two earlier cohorts have adjusted to social and economic positions in the United States from which they perceived and evaluated the newcomers. Many of the older immigrants often perceived the newcomers in a very negative light. For example, one interviewee, who came to the United States as a child after World War II, observed that the newcomers had a different mentality: "they expected the government to support them." An interviewee who moved to the United States about 24 years ago observed, "most of us did not have it easy, we took any work, $2.25 minimum wages and we were proud that we had something. The newer Polonia, you can't be surprised, they had more, even we tried to find them work,

$5.00 an hour, 'oh no, he will not take such work, he had that much in Poland. '" They perceive the new immigrants as wanting to achieve immediately what the older immigrants worked for over time. In their eyes, the recent immigrants perceive their market and symbolic value as higher, upsetting the immigrant structure in which those who had been in the United States longer should have a higher status. The older immigrants are protecting their place in the U.S. economic structure and investing in their ability to move up over time.

Although on the one hand, some of the older immigrants admit resentment when the newcomers are indeed successful, on the other, they do not appreciate recent immigrants' taking and retaining low-paying, low-status jobs. They reject these practices as situating Poles or Polish Americans on a lower status within the United States and reinforcing the assumption that Poles do dirty jobs. The older generation, "having to work hard to increase their social status and that of the community, . . . resent[ed] the ubiquitous presence of 'the Polish cleaning women'" (Lopata, 1994, p. 169). Another example can be found in the comments of an immigrant who had lived in the United States for almost 30 years. The immigrant complained that Poles who take jobs in the United States that are below their education level from Poland—for example, an engineer who works in a factory as a simple worker or a professor who works as a babysitter—"humiliate themselves if they do it long term." She continued, "I meet many Poles here who were educated in Poland, they had a social position there, they move here, get any job they can and they stay at that low level." Failing to learn English is especially indicative of the "low level." In this woman's eyes, these Poles do not occupy their proper place and act against their habitual dispositions, as perceived by others, upsetting the sense of hierarchy.

Members of the younger generation, in spite of the education level of many of them, do not have the luxury to reject these jobs. As newcomers, they often accept the lowest level of entry into the new economic system; their actions are driven by necessity. In the eyes of older immigrants, who are relatively freer from necessity, the newcomers who have credentials to occupy higher positions in the U.S. social and economic structures not only drop even lower in social ranking but fail to maintain appropriate structures of distinction. Taking the time to learn English was especially stressed as indicative of immigrant standing.

The older immigrants were clearly concerned about the status of Poles as a group in the United States. The immigrant cited above emphasized that those Poles who do not learn English do not adjust well and end up unhappy. She continued, "we Poles really can hold our head high because we have many things to be proud of. But one has to learn the language to communicate that." She clearly perceives Polishness in terms of cultural capital both within the Polish community and in relations with outsiders. In addition to being concerned about the group position, these older immigrants are also experiencing a habitus conflict, because although the newer immigrants occupied equivalent social positions in Poland, in the United States, they occupy lower positions, which becomes a marked difference.

My respondents developed understandings of the differences that divided them on the basis of the perception of ideological differences between capitalism and socialism. Economic immigrants often perceived different approaches to reality employed by the most recent immigrants as evidence of the influence of the socialist system on individuals who did not have as much drive for success and expected somebody else to secure higher-paying jobs for them. Members of these two groups have a different habitus, here referring to cultural differences engendered by socialization in a capitalist or socialist system of production, which leads them to respond to the world as well as to each other in different ways. Experiences and ideological identification with the U.S. experiences as immigrants in the United States, as well as their different preemigration experiences in Poland, create schemata of distinction. As a participant born in the United States whose parents were World War II immigrants explained, "they were brought up in the system where the objective was to work around the system and to exploit the system . . . that unfortunately became a culture." Distinctions between these groups are made on the basis of their dispositions resulting from adaptation to different conditions of existence. These dispositions engender specific schemes of perceptions. The participant quoted above uses the term *culture* to indicate a lower way of life and sensibility, and the word *unfortunately* is associated with different material and cultural conditions.

The older immigrants also become upset when the more recent immigrants complain about their conditions in the United States or about the United States in general. A respondent born in the United States verbalized sentiments shared by those who have spent a considerable amount of time in the United States: "I can't stand when Poles come here and complain about America, if you don't like it here, the door is open, nobody keeps you here chained." A different respondent was concerned about some Poles who come over to the United States, "milk the system," and "give us a bad name." Other Polish immigrants are uncomfortable about Poles who do not show the highest standard of work ethics. An immigrant who had spent almost 30 years in the United States observed that "there are many good Poles, but there are many rejects, Poland did not want them and America took them."

It is evident from these descriptions that the older cohort identifies ideologically not only with the United States but also with their place within the U.S. cultural and economic system. The older immigrants are invested in their own self-reliance and the story of their success, and they perceive the more recent immigrants' lack of familiarity with the system, different expectations, and possible initial lack of success as a basis of social and political distinctions. This sense of habitus as an embodied knowledge of one's place and as a set of principles to make sense of the world is visible in respondents' admissions that they had more commonality with those who came to the United States at the same time. This is attributable both to the immigration experience and to their common reasons for immigration and experience in Poland. In these narratives, cultural distinctions are bound up not only with economic distinctions but also with political distinctions; furthermore, cultural distinctions engender different practices, perceptions, and expectations.

Distinctions also emerge between economic immigrants and political/ professional immigrants. Economic immigrants position themselves as self-reliant achievers who were able to rise above their low economic positions in the United States. Political and professional immigrants frame their immigrant identities as matters of choice rather than economic necessity, despite the fact that many of those who claimed the label of political immigrants were actually economically motivated. Framing identity as a political and professional choice is a self-presentation strategy that relies on privilege and establishes difference from those immigrants who were driven by economic necessity. Professional immigrants I interviewed spoke negatively about the focus on material achievements of economic immigrants (their material achievement was just a by-product!) and about their reliance on tight ethnic communities. These professionals present themselves as cosmopolitans who can choose to be culturally invisible or to enact their ethnic identities at will (Drzewiecka & Nakayama, 1998; Portes & Rumbaut, 1996). Immigrant classifications, such as political (asylees) or economic immigrant, represent a class of positions that are endowed with cultural capital. The distinction between material necessity and an ideological need situates immigrants in different subject positions within a social field. Those immigrants who escape poverty are driven by necessity; they start at the lowest level, have nothing to go back to, and are less educated. Political immigrants are casualties of history; not limited by material conditions, they have been free to pursue higher-order ideological needs. In Bourdieu's words, the economic necessity for their immigration is translated into political virtue, reflecting a struggle for a higher position within a social field.

The notion of heterogeneity of immigrant positions within and between social and economic structures enables an extension of the concept of habitus as a system of dispositions that develops in a specific social, economic, and political system and that leads to familiarity and commonality of perceptions within immigrant cohorts and to distinctions between cohorts. However, the cohorts are not homogeneous themselves; they are divided by continuing preemigration class positions and by the habitus associated with these positions.

Class and Cultural Capital

Many distinctions within Polonia focus on social class and background as an indication of cultural differences. These distinctions take place across and within immigration cohorts, demonstrating that there are both fragmentations and connections within immigrant cohorts. Immigrants who occupy different social and economic positions identify with different aspects of Polish culture and struggle over how Polish culture should be defined. These distinctions are sometimes explicit, referring to a specific preemigration class, or implicit, referring to taken-for-granted indicators of class and social positions.

One of the participants who was born in the United States remembered that as he was growing up, his parents did not associate with other Polish immigrants because "they felt that they were peasants" and "they had no desire for us to somehow feel . . . that we should have some sort of identity with that part of Poland." This schema of distinction was engendered in him by his parents. Strong Polish accents were seen by his parents as a sign of lower education and social standing. He recollects his mother's distaste when one of the Polish organizations for which she designed a locale attempted to lower the cost by deciding on only one bathroom. "They kept on trying to cut some corners, and do silly things . . . she did not want to have anything to do with that, and quite frankly they [his parents] just did not feel that the best of Poland came to the United States."

He added that it was "that kind of thing" that kept his parents away from other Polish immigrants.

The same respondent just discussed, who did not identify with the majority of Polish immigrants, was also bothered by what he perceived as bad manners and vulgar language. He grew up speaking English and lost the ability to understand Polish. Now in his 40s, he is reclaiming the cultural capital; he takes Polish language lessons and has traveled to Poland, but he acknowledges that his vocabulary is very limited. In spite of this, he described a conversation with some immigrants in which he was sure they used a wrong Polish word for a sprinkler: "sometimes you know, they will make up words and they will have ways to express things that you know, it won't be, it is either incorrect or they just made it up, or they refuse to get the right word down . . . I have this large four volume Polish-English dictionary . . . They use slang words, very vulgar language to describe something . . . it's difficult to explain." The incorrect usage seemed to imply a lower level of education and a lack of sophistication. Even though his parents despised other Polish immigrants based on their class position, they maintained their own identification with Poland, *their* Poland, which they transferred to their son. In this context, culture and ethnicity become a hegemonic terrain through which a hierarchical configuration of differences is established. Some parts of Polish culture are more right and authentic, and these come to represent the culture as whole. Cultures are neither homogeneous nor fixed; they are sites of constant tensions between differential positions. His last comment in the previous quote is important in that economic and cultural distinctions are difficult to define or describe: They are most often simply felt and understood implicitly as representing embodied mastery of culture.

Several participants observed that many Polish immigrants did not want to admit that they were from villages and claimed that they were from Marszalkowska (a well-known street) in Warsaw or from other big cities. Apparently, these immigrants perceived immigration as an opportunity to break out of their social status in Poland. However, they were not entirely successful, because, in the words of one participant, "you can kind of tell," and in words of another, "you can feel through the skin, your background betrays you." Interestingly, these two participants were themselves from small towns and villages. The participants recognize such distinctions and apply them to themselves as well as to others; however, they challenge the need to be elitist, stressing that they were not ashamed of their own roots. One participant spoke very negatively about the elitism among some groups of Polish immigrants. Another one, however, observed, "I do not like when people try to raise themselves above others, some do it: 'I am from the West, I am from an aristocratic family, I am this, I am that.'" These respondents maintain social hierarchies by excluding themselves from what they are excluded from.

Taste, according to Bourdieu (1984), is "the source of system of distinctive features which cannot fail to be perceived as a systematic expression of a particular class of conditions of existence, i.e., as a distinctive life-style" (p. 175). Habitus is based on implicit distinctions that survive immigration and on changes in economic status, and both of these serve to establish positions of inferiority or superiority. "That kind of stuff" and "you can kind of tell" exemplify both the implicitness and the durability of habitus distinctions, which are defined through taste and are difficult to specify but discernible with even a limited knowledge of the Polish language. Taste fixes identities within a terrain of culture and is constructed as a hierarchy of positions articulated through economic conditions and class positions. Things "just do not look right . . . they look cheap"; they betray life based on necessity rather than luxury.

These distinctions become a basis for exclusions that imply inferiority and lower status overriding impulses to unite in a new environment on the basis of identity. Bourdieu (1984) refers to this effect as class racism, because classes of people are perceived as inherently worse. The notions of habitus and taste lead to splitting and distinctions among groups. These distinctions are points of contention between groups; they matter precisely because of identity, because the word *Polish* implies an identity relation between differently situated groups that do not identify with each other. These groups define *Polish* in fixed ways, through emphasizing the perceived superiority of "our" cultural practices, taste, and education. Each group's definition of *Polish* is articulated through relations of difference compared with other Poles, and the term becomes a site of both identity and difference.

This notion of stratification within the cultural field is very visible in the narrative of a different participant, who came to the United States about 15 years ago. She observed that immigration momentarily collapsed social distinctions:

When you grow up in Poland, you move in a certain orbit. When you immigrate, the only thing that you have in common, the only thing that you know about the other person is that they speak Polish. First meeting, you have to qualify how well they speak Polish. That shows you how they were brought up, when they were brought up, what's their education, do they speak a dialect, do they speak grammatically? You meet people accidentally and the only thing you have in common is Polish heritage or language, you have to rebuild your social structure that you had in Poland from scratch.

She pointed out that the structure and social relations have to be rebuilt, because having a Polish background in common is simply not enough to establish connection and commonality. Preemigration educational status as represented by language use becomes a part of symbolic capital, which is the basis of social distinctions. The issue of habitus becomes particularly visible in her concern about my classification system (she brought this topic up without any prompting from me; indeed, she assumed that I had a classification system), because she perceived herself as being quite different from other Polish immigrants. She told me that I would need to construct specific categories when analyzing my data, because people are not all the same. She said that she was different from other immigrants, both because she did not immigrate for economic reasons and because she attended one of the top gymnasiums in Poland, one famous for its political consciousness and high educational standards. She did not want to be lumped with those immigrants who had a lower status. Another participant similarly situates himself outside of the Polish community, which he describes as "poorly educated." He finds it difficult to establish friendships with others in the Polish community, because, he says, "I am one of the very few Polish professionals in the community and I really do not have a lot in common with most of these people." Professional status is indicated by more than a particular kind of employment. It is also indicated by one's social habitus, opinions, values, and perspectives.

As this analysis shows, being from Poland and speaking Polish are not enough to establish a commonality. The educational background, class background, use of language, cultural practices, and other less tangible indicators of social lifestyles become indicators of structural ordering of the cultural group. It is important to reiterate that specific ethnic or cultural practices are arbitrary and are not inherently better or worse but function within multiple hierarchies. Such practices acquire specific value through social reproduction and higher valuation by the educated higher classes. The position of subjects along axes of power endows practices they engage in with symbolic values.

Cultural Incorporation

Differing ways of cultural incorporation are also an issue in habitus struggles. Immigrants differ in their maintenance and incorporation of cultural practices. The resulting cultural field is marked by hybridity, as cultural practices and products created within uneven power relations between different classes and cohorts of immigrants.

A participant who came to the United States about 15 years ago observed that she did not have much in common anymore with her once close friends. As she said, "They live seemingly in Poland, seemingly in the U.S., mixed up, not very happy." She was upset when her friend refused to speak English in situations where her U.S. American husband was present. She decided that "they Americanized in a wrong way, actually we do not have anything in common any more." Her friend was reportedly appalled that she mixed Polish and U.S. cultural traditions, for example, using both a Polish and a U.S. Santa and celebrating Easter with both traditional Polish Easter rituals and a U.S. egg hunt. This respondent and her friend place different values on cultural maintenance and incorporation, which leads to struggles over cultural authenticity and cultural distinctions. These distinctions separate this participant from the Polish community, which she perceives as being, on the whole, of lower status. She said that after initially maintaining social relations with some Poles in the United States, she separated herself from them, because she did not appreciate their values. It is interesting that she saw their values (she identifies them as concerned with accumulating commodities) as dominant in the Polish society and she "did not care for them even in Poland." Nevertheless, this participant also feels separated from the community that does not perceive her as Polish. She has been told that she is not Polish because she is married to an American, does not attend the Polish church, and does not send her children to the Polish school. As she explained, she is not interested in sending her children to the Polish school because "these women do not speak correct Polish." She continued, "They were very nice, gave me some Polish cake, but this is right next to the Church, all mixed up, for me, going to the Polish Church or eating Polish cake does not mean that I am Polish."

I asked the same respondent what it meant for her to be Polish. She replied, "First of all, you must know Polish history . . . you have to understand what is going on with us, you have to be interested in Polish culture and politics, have the Polish spirit." She perceived the Polish community as expressing their Polishness through less important practices, food and religion. However, although she clearly spells out what it means for her to be Polish and describes herself as Polish, she also perceives those who oppose her cultural mixing of practices and traditions as less sophisticated and provincial—as less "Polish."

A different participant said that she did not read Polish newspapers from Chicago, because she did not understand or care for the issues they discuss, particularly discussions about politics within Polonia, complaints about Poles in Chicago, or information about the Polish government. Another participant claimed that she had more in common with Poles in Poland, because Poles in the United States change and try too hard to become Americans.

A respondent born in the United States explained that he did not practice everyday Polish culture, such as Polish cooking, partly because of his family's higher-class position in prewar Poland, where his mother grew up in a family with servants and never had a chance to learn to cook. His parents did not encourage their children to speak Polish because of the perceived lower status of children of other immigrants who spoke English with a heavy accent. In this case, the distinction was made on the basis of a habitus that already incorporated U.S. structures situating immigrants in a hierarchy based on their ability to speak English. On the other hand, this immigrant's parents taught him to be proud of his "glorious family history" and maintained contact with family in Poland. He also noted that one of his parents' friends in the United States was from a lower class, but a medal awarded to him for military bravery during World War II redeemed him in their eyes. This participant was troubled by the fact that maintaining these social distinctions was against "the American ideal," and he could never talk about them with his U.S. friends.

Hybridity (Lowe, 1996) is evident in the struggle over what is Polish, because the everyday lives described by participants represent different patterns of cultural incorporation in the context of uneven power relations between differentially situated groups. These cases show that habitus is a structure that incorporates new experiences as it continues to structure them. Cultural hybridity changes one's habitus, and those who once occupied similar positions become situated differently. These combined differences lead to many conflicts described by participants as occurring within the Polish community over such issues as the Polish church, Polish radio, the use of Polish or English during meetings of the Polish-American Congress, and others. What is at stake is how things should be done and how Polishness should be defined and represented.

Coming from different social classes as well as from different political convictions, the immigrants I interviewed have their own "Polands," which come into conflict. Political convictions are an important part of these conflicts; as one participant observed, "Two Poles belong to three political parties," stressing that Poles argue too much over everything. Polish immigrants struggle over what should be considered Polish. Many hang on to rigid definitions of Poland and Polishness; as one respondent observed, she "has to be very delicate criticizing anything that's Polish because people are very sensitive." This last comment especially shows that cultural identity is an object of symbolic capital investment and that groups are divided by politics of these investment not only within group relationships but also in relation to other groups.

CONCLUSIONS

This chapter argues that immigrant ethnic formations are fraught with tensions due to heterogeneity, multiplicity, and hybridity. They are articulated through differences and distinctions within the group that are made on the basis of cultural capital, habitus. Cultural capital is amassed around the notion of Polishness by immigrants situated differentially in terms of immigrant cohort, class, and cultural incorporation. Cohort class and incorporation of a "new" culture contribute to the creation of a structure, a habitus, social dispositions, principles, opinions, and an understanding of one's own location; these in turn generate practices and the capacity to distinguish between these practices and those who use them. Culture and ethnicity, as generative structures, are a part of habitual distinctions, because they provide means of establishing cultural and ethnic differences. Ethnicity is constructed across differences in habitus, which engenders distinctions on the basis of cultural capital. The concepts of heterogeneity, multiplicity, and hybridity enable us to understand how habitus distinctions are generated in the context of immigrant transitions between different economic and social structures. Such a relationship between ethnicity and habitus explains differences within ethnic groups as well as struggles over the meaning of ethnic identity by situating otherness *within* rather than in an us/them binary.

This chapter argues that habitus is created on the basis of immigrant cohort, preemigration class positions, and different patterns of cultural incorporation. Immigration cohort becomes a powerful basis for habitus distinctions as preemigration experiences, experiences in the United

States during a specific socioeconomic period, and present economic position generate a different view of the world and a different definition of what Polish is. Habitus is defined as a location within a specific sociocultural and economic system of production that structures a different way of life and, more important, perceptions of that different way of life and that finally engenders identification by interpellating individuals into subject positions. The notion of habitus is extended to refer to cultural differences generated by socialization in a capitalist or socialist system of production, which also engenders different views of the social world.

Habitus is also generated on the basis of social class and background as an indication of cultural differences. These distinctions are sometimes explicit, referring to specific preemigration class, and sometimes implicit, referring to taken-for-granted indicators of class and social positions. Habitus is based on implicit distinctions that survive immigration and changes in economic status and serve to establish inferiority/superiority positions. Taste fixes identities within a terrain of culture constructed as a hierarchy of positions articulated through economic conditions and class positions.

Habitus constantly regenerates, and it is restructured through new cultural experiences as it continues to structure them. Cultural incorporation changes one's habitus, and those who previously occupied similar positions are now situated differently. These combined differences lead to many conflicts within the Polish community; what is at stake is how things should be done and how Polishness should be defined and represented. Coming from different social classes as well as from different political convictions, the immigrants I interviewed have their own Polands, which come into conflict.

This analysis has several implications for the notions of culture, ethnicity, and identity. Culture and ethnicity have to be understood not as homogeneous, fixed, and discrete fields but as terrain bound up with material and economic conditions, political differences, and class positions that serve as axes of power along which identities are articulated (Lowe, 1996). In this cultural terrain, identities are articulated through domination and subordination of some identities over others. Ethnic and cultural formations are heterogeneous; multiplicities of immigrant positions are sites of exclusions and separation. These divisions splinter the social field of a community and are an expression of tensions between belonging and exclusion, commonality and difference. Finally, hybridity leads to the contestation of ethnic practices in the context of continued cultural changes. As Talai (1988) observes, ambiguities and differences in ethnic identification actually articulate a sense of commonality. Immigrants are thus connected in their struggles over different ways of being Polish.

REFERENCES

Balibar, E (1991). The nation form: History and ideology. In E. Balibar & I. Wallerstein (Eds.), *Race, nation, class: Ambiguous identities* (pp. 86-106). New York: Verso.

Bentley, G. (1987). Ethnicity and practice. *Comparative Studies in Society and History, 29*, 24-55.

Bentley, G. (1991). Response to Yelvington. *Comparative Studies in Society and History, 33*, 169-175.

Bottomley, G. (1991). Culture, ethnicity, and the politics/poetics of representation. *Diaspora, 3*, 303-320.

Bourdieu, P. (1977). *Outline of a theory of practice* (R. Nice, Trans.). Cambridge, UK: Cambridge University Press.

Bourdieu, P. (1984). *Distinction: A social critique of the judgement of taste* (R. Nice, Trans.). Cambridge, MA: Harvard University Press.

Bourdieu, P. (1991). *Language and symbolic power.* Cambridge, MA: Harvard University Press.

Collier, M. J. (1998). Researching cultural identity: Reconciling interpretive and postcolonial perspectives. In D. V. Tanno & A. González (Eds.), *Communication and identity across cultures* (International and Intercultural Communication Annual, Vol. 21, pp. 122-147). Thousand Oaks, CA: Sage.

Collier, M. J., & Thomas, M. (1988). Cultural identity: An interpretive perspective. In Y. Y. Kim & W. B. Gudykunst (Eds.), *Theories in intercultural communication* (pp. 99-122). Newbury Park, CA: Sage.

Delgado, F. P. (1998). Chicano ideology revisited: Rap music and the (re)articulation of Chicanismo. *Western Journal of Communication, 62*, 95-113.

Drzewiecka, J. A., & Nakayama, T. K. (1998). City sites: Postmodern urban space and the communication of identity. *Southern Journal of Communication, 64*, 20-31.

Eder, K. (1993). *The new politics of class: Social movements and cultural dynamics in advanced societies.* Newbury Park, CA: Sage.

Ganguly, K. (1992). Migrant identities: Personal memory and the construction of selfhood. *Cultural Studies, 6*(1), 27-50.

Hall, S. (1986). Cultural studies: Two paradigms. In R. Collins, J. Curran, N. Garnham, P. Scannell, P. Schlesinger, & C. Parks (Eds.), *Media, culture and society: A critical reader* (pp. 33-48). Newbury Park: Sage.

Hall, S. (1990/1994). Cultural identity and diaspora. In P. Williams & L. Chrisman (Eds.), *Colonial discourse and post-colonial theory* (pp. 392-403). New York: Columbia University Press.

Hall, S. (1991). The local and the global: Globalization and ethnicity. In A. D. King (Ed.), *Culture, globalization and the world-system: Contemporary conditions for the representation of identity* (pp. 19-39). Binghamton, NY: Department of Art and Art History, State University of New York.

Harker, R., Mahar, C., & Wilkes, C. (1990). *An introduction to the works of Pierre Bourdieu: The practice of theory.* London: Macmillan.

Hecht, M. (1993). 2002—A research odyssey: Toward the development of a communication theory of identity. *Communication Monographs, 60,* 76-82.

Hecht, M. L., Collier, M. J., Ribeau, S. A. (1993). *African American communication: Ethnic identity and cultural interpretation.* Newbury Park, CA: Sage.

Hegde, R. S. (1998a). Swinging the trapeze: The negotiation of identity among Asian Indian immigrant women in the United States. In D. V. Tanno & A. González (Eds.), *Communication and identity across cultures* (International and Intercultural Communication Annual, Vol. 21, pp. 34-55). Thousand Oaks, CA: Sage.

Hegde, R. S. (1998b). Translated enactments: The relational configuration of the Asian Indian immigrant experience. In J. N. Martin, T. K. Nakayama, & L. A. Flores (Eds.), *Readings in cultural contexts* (pp. 315-321). Mountain View, CA: Mayfield.

Holmer-Nadesan, M. (1996). Organizational identity and space of action. *Organization Studies, 17*(1), 49-81.

Houston, M. (1992). The politics of difference: Race, class, and women's communication. In L. F. Rakow (Ed.), *Women making meaning: New feminist directions in communication* (pp. 45-59). New York: Routledge.

Hutchinson, J., & Smith, A. D. (1996). *Ethnicity.* New York: Oxford University Press.

Jaroszynska-Kirchmann, A. D. (1996). Displaced persons, émigrés, refugees, and other Polish immigrants: World War II through the Solidarity Era. In J. J. Bukowczyk (Ed.), *Polish Americans and their history: Community, culture and politics* (pp. 152-179). Pittsburgh, PA: University of Pittsburgh Press.

Jenkins, R. (1997). *Rethinking ethnicity: Arguments and explorations.* Thousand Oaks, CA: Sage.

Lee, W. S. (1998). Patriotic breeders or colonized converts: A postcolonial feminist approach to antifootbinding discourse in China. In D. V. Tanno & A. González (Eds.), *Communication and identity across cultures* (International and Intercultural Communication Annual, Vol. 21, pp. 11-33). Thousand Oaks, CA: Sage.

Lincoln, Y. S., & Guba, E. G. (1985). *Naturalistic inquiry.* Newbury Park, CA: Sage.

LiPuma, E. (1993). Culture and the concept of culture in a theory of practice. In C. Calhoun, E. LiPuma, & M. Postone (Eds.), *Bourdieu: Critical perspectives* (pp. 14-34). Chicago: University of Chicago Press.

Lofland, J., & Lofland, L. H. (1995). *Analyzing social settings.* Belmont, CA: Wadsworth.

Lopata, H. Z. (1994). *Polish Americans.* New Brunswick, NJ: Transaction.

Lowe, L. (1996). *Immigrant acts.* Durham, NC: Duke University Press.

Martin, J., Krizek, R. L., Nakayama, T. K., & Bradford, L. (1996). Exploring whiteness: A study of self-labels for white Americans. *Communication Quarterly, 44,* 125-144.

Miller, K. A. (1990). Class, culture, and immigrant group identity in the United States: The case of Irish-American ethnicity. In V. Yans-McLaughlin (Ed.), *Immigration reconsidered: History, sociology and politics* (pp. 96-129). New York: Oxford University Press.

Nakayama, T. (1994). Dis/orienting identities: Asian Americans, history and intercultural communication. In A. González, M. Houston, & V. Chen (Eds.), *Our voices: Essays in culture, ethnicity, and communication* (pp. 12-17). Los Angeles: Roxbury.

Pienkos, D. E. (1984). *PNA: A centennial history of the Polish National Alliance of the United States of North America.* New York: Columbia University Press.

Polzin, T. (1982). The Polish Americans. In D. L. Cuddy (Ed.), *Contemporary American immigration: Interpretive essays.* Boston: Twayne.

Portes, A., & Rumbaut, R. G. (1996). *Immigrant America: A portrait* (2nd ed.). Berkeley: University of California Press.

Preston, P. W. (1997). *Political/cultural identity: Citizens and nations in a global era.* London: Sage.

Pula, J. S. (1995). *Polish Americans: An ethnic community.* New York: Simon and Schuster/Macmillan.

Talai, V. A. (1988). When ethnic identity is a mixed blessing: Armenians in London. *Ethnos, 53,* 50-62.

Tanno, D. (1994). Names, narratives, and the evolution of ethnic identity. In A. González, M. Houston, & V. Chen (Eds.), *Our voices: Essays in culture, ethnicity, and communication* (pp. 28-34). Los Angeles: Roxbury.

Yelvington, K. A. (1991). Ethnicity as practice? A comment on Bentley. *Comparative Studies in Society and History, 33,* 158-168.

11

A Face-Driven Account
of Identity Exchanges in
Israeli-Palestinian "Dialogue" Events

YAEL-JANETTE ZUPNIK • *University of Michigan at*
Ann Arbor

INTRODUCTION

Intergroup conflict has been a pervasive and ongoing world concern as well as a major subject of investigation in the human sciences (Vayrynen, 1991). Practical and theoretical concerns have focused on the characterization of conflict between groups and the potential means of resolving such strife. However, these approaches have often ignored analyses of the actual verbal communication between members of groups in conflict.

Conversely, within the field of discourse analysis, there have been attempts to analyze the structure and function of conflict talk of varying types (Labov & Fanshel, 1977; Tannen, 1990; Schiffrin, 1984; Goodwin, 1990). For example, researchers have analyzed the various participant relationships set up among interlocutors in therapeutic situations, friendly interactions among neighbors and friends, and interactions among children (Goodwin, 1990). Fine-grained analyses of these sort have shown how various language structures function within the verbal communication process. For example, it has been suggested that arguments among Jews function as a form of sociability meant to promote rather than hinder group relations (Schiffrin, 1984). Other studies have shown that boys and girls have access to similar verbal strategies of conflict, such as the use of stories to set up alliances in disputes (Goodwin, 1990).

These studies have furthered our understanding of conflict discourse and of the subtle means employed by interlocutors in the construction of such verbal situations. However, because of the problem of access to in situ conflict between groups in severe political conflict, problems in the generalization of such findings have been suggested (Grimshaw, 1990). In addition, analyses of conflict discourse, and discourse analysis in general, have often been criticized for their lack of recourse to social and sociological theories and principles to explain discourse findings. The present study addresses some of these gaps by analyzing in situ meetings between Israelis and Palestinians occurring during the Palestinian Uprising against the Israeli occupation of Arab lands. Using a convergence of tools from discourse analysis, pragmatics, sociology, and ethnography, the study demonstrates how the conflicting goals of the two groups are instantiated in and constituted by particular key discourse exchanges.

Specifically, the purpose of the present study is to illustrate how a key discourse construct is analyzed quantitatively (Zupnik, 2000) by focusing on the sociopolitical identity-display to the promotion, maintenance, and defense of the social "faces" that participants try to create and enact in dialogue events.

The earlier quantitative work indicated the significant differences in the use of the discourse construct by the two groups. These differences were suggested to be caused by the differing goals of members of the two groups for attending events. The present study, in contrast, focuses on the interactive nature of the discourse construct already uncovered; specifically, it shows how particular conversational sequences that employ the construct of sociopolitical identity-display demonstrate its significance for the social construction of participants in the events. A description of the data for the present analysis and background on the Israeli-Palestinian "dialogue" events is first provided.

The Israeli-Palestinian Dialogue Speech Event

The *dialogue speech event* refers to regularly planned, ongoing meetings that take place, usually in English, between Palestinians of the Occupied Territories (OT)[1] and Israelis from within Israel proper. These meetings came into existence with the onset of the *intifada* (uprising), the Palestinian Arab rebellion against the Israeli occupation of the West Bank and Gaza Strip. I refer here solely to meetings between these two groups, though dialogues also occur between Israeli Jews and Palestinians who are citizens of Israel, the latter group composing 17% of the Israeli population. In addition, the observed meetings are conducted in

English, because neither group has enough competence in the language of the other to speak in either Hebrew or Arabic.

Historical Background

At this point, additional background of historical events is in order.[2] The lands termed the Occupied Territories came about as a result of the 1967 "Six-Day War" between Israel and several Arab nations. After the war, Israel occupied various lands beyond its original borders, also known as the "green line." The following lands were occupied: west into Jordan—East Jerusalem and parts of the West Bank of the Jordan River; north into Syria—the Golan Heights; and south into Egypt—the Sinai Peninsula and Gaza Strip.

As a result of peace accords with Egypt in the 1970s, the entire Sinai Peninsula was returned to Egypt. Though throughout the decades there have clandestine attempts at negotiations over lands, no actual agreement was reached until the Oslo Peace Accords in 1993. In that agreement, it was agreed that in return for peaceful relationships with the Palestinians, Israel would give over to Palestinian control most of the lands occupied on the West Bank and Gaza Strip, which are almost entirely populated by Palestinians, but in which thousands of Israelis live as well. These Israelis, who moved to the OT after the 1967 war, are called "the settlers."

The Palestinian Uprising (the *intifada*) began in 1987. The Palestinians, who had been under Israeli occupation for 20 years, rebelled against the military government controlling their lives. Much of the Palestinian rebellion involved throwing stones, burning tires, and nonviolent activities. However, there were also numerous violent confrontations with Israeli authorities. As a result of the *intifada,* thousands of Palestinian civilians were killed, and many more were incarcerated. On the Israeli side, there were hundreds of casualties, mostly among soldiers and among settlers of the OT.

It was during the period of the *intifada* itself that Israeli-Palestinian dialogues were born. Here and there throughout the OT and within Israel proper, there were attempts among moderates of both sides to make contact and discuss the problems between them. Israelis and Palestinians involved in the events often state that it was as a result of the violent interaction of the *intifada* that verbal dialogue was attempted.

According to participants on both sides, the general, overt purpose of the Israeli-Palestinian dialogue speech events is to bring about acquaintanceship and communication between the two groups. In all cases, these events have come about as a result of grassroots movements among individuals on both sides of the conflict. Informal contact is made between members of the two sides, and these members then jointly decide how to create such regularly planned events and how to ensure participation by others.

Dialogue meetings constitute one type of ongoing intergroup event characteristic of the "pre-Oslo peace accords" era. Others include organizations in which the agenda is to work on specific tasks together, such as the resolution of human rights violations in the OT. Additional events are based on similar professions, such as meetings among writers or psychologists. There are also nonformalized meetings that take place for the purpose of transacting business; however, these interactions are not called "dialogue groups."

Approximately 10 different types of dialogue events between Israelis and Palestinians of the OT were known to exist during the years of the *intifada*. In almost all these cases, the language of dialogue was English. The groups varied along the dimensions of geographical location (Israel or the OT), frequency of meetings (biweekly to several times a year), consistency of participation by individual interlocutors, political affiliations of participants, and religion of the Palestinians (Moslem, Christian, or both). All meetings lasted approximately 100 min. Since the period of the *intifada*, many of these dialogues have disbanded; some now exist in the setting of Israeli universities between students from the two sides.

Participants of the dialogues during the period of the *intifada* were usually from the middle to upper-middle class of both societies, ranging in age from 30 to 60 years. Both groups were composed of politically moderate, mostly college-educated professionals, usually with very good communicative competence in English.

METHODOLOGY

Over a 9-month period during the *intifada*, participant-observation of 24 Israeli-Palestinian dialogue events was undertaken. Fourteen of these were audiotaped, and two were videotaped. Individual interviews were conducted separately, in English, with each of the 24 participants. Interviews were open-ended. Participants were asked to describe demographic facts about themselves, their goals in participating in events, and the goals of the other side. In addition, participants listened to playbacks of excerpts of the audiotapes and were asked to interpret the intentions of interlocutors in particular exchanges, whether the exchanges included the interviewee him- or herself, or not.[3]

In this chapter I deal with one dialogue event type observed: the "Hamla" dialogue speech event. Twelve such events were observed, and nine of these were audiotaped. Interviews/playback sessions were conducted with six Jewish Israeli and five Christian Palestinian participants. The specific data from one particular event of this type are dealt with in this chapter. Most of the events take place in a particular village on the West Bank of the OT, which I will call "Hamla," originally in the homes of the Palestinians and later in a center built for the specific purpose of dialogue events.[4] Israelis travel to Hamla in organized transportation. Less frequent are events that take place in Israel in the homes of various regularly attending Israelis. In these cases, Palestinians travel into Israel to meet the Israelis. This is considered to be the longest existing and best-known of the Israeli-Palestinian dialogue event types, and the groups have been meeting regularly since the onset of the *intifada.*

Security issues have affected the frequency of events. Both travel by Israelis into the OT and travel by the Palestinians into Israel are considered dangerous for the groups. In this connection, it should be noted that all the Israeli-Palestinian dialogue events I observed and participated in were relatively clandestine. Though they were not completely secret, neither were they generally known; knowledge of them passed by word of mouth.

Earlier on in the history of the Hamla events, events took place twice a week. Later on, they took place twice a month or once a month. Often the decision to hold an event was determined by the political events in the OT; during periods of strife, meetings would be cancelled. In addition, during such periods, Palestinians were barred from entering Israel. Often Israelis as well were not allowed to enter into the OT; in both cases, such decisions were made by the Israeli Jewish authorities.

Participants and Dialogue Events

The population of the Hamla events consisted of a predominantly (90%) Christian population on the Palestinian side. The Christian community makes up 80% of the population of the village of Hamla. Although in the OT as a whole, Christians make up only 8% of the population, there are many villages in the OT, particularly in the West Bank, that are almost completely Christian. Many of them are located in the area of Bethlehem. The Christian Palestinians are usually perceived by Israelis as being more moderate than Muslim Palestinians.[5]

The Israelis in the events were all Jewish. In addition, over time, an additional group became participants in the events: visitors to Israel or the OT. These visitors were usually Christian or Jewish. They participated in events just as the indigenous participants did.

The consistency of participation in the Hamla dialogue events varied. First, there was an Israeli and Palestinian "core" group of participants that held planning meetings and was responsible for ensuring participation by members of their "side." A different subset of interlocutors attended fairly consistently for certain periods of time. On the Palestinian side, such interlocutors attended regularly, though many took breaks during the long period of the dialogue's existence. On the Israeli side, regular attendance was usually limited to about half a year of attendance, that is, for about 10 to 20 events.

The number of participants in any one Hamla event varied from a minimum of about 12 participants to 30 participants. The distribution was usually a third Palestinian, a third Israeli, and a third visitors to the region.

The level of acquaintanceship varied among the participants. The Hamla Palestinian participants knew each other very well, because they lived in the same village. The next group highly familiar to each other was the intergroup core participants, who had planned events together since 1988, when the group began meeting regularly. Finally, usually one of the Israeli participants knew one of the core Israeli members, because the latter would invite the former to attend the events. The Israeli Jews did not typically know the other Israeli Jewish members attending the events. However, during the organized transportation into the OT, they became more familiar with each other.

My background needs to be accounted for; I am an Israeli American, bicultural, having intermittently lived half my life in Israel, since the age of 6. Access to dialogue meetings was gained through acquaintance with a well-known leftist Israeli political activist.

Political Orientations and Goals

Interviews and events indicate that both groups of interlocutors are made up of political moderates.[6] The way such moderation is instantiated in each of the two groups is discussed next.

Palestinians. In the interviews, the Palestinian (P) participants identify themselves with the Palestine Liberation Organization (PLO), which represents 80% of the Palestinian population of the OT. Thus, Palestinian participants are part of the political majority. In addition, Palestinians state in events and interviews that they view themselves as representing most of the Palestinian population. Many of the Hamla Palestinian interlocutors identified themselves with less moderate factions within the PLO, that is, with those factions less conciliatory toward Israel. This may typify the political stance of Christian Palestinians in the OT at the time: they were interested in displaying their close ties to the Palestinian cause above and beyond religious differences (Cragg, 1991). This context, including their self-categorization as members of a unified people, shapes their professed event goals, as noted later.

In interviews the Palestinians state that they wish to be perceived as human beings. They do not think the world or Israelis have so perceived them; rather, they have been perceived as terrorists. Most important, they express that they wish "to present their case" as victims who have a right to be recognized as a people and who have a right to their own state. They also emphasize their unity and their desire to present a united front. These goals are illustrated in the following excerpts:

> Ibrahim (P): Palestinians are not seen as human beings to the international public, they are seen as terrorists . . . the Palestinians have been presented to the world like a black box.

> The dialogues fit in with the purposes of the *intifada* . . . we were always trying to convey to them [Israelis] that their lives are at our expense . . . we have to take care of the unity of our society . . . our unity as Palestinians is a very strong and important issue to us and we won't sacrifice it.

> Abdel (P): We want to put across what we think, what the *intifada* means to us. It's my duty to do it. It's important for the national cause . . . to present my case.

> we have to keep a unified front . . . you'll get Israelis . . . will not recognize you as a person or as a nation, sometimes out of ignorance, sometimes out of belief . . . we are included with the rest of the Arab world, as if we don't have our own nation.

> Jaber (P): We all the time try to make them [Israelis] feel guilty.

*Israelis.*The Israeli Jewish participants are self-declared "Leftists" who believe in Palestinian rights, such as the right to statehood. At the time of these events, they constituted about 20 to 30% of the population of Israel. Because the government at the time was a right-wing one, they felt relatively powerless to bring about real change, in spite of participation in activities for peace. This context, including their self-categorization as moderates, shapes the event goals they espouse. Specifically, in interviews they state that they wish to create ties of solidarity and friendship with the Palestinians, including showing support for the Palestinian cause. They also wish to express distance from less-moderate Israelis. This position is illustrated in the following interview excerpts:

> Dov (IJ): I contribute by participating, by showing them that there are Israelis that listen to them, that think differently than the government . . . the issues, I discuss many times with Jews and Arabs . . . nothing new in it . . . I'm more interested in meeting with families . . . than these meetings . . . talking with one is better than groups . . . more intimate . . . more personal.
>
> David (IJ): Through a long-term meeting process I hoped to meet Palestinians beyond politics.
>
> Shalom (IJ): In a private home there is more of a real dialogue. I hoped for personal ties.
>
> Nicky (IJ): We're trying to tell them [Palestinians] that we're in this together.

Conflict in Goals

We note above a divergence and, indeed, conflict in goals for attending events. The conflict is not the obvious one expected, given the Israeli-Palestinian conflict; that is, it is not a conflict in which each side aims to convince the other about who is "right." Rather, Palestinians wish to fulfill political goals: to show themselves as united and worthy of statehood. Israeli goals are more social: they wish to forge close ties of solidarity with the Palestinians, in spite of the strife between them. Thus, one group seeks to achieve political goals, whereas the other group is aiming at social goals.

Although the goals are described in the one-to-one interviews, participants do not state these goals explicitly in the dialogue events. One objective of the present study, then, is to describe the ways in which these unstated goals are constituted in the discourse between the groups. Specifically, the conflict in goals is reflected in and constituted by the sequence of particular conversational exchanges of sociopolitical identity-displays (SPIDs).

Sociopolitical Identity-Displays

Earlier work on political discourse has dealt extensively with the use of first-person pronouns (i.e., *I*, *we*; e.g., Fairclough, 1989; Wilson, 1990; Zupnik, 1994). These have been found to be crucial in situating the political stances of speakers. For example, a speaker can display alliances to various kinds of groups by a vague use of *we*; he can also distinguish himself from the group as an individual by the use of *I*. In recent work on the use of political pronouns in Israeli-Palestinian dialogue events, the pragmatic discourse construct of the SPID has been put forth as one that instantiates particular stances and affiliations of speakers (Zupnik, 2000).[7]

The term *sociopolitical identity-display* refers to the verbal expression of the stance of the speaker relative to one of his or her dominant macro-affiliations, whether as an individual or as a member of a group. The anchoring of the speaker to such utterances is identified by the use of first-person pronouns: singular (*I*, *my*, *mine*) or plural (*we*, *our*, *ours*). Thus, when the speaker positions herself as an individual member of a particular group, she employs the singular *I*. When she positions herself as representative of the entire affiliation, she uses *we*. Of course, other elements could be suggested as verbal elements employed by interlocutors to set up relations between themselves and their utterances; however, I limit myself to pronouns as the elements that identify the SPIDs, because it is here that self-categorization of the speaker is clearest.

The semantic content of the conventional stances is also considered in the employment of the SPIDs, and the analysis demonstrates how these stances relate to the goals of participants from the two groups. Sociopolitical affiliations are identified by the semantic meaning of the verbal phrases linked to the pronouns. The phrases that I analyze deal with sociopolitical characteristics, such as sociopolitical actions or states. Earlier quantitative analysis has already identified three types of SPIDs: the personal, the intragroup, and the intergroup. These three types are described and illustrated below.

The Personal Sociopolitical Identity Display. In a personal SPID, the pronoun is linked to a sociopolitical affiliation by means of particular sociopolitical characteristics. In addition, the speaker is represented as an individual. This is encoded in the use of the singular pronouns (e.g., *I*, *my*).

For example, Yonnie, the Israeli mediator, responds to a question from Nasser, the Palestinian mediator, concerning the former's views of extremist Palestinians who oppose Israel's existence[8]:

> Yonnie (IJ): He's my political enemy-
> I don't means he's he's somebody
> that I'm going to go out and attack-
> I mean if if I- I
> Nasser (PA): to struggle against-
> Yonnie (IJ): I will struggle against his political goals- yes
> if his political goals is to destroy Israel-
> then I will struggle against his political goals-
> eh eh if it's a military goal-
> I'll struggle against it militarily-

Yonnie displays his personal sociopolitical identity. He takes on the role of an individual Israeli opposed to individual Palestinian extremists. This is evidenced in the first-person pronouns ("I," "my") and in the semantic content of the verbal phrases (e.g., "will struggle against"). That is, we can infer that the "I" refers to an Israeli, because it is an Israeli who would oppose the political and military goals of the Palestinians.

Although it is the use of the pronoun *I* in a sociopolitical context that identifies the personal SPID, some additional comments can be made concerning the conventional semantic content of the personal SPIDS. In general, both Israelis and Palestinians adopt a personal SPID of a politically moderate, peace-loving individual.

Intragroup Sociopolitical Identity Displays. In addition to the personal SPID, two types of group SPID have been identified, the first being an intragroup SPID. In the intragroup SPID, the speaker indexes an inclusive group identity, indexing members of her own sociopolitical affiliation.

For example, Nasser describes the history of Fundamentalism among Palestinians. Interlocutors have been discussing Muslim Fundamentalism, and Israelis have been asking Palestinians many questions on this topic. Below Nasser is relating his perception of the unique position of Palestinians versus other Arab peoples concerning the question of Fundamentalism.

Nasser (PA): we don't have the history of being fundamentalist
like what was going on in Egypt in Lebanon in Syria and Iraq-
we don't have this-
you know- we didn't have this problem in our history- in spite of-
we have been naturally Arabs-
but finally we didn't have a fundamentalist movement among-
the only distinguished movement we had all the time was nationalist-

Here we note that Nasser takes on an intragroup Palestinian identity. He situates himself as a member of this larger group, encoded in his use of the pronouns *we* and *our* to index the entire group of Palestinians. That he is referring to an inclusive Palestinian group is clear from the semantic meaning of verbal phrases, such as "don't have the history of being fundamentalist . . . like Egypt . . . Lebanon . . . Syria . . . Iraq." Given the sociopolitical context of the time, it can be inferred that it is only to Palestinians that he is referring.

This use by a Palestinian of an intragroup SPID that emphasizes the connection to the master group is conventional among Palestinians. The semantic content thus given by Palestinians to their intragroup SPID clearly allows them to achieve their goals of presenting themselves as a united people.

We see an example of Israeli use of the SPID below from an excerpt from Sara's turn at talk. She is an Israeli professional in her 40s. She is discussing elements of the Israeli policy in the OT at the time:

Sara: as long as we're in the territories-
we want to make sure
there's law and order-
and everything's okay
but in fact we want to get out of the territories-

Here we note that Sara takes on an intragroup identity display, an inclusive positioning that indexes all Israelis and expresses the institutional Israeli policy concerning the OT. This is clear from an analysis of the meaning of the verbal phrases "are in the territories" and "want to get out of the territories." During the period of time of this event, there was much discussion in Israel as a whole concerning the need to get out of the OT and particularly out of the Gaza Strip, where the violence was most serious and where many Israelis were killed in confrontations with the Palestinians. Here we note that Sara employs an intragroup SPID similar to that of the Palestinians: a group position that unites all elements including the speaker; for example, "we want to get out of the territories."

The Intergroup Sociopolitical Identity Display. A third type is the intergroup SPID. This display indexes members of two different sociopolitical groups, in this case, Israelis and Palestinians. It too is identified by the use of the first-person plural pronouns (e.g., *we*). This group affiliation "crosses enemy lines"; that is, it refers to a group of both Israelis and Palestinians. Examples of such intergroup affiliations are Israeli and Palestinian interlocutors of the events, all the moderate Israelis and Palestinians on both sides, or all the Israelis and Palestinians in general.

For example, Ibrahim, a Palestinian professional in his 40s, has just mentioned that just as Israelis have fears of Arabs (which they had been describing), so he has fears of Israelis:

Ibrahim (PA): to tell you the truth- I have the same fears-

Yonnie (IJ): [I think

Dov (IJ): [maybe

Shula (IJ): [that's why it's good that we're meeting

Dov: on both sides

David (IJ): on both sides and ( )

Dov: that's why we meet here

Here we see how the Israelis—Shula, Dov, and David—jointly take up an intergroup Israeli-Palestinian identity. This is encoded in the pronouns ("we") and the semantic content of the verbal phrases that refer to the intergroup meetings: "we are meeting," "why we meet here."

Another example of the intergroup identity-display can be seen from an earlier turn at talk by Shula:

Shula (IJ): maybe we can talk about the future

and not so much about the past-

we all agree that the situation is very bad-

Here we see that Shula indexes an intergroup scope for "we," as identified by the semantic content of the verbal phrases. These refer to the verbal interactions that take place between Israelis and Palestinians in such events, for example, talking about the political situation between them.

In general, similar verbal, semantic content is given to the intergroup SPIDS by both groups; the intergroup SPID shows that each is interested in achieving moderation, in achieving joint goals, and in doing so through conversation. However, the differences in the ways the Israelis and Palestinians employ the first two types of identity-displays can be explained by their differing goals (Zupnik, 2000). Israelis usually employ a personal SPID that distances them from other Israelis, whereas Palestinians employ a personal SPID that ties them strongly to the group. An earlier study (Zupnik, 2000) showed quantitatively that Israelis employ the personal and intergroup displays significantly more than the Palestinians do, whereas the Palestinians employ the intragroup identity-display significantly more than Israelis do.[9] These findings can again be explained by the macrogoals of interlocutors; that is, Israelis use the personal display to distinguish themselves from other Israelis, whereas they use the intergroup display to forge new ties of solidarity with Palestinians. Conversely, Palestinians use the intragroup display mostly to show unity among Palestinians, whereas they avoid the intergroup display.

Face

SPIDs constitute one strategy for manipulating face concerns of interlocutors, in that these face concerns are closely tied to the event goals of the two groups. The notion of face refers to the use initiated by Goffman (1967), who derived the notion both from the English folk term and from Durkheimian ideas concerning the relations of the self to society (Durkheim, 1915). In Goffman's view, face is something that all social actors invest in promoting and maintaining. There is also always the risk of "losing face." Thus, to a great extent, much of social interaction concerns the preservation of whatever face interlocutors promote and its defense when threatened. Certain kinds of speech activities intrinsically threaten face; for example, criticisms threaten the need for approval.

In the field of linguistics, research has been devoted to describing the patterned use of particular kinds of utterances the function of which is to manage face concerns of the speaker and the hearer (Brown & Levinson, 1978). In addition, face and the need to promote and maintain it have been found to be present across diverse cultural groups (Katriel, 1986). However, the research on face usually deals with utterance-level analyses, not with longer stretches of discourse. In addition, the notion of "group face" has not received adequate attention. In the present study, face concerns motivate the employment of extended stretches of discourse and SPIDs, and they function to defend the group as well as personal face concerns.

Face and the Israeli-Palestinian Dialogue Event

As all social agents are interested in putting forth particular "faces" in the world, so are the Israelis and Palestinians in the dialogue event.

Based on both my own long-term observations and my conversations and interviews with members of both groups, the atmosphere in these events is perceived to be tense. There are moments of joint laughter that break the tension, but in general, the atmosphere is far from relaxed. There are various reasons one can suggest for the tension, such as the face-to-face meeting with the "Other" and the fact that the topics discussed are usually highly volatile. In addition, the site of the dialogue is the Other's territory, which carries safety concerns for both sides. Thus, given all these tension-inducing factors, the dialogue is a socially complex and delicate undertaking.

The present study suggests that SPIDs function to create, maintain, and defend individual and group faces of Israelis and Palestinians in these dialogical interactions. Operationally, we might expect one SPID to trigger an opposing one by the other side, depending on the face that has been threatened. Thus, for example, the activation by an Israeli of an intergroup SPID might be responded to with a Palestinian intragroup SPID. Such a response might occur because an intergroup position by Israelis threatens the intragroup face of Palestinians, whose goals are to promote intragroup solidarity and to eschew close ties with Israelis.

Because SPID activations vary across diverse topics and utterances, they are not necessarily sequentially related. What follows, however, is a discourse analysis of three such SPID-focused exchanges in the event. These examples are analyzed, therefore, to illustrate the general claim that face concerns may motivate the employment of SPIDs in selected dialogue events.

Example 1

During the event, an extended discussion of Arab and Palestinian Fundamentalism is taking place. Israelis had already mentioned fears that other Israelis have of Fundamentalism. At the point in the interaction we note in the following example, Ibrahim, a Palestinian professional in his 40s, claims that in spite of the occupation, Palestinians have been trying to reach a compromise solution with Israelis, as evidenced by Palestinian attendance at peace talks in Madrid that had begun several months earlier. Several Israelis then respond:

1 Ibrahim (P): why- why our delegates are staying in Madrid

2 and going here and there

3 with all the threat against us-

4 I mean against-

5 the Israeli imprisonment of part of the movement-

6 and the harassment everybody is getting here-

7 the violation of our human rights etc. etc. . . . .

8 and on the other side- we don't feel that Israelis are moving towards

9 peace-

10 on the contrary- there has been a major shift toward the right-

11 everybody is on our side- is talking about peace-

12 while everybody on the other side is talking about fears-

13 talking about

14 Shula (IJ): no

15 Ibrahim: the *right*- the right of having the promised

16 land etc.

17 Dov (IJ): not everybody

18 Sara (IJ): not everybody

19 Dov: I think you're getting [carried away a little

20 Shula: [maybe you ( )

21 David (IJ): you're exaggerating in the same way in terms of

22 I think when we talked about

23 what percentage of the Palestinian population is Muslim or Muslim

24 fundamentalist-

25 and it's not ( ) compromise-

26 in a w- in a sense it's very similar in the Israeli population-

27 we probably have more or less the same percentage-

28 twenty to thirty percent of Israelis who are less flexible-

29 tending much more towards a fundamentalist- a Jewish fundamentalist

30 point of view

In Lines 1 through 13, Ibrahim employs an intragroup SPID by which he juxtaposes Palestinians to Israelis, whom he portrays as both frightened and extreme.

Note that in order to understand why the SPID activation extends from Lines 1 through 13, one must understand the way in which the boundaries of a SPID are set. A SPID begins at the first employment of a relevant sociopolitical first-person pronoun. It remains in play until there is explicit verbal evidence that the speaker has shifted out of the SPID. In Line 1, Ibrahim states, "why our delegates are going here and there." Given the context at the time of this event, it can be inferred that he is referring to delegates of Palestinians. Thus, here begins his employment of an intragroup SPID. He then remains in this SPID activation throughout his turn; there is no verbal evidence to indicate that he has shifted away from it. In Line 1, Ibrahim activates the intragroup SPID. When he goes on to discuss "going here and there," "all the threat against us," and "the violation of our human rights," he is still situated in the intragroup SPID. At the time, delegates of the Palestinians were meeting with Israelis in Madrid. Ibrahim confirmed this interpretation in the playback interview session with him.

Ibrahim's intragroup SPID includes conventional Palestinian juxtapositon of Palestinian and Israeli stances. This is indicated, for example, in Lines 8-12: "everybody on our side . . . talking about peace . . . everybody on the other side . . . talking about fears." In setting up this opposition between Palestinian proponents for peace and Israeli fears, Ibrahim threatens the face needs of his politically moderate Israeli interlocutors, who, as demonstrated in other parts of the dialogue, wish to be perceived as proponents for peace. His exclusionary stance (e.g., "everybody on our side . . . everybody on the other side") further threatens the intragroup face needs of moderate Israelis; that is, he ignores that Israeli moderates exist at all.

Thus, the group and individual Israeli moderate face has now been threatened. This threat to face motivates the Israeli reaction and thus the structure of the exchange. In particular, the threat to face here motivates the activation of an Israeli intergroup SPID. Specifically, Israelis initially react defensively, as shown in their negative responses in Lines 14, 17, and 18: "no," "not everybody." Subsequently, David employs the intergroup SPID in Lines 22 through 30. It is an intergroup SPID because it is Israelis and Palestinians together who have been talking ("when we talked about," Line 22) and who have similar numbers of extremists ("we probably have more or less the same percentages," Line 27).

David's enactment of this intergroup SPID seems to be motivated to defend both the personal and group face of moderate Israelis from Ibrahim's earlier criticism. Specifically, the use of the intergroup SPID promotes an intergroup face of Israelis and Palestinians: David portrays the two groups as similar in the proportion of extremists among them. Thus, the intergroup SPID serves to defend the Israeli moderate face and attempts to foster a new face: a grouping of Israelis and Palestinians as similar. Thus, the face concerns of the Israeli interlocutors may serve as motivation for the employment of the intergroup SPID and may explain the sequential structure of an intragroup Palestinian SPID followed by an intergroup Israeli SPID.

Example 2

The second example also concerns the topic of Fundamentalism, which was discussed at length in the event. Previously, Nasser (P) said that if there is popular support for Fundamentalism among Palestinians, it needs to be accepted. He also mentioned that he met Fundamentalists when he himself was in jail. See the consequent exchange between Nasser and David in the following:

1 Nasser (P): they are- you know uh-
2 they don't differ from the average Palestinian except a few differences
3 in politics and religion and social habits-
4 so what?
5 if uh- if he has certain social habits-
6 this- that doesn't disqualify him-
7 David (IJ): ( ) there is- like when I talk in Israel to a religious Jew especially a
8 religious Jew who- a nationalist religious Jew
9 I feel that there is a chasm a very- an abyss between me and this person-
10 don't you have this feeling?
11 Nasser: not exactly I don't think I don't think you can you can have uh
12 David: ( )
13 Nasser: you can have the similarity here
14 because our society here is not a secular one-
15 David: hmm
16 Nasser: you know- secularity came to you from uh the Jews
17 who came from Europe-
18 and many of them came here as secular Jews

19 David: yes

20 Nasser: not as religious Jews

21 our- our community is more religious- in- naturally-

In Lines 7 to 10, David activates a personal SPID of a moderate, secular Israeli. This can be inferred from the predicates linked to the singular pronoun *I*; for example, "feel there is a chasm" (between a nationalist religious Jew and David). Given the context of Israeli society, it is secular, moderate Israelis who feel distance from religious, nationalist Jews, who are opposed to giving up any of the OT. By the employment of this personal SPID, David sets himself up as an individual, distinct from more radical Israeli individuals. Included in his activation of a personal SPID is his question to Nasser in Line 10: "don't you have this feeling?" The presupposition of such a question is that Nasser must also feel distant from radical religious elements in Palestinian society.

Nasser's intragroup face appears threatened by David's personal SPID, presumably because David employs a personal SPID that refers to an individual, moderate Israeli. He then implies that Nasser is similar to him ("don't you have this feeling?"), thereby attempting to set up a closer relationship of solidarity between David and Nasser. However, given the goals of the Palestinians, this SPID move must threaten Nasser's intragroup face, which is based on promoting an inclusive Palestinian identity that does not include close ties to Israelis.

It then seems reasonable to infer that this may be a serious threat to Nasser's intragroup face, which motivates Nasser's enactment of an intragroup SPID in, for example, Lines 13-14 ("our society here is not a secular one") and in Lines 20-21 ("our community is more religious . . . naturally"). This intragroup SPID includes a contrast between Palestinian and Israeli society, encoded in referential contrasts between the Palestinians, characterized as religious, and Israelis, characterized as secular. For example, Nasser states that "our community is more religious" (Line 21). This then is a particularly striking instance of the display of the intragroup SPID, because it is employed by a Christian Palestinian on the topic of religion.

Example 3

Later in the same dialogue, Jaber (P) responds to the same Israeli personal SPID with a personal SPID.

1 Jaber (P): I want ( ) about the same topic-

2 actually as a rel-as a religious person-as a Christian person-

3 I don't have anything against Islam as a religion-

4 actually what we- people have- what others-

5 I mean in terms of what kind of stereotypes you have

6 or images you have about Islam

7 is uh reflected in the in in in the practices-

8 in the *mis*use of this religion by by uh people

9 who- uh you know uh Moslem people or leaders during maybe the

10 Ottomani period or some other periods

11 where they misused- uh the- this religion

12 I think- I'm I'm not so-

13 I don't know mu- much about Islam as a religion

14 but I know for a fact that it has democracy in it-

15 all religions by the way- you know god is not extreme in his religion

16 he all the time wants to spread justice- equality among people

17 and I don't think Islam as a religion is- is *that* extreme

18 but uh- many Moslems misuse Islam-

19 and that's the stereotype you have about Islam-

20 I'm not afraid if- I'm not afraid

21 if in the future Palestinian state there will be uh Moslem parties more than

22 the national parties- if of course-

23 I will be afraid

24 if they misuse this religion

25 but if they follow religion properly this religion properly

26 they also have I- they also have something about Christians- to protect

27 Christians

This excerpt illustrates one of the instances where a Hamla Palestinian explicitly refers to his own Christianity. Specifically, in Lines 2 through 27, Jaber employs a personal SPID to respond to the earlier Israeli inter-group SPID, here from the position of an individual Christian (e.g., Lines 2-3, "as a Christian person I don't have anything against Islam as a religion").

Given the context described earlier, one could assume that to respond to an Israeli personal SPID with any type of Palestinian personal SPID would defeat the goals of the Palestinians to portray themselves as a united group. Moreover, this should especially be the case when the personal Palestinian SPID evoked is one of an individual Christian. Yet, in contrast to what might be expected, it seems that Jaber does manage to employ the personal SPID to defend his intragroup face, because he employs the personal SPID in order to portray himself as a Christian advocate of Islam.

Lines 4-11 of his personal SPID activation serve as an account for his nonadversarial attitude toward Islam ("I don't have anything against," Line 3). This is juxtaposed to Israeli stereotypes of Islam that result from the actions of particular Muslim individuals ("stereotypes you have," Line 5). However, Lines 8-11 display the potential tension in this affiliation. Here he admits that there are problematic Muslims ("who- uh you know uh Muslim people or leaders . . . where they misused- uh the- this religion"). However, Jaber then continues setting himself up as an advocate for Islam. Within this move, he creates particular relationships and affiliations between groups, which do not allow for the exclusion of Islam. Specifically, he defends Islamic democracy (Lines 13-14), refers to Islam as one of many religions (Lines 15-17), and repeats utterances concerning the misuse of the religion by particular Muslims (Lines 18-19). Line 18, however, points again to the tension in this alignment. Again, he refers to Muslim misuse of religion ("but uh- many Muslims misuse Islam").

He then states that as long as Muslims follow the religion of Islam, he has no fears, because Islam also espouses the protection of Christians. Here again, potential tension between these alignments can be noted: "I will be afraid if they misuse this religion" (Lines 23-24). After this short aside, however, Jaber returns to play the role of the Christian advocate of Islam, suggesting that Muslims are protectors of Christians ("they have something . . . to protect Christians," Lines 26-27).

The previous discussion indicates that though there is some tension involved in this move, Jaber's personal SPID is embedded in the Palestinian group affiliation. As a result, he can employ this SPID to defend both his personal and intragroup faces: On the one hand, by employing the personal SPID, he can identify himself as an individual, moderate Christian. However, the nature of the group embeddedness of his personal SPID further allows him to defend his intragroup Palestinian face as well, and he presents himself as an advocate for Islam.

Thus, face concerns can be seen as perhaps motivating a SPID sequence. In this instance, David's use of a personal SPID probably threatened both Jaber's personal face as a moderate Christian and his intragroup face as a Palestinian. As a result, Jaber enacts a particular kind of personal SPID, which seems to function to defend his individual and group face concerns.

DISCUSSION

Three illustrations of sequential occurrences of SPIDs have been provided, the order of which can be explained by the various individual and group face concerns of interlocutors. The notion of face can explain the use and functioning of the SPIDs analyzed here.

These sequences of SPIDs reflect and constitute the interactive struggle over the unverbalized goals of interlocutors in the events. By the management of such potentially "oppositional" SPIDs, both groups attempt to accomplish their face goals. In other words, the Palestinians attempt to portray themselves as distinct and united, and they employ both individual and intragroup SPIDs to defend, promote, and maintain such a face. Israelis may be aiming to create social ties with Palestinians and to distance themselves from radical Israelis. As a result, they employ personal and intergroup SPIDs in order to create and maintain the face they wish to present to Palestinians. Thus, we note that though the two groups have divergent goals, they apply the same kinds of discourse constructs for the same social face ends.

The discourse analysis supplied here is based on limited excerpts from one Hamla dialogue event. Thus, one needs to address the potential generalizability of the present findings. Though other close microanalyses in progress have not been shown here, they do suggest that SPID use and its link to face concerns are prevalent in other settings of Israeli and Palestinian talk, for example, in speeches by Israelis and Palestinians and in interactions between them appearing in the mass media. Future research is needed to substantiate such claims.

Further, there is the question of the generalizability of the use of English by native speakers of Hebrew and Arabic. In the case of all three of these languages, first-person singular and plural pronouns are morphologically similar; that is, there is only one possibility for the singular pronoun (depending on the grammatical case; e.g., *I, my*) and one word for the plural (*we*). Thus, had the speakers been speaking in Hebrew or Arabic, their use of the pronouns would probably be the same: instead of *I* in English, for example, *ani* in Hebrew would be used. Although in some other languages one word for the plural pronoun (e.g., *we*) includes the speaker and another word does not, it may be necessary to carry out a more intricate analysis of the use of first-person pronouns in these more morphologically complex languages. Such analyses may lead to different SPID categories than the three noted in this study.[10]

Finally, this study is an exhaustive account neither of the functions of SPIDs nor of the possible discourse strategies that can be employed to fulfill complex face needs in intergroup conflictual events. Yet evidence for the link between a discourse construct and a social principle has been provided. In addition, this social-discourse connection may occur in other kinds of group settings. It seems reasonable to predict that identity-displays of various types would occur in all kinds of social-interactive situations, not only in conflictual ones. Thus, the concept of identity-displays, the notion of face, and the link between them could be applied to other settings as well, allowing for other fine-grained analyses of the ways in which interlocutors achieve their goals in face-to-face interaction by means of particular verbal sequences. Such settings could include interactions in the family, among friends in conversation, and in the work setting.

As is the case of most grassroots movements, Israeli-Palestinian dialogue events have been limited in scope to relatively few participants on either side. Some Palestinians and some Israelis continue the dialogues. But no grand movement of dialogues ever overtook events in the Israeli-Palestinian conflict. The peace process was instigated and carried out at the macrolevel, with the dialogue events having little or no influence. Nonetheless, the peace process began in Oslo and elsewhere, covertly, in private meetings taking place among individuals representing various institutions. The enactment of identity-displays and the complex face dynamics involved in intergroup talk probably were evident there as well. From a realpolitik standpoint, therefore, analyses of the dialogue events may have much to offer for understanding discourse dynamics involved in face-to-face interaction between institutional representatives of groups in conflict.

NOTES

1. The description is based on indigenous sources from both sides (Abu Am'r, 1988; Cohen, 1990; Kimmerling & Migdal, 1993; Qleibo, 1992; Said, 1989; Shehadeh, 1982; Shipler, 1986; Shiff & Ya'ari, 1989).

2. The term *Occupied Territories* will be maintained throughout, because during the period of observations, they were still under complete Israeli control. This has changed

since the onset of the Peace Process, and some of these territories now fall under the Palestinian Authority.

3. I maintain gender bias-free language throughout the chapter.

4. All names are pseudonyms.

5. For a description of the history of the Christian Palestinians in the Middle East, see for example Cragg (1991).

6. When presenting information from the dialogue itself, I retain the use of the present tense.

7. See Zupnik (2000) for extended discussion of sociopolitical identity-displays.

8. Transcription conventions are as follows:

-	0- to 1.5-second pause
?	sentence has final rising intonation
( )	garbled utterance
(what?)	unclear utterance
[	simultaneous utterance
]	

Line divisions are based on clausal boundaries.

9. The quantitative analysis (Zupnik, 2000) concerned the distribution of the amount of SPID talk for each of the three SPID categories: personal, intragroup, and intergroup. This analysis was undertaken for one entire Hamla dialogue speech event. Eight Palestinians, five Israelis, and four third-party participants were present. The number of SPID clauses employed by the eight Palestinians and five Israelis was calculated.

Chi-square analysis performed indicated clear differences between the two groups (chi-square = 58.79, $p < .001$). Palestinians devoted most of their SPID talk to the intragroup SPID; Israelis, on the other hand, devoted most of their SPID talk to the personal SPID and the least amount of talk to the intragroup SPID. The greatest difference between the groups was in the amount of talk devoted to intragroup SPID talk, with Palestinians employing it far more than Israelis.

10. Analyses assume that there is one observable identity foregrounded in the discourse at any particular moment. This does not mean that interlocutors may not be aware of more than one identity for the speaker at that moment, only that there is one that is verbally realized.

REFERENCES

Abu Am'r, Z. (1988, September/October). Notes on Palestinian political leadership: The "personalities" of the Occupied Territories. *Middle East Report,* 23-25.

Brown, P., & Levinson, S. C. (1978). Universals in language usage: Politeness phenomena. In E. Goody (Ed.), *Questions and politeness* (pp. 56-289). Cambridge, UK: Cambridge University Press.

Cohen, S. (1990, May/August). The Intifadah in Israel: Portents and precarious balance. *Middle East Report,* 16-25.

Cragg, K. (1991). *The Arab Christians: A history of the Middle East.* Louisville, KY: Westminster/John Knox Press.

Durkheim, E. (1915). *The elementary forms of the religious life.* New York: Macmillan.

Fairclough, N. (1989). *Language and power*. London: Longman.

Goffman, E. (1967). *Interaction ritual: Essays on face-to-face behaviour*. Garden City, NY: Doubleday.

Goodwin, M. H. (1990). *He-said-she-said: Talk as social organization among Black children*. Bloomington: Indiana University Press.

Grimshaw, A. (Ed.). (1990). *Conflict talk: Sociolinguistic investigations of arguments in conversation*. Cambridge, UK: Cambridge University Press.

Katriel, T. (1986). *Talking straight: Dugri speech in Israeli Sabra culture*. Cambridge, UK: Cambridge University Press.

Kimmerling, B., & Migdal, J. (1993). *Palestinians: The making of people*. New York: Free Press.

Labov, W., & Fanshel, D. (1977). *Therapeutic discourse*. New York: Academic Press.

Qleibo, A. (1992). *Before the mountains disappear: An ethnographic chronicle of the modern Palestinians*. Jerusalem: Al Ahram Press.

Said, E. (1989, May/June). From Intifadah to independence. *Middle East Report*, 12-16.

Schiff, Z., & Ya'ari, E. (1989). *Intifada: The Palestinian uprising—Israel's third front*. New York: Simon & Schuster.

Schiffrin, D. (1984). Jewish argument as sociability. *Language in Society, 13*, 311-335.

Shehadeh, R. (1982). *The third way: A journal of life in the West Bank*. London: Quartet Books.

Shipler, D. (1986). *Arab and Jew: Wounded spirits in a promised land*. New York: Times Books.

Tannen, D. (1990). Silence as conflict management in fiction and drama: Pinter's *Betrayal* and a short story, "Great Wits." In A. Grimshaw (Ed.), *Conflict talk* (pp. 260-279). Cambridge, UK: Cambridge University Press.

Vayrynen, R. (1991). *New directions in conflict theory: Conflict resolution and conflict transformation*. London: Sage.

Wilson, G. (1990). *Politically speaking: The pragmatic analysis of political language*. Oxford, UK: Basil Blackwell.

Zupnik, Y. -J. (1994). A pragmatic analysis of the use of person deixis in political discourse. *Journal of Pragmatics, 21*, 339-383.

Zupnik, Y. -J. (2000). The use of "sociopolitical identity-displays" in Israeli-Palestinian "dialogue events." *Journal of Pragmatics, 31*, 85-110.

12

"In the Beginning . . ."

Israeli Jews and Arabs Construct Intifadas and Selves

RIVKA RIBAK • *University of Haifa*

That traditions are invented, a literal oxymoron and for ages a well-kept secret, is now, ironically, taken for granted and well documented (Hobsbawm, 1983). Ranging from the Highlander kilt (Trevor-Roper, 1983) to Watergate (Schudson, 1992), from the commemoration of the Holocaust (Zelizer, 1998) to social-Zionist pioneering (Katriel, 1997), work on the deceivingly static and untouchable has uncovered its fluid contours and the politics of its construction. History is inescapably narrated, these works remind us, and so we study the practices that transform events and customs and traditions into stories—and back (see White, 1987). But how are these institutional efforts—be they self-appointed or officially authorized—met by their would-be listeners? How are Richard Nixon books and Israeli settlement museums received by their readers and visitors—and by those who refuse or resist them?

This chapter is concerned with the ways in which history is narrated in everyday conversation; it asks about the practices through which the past is employed in order to create a sense of self, to forge a collective identity, and to challenge alternative voices. Adopting a constructionist perspective (Gergen, 1982; Potter, 1996; Shotter, 1985; Wetherell & Potter, 1989), I view history here as a resource in an ongoing social conversation in which different people draw on different events to tell different stories and to silence others, discursively defining—and being defined by—their respective constructions. Identity work is accomplished, the chapter argues, as people construct alternative histories while at the same time constructing themselves as authors of these constructions and as the

AUTHOR'S NOTE: *The author thanks Tamar Liebes, Elihu Katz, Tamar Katriel, and Michael Schudson for their help and advice throughout.*

295

actors in them, as they continually negotiate and readjust their constructions.

Television news viewing may be regarded as a concrete instance in which such mainstream voices are faced with oppositional, challenging narratives and accounts. The living room can thus be seen as a liminal space where the public is rendered private and where the collective is individually—if simultaneously—consumed. Previous work on this encounter has highlighted audience resistance and vulnerability, identifying specific moments of textual openness (or closure) and the corresponding oppositional (or hegemonic) reading that they enabled (Hall, 1980; Liebes & Ribak, 1991, 1994; Morley, 1986). By contrast, this chapter conceives of the living room not as an accidental setting for the particular decoding of a particular text, but rather as constructive—as is the discourse that is produced in it—of the identities of its inhabitants. It is not accidental, that is, that specific people meet in specific places to discuss specific issues in specific ways; indeed, it is the practices that underlie and inform this encounter that this chapter seeks to explore.

In the spring of 1988, during the early stages of the Palestinian uprising, the *intifada,* and during the last days of the single-channel public-television monopoly, 65 Israeli families were interviewed following the broadcast of *Mabat,* then the only television evening news program in the country. The interviews were part of a larger project that studied patterns of political socialization among Israeli Jews and Arabs; the study relied on extensive surveys as well as in-depth interviews to examine similarities and differences within families and between generations and communities.[1] Based on the survey, which indicated that the younger generation was far less compromising than the older one and that television news viewing was a frequent occasion for political conversation, the interviews were intended to identify patterns in the negotiation of political identity between parents and their children, and between public and private voices, as they took place in the family context in front of the screen. And so interviewers visited the homes of 50 Jewish families in Jerusalem and 15 Arab families in Sakhnin during and following the television evening news program, documented their conversation throughout the program, and initiated the discussion that followed.[2] But this experience, although identical in design, was in fact markedly different for the 50 Jewish and 15 Arab families that participated in the study.[3]

Israeli Arabs—who compose almost one fifth of the Israeli population—were practically unknown to Israeli qualitative social research in 1988, and even surveys of the Israeli population today have largely ignored them. It is for this reason that the very inclusion and presence of Arabs in the study, aside from the requirements relating to language, are constructed differently in a community unused to, and admittedly suspicious of, unfamiliar visitors. And as their answers to the interview questions related to the news in general and to the *intifada* in particular demonstrate, these Arabs have accentuated this structural asymmetry by explicating Israeli Arabs' uneasy position vis-à-vis the Jewish Israeli center, from which they are by definition excluded, and vis-à-vis the Palestinian refugees in the territories, whose physical separation from Israeli Arabs was not without cultural and political ramifications.

The legal term *Present absentees,* which refers to refugees who resided in Israel in 1948 but failed to claim their property, is suggestive of Israeli Arabs' uneasy situation.[4] Israeli Arabs are Arabs in the eyes of Jews and Israelis in the eyes of Palestinians. Israeli Arabs are continually blamed for identifying with the enemy as they strive to manage a voice that will pacify distrustful others while remaining agreeable to critical insiders. Thus the stones of the *intifada,* though directed at Jews, forced Israeli Arabs, too, to examine their positions and loyalties, torn as they were between the relative convenience of their present lives in the Jewish state and their historical commitment to the plight of their Palestinian brothers and sisters.

The early days of the *intifada* and the last days of single-channel television broadcasting were thus particularly significant for Israeli political discourse, rendering the absent Arab—both Israeli and Palestinian—visible and putting an end to their denial and repression. Channel One's *Mabat*—an authoritative, public, government-owned medium—was suddenly compelled to narrate an intelligible story wherein the familiar actors had a sudden role reversal and wherein the less-known actors needed to be sensibly introduced. The program's huge, willingly captive audience—Israeli Jews, Arabs, and Palestinians—had to make that story their own. The interviews, conducted between March and May 1988, give us a glimpse of this process of political storytelling. Detailed transcriptions of the interviews, therefore, provide rich data for an analysis of the articulation of collective time frames in everyday discourse.

CONSTRUCTING THE *INTIFADA* AND THE SELF

Six months into the Palestinian uprising, Israelis' conversations following the evening news on television revolved around two interrelated issues: the *intifada* itself and its coverage in the media.[5] This Israeli discourse may be seen as an attempt to make sense of the events that took place in the territories, a concentrated effort to lend meaning to a violent, bewildering reality. But, taken as a whole, Israelis' *intifada* talk appears as disjointed and messy as the reality it sought to interpret: an inconsistent, contradictory account in which different *intifadas,* different media, and different Israelis strenuously coexist. Contrary to what we might have expected, however, the strain is not relieved when different *intifadas* and media are related to different Israelis. Instead, we find that Jews and Arabs, adults and adolescents, and extremists and moderates may all share and challenge constructions irrespective of their national, generational, or political identification.

For this reason, the following account takes discourse itself as its unit of analysis rather than individuals, communities, or cultures. Drawing on constructionists' concept of the *interpretive repertoire,* this analysis seeks to understand discursive differences not as a function of the social groups that produced them but as a result of local, evolving practices and purposes that underlie and define them. *Interpretive repertoires* are "recurrently used systems of terms used for characterizing and evaluating actions, events, and other phenomena" (Potter & Wetherell, 1987, p. 149).[6] What distinguishes interpretive repertoires from other social scientific attempts to explain variance in attitudes and opinions is, first, their emphasis on language, which reduces the threat of psychological reductionism. Focusing on discourse as such, interpretive repertoires need not resort to cognitive constructs in order to explain how accounts are produced and what functions underlie variability in their construction.

Second, interpretive repertoires are "not construed as entities *intrinsically* linked to social groups" (Potter & Wetherell, 1987, p. 156). Conceiving of group membership as "occasioned phenomena," constructionists render it impossible to identify discourses (or the individuals who produce them) as representative of or belonging to particular groups that precede and are independent of these discourses.[7] Implicated in the words that they themselves employ, the question to ask, then, is not how different groups construct different discourses, but rather how discourses construct those groups that choose to practice them. When Israelis' discourses narrate the *intifada* as a historical inevitability or when they portray it as an arbitrary violation of law and order, these discourses construct the worlds and the identities that the speakers then assume and inhabit. This analysis is concerned with the practices and the purposes that predicate these different constructions.

Yet interpretive repertoires have their own share of conflict and contradiction, and although constructionists tend to portray each interpretive repertoire as relatively uniform and monolithic, repertoires in Israelis' *intifada* discourse are continuously challenged from *within* (see Bakhtin, 1981; Billig, 1987; Billig et al., 1988). Indeed, as I will show, it is these challenges that mark the edges of each repertoire and that tell us about its discursive power and effectiveness. The edges of the repertoire, in other words, are the edges of its collective resonance. And so as we move on to examine some recurring themes in Israelis' discourse about the *intifada,* we ask, first, what repertoires they construct and what they achieve through these particular constructions; second, we ask whether these repertoires contain (or co-opt?) alternative voices, and how strong they are.

A reading of the interviews[8] suggests two contrasting constructions of the *intifada.* Characterized by its reliance on history as a source of authority, the *evolution* repertoire sympathizes with the Palestinian cause and maintains a relatively uniform structure. The *eruption* repertoire, on the other hand, may be distinguished by its very diversity and disorganization, producing a fragmented, decontextualized account of the uprising in an ethnocentric, unsympathetic voice. It is perhaps not surprising that these constructions are in effect community-specific, such that the first is practically exclusive to Israeli Arabs, whereas the second may be found only among Israeli Jews. And in this overlap between communities and repertoires, deviations in the form of historical accounts among Arabs and in the form of empathic narratives among Jews become significant markers, indicating both the force and the limitations of each construction.

The Evolution of the Intifada

The evolution repertoire, then, consists of a single tale that is repeated, with minor but significant changes, in all Israeli Arab families. It is a story of prolonged occupation, first by Jordan and Egypt and then by Israel, that has lead to great suffering and frustration, which have in turn made the Palestinians "turn to the stone":

M:[9] It [the *intifada*] is about a people [nation] who since 1948 did not know independence. In 1948 it was occupied and became under Jordanian rule and in 1967 under Israeli rule. And believe me, there is no difference between the Jordanian occupation and the Israeli occupation. Therefore after a period of 20 years, and this people [nation] has intellectuals and they are the ones who pull the strings today in the [West] Bank and Gaza. They want a state rather than be under the Israeli or Jordanian occupation.

S: What happens in the territories is that the youth today are the leaders. The youths and the students of the [high] schools want to show the entire world that there is a people [nation] in the [West] Bank who is alive and who wants an independent state. Therefore they hoped that the Arab world and Israel would help them. But what [happened]? Twenty years of desperation. Therefore at one point they despaired and got up and said, we are still alive. (#2,006)[10]

F: Gaza and the [West] Bank are Palestinian land. In '48 the Jordanian army took over the Bank and Egypt [took over] Gaza and this situation remained until 1967, at the time when Israel occupied Gaza and the [West] Bank. Today the population regards the PLO [Palestine Liberation Organization] as [its] representative and they want a state, and Israel of course does not allow and opposes it. The people [nation] there are depressed and they are treated disrespectfully, therefore they oppose and protest this. And today there is what is taking place in the [West] Bank and Gaza, the *intifada*: A people [nation] against the occupation, wanting to throw it away and establish a state of its own.

S: Israel oppresses the people in Gaza and the [West] Bank. And the people [nation] there opposes and does not want Israel.

F: What does the people [nation] want?

S: It wants a state of its own. (#2,008)

But although uniform and cohesive as a family production, the evolution repertoire allows different family members to construct their own histories and to find their own positions within them. Israeli Arab adults typically provide the introduction to the story, going back to 1948 to produce a cyclical narrative in which an arbitrary occupation by Jordan and Egypt begets an arbitrary occupation by Israel, such that one people (nation) are the permanent victims of a succession of willful aggressors.[11] Their children supply the more recent part of the story. Beginning their tale with the 1967 war and the experience of the 20 years that followed, they construct the war as an apocalyptic event that fundamentally, irrevocably changed the course of events that came in its wake.[12] And as they talk about different times, they also talk about different regional politics. Thus, whereas the parents insist that neither Jordan nor Egypt attempted to help the Palestinian refugees, "riding on the problem as one would ride on a horse" (#2,009), from the adolescents' perspective, the Arab countries did assist the Palestinians, but now that they have (for unspecified reasons)[13] stopped helping, the Palestinians have become desperate and have taken the initiative:

> S: In the [West] Bank and Gaza there are citizens who couldn't suffer this situation. People [nation] without houses and food, and difficult situation. The Arab states, like Jordan, who gave them assistance, have stopped, and they are in a difficult situation. Therefore they want a state of their own, that expresses their hopes and their future.

> M: It [the *intifada*] is about a million and a half people [nation] who used to live under the rule of Egypt and Jordan and today they are under Israeli rule for more than 20 years, therefore they look for respect and identity. They've had enough. Therefore they made the *intifada,* so that the world will hear and will help them, that is, will pressure Israel. But nothing is certain. (#2,013)

> F: I don't know, sometimes it's hard to explain. Gaza and the [West] Bank are the heart of the problem today. There are more than a million and a half people [nation] there, who strive for freedom. The story began in 1948. Then Egypt ruled over Gaza and Jordan and the king ruled over the [West] Bank by force. It is [well] known what happened in 1967, and since then the territories are under Israeli rule. For 20 years everybody thought that it was OK, and suddenly the events [*me'ora'ot*] started, and that is a sign that life there is not OK. And the people [nation] there have aspirations, and these are the establishment of a state. If I were Jewish, I would do everything so that the state would return the territories. It is a burden and a problem for the state of Israel. I think this way; I don't know what will happen in the future.

> S: I would explain this [*intifada*] item, that Gaza and the [West] Bank are under Israeli occupation since 1967, and the people [nation] is dissatisfied politically and on all other accounts. It is governed by another people [nation] or another government, and it wants to establish a state of its own. Under the state of Israel it suffered for a long time, therefore it had enough of this situation and it made the *intifada,* in order to move things and to achieve its rights. (#2,015)

The Threat of Decontextualizing

These generational differences outline the boundaries of this reper-toire, as they suggest different understandings and uses of the historical. Among Israeli Arab adults, history is employed as a means of situating their argument on objective grounds: These are the facts, based on rea-son, and facts cannot be argued. Facts, moreover, allow Israeli Arab adults to at once excuse power and criticize it, as they place Israeli treat-ment of the Palestinian refugees in the context of Israel's Arab predeces-sors and emphasize the need for change. Their children, on the other hand, employ historical markers ("since 1967") without narrating them in chronological continuity, thereby producing a discourse that leaves no room for negotiation or compromise. By focusing on a single historical moment, they transform the tale of the Palestinian people from a fatalis-tic saga of destined, recurring oppression to an account that assigns spe-cific blame and demands concrete reparation. It is not objectivity, there-fore, that Israeli Arab youths rely on, but a sense of inalienable rights and absolute justice in the face of repressive power.[14]

It is not only through their use of the historical that Israeli Arab adults depoliticize their account of the *intifada*. Unlike their children, they frame the uprising in safer, more traditional terms of suffering and honor: "The people [nation] there have suffered and are suffering and are therefore in a situation of desperation" (#2,003), or "Their tragedy is that they are not happy because they want respect and life" (#2,010). The youths' narratives, by contrast, are dotted with references to *revolution, nation, power,* and *oppression,* concepts that are typically absent from adults' accounts and that shift the discourse from human compassion to political action (as well as, perhaps, from East to West[15]). Having freed themselves from their parents' burdens of memory and wariness, the youths are far more explicit in portraying their positions and sympathies:

> S: The *intifada* is a revolution of a people [nation] that was occupied in 1967 and that wanted to express their suffering and desperation. The territories belong to the Palestinian state that will be established beside the state of Israel. (#2,002)

> S: The situation in the [West] Bank and Gaza is the revolution of the Palestinian people [nation]. They are under an oppressive Israeli rule, and they made the *intifada*. (#2,007)

Even when its spokespersons are less outspoken, however, the evolution repertoire is conscientiously sympathetic to the Palestinian cause, insisting on Palestinian brotherhood despite apparent divisions. This insistence seems rather fragile, but their words in the following passages seem to deny its significance and point to the dualities of brotherhood and separateness and of participation and hesitation. Apparently shifting between support and guilt, they justify the *intifada* as a matter of course while carefully excusing their absence from it.[16] Thus, to account for what may be seen as neglect and inadequate advocacy and identification throughout the years, Israeli Arabs insert themselves into their historical narrative by noting that they never realized how bad things were until the *intifada* began: "I always thought that the situation in the [West] Bank was well and comfortable. I used to go to Nablus and I thought all was well" (#2,004); "We all thought that these people were living OK and [that they were] happy. You go to Haifa and Tel Aviv and everywhere, and you see people from the [West] Bank. And everybody thought that the story of the territories was over" (#2,005); and, "Life [after the 1967 war] continued and suddenly the situation turned upside down and we saw that the people there are not happy and are not living well; therefore, a new and a difficult situation was created" (#2,010). Having excused any delay or hesitancy in their support,[17] Israeli Arabs are now in the position to justify why their brothers and sisters are acting as they are.

The Eruption of the **Intifada**

We find no such master narrative among Israeli Jews, whose discourse about the *intifada* is less disciplined and structured. Yet the lines are clearly drawn here as well, and in order to remain within the consensus, speakers must maintain an ethnocentric perspective and beware of any suggestion of sympathy toward the Palestinian cause; attempts at trespassing are not tolerated.

Hesitating over national identity, the evolution repertoire resorts to history as a source of (discursive) strength; the eruption repertoire, on the other hand, positions national identity as a given and treats history in a more casual, perhaps irreverent—but never haphazard—manner. Systematically fragmenting time, this repertoire moves back and forth between past and future, taking care never to embed the *intifada* within a chronology that would render it meaningful and always to link it to its unthinkable inevitable consequences. Thus, Israeli Jews employ their own constructions of the past in order to trivialize and marginalize the *intifada*, and they use their reconstructions of Arabs' explanations in order to subjunctively portray a future frightening enough to justify the oppression of the trivial—yet existentially dangerous—*intifada*.

References to the causes of the *intifada* in the eruption repertoire are ambiguous and arbitrary, thereby constructing an uprising that is similarly vague and irrational: "In the beginning," according to one youth, "only some—someone threw a stone; I remember, we had to write a paper about it. And then explosive envelopes began to arrive, from Turkey, and then—there, it began to develop" (#1,190). Like Israeli Arabs, Jews here appeal to ignorance of any growing desperation among the Palestinians in the occupied territories; however, Israeli Arabs excuse themselves by saying that although they thought all was well, they realized later that they were wrong. Jews blame the uprisers when insisting that all *was* well, and that *the Palestinians* made them think that they were wrong: "Twenty years they've lived here—all was well. After 20 years they get up and uprise [*kamim vemitkomemim*]?" (#1,217).

Israeli Jews' discourse positions them as offended and surprised[18] that the Palestinian refugees have taken advantage of momentary—but perhaps symptomatic—vulnerability. The *intifada* began, in this construction,

> perhaps then, when terrorists penetrated a military compound in the north, and saw that we are not as strong as . . . they once thought, and suddenly they got self-confidence, and it's like a snow ball that began to roll, that . . . all sorts of things that were inhibited within them out of fear, suddenly rushed out. (#1,079)

But, looking back, Jews admit that they were never really strong, and it is their weakness and indecision that underlie the *intifada*:

> Because the Arabs sense the weakness of Israel, then they act out [*mevatsim*] what . . . they can act out stone-throwing, all this. There is no response, a strong one, of the IDF [Israel Defense Force: the Israeli army]. (#1,187)

> All this is a result of the fact that we give them too much freedom of action, and teach them how . . . teach them how . . . Show them we are afraid! (#1,094)

The Arabs realized that even if a soldier has a gun, then he's not exactly threatening, and then they started, they started to use more force. [ ] There is a given political situation in which for many years the state of Israel sits, sits in the territories which it never decided what to do with. (#1,175)

We left [*hish'arnu*], intentionally or unintentionally, but in any case foolishly, we left uncertainty among the Arabs, that is, since the Arabs are unclear about the relation between Israel and Judea and Samaria, at least legally and politically, then they have no reason, after 20 years, not to draw question marks, in the shape of stones. (#1,199)

And so in fact the *intifada* was brought about by "us," the Jews say—by Jewish leaders ("The one who set up the Palestinian problem is one of us, our head, as they say, in those days, and it is Ben Gurion," #1,152) and by Jews' failure to articulate and implement their policies regarding the territories ("We don't know ourselves, in our country; we still don't know what we, ourselves, want; we can't reach any agreement about what we want to do," #1,244; "The events of the last months are a result [ ] of the ambiguity in which the Arabs in the territories are in: In practice, the policy of Israel is unclear to them," #1,199).

Self-blame in this discourse is very specific and pointed: Israeli Jews blame their leaders for creating and exposing weakness and for having failed to eliminate "The Palestinian Problem" when they could and should have. Taking care not to blame themselves for their part in the occupation, not to admit that perhaps their weakness is a result of the occupation, Jews' discourse, rather than self-blaming, is an indictment of the Palestinians, who imposed this situation on them: "Instead of educating the[ir children] to the flower and the book, they force our soldiers to do things against all we were educated for, and want, in our country" (#1,116). It is in this sense that this discourse is ethnocentric: Not once, when trying to come up with the reasons for the *intifada,* do Jews adopt the Arab or Palestinian point of view, nor do the Arabs or Palestinians empathize with the Jewish perspective. The *intifada* began, in this repertoire, because Jews' attempts to rule the Palestinians were too hesitant and indecisive, and these attempts have therefore failed.

The eruption repertoire, which gives little consideration to the historical causes of the *intifada,* appears preoccupied with its potential future outcomes.[19] Again and again Jews second-guess—or rather, report[20]—

Palestinians' aspirations, based mostly on the Palestinian Covenant or on their claims of first-hand knowledge of Arab mentality:

> F: The Arabs give us trouble; if they were quiet, there was no trouble.
>
> S: You don't want to give them rights.
>
> F: They don't demand rights.
>
> S: They do.
>
> F: They demand that we leave the [West] Bank.
>
> S: They demand their right for self-determination. A right for self-determination is what they demand.
>
> F: They do all this today so that we'll leave the [West] Bank. They don't want self-determination and no nothing [*velo batich*]. They want us to leave the [West] Bank.
>
> S: No, they want to establish the Greater Palestine.
>
> F: Yes.
>
> S: Well, this is self-determination. (#1,071)
>
> S: Now they want a state of their own within our state.
>
> M: Sweetie, they don't want a state within our state, they want to throw us to the sea and get *our* state. This is the problem, because they don't agree to anything.
>
> S: And we're not willing to do that. We have this situation because we're not willing to give them a state, because if you give them a state, they'll want military force, and this will lead to war very quickly. (#1,116)

Keeping the *intifada* irrational and unfathomable, the eruption repertoire never acknowledges aspiration, clearly distinguishing the uprising from any understandable ideas that might have motivated it. Palestinian demands are used here not to explain the *intifada* but to illustrate what would be the result of Jews' surrendering to them. By manipulating temporal order, the demands are presented not as preceding (and giving sense to) action, but as abstract, untouchable entities that belong to an unthinkable future. In this future, the Palestinians have rights and a state of their own. However, because the real goal of Palestinians is to get rid of the Jews ("We want Palestine; and you—to the sea," #1,217), the rights and the state are portrayed as a tale told for the naive, an introduction or first step for what is to follow: a Palestinian state instead of the state of Israel.[21] This two-stage plan is invoked again and again in no uncertain terms:

They are not satisfied with minor border adjustments [*tikunei gvul*]; they're not. . . . They want Jaffa as well, and they want all the parts. They want to return to their houses, where they used to live. (#1,149)

They want our country—they always say, we want first Jaffa, then Jerusalem, then Tel Aviv. (#1,275)

—They want the territories, but all the territories, every meter of this country. There are many who are not willing to give, because many were killed on every territory.

—On every millimeter.

—On every millimeter. And if they give it, it's simply, the Arabs afterwards will want more and more. And the country will simply give. (#1,257)

The Threat of Empathy

Mistrusting of the other, those evoking the eruption repertoire insist that if the Arabs are "given one finger, they want the whole hand" (#1,398). This is presented as common knowledge, as a challenge not to the Arabs, but to those Jews who believe them and who, through their irresponsible trust, endanger the entire community. Such innocence is not tolerated in this discourse, and any signs of empathy are vehemently resisted. Undermining ethnocentric strength, such naïveté outlines the edges of this repertoire, clearly marking the borders of the consensus. Subjunctive role playing and challenges that suggest points of resemblance between Palestinians and Jews or that question the differences between them are therefore particularly revealing:

D: If you wanted to establish a state, you would do exactly the same thing.

M: How can you compare to them?

F: You have to understand one thing, the Etsel [Irgun] and the *Lechi* [Stern Group; two marginal prestate terrorist groups whose image was rehabilitated following the ascent of the Israeli right to power in 1977] didn't go to murder neither women, nor children. They fought the [British] empire. They didn't throw stones on children and didn't come and . . . [everybody shouts] (#1,249)

M: As I was saying, no Arab ever threw a stone at me, but some Jews did. On Shabbat I got hit by a stone, on my car, and they threw a garbage dumpster at me, and they almost jumped at us. [ ] On Lag BaOmer [a holiday celebrated by bonfires]. . . . I went to a friend's today and she told me that on Lag BaOmer she went to see a bonfire in Me'a She'arim [an ultrareligious neighborhood] . . . not Me'a She'arim, but closer to the center of town, and she said that the religious there started a bonfire, lit it and burned the Israeli flag. [ ]

D: Anyway, they [Arabs] are in our country, what do you want, they oppose the establishment of our state. [ ]

M: These religious . . . the fanatics . . .

F: Isn't there a difference?? The Arabs want to deport you from the country, isn't there a difference?? Between the religious? To say they are worse than the Arabs?? (#1,082)

Highly threatening, such comparisons of Jews' and Palestinians' struggles and violence are rejected out of hand, and the ill-conceived allusion serves as an opportunity to forcefully reiterate important differences between the two.[22] Using an irreverent—and dangerously universalistic—rhetoric of analogy (*gzera shava*), voices from the margins of the eruption repertoire suggest that perhaps Palestinian politics and practices are not substantively different from Jews' and that perhaps, based on this similarity, Jews might try to understand them.[23] But the mainstream immediately calls these voices to order by drawing on the much more powerful and apparently unanswerable tactic of *lehavdil* (draw a distinction), which is traditionally used to denote the difference between the sacred and the profane.[24] The Arabs, it is posited, are essentially, substantively distinguished from the Jews; contrasting the logical operation of analogy with the moral claim of *lehavdil,* the eruption repertoire insists that regardless of how similar Jews and Palestinians may appear on the surface, underlying differences render any comparison rhetorically useless and, moreover, communally offensive. Interestingly, it is typically those who propose a comparison known to violate social taboos who disclaim their challenge by prefacing it with *lehavdil.* Here, however, challenges to the consensus are voiced without qualifications, and it is left to the scandalized center to reclaim its rightful, total position.

To do this, the eruption repertoire carefully explains away any manifestation of violence on the Jewish side, employing both excuses and justifications to present Jews as the true victims in this story (and in history in general).[25] Using these two logically incompatible mechanisms interchangeably, this repertoire renders Jews' violence at times as an understandable response to Palestinians' provocation and at times as an imperative, legitimate means of maintaining what belongs to the Jews by right. Although, as one woman says, "I'm not exactly proud of what's happening but I don't feel any obligation to apologize" (#1,276), the depiction of Israeli soldiers' aggression toward Palestinians, often women, elderly, and youths, does seem to require an explanation, and the eruption repertoire employs the following formula:

> Abroad, they always show how the soldiers chase the Arabs, rather than what the Arabs do before. (#1,001)

> Our soldiers sit and work. They work very hard in the face of recurrent provocations of the residents there. And they treat them with kid gloves relative to any other army in the world that would encounter that situation. And they simply show it disproportionately, everything that's taking place there. (#1,094)

> If a soldier sits with his gun, [and] he's stoned, he's shouted at, he's cursed, and he opens fire, this, I don't think that in any nation in the world, they wouldn't make a thing out of it; in any army in the world. So I think that the very fact that they throw stones and we respond as we respond, in my opinion we are very moderate about this, very moderate about this. (#1,095)

To render Israeli actions excusable, the eruption repertoire systematically recontextualizes televised portrayals of soldiers' aggression, insisting that the acts of violence are always discrete, disconnected, and invariably local: an immediate response to Palestinian provocation, which is typically—but not accidentally—absent from the screen. By presenting Jewish aggression as a reaction to Palestinians aggression, and by situating both at the level of the dyadic confrontation between the Israeli soldier and the Palestinian upriser, this account shifts the blame to the other side and constructs Jewish violence as reactive, almost instinctual (and thus natural) acts that (unfortunately) do not express or implement any government policy that encourages such aggression.

Justifications, on the other hand, rely heavily on history in order to present Jews' violence as a necessary, unavoidable means of maintaining their (democratic) rule over their land and, perhaps ironically, of keeping God's promise to give them this land:

> [King Hussein] wouldn't have finished it. He would have silenced them for a month, 6 months, a year, 5 years, but he wouldn't have finished them, because in fact he has no reason to be in Judea and Samaria. He has no connection—not historical, not political, not emotional—he has no connection like we do. We, when we are hit by stones, we know why. (#1,199)

They have a right . . . to live in the Land of Israel. But they don't own this land. They don't have ownership. If somebody doesn't like it here—he can go. The Palestinian State is in Jordan, not here. Here they live . . . by sufferance. Sufferance, not right. Because the place . . . all this area, Judea and Samaria, it belongs, from the time of the Bible it belongs to Israel. (#1,190)

If they come here to visit, they come to my house [ ] . . . in their weddings, we're happy with them, we come with them, all up to a point. But not to harm [*lifgo'a*] the state. As far as the state is concerned, that they want to eliminate us—this deeply offends [*poge'a*] me. We need to totally . . . hit them hard, heavy punishments, unbearable, so that they know: up to here, enough. (#1,161)

Do you have another place to go to? We have nowhere! This country [land] is ours. We don't have another country, and this is home, and it's impossible to throw us out of our home. [ ] This is a struggle for our survival in this state. (#1,149)

The preference to excuse soldiers' violence rather than to justify it could have been interpreted as yet another, perhaps more subtle, challenge to the dominant repertoire. Excuses, according to this interpretation, do not display enough patriotism; in order to remain within the ethnocentric consensus, one ought to justify, not merely excuse, the government's repression of the *intifada.* But excuses do not provoke the heated responses that empathy and sympathy do, providing not an alternative view, but rather an additional perspective with which to argue the same case. Instead of saying something fundamentally different about the *intifada,* excuses and justifications each talk about different aspects of it; thus, despite the fact that excuses condemn the acts in question (and therefore minimize responsibility for them) and that justifications accept these acts (and the responsibility for them), the eruption repertoire can draw on both, using excuses to account for soldiers' violent practices as shown on the screen and justifications to explain the principles underlying the government's policies.

Rather than a political challenge, then, excuses should be seen as yet another tactic in a collective public relations campaign that family members joined when they were asked to "explain the *intifada* to a relative or a guest from abroad who doesn't understand what's going on." Once they were positioned by the interviewer as semiofficial spokespersons, the presence of imagined others silenced the internal debate over substance:

—Dad, how would you explain it to him?

—It depends on which guest. If it were a good friend, I would explain to him the different sides about . . . two main orientations in Israel: those who want to keep the territories and ignore the . . . hide their head in the sand, and others who want to solve the problem. But if he were a general tourist, a Christian or something, I would try to explain to him the other side, that is, our commitment and the other side that never wants to reach an agreement. So my explanation depends of the person I need to talk to. (#1,008)

—First I would examine who the relative from abroad is, how related he is. I would try to describe things . . . like television presents the . . . "The army investigates [the killing of two Palestinians in Nablus]." Everybody investigates. So we blur [*metashteshim*]. We say, look, we're living, we're eating, there are cakes, have some. . . . But the truth is that if you go deeper into the conversation, even if he's not related, you're somehow obliged to tell him what's happening, at least according to your feelings. At the same time, you emphasize that we can go on living, and the fact is that we are living. [ ]

—About the territories . . . if I explained it to a relative I would, that is, at some point I would begin to get defensive. Because somebody from outside, I think that it's very hard for him to understand Israelis' situation. [ ] I would tell him that I understand the Palestinian people, that they want self-determination, they want a state, [ ] and they want independence, and they want normal life, and they don't want to continue living in miserable [*dfukim*] places. And I would tell him that as much as it hurts me and as much as I understand them, they should understand us as well, that after all we have a state and we want to keep it. And that if the Palestinian people wants to kill us or throw us to the sea, then I cannot justify it nor understand it. If she [the relative] stands from outside and says: Why don't you give them a state, or: Why don't you give them independence, then it's easy for her to say; but let her live here and see that it isn't so simple.

—OK, I just want to say one sentence. Now, if you were sitting here with the microphone and you were speaking a foreign language, you would come from, I don't know, some television, radio company abroad, there is no doubt that I would tell you different things; and it matters, who interviews. Certainly I would say, I first want to live, I deeply respect the Palestinian people, I first want to live, so I have no choice, if he throws a stone at me, I will catch him. [ ] Naturally, when you're sitting with an Israeli interviewer, and regardless, naturally you feel you're yourself, you're sitting amongst your own people. [ ] But if you came and you said, Listen, I'm going to publish a story or an interview with you—OK, doubtless I would come and say what [my daughter] just said, and she said it much nicer than I did, I would say, "Sorry, we have to live." (#1,353)

Accounts of the *intifada,* then, are portrayed as discursive tools, not as reflections of deeply held beliefs. According to this construction, accounts do not express (or determine) one's political position but are instead intentional means of influencing (or determining) others' perceptions. And although Israeli Jews insist that there are many ways to account for the *intifada,* the presence of outsiders invariably pushes Israeli Jews toward the consensual, representative voice of the eruption repertoire.

CONCLUSION

In this chapter, I explored the use of historical narratives in everyday conversation, arguing, first, that conversation not only affects the Other, but also is a construction of self, and second, that it is not only one's words that construct one's selfhoods, but the words of others as well. This interdependence of self and other and discourse underlies this analysis of Israelis' conversation about the *intifada.* The interpretive repertoires they use are thus seen not as fixed, self-contained frameworks, waiting to be used and discarded at will, but rather as tentative constructions that are constantly articulated and reworked, moments in which hegemony is challenged and reasserted and where alternative voices may be heard and silenced.

Israelis' *intifada* discourse constructs two coherent selves—the Israeli Jewish and the Israeli Arab. These identities may be seen as the main theme of the conversation and as the organizing principle of the self, such that all other identifications—for example, political and generational[26]— are subsumed under this division and such that trespassing at this point is practically unthinkable. But there is no dialogue in this construction, because, despite its intertwined nature, Jews and Arabs engage in it separately, each in their respective living rooms, and the constructions are not pressed to consider any concrete Other who may challenge or question them.[27]

The distinction between moderation and extremism, on the other hand, could be articulated in a dialogue with a concrete Other, although much like the Arab/Jew binary, extremism and moderation were more often constructed in relation to imagined Others than to real ones.[28] Significantly, the Others' absence from the living room, which may account for the unfavorable portrayals of them, is accompanied by their silence in the public sphere and by their failure to articulate a repertoire that would provide a coherent alternative to the mainstream. Aside from Israeli

Arab youths' contribution to the evolution repertoire, the Israeli Arabs' discourse is a voice of moderation, and alternative courses of action are mentioned mainly to be condemned ("These religious zealots are the most dangerous. . . . [They] are against Islam, against the Arabs and against the Communist Party and the left in general," #2,005; "[The demonstration of the Progressive Party in the outskirts of Kalkilya] shows that the Progressive Party does it only as preelection propaganda," #2,012). Arabs, however, briefly mention divisions among Jews, but the importance of these divisions is debated and uncertain ("I'm sure Peres will bring peace; the Likud doesn't want to, the Labor does.—That's not true, the difference between the Labor and the Likud isn't so clear!" #2,004).

They may be right, because Jews' discourse, though far from monolithic, is overwhelmingly consensual. Within this conversation, there is a wealth of references to the left (which is alternately constructed as childish and naive, cynical and self-hating, conscientious and unrealistic, and dangerous and irresponsible). But although the consensus is reiterated and reaffirmed, and although the left is delegitimized and excommunicated (at least until it sees the light and mends its ways), this threatening, horrifying beast ("Look, there are people . . . [left-wing leaders who are] cancer, do you know what cancer is?" #1,217) remains silent.[29] At best, the left voices marginal alternatives to the dominant discourse, but it is impossible to identify a left-wing Jewish repertoire that argues moderation. Instead, these marginal positions are articulated within repertoires defined by conservative concerns (security, censorship) and designed to advocate uncompromising positions; they thus propose an alternative within an agenda set for other, indeed opposite, purposes. And so although Jews' discourse *constructs* a Jewish right wing (the natural, self-evident truth) and left wing (the subversive threat), it in effect *consists* of a consensual mainstream and some occasional, marginal challenges.

Two things seem to render this mainstream attractive. First of all, it is positioned as consensual. Again and again throughout the conversation, the center is celebrated as the obvious, taken-for-granted way of seeing things or as the way that, through this celebration, has become natural and self-evident. Every challenge to this consensus is then dismissed in a manner that constructs the challenge not as pluralistic, but rather as *unpatriotic*. The achievement—and the attraction—of this discourse, then, is not the articulation of extreme nationalism, but rather the affirmation of the center through the definition of insider and outsiders and through the specification of entry and exit rules (if one is sympathetic, one is an insider and thus may criticize, although criticism in some conditions may indicate outsider status, etc.). Predicated on the notion of *lehavdil,* this discourse seeks to construct a Jewish consensus; extremist rhetoric is therefore restrained for the sake of harmony and community.

Second, the mainstream is positioned as total, obvious, simple. Using a well-structured, calculated rhetoric that trivializes any alternative, the discourse constructs as simple and indisputable the choices that need to be made. Thus, once the Arabs' two-stage plan is outlined, once their intention to throw Jews to the sea is invoked, the choice that is constructed between "them" and "us" is emptied of meaning. This does not suggest, however, that this choice has indeed become meaningless; on the contrary, the dilemma remains practically insoluble. But the way in which it is introduced, the context in which it is embedded, and the binary in which it is described all combine to construct the solution as a rational inevitability. It is neither the concluding dilemma, then, nor the premises on which it rests, that are simple; instead, it is their interdependence, and the acceptance of the premises for resolving the dilemma, that construct these arguments as simple and self-evident.

There is room for hope, however, since—as Raymond Williams has argued—hegemony is never total, and this mainstream turned out to be less attractive than this chapter seemingly constructs it to be. The margins, it appears, were not altogether silenced, because, since these interviews took place, the Israeli left has won two election campaigns, and negotiations with the Palestinians are now underway. Thus, although theories of power conceive of hegemony as invincible (and irresistible), constructionist and interpretive accounts insist on variability and difference: there is one television news program, but there are many decodings; similarly, there is one authoritative historical narrative, but it is retold and reconstructed so as to constitute changing selves and communities.

NOTES

1. The project was conceived and directed by Dr. Tamar Liebes, and it benefited from the advice of Professor Elihu Katz (for selected earlier papers, see Liebes, Katz & Ribak, 1991, and Liebes & Ribak, 1991, 1994). The Spencer Foundation funded the project, and The Guttman Institute for Applied Social Research conducted the field work.

2. The discussions needed little encouragement and were on the whole unstructured. To start interviews, when necessary, one family member was asked to retell the news to another as if he or she had missed it; if the conversation came to a halt, family members were asked to explain the *intifada* to a relative from abroad, a task that will be analyzed later in the chapter.

3. Interviews with Jewish families were conducted in Jerusalem by the author (half) and assistants. Interviews with Israeli Arab families were conducted in Sakhnin by an Arab assistant from Sakhnin and were translated by him into Hebrew. The Jewish families were a representative subsample taken from a survey of 400 parents and their adolescent children in Jerusalem. Subsampling from the counterpart 200 Israeli Arab families who were surveyed in Nazareth was impossible for technical (but illuminating, see Ribak, 1997) reasons; therefore, a sample of 15 families in Sakhnin was surveyed and then interviewed. For details, see Ribak, 1993.

4. *Present Absentees* (*Sleeping on a Wire*) (1992) is the title of a book by David Grossman, consisting of interviews with Israeli and Palestinian Arabs. On the ideological and practical significance of the distinctions between Israeli Arabs, Arab Israelis, Palestinian Israelis, and Palestinians, see Rabinowitz, 1993.

5. It is possible to argue, of course, that the focus on the *intifada* and its coverage can be explained by the survey that preceded it and by the fact that the conversation took place immediately following the television news program. Although the first constraint needs to be taken into consideration, the second is prescribed by the rationale underlying the design. Note that in the survey, respondents—both Jewish and Arab—indicated that they regularly watch the television news program; that they watch it with other family members; and that they tend to discuss and to argue over issues raised in the program. The design, then, merely accentuated and explicated practices that normally are perhaps more subtle and implicit.

6. See also Wetherell and Potter (1989) and Gilbert and Mulkay (1984). Ann Swidler's discussion of "cultural strategies of action" (1986) is relevant here as well.

7. This, in a way, is a response to the interpretation of contradictions in survey responses as indicating political immaturity and inadequacy, common in studies of political behavior (cf. Converse, 1964).

8. Regarding method, the analysis proceeded from an initial stage of reading and rereading the transcripts, which was followed by two related stages: identifying patterns in the variability of the content or the construction of the accounts, and then, having interpreted these patterns in terms of the discursive functions they fulfil and the consequences they may have, validating these hypotheses in the transcripts. For more on this process, see Potter and Wetherell (1987).

9. When required in order to explain variability (or when the excerpt quotes more than two family members), speakers are identified in terms of their position in the family (i.e., *M* stands for mother, *F* for father, *S* for son, and *D* for daughter). In all other excerpts, information regarding the generation and the sex of speakers was omitted so as not to blur the focus on communities and repertoires. In terms of translation, care was taken to keep the English as close to the form and content of the original as possible.

10. Numbers following quotations are family identification codes.

11. In these interviews, Israeli Arabs, as a rule, avoid mentioning anything prior to 1948.

12. On the significance of *apocalyptic* and *serial* time orientations, see Back and Gergen (1963).

13. Note that the evolution repertoire invariably renders occupation as arbitrary and inexplicable. Never articulating the reasons that brought about Jordanian, Egyptian, or Israeli aggression, this repertoire renders occupation irrational and yet at the same time normal, an action that does not require justifications or excuses. It is only Palestinian aggression (never described as such) that is repeatedly accounted for, and in this sense,

Palestinian aggression is what is constructed as a deviation. See Scott and Lyman (1968) and Note 16 of this chapter.

14. The youths' use of *therefore* similarly suggests that they rely on absolute justice, rather than factual chronology, as the premise of their argument.

15. I thank Tamar Katriel for pointing this out.

16. On the significance of justifications as distinguished from excuses, see Scott and Lyman (1968). Essentially, these are two forms of explaining what is considered (and what thus becomes) deviant. When justifying, one accepts responsibility for the acts in question but denies the pejorative quality associated with it. When excusing, on the other hand, one admits that the act in question is bad but denies full responsibility on various grounds. See also Semin and Manstead (1983). As applied to the *intifada,* see Cohen (1988).

17. Note that among Israeli Arabs, participation here does not go beyond discursive support. The father in one of the families may have indicated the reasons for this when he declared, "We, the Arabs of Israel, are Israeli, and our story is over. We have no connection to the state that will be established there. We shall die here and not go anywhere" (#2,005).

18. This is of course paradoxical because, in line with their own construction of Arab mentality, they should have known better. In the discourse of Jews, it is their familiarity with the nature of Arabs, rather than their familiarity with the nature of the occupation, that should have prepared them for the *intifada.*

19. The future is invoked to highlight dangers from within as well. Repeatedly, the eruption repertoire conjures up scenarios detailing the catastrophes that will doubtless occur once left-wing governments are given power ("The Labor will return the entire land of Israel! [ ] We'll have to come to Neve Ya'akov with a visa, we'll have to come, if there's a government . . . there'll be a Palestinian state, this is . . . this is what Peres wants," #1,190).

20. On the advantages of using reported speech, see Tannen (1989) and Bakhtin (1981).

21. Taking into account all instances in which Jews specified "what the Arabs want," we learn that according to Jews, "they" want a state of their own (mentioned 20 times), they want to complete a two-stage plan (17 times), they want to get rid of us and throw us to the sea (15 times), they want human and civil rights (10 times), and they have some additional, less impressive—and less frequent—desires (to shock the public, to mess around [*lehitpare'a*]).

22. Attempts to compare, not Jewish and Palestinian violence and deviation, but Jewish and Palestinian normality similarly fail:

> M: I've had Arabs students, so I know: Nice people! People—they are human beings! Like anybody else! They want to live! So let them live! I know they always chose Jewish schools rather than Arab schools, they are so grateful for what you do for them.
>
> D: Well, these are Arabs?! Ten—ten percent are like that! (#1,082)

23. Analogy is used by the center as well, particularly in the *We're Afraid* repertoire (see Ribak, 1993), which draws on a rhetoric of equal rights to argue Jewish inferiority relative to Arabs. In the eruption repertoire, this rhetoric is employed in order to point out that *they* don't have a Peace Now movement (#1,217) and that *they* are not democratic (#1,215)—politics that are criticized for their naïveté in *our* camp, and for their absence in *their* camp.

24. Liebes and Katz (1988) explain that *lehavdil,* which connotes "if you will forgive the comparison," is used "to qualify an otherwise valid analogy between something sacred and important and something profane or trivial" (p. 124).

25. The notion that Jews are the perpetual victims of history appears to parallel Israeli Arabs' portrayal of the Palestinians. Rhetorically, however, the tales are structured differently, as the Palestinian fate of recurring occupations and oppressions is intimated narratively through a decidedly objective historical account. Among Jews, on the other hand, the theme of permanent persecution is not as prevalent but is far more explicit. Jews do not hesitate to say that "the whole world is against us" and mention anti-Semitism as well (cf. #1,149). Considering the centrality of the Holocaust in Israeli Jewish rhetoric (especially since Begin's ascendance to power in 1977), it is perhaps surprising that this theme is rarely mentioned in the interviews and is never used explicitly as a justification for the way the *intifada* is repressed (or for Israeli policies in general).

26. These, of course, are the identities that were of interest in this project, and these are thus the identities that were structured into the survey and that underlie this analysis. Of course, one may discuss here other identities as well: gender, religion (e.g., religious vs. secular, as well as Jews vs. Moslems), new (vs. old) comers to Israel, and class are the first that come to mind.

27. This needs to be qualified, because Israeli Arabs know that their conversations will be read (and analyzed) by Jews, whereas Jews had no reason to assume that Arabs might eavesdrop on their "private" conversation. This sense of outsiders' eyes or ears might have restrained Arabs' voices while allowing Jews to feel that theirs was an insiders' conversation.

28. The fact that the Other, both from within one's community and from without, is purely discursive is of course extremely problematic in social-psychological terms, because the lack of shared lived experiences arguably inhibits the move for change. Words, however, can do things as well.

29. It is possible, however, to find in mainstream discourse what appear as co-opted alternatives, used here to construct sham dilemmas (free speech or national security? human rights or our survival?); these are discussed in Ribak (1994).

REFERENCES

Back, K. W., & Gergen, K. J. (1963). Apocalyptic and serial time orientation and the structure of opinions. *Public Opinion Quarterly, 27,* 427-442.

Bakhtin, M. M. (1981). *The dialogic imagination* (M. Holquist, Ed.; M. Holquist & C. Emerson, Trans.). Austin: University of Texas Press.

Billig, M. (1987). *Arguing and thinking.* Cambridge, UK: Cambridge University Press.

Billig, M., Condor, S., Edwards, D., Gane, M., Middleton, D., & Radley, A. (1988). *Ideological dilemmas.* London: Sage.

Cohen, S. (1988). Criminology and the uprising. *Tikkun, 3,* 60-62, 95-96.

Converse, P. E. (1964). The nature of belief system in mass publics. In D. E. Apter (Ed.), *Ideology and discontent* (pp. 206-261). Glencoe, IL: Free Press.

Gergen, K. J. (1982). *Toward transformation in social knowledge.* New York: Springer.

Gilbert, G. N., & Mulkay, M. (1984). *Opening Pandora's box.* Cambridge: Cambridge University Press.

Grossman, D. (1992). *Nochechim-Nifkadim* [Sleeping on a wire]. Tel Aviv, Israel: HaKibbitz HaMeuchad.

Hall, S. (1980). Encoding/decoding. In S. Hall, D. Hobson, A. Lowe, & P. Willis (Eds.), *Culture, media, language: Working papers in cultural studies* (pp. 1972-1979). London: Hutchinson.

Hobsbawm, E. (1983). Introduction: Inventing traditions. In E. Hobsbawm & T. Ranger (Eds.), *The invention of tradition* (pp. 1-14). Cambridge, UK: Cambridge University Press.

Katriel, T. (1997). *Performing the past.* Mahwah, NJ: Lawrence Erlbaum.

Liebes, T., & Katz, E. (1988). *Dallas* and *Genesis*: Primordiality and seriality in popular culture. In J. W. Carey (Ed.), *Media, myths and narratives* (pp. 113-125). Newbury Park, CA: Sage.

Liebes, T., Katz, E., & Ribak, R. (1991). Ideological reproduction. *Political Behavior, 13,* 235-252.

Liebes, T., & Ribak, R. (1991). A mother's battle against TV news: A case study of political socialization. *Discourse and Society, 2,* 203-222.

Liebes, T., & Ribak, R. (1994). In defense of negotiated readings: How moderates on each side of the conflict interpret *intifada* news. *Journal of Communication, 44,* 108-124.

Morley, D. (1986). *Family television.* London: Comedia.

Potter, J. (1996). *Representing reality: Discourse, rhetoric and social construction.* London: Sage.

Potter, J., & Wetherell, M. (1987). *Discourse and social psychology.* London: Sage.

Rabinowitz, D. (1993). Nostalgia Mizrachit? Eich Hafchu HaPalastinim LeArviyei Israel [Oriental nostalgia? How the Palestinians transformed into "Israeli Arabs"]. *Te'oria Uvikoret* [Theory and Criticism], *4,* 141-151.

Ribak, R. (1993). *Decoding the news in a divided country: Political socialization among Israeli Jews and Palestinians.* Unpublished doctoral dissertation, University of California, San Diego.

Ribak, R. (1994, June). *Divisive and consensual constructions in the political discourse of Jews and Palestinians in Israel: Dilemmas and contradictions.* Paper presented at the Annual Conference of the International Society for the Study of Argumentation, Amsterdam.

Ribak, R. (1997). Socialization as and through conversation: Political discourse in Israeli families. *Comparative Education Review, 41,* 71-96.

Schudson, M. (1992). *Watergate in American memory.* New York: Basic Books.

Scott, M. B., & Lyman, S. M. (1968). Accounts. *American Sociological Review, 33,* 46-62.

Semin, G. R., & Manstead, A. S. R. (1983). *The accountability of conduct.* London: Academic Press.

Shotter, J. (1985). Social accountability and self speculation. In K. J. Gergen & K. E. Davis (Eds.), *The social construction of the person* (pp. 167-189). New York: Springer.

Swidler, A. (1986). Culture in action: Symbols and strategies. *American Sociological Review, 51,* 273-286.

Tannen, D. (1989). *Talking voices: Repetition, dialogue and imagery in conversational discourse.* Cambridge, UK: Cambridge University Press.

Trevor-Roper, H. (1983). The invention of tradition: The Highland tradition of Scotland. In E. Hobsbawm & T. Ranger (Eds.), *The invention of tradition* (pp. 15-41). Cambridge, UK: Cambridge University Press.

Wetherell, M., & Potter, J. (1989). Narrative characters and accounting for violence. In J. Shotter & K. J. Gergen (Eds.), *Texts of identity* (pp. 206-229). London: Sage.

White, H. (1987). *The content of form.* Baltimore: Johns Hopkins University Press.

Zelizer, B. (1998). *Remembering to forget.* Chicago: University of Chicago Press.

Index

About the Contributors

LING CHEN (PhD, The Ohio State University, 1991) is Associate Professor in the Department of Communication Studies at Hong Kong Baptist University. Her work appears in *Communication Monographs, Communication Reports, Howard Journal of Communication, International Journal of Intercultural Relations, Journal of Language and Social Interaction,* and *Journal of Management Communication,* among others. Her areas of interest include intercultural communication, language and social interaction, Chinese communication, and organization communication.

MARY JANE COLLIER (PhD, University of Southern California, 1982) is Professor and Chair of the Department of Human Communication Studies, School of Communication, at the University of Denver. Her research interests focus on cultural identities and discourses across multiple contexts. Her work appears in such journals as *Communication Monographs, International Journal of Intercultural Relations, Communication Quarterly,* and *Howard Journal of Communication*; her work also appears in various scholarly books and texts.

NANCY C. CORNWELL (PhD, University of Colorado, Boulder) is Assistant Professor of Communication and Women's Studies at Western Michigan University. Her current research, which includes developing a feminist philosophical approach to hate speech, has been published in *The Journal of Intergroup Relations* and has been presented at the national conferences of the International Communication Association, the National Communication Association, and the Association for Education in Journalism and Mass Communication.

JOLANTA A. DRZEWIECKA (PhD, Arizona State University, 1999) is Assistant Professor of Communication Studies in the E. Murrow School of Communication at Washington State University. Her research and teaching interests focus on intercultural communication and cultural studies and include issues of identity, immigration, tourism, representation, and difference.

LISA A. FLORES (PhD, University of Georgia, 1994) is Assistant Professor in the Department of Communication and the Ethnic Studies Program at the University of Utah. Her research interests include intercultural communication, rhetoric and culture, feminist theory and criticism, and Chicana/o studies. Her work has appeared in such journals as the *Quarterly Journal of Speech, Critical Studies in Mass Communication,* and *Southern Communication Journal.*

GUSTAV FRIEDRICH (PhD, University of Kansas, 1968) is Professor and Dean in the School of Communication, Information, and Library Studies at Rutgers University. His publications appear in such journals as *Communication Education, Communication Monographs, Journal of Communication,* and *Journal of Personality and Social Psychology,* and he is author/editor of 13 books. His honors and awards include O.U. presidential Professor, Kenneth E. Crook Faculty Award, Josh Lee Service Award, and Regents' Award for Superior Teaching. His research interests are in communication theory and in instructional and applied communication.

BRADFORD 'J' HALL (PhD, University of Washington, 1989) is Associate Professor in the Department of Communication and Journalism at the University of New Mexico. He is interested in cultural communication, intercultural conflict, organizational culture, and how people establish and maintain membership within a variety of communities. He has published in such journals as *Communication Monographs, Communication Theory, Human Relations, The International Journal of Intercultural Relations,* and *Human Communication Research.*

MAROUF HASIAN, JR. (PhD, University of Georgia, 1993) is Assistant Professor in the Department of Communication at the University of Utah.

TRUDY MILBURN (PhD, University of Massachusetts, Amherst) is Assistant Professor at Baruch College, City University of New York. She teaches several courses, including courses in culture and communication and in gender and communication. Her research focuses on culturally situated ways of constructing identity and membership. She has presented her research at several national and international conferences and has published in *Emerging Theories of Human Communication* (1997) and in *Earthtalk* (1996).

DREAMA MOON (PhD, Arizona State University) is Assistant Professor in the Communication Program at California State University, San Marcos. Her research interests include inter/cultural communication and critical theory, with a particular focus on the ways in which critical approaches can enhance studies of cultural identities and social discourses. Her research has appeared in a number of venues, most recently in the edited collection by Thomas K. Nakayama and Judith N. Martin, *Whiteness: The Communication of Social Identity*. She is currently working on a project that examines the communication of hate.

YOKO NADAMITSU (PhD, University of Oklahoma, 1996) is Assistant Professor in the Department of International Exchange Studies at Josai International University, Japan. Her work can be found in *Human Communication Studies* and *International Communication Studies*. Her honors and awards include the Ralph Cooley Award. Her research interests are in intercultural communication, language, and social interaction. This paper is based on her dissertation, which was codirected by the other two authors.

MARK P. ORBE (PhD, Ohio University) is Associate Professor of Communication and of Diversity and Women's Studies at Western Michigan University. His research, which examines the inextricable relationship between culture and communication in a variety of contexts, has been published in *Communication Quarterly, Communication Studies, Howard Journal of Communications, Communication Theory, Women's Studies in Communication, Southern Communica tion Journal, Western Journal of Communication,* and other interdisciplinary journals and edited books. His first book, *Constructing Co-Cultural Theory,* was published by Sage in 1998.

RIVKA RIBAK (PhD, University of California, San Diego, 1993) is Assistant Professor of Communication at the University of Haifa. She completed her dissertation, focusing on political socialization among Israeli Jewish and Palestinian families, in 1993 and has published her work in the *Journal of Communication, Comparative Education Review,* and elsewhere, as well as in Hebrew. She recently received a grant to study power relations in the family vis-à-vis domestic communication technologies.

RAKA SHOME is Assistant Professor of Communication Studies at Arizona State University, West Campus.

KIESHA T. WARREN (MA, Indiana State University) is a PhD student in the Department of Sociology at Western Michigan University. Her primary area of study is applied sociology/criminology; specifically, her current research interests focus on examining the role of culture and communication processes within inter- and intragroup relations. Her research has been published in *The Journal of Intergroup Relations* and has been presented at national and international conferences.

YUMIKO YOKOCHI (MA, University of New Mexico, 1999) is currently working for Nikko Securities Company International. She is interested in intercultural communication, especially as it applies to Japanese and U.S. American relations. She has conducted numerous workshops on intercultural communication and has presented research at conferences sponsored by the International Communication Association, National Communication Association, and Western States Communication Association.

YAEL-JANETTE ZUPNIK (PhD, Boston University) currently holds an appointment at the University of Michigan at Ann Arbor. She has been a recipient of a postdoctoral fellowship from the Israeli Council of Higher Education and subsequently Visiting Assistant Professor in the English and Communication Departments of Tel-Aviv University. Her areas of interest include discourse analysis, pragmatics, and cross-cultural communication. Previous publications have appeared in the *Journal of Pragmatics* and *Language in Society.* She has previously taught at Harvard University, Boston University, and the Hebrew University of Jerusalem.